THE UNTOLD STORY OF THE SPIRIT OF ST. LOUIS

To Chuck Faber, with Best personal regards,

"Ev" Cassagneres

By

EV CASSAGNERES

Flying Books International

121 5th Avenue NW • New Brighton, MN 55112

Logo by Kate Mahoney

The Untold Story of the Spirit of St. Louis

From the Drawing Board to the Smithsonian

Ev Cassagneres

FLYING BOOKS INTERNATIONAL, Publishers & Wholesalers
121 5th Avenue NW, Suite 300, New Brighton, MN **55112**
651-635-0100

The Untold Story of the Spirit of St. Louis

Flying Books International,
Publishers & Wholesalers

Library of Congress Cataloging in Publication Data

Cassagneres, Ev 1928-
The Untold Story of the Spirit of St. Louis/Ev Cassagneres.
p. cm.
Includes bibliographical references.
ISBN 0-911139-32-X (alk. paper)
1. Lindbergh, Charles A. (Charles Augustus), 1902-1974 – Journeys. 2. Spirit of St. Louis (Airplane)
3. Transatlantic flights. 4. Aeronautics, Commercial. I. Title.

TL540.L5 C37 2002
629.13'0911 – dc21 **2002024282**

Printed and bound in the United States of America

Front cover: *Lucky Lindy*. Painting by Stan Stokes. Charles A. Lindbergh begins his solo trans-Atlantic flight, taking off in his Ryan NYP—the Spirit of St. Louis—from Roosevelt Field, Long Island, New York, May 20, 1927.

Stokes print available from HistoricAviation.com, or call toll free: 800-225-5575.

Back cover: Charles Lindbergh and the Ryan NYP in front of the National Guard hangar in St. Louis, upon his arrival from San Diego, May 11, 1927, prior to the Atlantic flight. (Louis M. Lowry)

Art Director: Noel Allard
Publisher: G.E. Herrick

TABLE OF CONTENTS

DEDICATION

This book is dedicated to the men and women responsible for the design, building and care of the *Spirit of St. Louis*, during its flying life including the care and feeding and curatorial requirements at the National Air & Space Museum in Washington, DC.

The book is also dedicated to my family for their patience when time spent on the book could have been time spent with them.

The Author

ACKNOWLEDGEMENTS

This book, and a later volume about Lindbergh's post record-flight tours, have not been written by myself only. The various abilities of many people and organizations have contributed and become part of whatever success this work may represent. Their cooperation and interest is without parallel. They have all been true collaborators. Their generous gifts of time, talent, experience, resources, and encouragement in varying degrees, have been a source of immense help and inspiration.

I owe these special individuals and groups my deepest gratitude and appreciation, for without them I could not possibly have put this story together.

Having spent over thirty-five years in extensive and exhaustive research, worldwide travel, telephone calls and letters by the thousands, I have found that a project of this complexity requires almost as many people and skills as was required to keep the *Spirit of St. Louis* in the air during its flying life as well as preserved in Washington, DC.

Countless people went out of their way to have me as a guest in their home, feed me, and transport me from place to place. Often they would provide further leads or contacts, make suggestions, and offer access to their own personal archives or photographic collections.

Literally hundreds of people played crucial roles in this work. Hundreds more took time to write by either longhand, typewriter, or computer, letters with detailed help and answers to my many questions. Many of these people would either donate or loan long-cherished photographs from their family photo albums, scrapbooks, or shoe boxes.

Encouragement from family, friends, business associates, pilots, authors, researchers and historians, writers, (professionals and non-professionals), librarians, and even strangers, has been enormous. This alone has kept me going even at times when I was ready to give up in moments of discouragement. Space does not permit me to give credit to each and every individual.

Members of my immediate family deserve special mention for the hours, days, and weeks away from them. Often while in such deep thought while in their company, I hardly knew they were even in the same room. However their quiet support gave me the strength and determination to keep going to complete the work.

Over the years I tracked down and made contact with scores of people "who were there", many of whom worked on the NYP in one capacity or another, or knew Lindbergh personally.

Countless hours have been spent scrutinizing photographs and their captions, checking and double checking stories, anecdotes, and printed material for accuracy, details, and thoroughness to pinpoint dates and other data.

In the course of this project I become familiar with countless other published materials on Lindbergh, the man, the airplane "*Spirit of St. Louis*" and the New York to Paris flight.

I have gathered primary data on the effect of the Lindbergh/*Spirit of St. Louis* flights on the development of air travel and aviation in general.

I would like to give special mention to Charles A. and Anne Morrow Lindbergh, Reeve Lindbergh Tripp, Wendy Lindbergh, and Lars Lindbergh for their personal interest and help. The Lindbergh family was always available whenever the need for help arose.

A special thanks to Ruth Bauer, Ph.D. and her husband, Hans, son Paul, and daughter Betsy, for their friendship and encouragement. A special thanks to Ruth for her devotion, patience, and expertise, putting all of the manuscript on computer disc, while working from my rough typewritten drafts with all of its chicken scratches, and most of all for her untiring encouragement over so many years.

A special thanks to my good friend Candace McM. Routh, a business communications consultant, for her many hours of editing, constructive criticism and suggestions.

Finally, I would like to express my deepest gratitude and appreciation to both Greg Herrick and Noel Allard: to Greg for his long time interest in Lindbergh and in the preservation of many rare antique/classic aircraft, and for making it possible to have Historic Aviation publish this work. He is to be commended. And to Noel for his long time interest and editorial expertise in the preservation of our American aviation heritage, and especially for his editorial work on this book.

Two other close friends who need special mention are Ken Cassens and Dale Caldwell. I consider both to be extremely knowledgeable NYP historians.

Ken Cassens has been building up the most accurate flying replica in existence. This one will be used in regular flight operations at the Old Rhinebeck aerodrome, Rhinebeck, New York. Ken's workmanship and attention to the most minute detail has been of tremendous help in my own research. He has picked up on some details that I have missed.

By the same token, Dale Caldwell has done the same, only with regard to the exact detailed drawings seen in this book. Also, Dale quite often has called my attention to a particular detail that I overlooked. As a long time senior draftsman myself, I can say that Dale's draftsmanship is nothing short of superb. His drawings of the NYP are, in my estimation, the most accurate in existence. I owe much gratitude and appreciation to both of these gentlemen.

I would like to express my appreciation to Bonnie Czuchra of Elite Travel, Inc. of Cheshire, Connecticut for her help in arranging my travel schedule to places far and wide to do research on this book. Most of the time she was able to get me a window seat so that I could see and appreciate some of the countryside, before or aft of the wing, of course. I would never pull the shade down while flying over this beautiful land.

PARTIAL LISTING OF PEOPLE

Charles A. Lindbergh, John Underwood, Anne Morrow Lindbergh, William T. Larkins, Reeve Lindbergh Tripp, Peter M. Bowers, Lars Lindbergh, Richard Sanders Allen, Wendy Lindbergh, Dr. Paul E. Garber, Claude Ryan, Dan Hagedorn, Jerry Ryan, Robert van der Linden, William Wagner, Kirsten J. Cassagneres Salvador, Ray Wagner, Eline O. Cassagneres, Elizabeth Ferguson, Bryan Ev Cassagneres, Ed Morrow, Judith Schiff, Yale U., "Dapper" Dan Burnett, David Bilodeau, Yale U., Oce and Lorna Dotson, Cole Palen, Jon Harme van der Linde, Ken Cassens, Walter O. Locke, James Hare, Douglas Corrigan, Dale Caldwell, Clair Rand, John Barker, Martin Jensen, Dan Taylor, Arthur Mankey, George Gentsch, Adalaide Prudden, Nel MacCraken, Donald Keyhoe, Roger Thiel, Carol Keyhoe, Larry Ross, Richard Hall, James Stewart (actor), Donald A. Hall, Robert Arehart, Donald Hall, Jr., Frank Greene, Nova Hall, William M. Foley, O. R. McNeal, Donald Richardson, Jack Cox, Laura Longacre, Mrs. Clyde Wann, Warren Shipp, Kenneth Boedecker, Col. Richard Gimbel, Kenneth Lane, Rogers Studio, Clarence Chamberlin, Mrs. Allen W. McCann, Jr., Ruth Kennough Clemens, Mrs. Frank Hawks, Helen Hendrix,

Donald Ives, Walter J. Jones, Melvin Rice, Stanley Jones, Mrs. Ruth Morrison, Carl Hatfield, Dan Chisholm, Douglas Kelly, William Feeney, William F. Chana, Fred L. Barber, Harlan "Bud" Gurney, Binka Bone, Charles Hansen, Pierre Hollander, George Hammond, Ed Eilertsen, Cliff Petzen, Dennis Parks, Leon Klink, Tom Poberezny, Otto Timm, Susan A. Lurvey, Loren "Deak" Lyman, Robin Williams, Ed Granville , Lucy Wilkins, Carl Schory, Ray Howland, Howell Miller, John Vavrek, Igor I. Sikorsky, Jr., Donna Recko, Sergei I. Sikorsky, David Walters, Tom Matthews, Eusabio Zambrano, MD, Robert B. Meyer, Jr., John Chamberlain, Harvey Lippincott, Clarence M. Young, A. Scott Berg, William H. Gates, Neil Armstrong, William Louis Nungesser, Jansz V. (Jack) Vander Veer, Francis J. Menez, Richard A. Washburn, Roy Meyers, Carlos Rosa Mejia, Dan Witkoff, Paul W. Looney, John E. Anstensen, Tom Heitzman, Maryann Bury, Charles F. Schultz, James B. Horne, Arvela Horne, Barbara Horne, Alice A. Brewer, Esq., George Rosen, Alek P. Szecsy, Esq., Merwin L. Hill, Jean Lucy, Charlene Badeau, Harold H. Mandly, III, William H. Shay, Jr., Ralph Ehrenberg, Paul Shay, Steve Moisen, John Reznikoff, Norbert Cupp, Stanley King, Dewey France, Joshua Stoff, Steve Mulligan.

ENGLAND

Marion & Phil Munson, Eric Webster, Pam and Ray Billings, Colin Smith, Doug Cluett, John Thorn, Peter Cooksley, Ian Nutley, Peter Newstone, Arthur Freeman, Peter Little , Rudolph Paltauf, Sir Peter Masefield, Fred Deal, Tony Trevor, Donald Bruce Holmes, Eileen and Keith Howard, Charles Oman.

FRANCE

Stephan Nicolaou, Ronald M. A. Hirst, Tatiana Capretz, Andre Dumas, Roger Giraud, Francis Storez, Paul M. Lambermont, Bernard Millot, George Simon, Mrs. Francoise do Peyrelongue Kalognomos

BELGIUM

Dr. Gustaaf Janssens, Jean Dillen, Marc Mommaerts, His Royal Highness Prince Philippe

JAPAN

Fumio Habuto, Pete Horiuchi, Jim Marquis, Capt. George H. Kronmiller, Shuichi Manei, Yoshiro Ikari, E. Sekigawa, Mainichi Shimbun newspaper

ASSOCIATIONS—ADMINISTRATIONS—INSTITUTIONS—ARMED FORCES—CORPORATIONS

Ryan Aeronautical Company, Ryan Aeronautical Library, San Diego Aero Space Museum, National Air and Space Museum, American Aviation Historical Society, Federal Aviation Administration, National Archives, Library of Congress, Daniel Guggenheim Foundation, National Geographic Society, Experimental Aircraft Association, Aircraft Owners & Pilots Association, National Aeronautic Association, Airguide Publications, Inc., Jeppesen Sanderson, Inc., National Oceanic and Atmospheric Administration, Aviation Publication Service, United States Air Force Museum, Wright-Patterson Air Force Museum, National Aeronautics & Space Administration, Pentagon—Office of the Assistant Secretary of Defense, Connecticut Aeronautical Historical Association, Pratt & Whitney Aircraft Company, Sikorsky Aircraft Company, Hamilton Standard Propeller Company, Yale University, Sterling Memorial Library, Manuscripts and Archives; U.S. Air Force Association—Charles A. Lindbergh Chapter, United States Air Force, United States Navy, United States Army, Office of Naval Records and Archives, Washington Navy Yard, Missouri Historical Society, Minnesota Historical Society, Charles A. Lindbergh Museum and Interpretation Center, Little Falls, Minnesota, The Charles A. and Anne Morrow Lindbergh Foundation, C.A.L./NX211 Collectors Society, Martin Luther King Library of Washington, DC, Anacostia Naval Air Station, Delta Airlines, Swissair Airlines, Canadian Aviation Historical Association, *Asahi Shimbun and Mainichi Shimbun* Tokyo, Japan (newspapers), Tallmantz Aviation, Henry Ford Museum, Warner Brothers Pictures, Title Insurance and Trust Company, Switlik Parachutes, Old Rhinebeck Aerodrome, Cradle of Aviation Museum, Museum of Flight, Mobil Corporation (Sandra Y. Jackson, Paul D. Ledvina), Kollsman Instrument Company,

National Aviation Museum—Ottawa, Ontario, Canada
National Library of Canada—Ottawa, Ontario, Canada
National Archives of Canada—Ottawa, Ontario, Canada
Royal Air Force Museum
Fleet Air Arm—Somerset, England
Public Records Office—Kew, London
Royal Aero Club—London
Buckingham Palace—London
Royal Aeronautical Society—London
London Society of Air Britain
British Library—London
United States Embassy—London
British Broadcasting Corp. (BBC)—London
Illustrated *London News* Library—London
Daily Telegraph Newspaper—London
Naval Museum—Portsmouth, England
Gosport Museum—Gosport, England
Gosport Library—Gosport, England
Royal Archives—Windsor Castle, England
Aeroplane Magazine, England
Flight International magazine—England
Aviation Museum—Southampton, England
Marine Museum—Southampton, England
Science Museum—London
Imperial War Museum—London
The British Newspaper Library—London (Colindale)
Hampshire Central Library—Portsmouth, England
Hulton Picture Library—London
Quadrant—London

American Embassies of the countries of Mexico, Belize, Guatemala, Honduras, Salvador, Costa Rica, Panama, Colombia, Venezuela, Dominican Republic, Haiti, Cuba.

Further listings and credits may be found in the contents of footnotes and endnotes.

PHOTOGRAPHIC SOURCES AND CREDITS

Every effort has been made to credit the original photographer or any other appropriate person. However, photographs are frequently traded or sold, and the individual who snapped the camera shutter is often lost to history. For that reason the person who supplied the photo to this author is named in many cases where the original photographer is not known or doubt exists as to who the original photographer was.

Some photographs can be credited to the original photographer, such as Major Erickson of San Diego. Others were supplied by Ryan Company employees, pilots, Ryan or other aircraft owners, aviation enthusiasts/historians, collectors, people from the general public, libraries, historical archives, museums, educational institutions, commercial photographers, or commercial photo archives.

I wish to credit Ryan Aeronautical Library, Ryan Aeronautical Corporation, San Diego Aero Space Museum, National Air and Space Museum, National Archives, Library of Congress, Leo B. Kimball Collection, Pratt & Whitney Aircraft Company, Charles A. and Anne Morrow Lindbergh Foundation, Missouri Historical Society, Minnesota Historical Society, Charles A. Lindbergh Museum, Little Falls, Minnesota, Cradle of Aviation

Museum, Yale University Manuscripts & Archives, Experimental Aircraft Association, Donald Hall Collection, Donald E. Keyhoe Collection, National Geographic Society, Miscellaneous Libraries, Universities, Schools, Institutions, individuals, private collections, Bettman Archives, Underwood and Underwood.

In my teens, while living across the street from a pioneer aircraft engine designer, who become my mentor, I was thrilled beyond all imagination when he offered his sizable collection of original glossy, often professionally taken, old aircraft photo and negative collection, which included scores of NYP pictures. His name was Leo B. Kimball, designer of the Kimball "Beetle" radial engine. Many of these NYP photos I had never seen before or since. He gave them to me with the understanding that I would preserve them as best I could, and I have respected that wish.

Often a photo was found at a flea market or some other obscure location, with no information on the back. At a later date the same photo was found in a commercial photographic archive, for which there was a very high price for a copy, plus a high fee for publishing rights. Due to the lack of sufficient funds for this project, I often chose to use the same photo that was found at sources named above, as this photo quality was as good as the commercially supplied one. In some cases there are many duplicate photos of Lindbergh and the NYP, which were printed by the hundreds in 1927 or later. This author has found that many of them ended up in private collections, but others found their way into commercial photographic archives, for which a large fee was charged for a print and publishing rights on top of that.

So it has been most difficult to make decisions regarding what photos to use for this book, to more completely tell the story.

After this book is published I am certain that someone will appear who might know the answer to some questions I have been unable to answer before going to press. In addition, there is likely someone out there who will challenge some point I have made. Such people will say, "Why didn't you contact me?" I would have, had I known of their existence.

If I have made life a bit easier for the next generation of aviation historians, who may show an interest in continuing the research on the NYP, then this work has not been in vain.

Therefore, this book should not be considered complete or official in spite of the years of research. It is more extensive, however, than any previous publication on the subject.

As for the airframe of the NYP, it was a basic, contemporary vehicle, not too different from the scores of better or lesser types of the day. One of the keys to the design success of the NYP, however, was the unfailing Wright J-5 "Whirlwind" engine.

The NYP came to represent an historical turning point. The world was at peace, and man had seemingly triumphed over nature, and especially the vast Atlantic Ocean. The NYP was physical justification for man's and the aviation community's optimism, and the perfect backdrop for the advancement of air travel to what we have today.

AUTHOR'S NOTE

Over the course of many years, I have often been asked what inspired my deep interest in Charles Lindbergh and the *Spirit of St. Louis*.

During the 1930s, I was one of that great throng of air-minded young Americans who would run outdoors at every opportunity to gaze upward at any airplane that might be passing overhead. I found I could not take my eyes off the plane until it passed over the horizon and disappeared completely from sight. The shape, the sound, the direction and altitude of every plane would be deeply recorded in my memory. I kept scrapbooks, built stick and tissue and solid models, rode my trusty bicycle many miles to local airports to watch the aviators fly their beautiful machines, dreaming about the day I might join their ranks.

I spent long hours reading model airplane magazines and books on flying. I had a particular fascination with Lindbergh and his flight from New York to Paris in 1927. In the course of my reading, I began to notice discrepancies and inconsistencies in writings about the famous flight, the design and building of the *Spirit* and Lindbergh's goodwill tours.

After I became a pilot in 1945, I continued to read about Lindbergh and the *Spirit of St. Louis* and noticed that the errors continued to proliferate. In 1956 I had the opportunity to "check out" in a classic 1936 Ryan ST. From that moment, I was compelled—I had to learn all I could about the history of the *Spirit*, its manufacturer and its development.

I had always been inspired by Lindbergh and wondered how this little-known airmail pilot managed to become involved in the seminal 1927 trans-Atlantic flight. In light of the conflicting information I had already encountered, I developed an irresistible urge to dig deeper and find out the true story. I felt driven to fit the pieces together; not just to learn more, but also to better understand this key chapter of aviation and the crucial role that a small airplane and its pilot played in the future of commercial air travel and aviation in general.

In the thirty-five years I have been involved in this project, it has continued to be both fascinating and satisfying—intellectually as well as emotionally. Perhaps it is just a basic human need to learn about the past in order to more fully appreciate the present and anticipate the future.

Researching the history of the *Spirit* was not without its challenges. I had to spend much time tracking down official documentation. When I did find original material (much of it dated 1927 and 1928,) I often had to spend additional time scrutinizing this information to ascertain its accuracy and authenticity.

Data transcription often leads to typographical errors, misunderstandings and flat-out guesses. I attempted to distinguish fact from error throughout this research. Fortunately I have had access to a vast amount of historical, technical and photographic material which helped greatly in this effort.

Most important as accurate and trustworthy sources of information have, of course, been any writings by Charles Lindbergh, his wife Anne Morrow Lindbergh, or their daughter, Reeve Lindbergh Tripp. In addition, I have had the invaluable experience of spending time with the Lindbergh family, all of whom have generously shared from their hearts and personal archives.

I have also interviewed many people "who were there," via letter, telephone, in person and on tape, and listened to their stories and observations of how the experience affected their lives. I have collected photographs of the *Spirit* taken every place it ever landed, as well as the newspaper stories of Lindbergh's visits to every town, city or country stopped in or overflown on his tours. I was especially watchful for errors in these newspaper stories. Unfortunately, in many cases, those are the only sources I was able to find on the events. I have attempted to qualify any information in this text that I feel questionable.

The original intent of this work was to convey a detailed documentation, as complete and accurate as possible, of the concept, design, and flying life of the *Spirit of St. Louis.* because Lindbergh was the man responsible for the creation of the *Spirit* and determined every aspect of its flying life, I have also addressed, in short, his life leading up to that time.

This book is full of anecdotes, legend, and cold facts. I have attempted to weave all three elements into a useful story.

In 1968, upon learning of my project, Lindbergh invited me to his home where he provided much valuable first-hand information. Since his death in 1974, his family has continued their interest in the progress of the project. Thus, my perception of Lindbergh is derived from knowing him personally, and I have tried to convey that image in this book.

In his own book, *The Spirit of St. Louis*, on page 548, Lindbergh wrote, "No work is infallible; desire, records and memory combined cannot produce exactness in every instance; but sufficient effort has been expended on the pages of this book to warrant that in the majority of cases where there is conflict, accuracy will rest with the account carried herein." I would like to feel that way about my book as well.

Early in this project I needed to address several questions to which I felt only Lindbergh would have the answers. But aware of his great desire for privacy I couldn't imagine how I would ever meet him.

Carl Schory, formerly of the National Aeronautic Association, suggested that I contact one of Lindbergh's close friends, Loren "Deak" Lyman, who lived near Lindbergh in Connecticut. I did, and three years later (February 1968,) Mr Lyman felt the time was right for me to write to Lindbergh to request a meeting, using Lyman as a reference.

To my great surprise and pleasure, I soon received a telephone call from Lindbergh himself, inviting my wife and me to join him and his wife, Anne at their home for supper and a discussion of my project. During that meeting, on the eve of February 28, Lindbergh and I began a friendship that continued until his death. I found him to be a true gentleman-pleasant, gracious and quite accessible, with an incredible memory for detail and a quick and restless intellect. he did not waste words, always getting right down to the point in his answers and observations.

Since his death in 1974, many other questions have surfaced as I continued to collect information. I truly wish he were here to provide the answers. I will always be grateful for his friendship and generosity in sharing his thoughts so freely whenever we met.

Ev Cassagneres
February 7, 2001

PREFACE

Everyone knows the basic story of Charles A. Lindbergh and his *Spirit of St. Louis* making the first solo trans-Atlantic flight from New York to Paris, France in 1927. But how many stop to think of the crucial role that the pilot and his airplane played in the future of commercial air travel and aviation technology today. What was learned as a result of that 1927-1928 effort laid the groundwork for modern aviation technology as we know it today.

In a converted San Diego, California fish cannery, there existed a small airplane manufacturing company, founded in 1922 by T. Claude Ryan, and known as the Ryan Flying Company and Los Angeles-San Diego Airline, which later became Ryan Airlines, Inc. In late 1926, the company had a high-wing monoplane, the Ryan M-1, in production. Several M-1s were flying airmail service on a regular basis between Los Angeles and Seattle for Pacific Air Transport (P.A.T.) an airmail carrier.

On February 3, 1927, the Robertson Aircraft Corporation of Anglum, Missouri sent Ryan Airlines a telegram inquiring whether the small West Coast firm could build a Wright engine-powered airplane capable of flying from New York to Paris non-stop. The wire was signed by Charles A. Lindbergh, chief pilot. Lindbergh would be competing for a cash prize offered by entrepreneur Raymond Orteig for the first pilot to make the solo non-stop crossing.

It was clear that Ryan would have to re-engineer their existing M-1, incorporating aspects of a newly designed larger Ryan B-1 "Brougham," then under construction, for such a feat. They not only accomplished the engineering but did it in record time under the watchful eye of the daring pilot. The airplane proved to be up to the task, and the flight was so earth-shaking that the whole world was taken up by the marvel of the flight. The public demanded that Lindbergh follow up his feat by flying the *Spirit* around the country and into Canada, South America, and the Caribbean after his return.

Much has been written over the years about Lindbergh, but little attention has been paid to the airplane itself and the role it played in aviation's development. This book has been written to fill that need.

Space in this first Volume does not permit a thorough history of the "Goodwill Tours" of 1927-1928, but the Tours will be covered in detail in a subsequent volume to be published in the near future.

FOREWORD

(Reeve Lindbergh)

April 24, 2002

Dear Ev,

I have been trying to write a formal introduction for the new edition of your book about the *"Spirit,"* but I'm having trouble. You and I are old friends now, after all, and I just can't seem to find the formal words and phrases I'd normally use for this literary exercise.

And besides, Ev, what do I know about airplanes? I'm not a pilot, just a pilot's daughter. No, make that plural—I"m just the daughter of two pilots. Charles A. and Anne Morrow Lindbergh were both aviation pioneers, and I am still amazed by all they did during those wonderful early years in the air. I salute those two, my own beloved aviation pioneers. I miss them very much, and it is a joy to think of them—who knows?—soaring together again now, somewhere.

Whatever I learned about aviation I learned directly from them, of course, from what they remembered and said and wrote. But there was one flight that my mother did not know much about, and that my father did not talk much about, and that was the most famous flight of all.

"Read my book!" Charles Lindbergh would admonish his children, when we asked questions about the *"Spirit's"* flight, as you know. I did read his book—all of them—eventually, and now I read them over again, but as I grew up I also learned from other people. You have been one of the first and foremost of the teachers, for me and for so many others. *Thank you, Ev.*

Thank you for bringing me my own family history in such a careful, caring, meticulous way. Thank you for your devotion to this airplane and this story, every nuance and detail, over the decades. Thank you for your kindness to my family, for making sure that each generation in its turn learns the story, as I did. Thanks for caring, and thanks, above all, for your own wonderful "Spirit." I don't know if I ever told you how much it means to me, so I am telling you now.

Blessings always,

Reeve Lindbergh

Reeve

CHAPTER 1

Raymond Orteig and the Prize That Started It All

Since the beginning of time, humanity has always been curious, adventuresome, questioning, inquisitive, with a strong drive to see what was over the next hill, around the next corner, on the other side of a continent or body of water, be it an ocean, large lake or sound.

Large expanses of ocean have thrilled and challenged us for eons. What is out there? Who is on the other side? What is on the other side? How can we get over there?

Eventually man built vessels that were capable of sailing across these great expanses of water, sometimes taking months to reach "the other side." As time went on, time itself became a very important factor in our daily living style; a precious guide to how, what and where we did the business of living. So did the development of how we transported ourselves over these large expanses of ocean and land, and finally the wheel, the steam engine and the flying machine came into existence.

Now people on both sides of these great oceans began to wonder and actually plan how they could get to the "other side" more quickly, more conveniently, more comfortably and more safely.

These efforts would turn a fresh page in the world's history, one which would transform life as we presently know it. It might be known as the "distance devouring era" in which humanity would feel like supermen.

Today science sends our words flashing over cables, through empty space. Thanks to television and other technological advances we are able to actually see people in real time anywhere in the world, thousands of miles away.

This "new age" would be an immensely faster, high-flying age, the age of colossal "ships with wings." These winged monsters would ascend majestically to seek higher "wind-ways," miles above our heads, with hundreds of passengers in great "saloons."

So began our quest for actually flying across these oceans, with the Atlantic Ocean being the first attempted. So sit back, get comfortable in your favorite living room chair, and read how this all came to pass, and what part Charles A. Lindbergh played in this phenomenal development of over-water air transportation, especially as we know it today.

RAYMOND ORTEIG

High in the beautiful French Pyrenees, is the small town of Louvie-Juzon. The main occupation of many of the people in this mountain town was sheepherding. One such family, the Orteigs, had a son born on October 26, 1870, and named him Raymond, who, as he grew up also became a sheepherder.

During these early years one of his grandmothers had suggested "You should set off to America, that new and promised land, where golden opportunities abound for the industrious." [1] Raymond never forgot those words of wisdom.

He married Marie Ruisques on October 26, 1892, and eventually the couple immigrated to America. By 1919 Raymond Orteig, at the age of 49, had made a place for himself in America as a successful businessman. He was a friendly man who had operated both the Brevoort and Lafayette Hotels in New York City. The Brevoort was near Washington Square in Greenwich Village and the Lafayette on University Place at 9th Street in Manhattan.

Upon reflection, Orteig felt that he would like to contribute something to the strengthening of the bonds of friendship between his native France and the United States, the country of his adoption. He had learned to love America.

On February 3, 1919, Eddie Rickenbacker, America's leading air ace of WW I, was the honored guest at a lavish banquet in the ballroom of the Waldorf-Astoria Hotel in New York City. Among the guests that evening was the French-American, Raymond Orteig. Little did anyone at that event realize that Orteig was to launch another American hero into sudden fame and a lasting place in world history. That story, with all its suspense, color and emotion, was about to unfold.

Various speeches at that dinner strongly indicated that Franco-American friendship and brotherhood of airmen had been established between these flyers of both nations over the Western Front. Rickenbacker had actually looked forward to the day the two nations could be permanently linked together by air. Orteig was quite impressed with these possibilities.

Aviation was the big story-within-the-story of World War I. Despite the air casualties and the suffering of doughboys in the trenches, the exhilaration, the fever associated with this remarkable new freedom in the skies could not be denied. Between Orville Wright's historic 12-second flight on December 17, 1903, and this celebration honoring Rickenbacker was a span of only sixteen years.

By the time Eddie Rickenbacker, internationally known as an auto racing driver, arrived in Europe in 1917, the air war was in full swing. Within two months Rickenbacker, assigned as chauffeur to General John J. Pershing, arranged a transfer to the fledgling American Air Service. He eventually became the leading American air ace by shooting down twenty-six enemy aircraft.

But the focus of the party to welcome Rickenbacker home was away from the harsh realities of war and toward the hopes for a dawning of peace in a world made safe for democracy. Speed, prowess, cooperation, progress; these were the themes woven through the stirring speeches made that night.

Rickenbacker himself spoke movingly of the comradeship among the French and Americans "over there." The crowd was caught up in his visions of the day when aircraft would link the two peoples in commerce via international flights.

Orteig was no doubt aware of both French and American contributions to the infant science of aviation. Rickenbacker's speech that night welded both Orteig's loyalties—to his native soil and his adopted home.

So impressed was Orteig by the idea of continued Franco-American comradeship in the air that on May 22, 1919, he announced a $25,000 prize (worth ten times that in today's dollars "to be awarded to the first aviator who shall cross the Atlantic in a land or water aircraft (heavier-than-air) from Paris or the shores of

France to New York, or from New York to Paris or the shores of France, without stop."[2] The prize would go to the flier who pioneered the route from New York to Paris in either direction. The distance; 3610 statute miles. The offer was good for five years.

Orteig felt that France would play a part in the development of long-distance flying. France had been recognized as the cradle of aviation in the sense that it had been the site of early attempts to conquer the skies; for instance, the early experiments by the brothers Joseph and Etienne Montgolfier in 1783 with balloons, and later Gabriel Voisin and Louis Bleriot.

A racing mania gripped the world in the first decades of the twentieth century. Ten years prior to the Wrights' first successful flight, another marvelous machine—the automobile—had begun to captivate the public. Competition to prove superior durability and reliable performance sparked scores of auto races and endurance "tours". Cross-country they sped, up mountains, around race tracks, and even around the world (the cars being carried by ship across the oceans.) Newspaper headlines carried the thrilling news of these remarkable events.

With the development of the Wright flying machine, racing took to the air. In 1910, Glenn Curtiss won $10,000 for the first continuous flight from Albany to New York City.

Less than a month after Orteig's announcement, two British aviators, John Alcock and Arthur W. Brown, collected $50,000 (£10,000) for the first nonstop trans-Atlantic flight, from Newfoundland to Ireland, a distance of 1,934 miles, in 16 hours and 28 minutes, flying a converted twin-engine Vickers Vimy bomber.

Meanwhile, New York-to-California air racing became a national craze. Stunt flying drew crowds of sedately dressed spectators. On the more practical side, airmail service was being established by the U.S. Post Office.

However, in spite of all these impressive events, Orteig's was considered "the" race to win. It was glamorous; New York-to-Paris, very chic. It piqued the already strong and friendly rivalry between French and American aviators. Most importantly, it challenged the aviation world with a tough assignment—to build an airplane capable of flying 3610 miles nonstop over water, and to find aviators with the courage and daring to attempt the feat.

Orteig's proposition was, in fact, some eight years ahead of the technology. The original term of the contest announced in May 1919 was for five years, but not one contestant came forward. Engine technology simply was not up to the challenge. Developing lightweight engines had been a major hurdle in the advancement of aviation from the beginning.

Six years after his first announcement, Orteig renewed his offer and stipulated that the flight should be made under the rules of the newly formed National Aeronautical Association of the United States of America and the Federation Aeronautique Internationale of Paris. In response to Orteig's renewed offer, Rene Fonck promptly announced that he would fly New York-to-Paris in an airplane specially built by famous pioneer, Igor I. Sikorsky.

Fonck was a renowned French air ace who had become the highest scoring Allied ace of World War I with 75 victories. Sikorsky was a Russian airplane designer who had made world news in 1913 when he built and flew the world's first multi-engine aircraft, the four engine "Grand."

But an unknown airmail pilot who hailed from Little Falls, Minnesota (population 5200) and an innovative but obscure airplane manufacturer, operating out of a former fish cannery in southern California, had other ideas. So did a few other contestants.

The race was on!

FOOTNOTES

1. "We Saw Lindbergh take Off," by Jean B. Orteig, New York, NY, May 1977, page 4. A personal account on the 50th anniversary.

2. The Raymond Orteig $25,000 Prize, Paris-New York, New York-Paris, Trans-Atlantic Flight, Official "Entry Form" title page. Army and Navy Club of America, New York City.

ENDNOTES

Seed Money, the Guggenheim Story, Milton Lomask, Farrar, Straus and Company, New York, 1964.

The Guggenheims, An American Epic, John H. Davis, William Morrow and Company, Inc., New York, NY, 1978.

America Fledges Wings, "Guggenheim," The History of the Daniel Guggenheim Fund for the Promotion of Aeronautics, Reginald M. Cleveland, Pitman Publishing Corporation, New York & Chicago, 1942.

Who Was Who, Vol. I, 1897-1942, page 919, Yale University, Manuscripts and Archives, New Haven, CT.

Curtiss, The Hammondsport Era, 1907-1915, Louis S. Casey, Crown Publishers, Inc., New York, 1981.

The Pathfinders, David Nevin, Time-Life Books, Inc., Chicago, IL, 1980.

CHAPTER 2

Other Transatlantic Flights

Lindbergh was not the first man to successfully fly an airplane across the Atlantic Ocean, as often believed. Lindbergh was the first aviator to fly "solo" across the Atlantic, from west to east, from the continent of North America to the European continent, successfully, non-stop.

It appears there were 101 people who flew the Atlantic before Lindbergh.

Of all the high flying hurdles still to be jumped, the Atlantic Ocean offered the greatest rewards and challenges. These tremendous distances and fierce weather conditions would prove a true test of men and aircraft of that time. If this ocean could be conquered by air it would surely pave the way for a regular transatlantic air route that would bring the two continents within hours of each other, instead of months.

New Hampshire meteorologist and scientific genius, Professor Thaddeus Sobieski Constantine (Coulincourt) Lowe, (1832 - 1913), as early as 1860, visited the Smithsonian Institution in Washington, DC. [1] He came to present a plan to their officials of his desire to fly across the Atlantic Ocean in some kind of steerable balloon of his own design. The balloon was named the "Great Western," (formerly "The City of New York") It was of 725,000 cu. ft. capacity. It would lift an estimated 22½ tons. [2]

They did not approve of such a venture and suggested he make an overland flight in order to test his theories before attempting what they considered such a hazardous long distance over water flight. He never did make such a flight.

In 1910 an American journalist, Walter Wellman, accompanied by Melvin Vaniman, was the first to attempt an Atlantic flight in the dirigible "America." The airship was equipped with a specially constructed wireless apparatus supplied by Marconi Wireless Telegraph Company. The balloonists departed from Atlantic City but came down 400 miles at sea, drifting helplessly with the wind after the engine quit.

In 1913, Alfred Harmsworth (later Lord Northcliffe,) British publisher of the *London Daily Mail* and *The Times* newspapers, had offered a prize of 10,000 pounds ($50,000.) to the first airman, or airmen, to fly non-stop across the Atlantic. Northcliffe's intent was to stimulate aeronautical advances. The shortest distance across the Atlantic Ocean was some 1900 statute miles, between Newfoundland, the eastern prominence of North America, and Ireland. When no attempts were made, the offer was renewed in 1919.

The very first successful transatlantic flight in a heavier-then-air flying machine, involved three American built Curtiss flying boats.

The US Navy had decided to demonstrate the power and range of these new large aircraft, and worked closely with the Curtiss company in Buffalo, New York. Designed by both Navy and Curtiss engineers, under the supervision of G. C. Westervelt, they emerged as the NC-1, NC-2, NC-3 and NC-4. The NC stood for Navy Curtiss 1 (etc.) and were often referred to as the "Nancies." They were of all wood construction, fabric covered, and each was powered with four Liberty V-12-A engines of 449 horsepower.

As plans developed for the Atlantic flight, NC-2 was dismantled to provide spare parts for the other three flying boats.

The NC's were under the overall command of one of the Navy's most illustrious aviators, Commander John H. Towers, who became the pilot in command of NC-3, the flagship.

Lt. Cmdr. Patrick N. L. "Pat" Bellinger was in command of the NC-1, and Lt. Cmdr. Albert C. "Putty" Read was pilot of the NC-4.

Under the full command of the United States Navy's Seaplane Division One, the three NC's on May 8, 1919, took off from NAS Rockaway, on Long Island, New York at 10:00 a.m. and flew directly to Halifax, Nova Scotia. NC-4 had engine trouble and returned to Chatham, Massachusetts for repairs and then went on to Halifax on the 14th.[3]

Here is the monstrous Curtiss NC-4, the most famous of the NC's, on a dolly and track system to get it into the water. ***(John Underwood)***

On the 15th the three flying boats flew up to Trepassey Bay, in the southeast corner of the island of Newfoundland, Canada.

After careful preparation all three took off at 6:00 a.m. the next day and headed southeast for the Azores, their next planned stop. This would be the largest over-water flight of the trip. After more than fifteen hours in the air, the aircraft neared the Azores, and at 23:23 GCT, NC-4 completed the flight when Read and his crew landed at Horta, on the Island of Fayal, Azores without incident.

However, NC-1 and NC-3 were not so fortunate. Due to some fog, the commanders of these aircraft decided to land in the heavy seas to determine their position. They both suffered severe damage to the aircraft from the heavy seas and were unable to take off again. The crew of NC-1 was rescued by the Greek freighter, Ionia. Abandoned, the NC-1 eventually sank. Severely damaged, the NC-3 half-sailed, half-taxied, the final 205 miles to Ponta Delgada, Sao Miguel, Azores—a tour de force of navigation.

The NC-4 proved to be a faster, luckier airplane than the other two. Fog blanketed the sea near the Azores but the airplane made it to Horta covering the 1380 miles at an average speed of 74.8 knots.

Taking off from Horta on the 27th at 8:01 p.m., the NC-4 landed in the harbor of Lisbon, Portugal, after a flight of nine hours and forty-five minutes.

The final leg of the flight took the NC-4 eventually to Plymouth, England on May 31, 1919. Putty Read was tagged "The Christopher Columbus of Aviation" by a popular magazine and became a hero.

On June 14 and 15, two British flyers, Captain John Alcock, then about 27 years old, and thirty-three year old Lieutenant Arthur Whitten "Teddie" Brown, whose parents were American, successfully flew a Vickers Vimy, a large twin-engine bi-plane bomber of the day, from Lester's Field, Quidi Vidi, near St. Johns, Newfoundland to Clifden, County Galway, Ireland, a distance of 1934 statute miles (1650 nautical miles) in 16 hours 28 minutes, at an average speed of 117 mph, to win *The London Daily Mail* prize. At the presentation ceremony, Winston Churchill, who presented the prize, remarked—"I really do not know what we should admire the most in our guests, their audacity or their good fortune."

On July 2 and 6, 1919, Royal Air Force Major George H. Scott flew from East Fortune, near Edinburgh, Scotland to Roosevelt Field, Mineola, Long Island, New York in the British rigid airship R-34, a gas filled dirigible. The flight covered 3604 statute miles (3128 nautical miles) at an average speed of 33.3 mph. The airship had a crew of 27, an American observer, one stowaway, (William Ballantyne) and two other passengers. One person on board the R-34 became the first man to arrive on U. S. soil by air. He was Maj. J.E.M. Pritchard. As the R-34 was arriving over Mineola, the original ground landing crew had been dispatched to Boston, where they thought the R-34 was planning to land. So Pritchard parachuted out of the R-34 over Mineola in order to supervise an inexperienced landing crew. After landing, he was asked what his first impression of America was, and he replied—"Hard."

Here can be seen the 643 ft long British rigid airship R-34 that made the first trans-Atlantic airship flight **(Smithsonian Institution)**

On July 9 through 13, 1919, the R-34 again flew with Major Scott and a crew of thirty, from New York back to Pulham, Norfolk, England. On this flight they covered 3816 statute miles (3314 nautical miles) at an average speed of 50.8 mph. They flew sixty-one hours and thirty-three minutes.

There were no crossings of the North Atlantic by either heavier than air or lighter than air machines from 1920 through 1923.

In 1924 the United States Army made a very successful first flight around the world. The aircraft were four single engine Douglas DWC "World Cruisers" built by the Douglas Aircraft Company at Santa Monica, California. Each was powered by the Liberty V-12-A of 449 hp. The planes were named the Seattle, Boston, New Orleans and Chicago. They cost just under $20,000. each, and could cruise at 100 mph. They were designed to use either wheels or floats, depending on what was appropriate to the local terrain.

Under the command of Major Frederick L. Martin, all four started out from Seattle on April 6, 1924, and headed north-west for a westward trip around the globe. The Seattle crashed into a mountain peak in Alaska, but the crew survived.

By the 16th of July the other three made it to Croydon, England. Finally all three airplanes flew from the Orkney Islands to Iceland, Greenland, Labrador, Newfoundland, Nova Scotia and on to Maine for another successful crossing of the Atlantic Ocean.

On October 12 through 15, 1924, Dr. Hugo Eckener flew the Zeppelin LZ-126 with a crew of 27 plus 4 United States Navy observers, from Friedrichshafen, Germany, on the shores of Lake Constance, to the U.S. Naval Air Station at Lakehurst, New Jersey. The Zeppelin was built in Germany for the U.S. Navy and would eventually be commanded by Cmdr. G.W. Steele, one of the officers on board during the crossing. The LZ-126 covered 4010 statute miles at an average speed of 49.3 mph. It was powered by five Maybach engines of 300 hp. Eventually this lighter than air ship became the U.S. Navy ZR-3 and was commissioned the Los Angeles. After eight years of service and 5368 hours logged on 331 flights, the air ship was decommissioned with honors at Lakehurst in June 1932.

There were no more successful Atlantic crossings by air in 1925 and 1926.

In 1927 Raymond Orteig renewed his prize offer, hoping to make the world more aviation and air travel conscious.

At dawn on May 8, 1927, two very gallant French aviators left Le Bourget Aerodrome, just northeast of Paris, in a French built Levasseur P.L. 8, hoping to take the Orteig Prize. The two flyers were Capt. Charles Nungesser, a World War I ace and Capt. Francois Coli, navigator. The airplane was affectionately named the "White Bird" (L'Oiseau Blanc) They were attempting to fly east to west, against prevailing winds. No trace of them has ever been found, and it is only speculation that they perhaps made it to Newfoundland or the vast Maine woods, having possibly crashed somewhere in the wilderness of those areas. They used a landing gear that could be jettisoned, which exists today in the Musee d'la Air at Le Bourget. This reduced the drag and load after take-off.

On February 13, 1927, three Italian aviators left the seaplane base, Cagliari, in Sardinia, Italy aboard the Italian built Savoia Marchetti SM-55, named the Santa Maria, and flew south to Africa, and from Cape Verde Islands on across the South Atlantic Ocean to Brazil. The airplane was under the command of Francisco De Pinedo (Marquese de Pinedo, from a noble Neapolitan family) who was accompanied by two mechanics (Del Prete & Zacchetti). The Savoia was powered by four Isotta-Fraschini ASSO 500, water-cooled, V-12 engines of 500 hp each. Eventually the aircraft was flown north via the Caribbean to New Orleans, and across the United States to Arizona. While refueling in Theodore Roosevelt Lake near Phoenix, the fuel coated water ignited due to a careless smoker, and the airplane was destroyed.

A second Savoia Marchetti SM-55, the Santa Maria II, was flown from Italy to New York by the same three airmen only three days after Lindbergh's flight, on May 23, 1927, and eventually was flown from flew from Trepassey Bay, Newfoundland to Italy via the Azores and Portugal. This is a little known flight, probably because of the publicity of Lindbergh's success.

The largest single passenger movement in the history of trans-Atlantic travel reached the end of its first phase on June 3, 1927, with the arrival of six large Cunarders, the Caronia, Carmania, Lancastria, Samaria, and Transylvania, off the coast of Dover, England. The ships were carrying three thousand Rotarians from America to the Rotary Convention in Ostend, Belgium.

This armada steamed out of New York harbor on May 18th, two days before Lindbergh's departure. This was the largest party that had ever crossed the Atlantic.

Note: Distances and flying times shown in this chapter are debatable. This is due in part to the inaccuracies of distance measuring methods of the time, the lack of straight line flights due to weather detours, and variations in altitude.

FOOTNOTES

1. Lighter-Than-Air Flight, C.V. Glines. USAF, Franklin Watts, Inc., New York, NY, 1965, page101

2. *The 91 before Lindbergh,* Peter Allen, Flying Books, Eagan, MN 1985, page 3. (First published in England in 1984 by Airlife Publishing, LTD.)

3. *United States Naval Aviation 1910-1970.* Prepared at the direction of the Deputy Chief of Naval Operations (Air) and the Commander, Naval Air Systems Command, 1970. page 36.

ENDNOTES

Thaddeus Lowe, *America's One-Man Air Corps,* Mary Hoehling, Kingston House, Chicago, 1958. Also published by Julian Messner, Inc. New York, pages 58, 187 and title page.

The Pathfinders, David Nevin, Time-Life Books, Inc. Chicago, IL, 1980.

The First World Flight, Lowell Thomas, Houghton Mifflin Company, Boston and New York, 1925.

Aerosphere 1939, Glenn D. Angle, Aircraft Publishers, New York and Detroit, 1940.

Pioneer of Flight, Henry T. Wallhauser, Hammond, Inc., 1969.

Southern Daily Echo (newspaper) Southampton, England, Thursday, June 2, 1927, "Round the Port." Making History. Found at Central Library, London (The British Library)

Also published by Julian Messner, inc. New York.

The Pathfinders by David Nevin, Time-Life Books, Inc. Chicago, Illinois, 1980

The First World Flight by Lowell Thomas, Houghton-Mifflin Company, Boston and New York, 1925

Aerosphere 1939 by Glenn D. Angle, Aircraft Publishers, New York and Detroit, 1940

Pioneer of Flight by Henry T. Wallhauser, Hammond, Inc. 1969

Southern Daily Echo (newspaper) Southampton, England, Thursday, June 2, 1927, "Round the Port." Making History. Found at Central Library, London (The British Library)

Shown here is Alcock and Brown's Vickers Vimy remodeled bomber that flew the Atlantic in 1919. ***(Cassagneres collection)***

The Douglas DWC "World Cruiser" No. 4 "New Orleans", with its Liberty V-12-A single engine. A large airplane in its day. ***(John Underwood)***

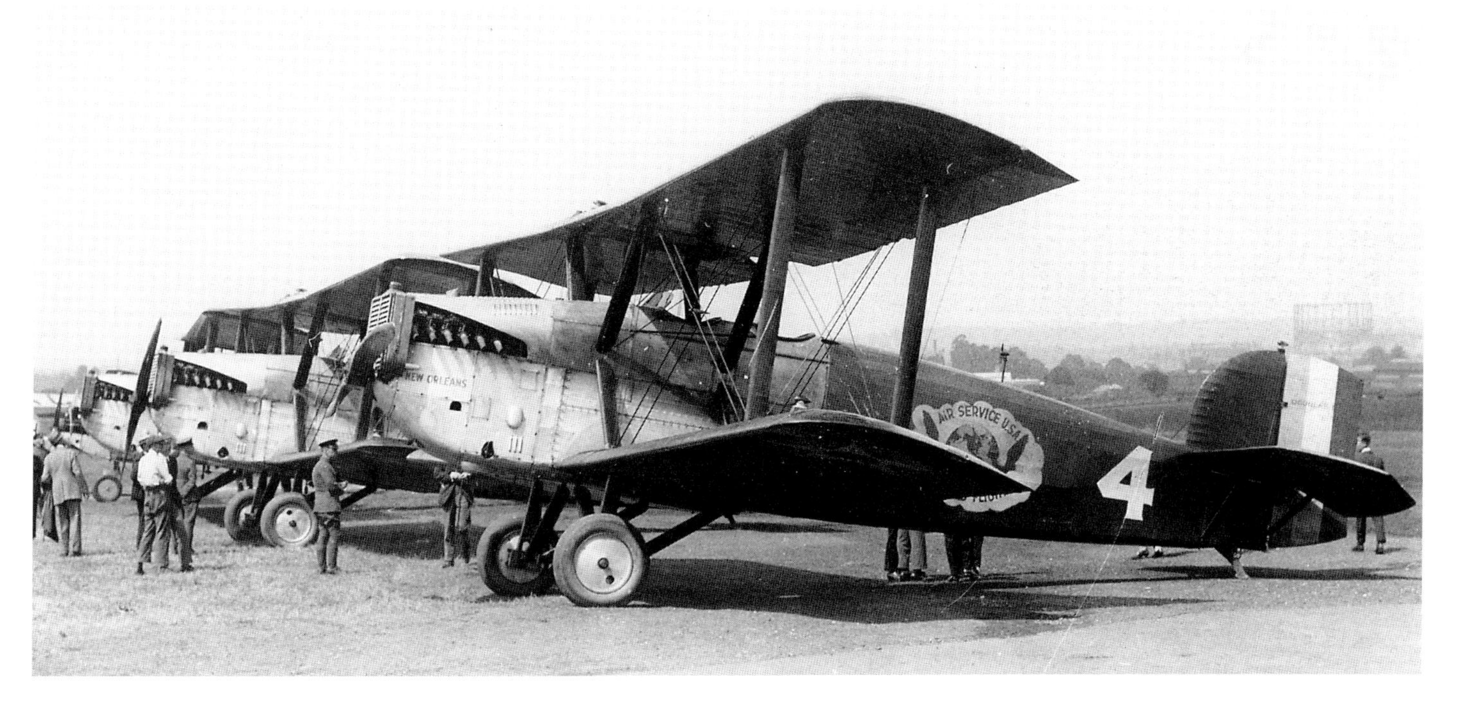

CHAPTER 3

Lindbergh—The Man

Although Charles A. Lindbergh's ancestry began in Sweden, the name Lindbergh did not originate in that Scandinavian country, but actually in the north central United States, after Charles's grandfather, Ola Mansson had left Sweden to settle in Minnesota in the summer of 1859.

Ola Mansson was born May 12th, 1808 in Gardosa, between Smedstorp and Garsnas, (southeast part of Skane, in southern Sweden). He was married in 1833 to Ingar Jonsdotte with whom he had ten children. [1]

In Sweden Ola was a prominent citizen, a self-educated scholar and one of the members of the Swedish Riksdag (Parliament). From about 1847 to 1858 he represented a district in Skane, Kristianstad Lan, in the southern part of Sweden. In addition, he was an officer of the Bank of Sweden. [2]

In 1859 Ola was accused of illegal dealings while in his bank position, and after being cleared of the charges decided to migrate to the United States to begin a new life.

In the meantime Ola had domestic trouble and remarried Louisa Carline, (born Louisa Kallen) and on January 20, 1859 they had a son, Charles August.

At about this time the people of Sweden were slowly changing over from the old-fashioned system of patronymics of adding the suffix SON or DOTTIR, to the father's first name—to the standard surname Lindberg. Ola decided to do just that, and at the same time he changed his first name. He became August Lindberg.

After their arrival in the United States, Ola and his second wife anglicized their last name by adding the letter "h," becoming Lindbergh. They felt it actually looked and sounded better and would add some sort of elegance, thereby giving them a more formal introduction to the higher society. This they also felt would open up opportunities in a country where they would normally be unknown. A higher standard of living such as they enjoyed in their native country could be attained.

The "new" Lindberghs settled on the Sauk River near the town of Melrose, Stearns County, Minnesota, becoming farmers. The countryside, with its many lakes and streams, reminded them of where they had lived in Sweden. They had six more children, three of them dying in infancy.

At the age of 51 Ola and his wife Louisa, with little money and a minimum of equipment, began their business of farming. This new life was not without its hardships, and young Charles developed the same determination and drive to succeed in life under extremely difficult circumstances, as his father had shown him.

By learning to do hunting and trapping and getting a job on the railroad, Charles saved enough money to pay for his law school tuition at the University of Michigan, which he began in 1881.

After graduation in 1883 from a two year course he eventually was admitted to the Minnesota bar, where he worked as a law clerk in St. Cloud. He later opened his own law office in Little Falls.

His law business together with real estate interests prospered. Finally, Louise (nee Louisa) and August (nee Ola) sold the farm and moved to Little Falls to be with their successful son. August died on October 14, 1893 and Louise in April, 1921.

C.A., as he was known, married Mary La Fond (born May 1, 1867) and had three children; Lillian, Edith, and Eva. Mary died

Charles A. Lindbergh in his barnstorming days, with friend Leon Klink (on Lindbergh's right) and a Curtiss Jenny in the background. ***(Minnesota Historical Society)***

on April 16, 1898 and C.A. later acquired 110 acres of land on the Mississippi River and built a home there. Three years later, still a widower, C.A. met Evangeline Lodge Land (born 1875) from Detroit, who came to Little Falls to begin a career as a teacher of chemistry at the local high school. Evangeline was also a University of Michigan graduate. The two decided to marry. The wedding took place in Detroit on March 27, 1901. After a honeymoon out West they returned to Little Falls and the property on the banks of the Mississippi and moved into their new home. Then on February 4, 1902 in Detroit Charles Augustus was born.

Charles Sr. had early established a reputation for honesty and principle, even at great personal cost. His mother was an attractive, high-spirited and gifted young woman, accustomed to scientific thinking. Her father, Dr. Charles Henry Land, was renowned for pioneering in the art of porcelain dentistry.

The traits of the parents—the hardiness and integrity of the father and the scientific curiosity and spirit of the mother—would be indelibly ingrained in their son. The father was an incurable prankster as well.

Years later, following his famous flight, people marveled at young Charles' ease in the company of the eminent who gathered around him, such as in Paris, Brussels, and London, England. The answer lay in his strength of character and in his previous experience. From the time that he was four years old until he was fourteen, his father served as a US Congressman. Growing up in Washington, young Charles was accustomed to seeing and meeting important people, including statesmen and Presidents.

The summers of his youth were spent on the family farm in Minnesota and on camping trips. Under his father's tutelage he developed a strong sense of responsibility, independence and a love of nature. He saw his first airplane when he was ten, and his interest in aviation grew until he was old enough to enter college. He wanted to study aeronautics at MIT, but he wasn't able to pass the entrance requirements. He enrolled at the University of Wisconsin at Madison. Although he was intelligent, academic life was difficult. Theories and formulas took a poor second to the excitement of the outdoor world which beckoned him to explore it on his motorcycle. His freshman grades were mediocre and slid further down in the first semester of his sophomore year. He was not asked to return. The door to aviation via formal schooling had closed. But that only permitted him to do what he really wanted, to be around "real" aircraft.

In April 1922 he became a flying student at the Nebraska Aircraft Corporation at Lincoln. The school was part of the factory which produced the popular Lincoln-Standard biplanes.

Lindbergh experienced his very first airplane ride at Lincoln on April 9, 1922. The flight was in a Lincoln-Standard J-1 "Tourabout", open cockpit bi-plane. He shared the front passenger cockpit with 16 year old Harlan A. "Bud" Gurney, a local lad who worked at the field, and who also loved airplanes. The pilot that day was Otto Timm. Lindbergh and Gurney developed a friendship that lasted for the rest of their lives.

That first flight was enough to convince Lindbergh that this was the way to go in life, to fly, and to live aviation to its fullest.

While working around and on airplanes, he began his first flying lessons. The instructor assigned to him at that time was Ira O. Biffle, sometimes known as "Biff" amongst the local flyers.

By the end of May Lindbergh, often referred to as a natural, was clearly ready to solo. During this learning process he found the experience rather frustrating, due to Biff not always showing up at the appointed time, or when he did, the flying conditions were not just right, for one reason or another. He had accumulated about eight hours of dual, but he did not solo at that point. Ray Page, the owner of the operation, stipulated that Lindbergh

An MB-3 early fighter, shown at Brooks or Kelly Field in Texas, often flown in training by Lindbergh. ***(Minnesota Historical Society)***

would have to put up a $500 bond before he could take the chance of letting him solo. "Slim" (as he was nicknamed by friend Gurney) did not have that kind of money, so he had to decline the opportunity. At the same time Page sold one of the training airplanes to Erold G. Bahl, noted local and respected flyer, who was planning a 'barnstorming' tour. Lindbergh signed up with the Bahl operation as a helper, in order to gain further experience in the flying game. He went to work as a barker, mechanic and wing-walker.

The troupe returned to Lincoln in June, and Lindbergh was hired back at the factory doing odd jobs. While in Lincoln he had met Lt. Charles Hardin, who made parachutes. Through this contact he developed an interest in these safety devices and eventually made his first jump. It was a 'double' jump, in which he had two parachutes, one of which he opened after leaving the airplane, and then cut it loose. He then pulled the rip chord for the second one and after a long delay the second finally opened, and he landed safely.

It did not take long for Lindbergh to be offered a job barnstorming again, only this time with a wheat farmer from Bird City, Kansas by the name of "Banty" Rogers, and a pilot known as Harold J. "Shorty" Lynch. Lindbergh was hired as a mechanic as well as parachute jumper and wing-walker. They barnstormed through Kansas, Nebraska, Wyoming and Colorado, all that summer and fall of 1922.

In the spring of 1923 young Lindbergh went to Souther Field in Americus, Georgia, where he purchased a war surplus Curtiss OX-5 Jenny with $500. loaned by his father. When the airplane had been assembled and tuned up, he made an abortive first solo which ended abruptly on one wheel and a wing skid. A friendly pilot by the name of Henderson saw his distress and gave him some dual time in the unfamiliar plane. Lindbergh flew with this experienced pilot for about thirty minutes doing several take-offs and landings. The stranger felt "Slim" was only a bit rusty and would do fine after that. Henderson also suggested he wait until evening when the air would be smoother to make a few solo flights. That evening, with his confidence up, Lindbergh did just fine on his first real flight alone. The exact date in April of 1923 is not known.

After a few days of practice he took off on a successful barnstorming tour of several Southern states, all the while working his way homeward to Minnesota.

It was on this trip north that he flew a very interesting female passenger, a prominent and beloved old country doctor, to treat a patient near the Wisconsin River.

Getting to these sick was often an adventure. One day Dr. Bertha Reynolds received a call from the little town of Clyde, a community located south of the Wisconsin River. That river was at flood stage, making it impossible to cross by bridge or boat. Dr. Bertha, as she was known, learned that a young barnstorming aviator had landed at the Lone Rock airport. She asked him if he could fly her across the river. So, at the age of fifty-five, she climbed into his open cockpit biplane, and asked, "What is your name, young man?" "Charles Lindbergh," he replied. "Well, Charles, I'm in a hurry, so let's be off."

They landed in a field near Clyde, and as Lindbergh tinkered with his airplane, Dr. Bertha attended to her patient. Soon they flew back across the river to Plain, where they landed in a school yard. As Dr. Bertha treated another patient, Lindbergh gave rides to the students.

Continuing on from there to Marshall, Minnesota "Slim" met his father, who was campaigning for re-election to Congress. The two made many flights together, the senior Lindbergh throwing out political handbills as they flew over the towns.

Once the campaign was over he spent the remainder of the summer barnstorming throughout Minnesota, northern Iowa and western Wisconsin. He spent some of this time giving flying lessons to his first student and later continued barnstorming in southern Minnesota with his mother. He had taken her up for her first flight in Janesville earlier that year.

One evening while he was waiting for passengers at a field in southern Minnesota, a young graduate of the Army Air Service Training school approached Lindbergh and tantalized him with the thought of gaining experience as an Army Cadet, flying the powerful and well-maintained DeHavilland airplanes. That night Lindbergh wrote a letter to the Chief of Air Service and a few days later received the necessary enrollment blanks from Washington. In January 1924, after completing and returning the forms, he received the authorization to appear before an examining board at Chanute Field, Rantoul, Illinois.

He continued to barnstorm, eventually finding himself at Lambert Field near St. Louis, Missouri. There he attended The International Air Races. His enthusiasm was sparked even more when he inspected and observed the many flights of high powered military aircraft. He became even more determined to let nothing interfere with his chances of becoming a flying cadet in the Army.

BROOKS FIELD

Lindbergh continued to barnstorm in Illinois, then sold his jenny, and in January made his way to Chanute Field to take entrance exams to be a flying cadet. He entered the March 15, 1924 class at Brooks Field in San Antonio, Texas. His heart and mind were into what he was doing, and he excelled in his class.

At that time the Army was using the popular Curtiss JN-4 "Jenny", powered with the 90 h.p. Curtiss OX-5, water cooled, V-8 engine. It was later replaced with the 150 h.p. Hispano-Suiza, affectionately referred to as the "Hisso".

Lindbergh's assigned flight instructor was Master Sergeant Bill Winston, an aviator who held the record for flying time in the Army with about thirty-three hundred hours.

It is believed that Lindbergh was the only cadet with previous flying experience, which helped him advance a bit more rapidly than some of the other students. The demands of military precision flying polished his skills even more, preparing him not only to serve his country but also for his future flying career.

As the class neared the end of the Brooks Field training, they passed their primary flying requirements. They were then checked out in more maneuverable and faster airplanes, such as TW-3's and Voughts, and finally De Haviland DH-4B's, powered with either the 150 h.p. Hispano-Suiza or the 400 h.p. 12 cylinder Liberty engine. At this point in their training they were concentrating on both cross-country navigating as well as formation flying. This was an introduction to both phases before going on to Kelly Field near San Antonio, Texas. Lindbergh graduated from Brooks with the second highest scores.

KELLY FIELD

In September 1924 Lindbergh was transferred to Kelly Field, San Antonio, for advanced training courses. Now he and his classmates were treated as potential officers rather than rookies. They had about seventy-five hours of flying time in their log books.

At Kelly Lindbergh got to advance into even more challenging airplanes such as the S.E.-5 scout, the M.B.-3, the Sperry messenger, the T.W.-5 two place transition airplane and twin engine Martin Bomber with twin Liberty engines.

It was at Kelly that Lindbergh experienced his first emergency parachute jump. This took place after a collision of SE-5's during a scheduled sham-combat attack.

After a year at Kelly, Lindbergh and seventeen of the original hundred and four cadets remained on graduation day. Lindbergh graduated first in his class and was given the coveted wings and a commission as a Second Lieutenant in the Air Service Reserve Corps.

It was during his military training that Lindbergh met Phil Love, another cadet whom he flew with later in his career, and Elmer F. Beckstrand, a cadet he teamed up with to play very funny practical jokes on fellow cadets, helping to balance the tensions of the everyday pressures of flight training.

BECOMES AIR MAIL PILOT

The day after he graduated from Kelly Field, "Slim" took a train to St. Louis, Missouri, with the intention of getting back into barnstorming.

*Lindbergh in winter flying suit for a cold winter's airmail flight in a Douglas M-2 mail plane **(United Technologies Archive)***

He obtained an OX-5 powered Standard and spent time flying all over Iowa, Illinois and Missouri.

It was at this time that the United States Post Office Department advertised several air mail contract routes for bid. One of these routes, CAM #2. (Contract Air Mail, route #2) was between St. Louis, Springfield & Peoria, Illinois, and Chicago, (a distance of two hundred seventy-eight miles). Lindbergh took note of this and continued to barnstorm until he learned who the winner of that contract would be. One of the bidders was the Robertson Aircraft Corporation based at Lambert Field outside St. Louis. They offered Lindbergh the position of Chief Pilot if they won the contract.

His barnstorming continued, and he traveled all around Iowa, Missouri and out to Colorado and other parts of the country.

At the end of October 1925 Lindbergh made his way back to St. Louis, where he spent the winter as a flight instructor for

Robertson Aircraft Corporation on their OX-5 Standards. Robertson had been awarded the air mail contract, but the actual operation was not to begin until the following Spring.

In November 1925, while at Robertson, Lindbergh enlisted in the 110th Observation Squadron of the 35th Division of the Missouri National Guard, where he was commissioned as a First Lieutenant. The squadron was based at Lambert Field, next to the Robertson operation.

Mostly on Sundays, their flying training day, he got to fly T.W.-3's and Jenny's again. He considered this a good opportunity to stay in tune with military flying and considered it a patriotic duty to keep fit for immediate service in case of a national emergency.

In the meantime Robertson, which was owned and operated by brothers Major William B. and Frank H. Robertson, purchased four DH-4 airplanes from Army salvage plus Liberty engines and rebuilt them in their shops. These English designed airplanes were built during World War I for bombing and observation purposes and had two cockpits, the front cockpit for the pilot and the rear for the observer. Robertson converted the DH's into single cockpit versions, putting the pilot in the rear and allowing for the mail in the forward cockpit area.

Lindbergh as Chief Pilot drew a salary of $3,600. a year. He and his friends Phil Love and Thomas Nelson as line pilots would handle the St. Louis-Chicago mail run.

Service was inaugurated along the 278 mile route on April 15, 1926.

Lindbergh experienced three additional emergency parachute jumps while at Robertson (his first being at Kelly Field.) The first of the three was during a test flight in an OX biplane constructed at St. Louis by one of the Robertson Aircraft engineers. Lindbergh could not get the airplane out of a flat, lunging spin.

The next two jumps were made while flying the mail between St. Louis and Chicago.

Lindbergh was gaining valuable experience as a professional aviator delivering mail in all kinds of winter and summer weather conditions. Unknown at the time, this background was to prepare him for the flight of all flights in aviation history.

The Lindbergh family was deeply rooted in courage. Lindbergh's father showed a Viking's love of adventure. His mother passed on that reticence, that unassuming modesty and yet that intelligent curiosity which, combined with a passion for mechanics, resulted in his being acclaimed the pilot and hero of all time and winning the hearts of people all over the world.

It was in September 1926 when "Slim" was piloting one of those surplus World War I DH-4s on a night flight from St. Louis to Chicago that he began thinking of a long distance flight over the Atlantic Ocean. The sun was just setting to the west, as his thoughts became the start of a master plan to attempt such an incredible feat.

"Suppose I really could stay up here and keep on flying. Suppose gasoline didn't weigh so much and I could put enough in the tanks to last for days. Suppose, like the man on the magic carpet I could fly anywhere I wanted to, anywhere in the world, to the North Pole or to China or to some jungle island if I wished. How much fuel could a plane carry if its fuselage were filled with tanks? Why does fuel have to be so heavy? If gasoline weighed only a pound per gallon instead of six, there'd be no limit to the places one could fly—if the engine kept on running."

His mind continued to wonder into the future of aviation and air travel. He was convinced and believed aviation did have a future and that businessmen needed to be convinced and to understand the possibilities of flight. They would understand the importance of financing an airline between New York and St. Louis for instance, or anywhere else for that matter.

They would understand how swiftly and safely passengers could fly, maybe even non-stop from one end of the country to the other in either direction. All kinds of records were out there to be broken, to prove this point, to prove his theories and projections and visions.

With very careful planning, one could build an airplane that could break the world's endurance record, and the transcontinental, and set a dozen marks for range and speed and weight.

"Possibly—my mind is startled at its thought—I could fly nonstop between New York and Paris."

PLANNING THE FLIGHT

Lindbergh realized that several public minded and spirited businessmen from the St. Louis area might be interested in the future of aviation enough to finance a record flight.

But first he would have to do some homework in the way of very careful investigation and planning.

First priority was what type of airplane would be best suited for this flight and how many engines would be necessary. Should it be a biplane or monoplane, wing on top or bottom. A monoplane made more sense due to the efficiency of less drag of flying and landing wires and multiple struts. The weight difference would negate the ability to carry more weight in fuel and could carry a greater load per square foot of surface at a higher speed.

A single engine would have the advantage of lesser frontal area so less resistance would result in a greater cruising range. There would be three times the risk of engine failure in a tri-motor airplane, and that extra engine would be dead weight (worth much fuel also) for the rest of the trip.

As Lindbergh so clearly reasoned, the reliability of the then modern air-cooled radial engine was so great that the chances of an immediate forced landing due to engine failure of a single engine would be more than counterbalanced by a longer cruising range. Consequently, there was the advantage of reaching the objective, even with unfavorable conditions. The engine he had in mind was the well proven Wright "Whirlwind" which had a reputation for rarely stopping, unlike the old Liberty engines he had flown behind so often.

He also felt that when it came to weather, flying over the ocean could not be much worse than conditions he had experienced so often in flying the mail at night in the dead of winter. With enough fuel he would never have to worry about fog, for instance, and if he did get caught he could simply keep on flying until he found clear weather.

As for navigation, he figured that if he just held to the correct course long enough he should arrive somewhere on the European coast.

And why should he not fly to Europe? He was almost twenty-five years old and had more than four years of piloting experience with almost 2000 hours of flight time logged. He had barnstormed all over the United States, fighting weather, and difficult wind conditions in the Rocky Mountains. He had training at two of the best Army flight training schools in America where he learned the basic elements of air navigation. He was a also Captain in the 110th Observation Squadron of the Missouri National Guard.

He contemplated such a flight though he found it rather overwhelming at times. He reasoned that he had had dreams before which became reality, although appearing insurmountable at the time. He had learned to fly an airplane, then become an air show pilot, wing-walker, parachute jumper, and later a military aviator and eventually an air mail flyer. He was quite successful at all of these endeavors and was able to deal with difficult weather conditions and navigation challenges. Clearly he had the potential to fly and navigate an airplane over the ocean to another continent if he had the right airplane.

So the decision was made to go ahead with this dream.

Lindbergh thought further about financial backing and the possibility of the Wright Aeronautical Corporation financing his project. They could profit by use of their engine. If the flight was successful their chances for high sales could be unlimited.

As Lindbergh awoke early one morning to prepare for another air mail run, he suddenly realized that this was not like other mornings. This was a special one in which he had special thoughts—"Oh, yes, this is the dawn of a new life, a life in which I'm going to fly across the ocean to Europe!"

Between Chicago's Maywood Field and St. Louis, his thoughts continued to center on a plan. He considered where he could find a suitable airplane and how he would find the information on its performance, such as cruise speed, take-off run distance, and fuel consumption. He had heard about the Bellanca (Wright-Bellanca) airplane being built in New Jersey and from information he had read it was supposed to be one of the most efficient aircraft on the market.

Where could he get information on the Wright-Bellanca? How quickly could he purchase one, and at what cost? These were simple but logical questions for someone planning such a flight.

Because he was just an air mail pilot and for the most part unknown in aviation circles of the time, he knew he could not just approach any airplane or engine manufacturer with the suggestion that they supply him with such equipment to fly over the ocean to Paris, France. They might possibly be interested in having their products be the first to fly to Paris, but they would look very carefully at who would be the pilot or crew. More than likely it would not be Charles Lindbergh. Choices of such qualified people were high in the New York area with Bert Acosta, Clarence Chamberlin, Commander Richard Byrd, and Col. Bernt Balchen for starters. Tough competition indeed.

He would need the backing of some pretty important and forward thinking business people before he could even consider approaching the Wright-Bellanca Company in New Jersey. He would need men not only with vision like his but also influence and money. But who?

Although he was interested in the Wright-Bellanca, he also considered the Fokker Company in New Jersey and the Huff-Deland firm in Ogdensburg, New York.

As for finances, he had two thousand dollars of his own in a savings account, a reserve he built up in case of some unforeseen emergency. Now that he was a rather experienced aviator, he felt he could take some risk in the use of these funds to promote his dream.

Now another plan had to be worked out—a plan to convince business minded people about the value of investing in aviation and air travel for the future, which he deeply believed in.

Lindbergh had picked his target. He was staying on track without looking back. He continued to think it through, to work out his plan. He truly believed that one should always, always try—a good philosophy for us all.

He was beginning to think about his best business contacts in St. Louis. A St. Louis connection and backing could put this big mid-west city on a worldwide map and into the foreground of aviation development. He would have to convince them that a modern and well designed airplane could be built that would be capable of making such a long over-water flight, non-stop.

He would also show them that such a successful flight would be capable of covering its own costs by winning the Orteig $25,000. prize. Making such a flight could open up all kinds of possibilities for air travel anywhere in the United States, or the world.

THE "WE" GROUP IN ST. LOUIS

Lindbergh's friendship with Frank Robertson had been made on earlier visits, when the Lambert Field pilots had been impressed by his abilities. When Lindbergh became established at the field, he found his spare time in demand as a flying instructor and test pilot. This gave him a name in area aviation and an introduction to two air-minded St. Louis businessmen who were to become partners in the *Spirit of St. Louis* organization, Harry Hall Knight and Earl C. Thompson.

Knight was president of the St. Louis Flying Club and an attorney and partner in the firm of Knight, Dysart & Gamble in St. Louis. Thompson was vice-president of the Indemnity Company of America and an amateur aviator, who owned a Laird airplane.

Lindbergh met first with Harry Knight at Knight's home in early February 1927. After "Slim" explained the pros and cons of such a flight and answered Mr. Knight's many questions, the senior businessman showed much interest and was encouraging but cautious due to his business expertise.

Lindbergh next approached Major Albert Bond Lambert for whom Lambert Field (presently Lambert-St. Louis International Airport) was named. Lambert was a Major in the Army Signal Corp., a former balloonist and Chairman of the St. Louis Chamber of Commerce Committee on Aeronautics. Lambert listened carefully to Lindbergh's plans and agreed to participated. He offered $1000. as a start toward finances.

William Bryan "Bill" Robertson was a Major in the Army Air Corps and Lindbergh's employer. Due to business losses Robertson could not offer much money, if any, but Lindbergh was more interested in the Robertson Aircraft Corporation agreeing to be part of the group backing his plans. His boss agreed and suggested that Lindbergh contact Harold M. Bixby, who at the time was President of the St. Louis Chamber of Commerce and Vice President of the State National Bank.

The following letter by Harold M. Bixby expresses his enthusiasm for enabling the initiation of this project.

Feb. 18, 1927

Memo for Board:

Charles A. Lindbergh, Air Mail Pilot on the St. Louis-Chicago Route, wants to make the first aeroplane flight from New York to Paris.

As you know, I have been very much interested in aviation for a long time past and have taken a number of trips in my plane in the interest of the Bank. Harry H. Knight, President of the Flying Club, Albert Bond Lambert, Earl Thompson, myself and several others are raising the necessary money to buy the plane with which Lindbergh will make the attempt. It will take some time to raise the required amount, but we must have the $15,000 immediately.

Will the State National Bank lend Harry Knight and me $15,000, we to endorse the note personally?

(Signed) Harold M. Bixby

KNIGHT LETTER TO DWIGHT MORROW

New York City

June 29, 1927

Dear Mr. Morrow:

In connection with Charles A. Lindbergh's trans-Atlantic flight, I am very glad to tell you just how it came about. In the early part of February, 1927, Lindbergh called on me in my office, accompanied by W. B. Robertson, and said that he had been considering for some time a flight across the ocean from New York to Paris for the Raymond Orteig $25,000 prize. He stated that he had discussed this matter with several people in St. Louis interested in aviation and that they had declared an interest in the flight but that nobody had taken a lead in the matter. He asked me if I could assist him in raising the money necessary to buy a plane and finance the entire transaction. After some discussion as to the details of his plan, lasting over a few days, I told him that I would undertake to do this. I had several conferences with Mr. Harold M. Bixby who then became interested in Lindbergh and his flight and we agreed to underwrite the undertaking and borrowed from the State National Bank in St. Louis $15,000, endorsing the note personally. We then obtained subscriptions from the following gentlemen in the amount set after their names:

A. B. Lambert,	$1,000.
H. F. Knight,	$1,000.
H. M. Bixby,	$1,000.
H. H. Knight,	$1,000.
W. B. Robertson	$1,000.
St. Louis Globe-Democrat	$1,000.
Earl C. Thompson	$500.
Charles A. Lindbergh	$2,000.
	$8,500.

You will note that the largest subscription is $2,000 from Lindbergh himself, which was the original contribution made by Lindbergh out of his earnings as an air mail flyer. It has always been the intention of Mr. Bixby and myself that this subscription should be returned, if enough money were received in excess of the amount necessary to finance the flight. We have, however, not yet told Lindbergh of this plan. He, as a matter of fact, is not only willing but eager to bear his full share of the expense.

Assuming that Lindbergh's subscription is returned to him, the total amount collected for the flight would be $6,500. The total expense is not yet accurately known. In fact, some expenses are still going on. I estimate roughly that the expenses will be approximately $16,000 to $17,000, including the expenses of Mr. Bixby and myself for special trips made in connection with the enterprise, telegrams, cables, telephone calls across the Atlantic, etc.

You were good enough to say, the other day, that you would be glad of the opportunity to participate in the expenses incident to the flight.

I would like to take this opportunity to express to you the sincere thanks of Colonel Lindbergh and his St. Louis associates for the great assistance you have been to all of us in this affair. [3]

Yours sincerely,

(Signed) Harry H. Knight

Mr. Dwight W. Morrow,
New York City

LINDBERGH GOES TO NEW YORK

Lindbergh telephoned the Wright Aeronautical Corporation and made an appointment to speak with them about the purchase of a Bellanca airplane powered by one of their engines for a flight from New York to Paris.

After a meeting in their Paterson, New Jersey offices, Wright executive introduced Lindbergh to Giuseppe Bellanca, designer of the Bellanca airplane. They discussed in detail the plan, and Bellanca fully understood the design concept and agreed to work along with Lindbergh on an airplane capable of such a flight.

Lindbergh returned to St. Louis and again met with Harry Knight, who shortly arranged a meeting with Lindbergh, Harold Bixby and himself.

The usual questions were gone over again in front of Bixby. The possibilities of working with Bellanca in New Jersey and the possible use of a Wright engine for the Bellanca airplane were discussed.

Lindbergh met again with Harold Bixby at his bank office in downtown St. Louis. The alert businessman assured Lindbergh that he and his friends were sold on the proposition and that they would handle the financial end if he would go ahead and make his plans to obtain a suitable airplane for the flight. Bixby further stated that they would work out the rest of the organization of this support group and asked that Lindbergh work on further details.

Now Lindbergh realized that if Bellanca was not able to come through he had better sound out other airplane manufacturers around the country. How about the Travel Air Company in Wichita, Kansas for one. They were producing a monoplane similar in configuration to the Wright-Bellanca. He had also read something about a company on the West Coast by the name of Ryan that was producing a high-wing monoplane being used on an air mail run for the Pacific Air Transport Company.

But when Lindbergh contacted the Travel Air Company they showed no interest. He then thought of Curtiss, Douglas, Martin, and Boeing in Seattle.

On February 3, 1927 he sent a telegram to the Ryan Airlines, Inc. in San Diego, California.

WESTERN UNION

RYAN AIRLINES INC. ANGLUM MO.
SAN DIEGO CALIFORNIA, FEB 3 1927

CAN YOU CONSTRUCT WHIRLWIND ENGINE PLANE CAPABLE FLYING NONSTOP BETWEEN NEW YORK AND PARIS STOP IF SO PLEASE STATE COST AND DELIVERY DATA

ROBERTSON AIRCRAFT CORP.

Their reply:

WESTERN UNION

SAN DIEGO CALIF. FEB. 4, 1927 6:16 PM
ROBERTSON AIRCRAFT CORP.
ANGLUM, MO.

CAN BUILD PLANE SIMILAR M ONE BUT LARGER WINGS CAPABLE OF MAKING FLIGHT COST ABOUT SIX THOUSAND WITHOUT MOTOR AND INSTRUMENTS DELIVERY ABOUT THREE MONTHS

RYAN AIRLINES

Lindbergh thought that with the engine it would cost about ten thousand dollars, quite well within their budget.

Here was a company, almost unknown like himself, who had shown an interest with an immediate reply. So he telegramed back to them —

WESTERN UNION

RYAN AIRLINES INC. ANGLUM, MO.
SAN DIEGO, CALIFORNIA FEB. 5, 1927 6:50 PM

COMPETITION MAKES TIME ESSENTIAL CAN YOU CONSTRUCT PLANE IN LESS THAN THREE MONTHS STOP PLEASE WIRE GENERAL SPECIFICATIONS,
ROBERTSON AIRCRAFT CORP.

Ryan's reply:

WESTERN UNION

SAN DIEGO CALIF.
3 PM FEB. 5, 1927
ROBERTSON AIRCRAFT CORP.
ANGLUM, MO.

GAS CAPACITY THREE HUNDRED EIGHTY GALLONS CRUISING SPEED ONE HUNDRED MILES PER HOUR LOADING ONLY TWELVE AND HALF POUNDS PER FOOT AND TWENTY POUNDS PER HORSE POWER STOP CAN COMPLETE IN TWO MONTHS FROM DATE OF ORDER IF NECESSARY STOP WILL REQUIRE FIFTY PERCENT DEPOSIT

RYAN AIRLINES

Lindbergh was impressed with these figures of fuel capacity and air speed with a 200 h.p. engine.

He showed all of these telegrams to Bixby and Knight, and they had questions about a company they have never heard of. But because they figured Ryan had probably never heard of them either, they would continue with their plans.

Because Ryan was willing to build a special airplane for this one flight, it put them way ahead of the other companies Lindbergh had contacted.

In the meantime another telegram arrived addressed to Lindbergh—

WESTERN UNION

PASSAIC NJ 11:10 AM 2-6-27

CHAS. A. LINDBERGH

ROBERTSON AIRCRAFT CORP.

ANGLUM, MO.

SORRY DELAYED AS HAVE BEEN OUT OF TOWN WILLING TO MAKE ATTRACTIVE PROPOSITION ON THE BELLANCA AIRPLANE FOR PARIS FLIGHT STOP SUGGEST YOU COME NEW YORK SOON POSSIBLE SO WE CAN GET TOGETHER IN QUICKEST MANNER STOP WIRE ME CARE COLUMBIA AIRCRAFT CORPORATION 5104 WOOLWORTH BUILDING NEW YORK.

BELLANCA

Lindbergh was planning to make a trip to the Ryan Company to get started on construction of the airplane, but since this latest contact with Bellanca came through he decided to forget Ryan for the moment and go ahead with arrangements with Bellanca.

Lindbergh made a second trip to New York to meet with Mr. Levine, who was chairman of the Board of Directors of the Columbia Aircraft Corporation and their pilot, Clarence Chamberlin. Apparently Giuseppe Bellanca had broken his relationship with the Wright Aeronautical Company at the time Levine offered to develop his airplane design for production.

The meeting went well and sounded extremely encouraging to Lindbergh, even to the point of offering the normally priced $25,000 airplane for $15,000, indicating a contribution of $10,000. toward the Paris flight for the Columbia Company.

With Bellanca's design abilities and the specifications and configuration of the Bellanca airplane, and with Lindbergh in charge of the building and the flight of this airplane, there is no doubt that he would have been successful in flying from New York to Paris, France in 1927.

Lindbergh returned to St. Louis, announcing the wonderful news of firming up a deal for an airplane to his financial backers.

They were excited and already coming up with ideas such as what to name the airplane. Bixby was the one who suggested they call it—"THE SPIRIT OF ST. LOUIS" (L'Esprit de Saint Louis), certainly appropriate considering the project. Little did Bixby know how well known that name would become over the years.

ORIGIN OF THE NAME ST. LOUIS

But let us digress to the origin of the naming of this large midwestern city, whose name was applied to the nose of the world's most famous airplane in aviation history.

Pierre Laclede, born in 1724 in the village of Bedous, in the lower Pyrenees, France, migrated to New Orleans in 1755 and became a trader by profession. In 1757 he formed a union with one Marie Therese Chouteau, separated from her husband with an infant son, (Rene') Auguste Chouteau. Together they moved north in 1763 to the east side of the Missouri River, where he established a trading post. 4

In 1764 he and his step-son established a village on the west side of the Missouri River, and named it St. Louis, in honor of Louis IX, one of the great kings of France.

King Louis, born in 1214, was a hero in every way. He came to the throne at age 12, and with his mother's tutoring became a pious, unselfish ruler. His reputation was that of a respectful, fair and just king.

Like Lindbergh, he traveled. He led a crusade to the Holy Land in 1248, and in 1270 another trip to Africa, where he died. He united the qualities of a "just and upright sovereign, a fearless warrior, and saint", according to biographical material. Louis was strong, idealistic, austere. His character and foundations were many. Twenty-seven years after his death in 1297 Louis was canonized; the man who was "every inch a king", thus became a saint in the Roman Catholic Church. The year of his canonization, 1297 carries the same digits as 1927, the year of Lindbergh's flight.

In France the "Fete St. Louis" (St. Louis Feast Day) is celebrated on August 25.

ORIGIN OF THE TERM "SPIRIT OF" ST. LOUIS

The name coined by Harold Bixby was not the very first time "*Spirit of St. Louis*"was created, however. It actually appeared for the first time in 1913. And in 1922 a movie was produced having as its title "The *Spirit of St. Louis*". Here is the story.

First conceived by the Chamber of Commerce of St. Louis in 1913 and revived by its predecessors in 1922-23 as a crusade for the good, the true, the beautiful and the proud, the city was to become a "New St. Louis." As stated by the Reverend Doctor W. C. Bitting, the City had emphasized virtues that could not be measured. Thus, he says, "A city is more than an assemblage of buildings with streets between them. It has a soul and an atmosphere and a social significance to which all material things should be made to minister."

A motion picture depicting the years from the city's beginning to the present was produced as a public spirited movement to acquaint the public with the city's heritage.

"The *Spirit of St. Louis*" was the first historical film of its kind ever produced by an American city. It was made by the Rothacker Film Manufacturing Company of Chicago and featured many highlights of the city's history and reflected the 'Spirit of Achievement."

Lindbergh then planned to return to New York with a check to purchase the Bellanca, have extra fuel tanks installed and fly it on a test flight to St. Louis with the opportunity to not only give it a thorough checkout, but show his backers the airplane he hoped would make history.

However, it was not to be, as further discussion in the offices of the Columbia Company that day would put Lindbergh in a state of shock.

When the subject of who the crew would be arose, Levine, Chamberlin and Bellanca made it clear that they would pick their own pilot for the flight.

Lindbergh returned to St. Louis and soon the plans were changed to sign with Ryan in San Diego, hoping they would not turn him down too for some strange reason.

If that were to happen, he discussed the possibility of giving up the whole idea of flying to Paris and that perhaps they should concentrate on a Pacific flight. There were no plans in the country to fly the Pacific so there would be plenty of time to design and build a special airplane for such an undertaking. This could be even a greater demonstration of the capabilities of aviation and air travel.

But Knight and Bixby, however, were not interested in a Pacific flight. They wanted to stick with their original plans of a flight to Paris and were certain that it could be accomplished as Lindbergh had outlined and suggested in the first place.

Other partners of this support group included friends of Bixby; Harry French Knight, father of Harry Hall Knight; Frank

H. Robertson, brother to William Robertson; J.D. Wooster Lambert, brother of Albert Bond "Doc" Lambert; and E. Lansing Ray, Editor and Publisher of the St. Louis Globe—Democrat newspaper.

It was Albert Bond Lambert who issued the first check to Lindbergh. Bixby and Harry Knight arranged for a bank loan that assured the purchase of the airplane. Knight also handled the entry forms for the Orteig prize.

After the first meeting on January 9, 1927 William Robertson, and his brother Frank advanced Lindbergh $1000. Soon the Knights and Harold Bixby had secured $15,000. on notes at The State National Bank of St. Louis and underwrote the project, taking subscriptions of from $500. to $1000. The money was deposited to the credit of the committee.

Lindbergh's target figure for the airplane was set at $15,000. which included equipment, fuel, and related expenses. $2000 of that would be from his own pocket.

A popular misconception which started with his first book entitled WE has been quoted throughout the world as meaning Lindbergh and the airplane *Spirit of St. Louis*, or "man and machine" as it were. However, in 1968 Lindbergh declared to the author in a letter that, "I never used the term "We" to refer to the *Spirit of St. Louis* and myself. This was a newspaper concoction or misconception. I use "We" to refer to the men, including myself, who were members of the *Spirit of St. Louis* organization by which the purchase of the plane and the costs of the flight to Paris were financed." [5]

FOOTNOTES

1. *Lindbergh Alone*, Brenden Gill, Harcourt Brace Jovanovich, New York and London, 1977, page 52.

2. Gardosa (directly translated means "without house") was a small group of farm houses. Ref: letter to author dated December 21, 1996 from Pierre Hollander, balsta, sweden.

3. Copy donated to the author July, 2000 by Constance U.Sanders, Alpharetta, GA.

4. *Dictionary of American Biography*, Vol. V, Hibben-Larkin, edited by Dumas malone. Charles Scribner's Sons, New York, pages 520-521.

5. Letter to the author dated April 7, 1968 from Charles A. Lindbergh, Darien, CT, page 3.

ENDNOTES

Some of the information in this chapter was gleaned from Lindbergh's *We, Spirit of St. Louis, Wartime Journals,* and his *Autobiography of Values*. Frequently he did "flashbacks" to his days as a barnstormer, military student and fighter pilot, and later as an instructor, test pilot and air mail pilot. This author found these publications to be accurate, thorough, informative and consistent.

Information found in these works was occasionally in disagreement with other publications by respected authors, some of whom specialized in their field (air mail, military aviation, passenger air-lines etc.). Therefore, this author used the Lindbergh writings as his primary sources of reference.

Charles A. Lindbergh, Autobiography of Values, Harcourt Brace Jovanovich, New York and London, 1976, 1977, 1978 by Harcourt Brace Jovanovich, Inc. and Anne Morrow Lindbergh

Lindbergh of Minnesota, A Political Biography by Bruce L. Larson, Foreword by Charles A. Lindbergh, Jr. Harcourt Brace Jovanovich, Inc. New York. 1971

Anne Morrow Lindbergh, her Life by Susan Hertog, Nan A. Talese, Doubleday, Random House, Inc., New York, 1999

Boyhood on the Upper Mississippi, A Reminiscent Letter, Minnesota Historical Society, St. Paul, MN, 1972

The Spirit of St. Louis, Charles a Lindbergh, Charles Scribner's Sons, New York, 1953.

Charles A. Lindbergh and the Battle Against American Intervention in World War II by Wayne S. Cole, Harcourt Brace Jovanovich, Inc., New York, NY, 1974

We, Charles A. Lindbergh, G.P. Putnam's Sons, New York and London, 1927

Letter from Charles A. Lindbergh to William P. McCracken, Jr. at Washington, DC. Written on July 21, 1968 from somewhere in Germany.

Earth Pilot to Celestial Pilot by Elmer Francis Beckstrand. Published by Elmer and Ina beckstrand, Orem, Utah (publication date unknown.) Copy in author's possession. From Elmer and Ina Beckstrand, 1995

Western Union Telegrams, dated February 4 and February 5, 1927 to Robertson Aircraft Corporation, Anglum, MO from Ryan Air Line, San Diego. Original

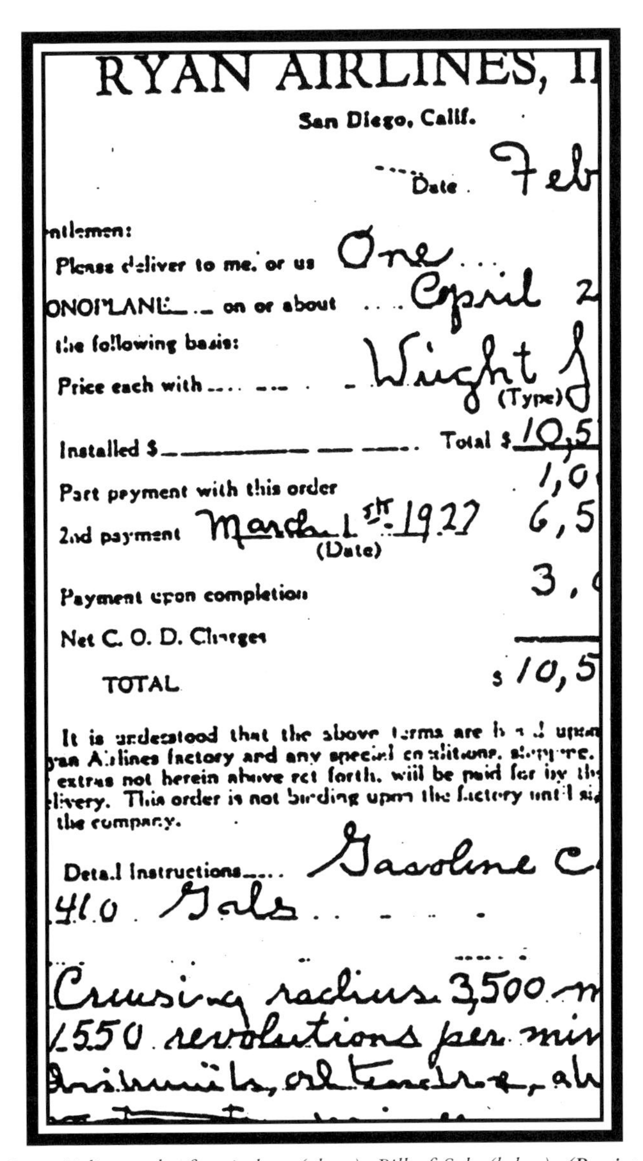

RYAN AIRLINES, I

San Diego, Calif.

Date Feb

ntlemen:

Please deliver to me or us One...

ONOPLANE on or about April 2

the following basis: Wright J

Price each with (Type)

Installed $ Total $ 10,5

Part payment with this order 1,0

2nd payment March 1st 1927 (Date) 6,5

Payment upon completion 3,

Net C. O. D. Charges

TOTAL $ 10,5

It is understood that the above terms are ... upon Ryan Airlines factory and any special conditions ... extras not herein above set forth, will be paid for by the ... livery. This order is not binding upon the factory until si... the company.

Detail Instructions.... Gasoline c

410 Gals

Cruising radius 3,500 m

1550 revolutions per min

Ryan Airlines order for airplane (above). Bill of Sale (below). ***(Receipts courtesy Missouri Historical Society)***

RYAN AIRLINES, INC.

BUILDERS OF AIRCRAFT

OPERATORS

LOS ANGELES - SAN DIEGO AIRLINE

SOLD TO
CHAS. LINDBERG,
ST. LOUIS, MO.

SAN DIEGO, CALIF. February 25 1927.

1	Special Ryan Monoplane with Wright J-5 Motor	$10580.00
	Payment with order $1000.00 " March 1st/27 6580.00 " April 28/27 3000.00 Total Pay't	$10580.00
	Received payment in full for the above RYAN AIRLINES. [signature]	LINDBERGH COLL. BOX 291 #45 ST. LOUIS

copy at Missouri Historical Society, St. Louis, MO

Dictionary of American Biography, Vol.V, Hibben-Larkin, edited by Dumad Malone. Charles Scribner's Sons, New York

The World Book Encyclopedia Vol. 12, Field Enterprises Educational Corporation, Chicago and other major cities worldwide. 1974

Annals of St. Louis, "In its early days, under the French and Spanish Dominations," compiled by Frederic L. Billon, from authentic data, St. Louis, printed for Billon 1886

Lion of the Valley, St. Louis, MO, James Neal Primm, Pruett Publishing Company, Boulder, CO

Miscellaneous St. Louis, MO newspaper articles dated from September 29, 1922 to October 22, 1923

Letter to author from Charles A. Lindbergh, dated April 7, 1968, Darien, CT

CHAPTER 4

The Ryan Company

After Lindbergh's consideration of having other aircraft builders supply an airplane and with competitive time running out, his next move was to approach the small Ryan company in San Diego, California.

But who was this Ryan Airlines, Inc.?

Tubal Claude Ryan, born January 3, 1898 in Parsons, Kansas, to parents William Marion Ryan and Ida Ziegler Ryan, dreamed of flying like so many young men. His inspiration had been an article in The American Boy magazine entitled, "How I Fly." This article described a flight in a French Bleriot monoplane.

The year 1911 produced much aviation activity. It had been only eight years since the Wright brothers had made their first successful flight at Kitty Hawk. Newspaper baron William Randolph Hearst had offered a prize of $50,000. to the first man who could fly coast-to-coast within a thirty day deadline. One-time motorcycle racer Calbraith Perry Rodgers was lured not only by the prize money, but also by the challenge such a flight would present. Little did he know how long such a flight could take. Nor did he know that he would on that flight pass over Parsons, Kansas, and ignite a flame in a little boy's heart. [1]

The sight of Cal Rodgers in his Wright Brothers Model EX, "Vin Fiz", appearing on the Eastern horizon as only a tiny speck, passing overhead, and then disappearing into the Western sky just about electrified the thirteen year old Ryan. He had actually seen a real airplane in the air being flown by a man!

Claude Ryan's father owned and ran the old Excelsior Steam Laundry on Main Street in Parsons, so Claude's first work experience was driving a horse-drawn laundry wagon over Parsons streets during school vacations. He had another job too, as a carrier for the Parsons Sun, the daily newspaper, earning seventy-five cents a week He was fired from that job for not reporting as instructed when a woman took over the position of circulation manager.

Tubal Claude Ryan, standing next to his DeHavilland DH-4, the young aviator used for aerial forest fire patrol over northern California and Oregon in 1921. ***(William Wagner)***

His first exposure to a self-propelled vehicle, occurred when his mother paid twenty-five cents for him to have a ride in Parsons' first automobile. The seven year old Ryan was one of its first passengers. About a year later a friend of the Ryan family bought a one-cylinder Oldsmobile. Claude spent hours watching the owner service this new modern mode of transportation. Sometime later Ryan "fooled around with the greasy parts" of a Model T Ford which this same friend had purchased.

But Claude did not have a chance to see another airplane again until the Ryan family decided to move west in 1912. While arrangements were being made for the move, his parents sent him on a summer vacation visit to his grandparents farm near Vancouver, Washington. Soon he learned of an airplane that was hangared in a tent at the Army's Vancouver barracks nearby. The plane was owned and flown by pioneer aviator Silas Christofferson. Although Ryan used to sneak into the tent and sit in the pilot's seat, he never did get a ride, even though he observed the airplane in the air many times as Christofferson flew across the broad Columbia River.

The Ryan family settled in Orange, California, where they had purchased an orange ranch. Claude landed a job delivering papers for the Orange Daily News and was able to cover the fifteen mile route on a Flying Merkle 7-hp motorcycle. He soon learned to service the Merkle as well as the family Model T Ford. It wasn't long before Claude Ryan developed into a crack mechanic.

In 1915 the family again made a major move, back to Parsons. Claude was now in high school, and even though his attentions were being directed towards the opposite sex, he could not take his mind off that first sight of Cal Rodgers over Parsons four years earlier. He had to fly.

On April 6, 1917, America entered World War I. It did not take much prodding for Claude Ryan to hop a train and head for Joplin, Missouri, to join up. He was nineteen then, but the Navy was only interested in twenty-one year olds at that time. So back to Parsons he went, still determined to fly.

Again the family moved back to the sunny orange groves of California. Claude drove the family "T" and did all the enroute repairs, which were frequent on that trip. Soon he learned that some of the recruiting requirements were being slackened, so he drove to San Diego to again try the Navy. He went straight to Rockwell Field on North Island, which was used by the Navy as well as the Army. The services said he needed two years of college, so he was again turned down for flight training.

Now he had to find some other way to learn to fly. He shopped around the Los Angeles area and came upon the "American School of Aviation." It was a shaky business at best, but in his desperation he signed up and paid his $500. for "400 minutes of flight training."

When he went to the flying field in Venice, he was startled to see two airplanes, one a flimsy-looking pusher. It could barely fly, and so was used by students for taxi training—known as the "French system" of learning to fly. Some months later Claude Ryan finally got his first ride in the other airplane. It was a push-

Shown is the highly modified Standard J-1 into what was to be known as the Ryan-Standard, powered with a 150 hp Hispano-Suiza water cooled engine. ***(Ryan Aeronautical Company)***

er powered by a Hall-Scott eight-cylinder 75 hp engine, flown by Joe Mattingly, one of the school's instructors. The flight was only a short one, in one direction across the field, at the hair-raising altitude of four or five feet. But Ryan flew, and that was the important thing.

His first real flight came a day later when he went up with Bill Bailey and flew over Venice at an altitude of 1000 feet. Now he just had to solo. Sometime later, and with no further instruction, he borrowed one of the school's planes, a Jenny JN4-D, and took it up. He climbed to twenty or twenty-five feet, and rather than attempt a turn around the field, decided to land. After a rather hard landing the plane went up on its nose at the end of the field. The only damage was to the broken propeller and Ryan's pride.

Ryan could not afford to replace the propeller and had to seek other possibilities to learn to fly.

Finding that the Army had dropped its age requirements, he took the entrance tests and passed. Shortly thereafter, November 8, 1918, a letter arrived with a request to report to Berkeley, California, for ground school. However, the Armistice was signed three days later, and when he called the base he was told to forget the whole deal.

He then worked in the family orange grove business and was admitted to Oregon State College at Corvallis in September 1919 to study mechanical engineering. There was no course in aeronautical engineering at that time. He went back to the family business during his summer vacation of 1920 and again applied for entrance to the Army Air Service. This time he was accepted for flight training and ordered to report to March Field near Riverside, California that Fall.

After arriving at March, he was impressed with the orderliness of the operation, well-maintained airplanes, clean shops and hangars; a sharp contrast to the sloppy operation at the flight school in Venice. Ryan was one of three of seventy-five cadets to complete the course and receive a pursuit pilot rating. He soloed in a JN6-H Jenny, having been let loose by his instructor, Lt. John Benton, after seven hours of dual. Eventually he got to fly both the SE-5 and Spad pursuit airplanes.

Now Claude Ryan could sink his hands into the "greasy parts" of airplanes and aviation. Instead of signing up for advanced training at Kelly Field, Claude volunteered for aerial forest fire patrol over northern California and Oregon in the late spring of 1921. This was an arrangement between the Army and the Forest Service. The airmen, part of the Ninth Aero Squadron, were to fly de Havilland DH-4 biplanes over the rugged mountains of the Sierra range reporting to Mather Field near Sacramento.

Here can be seen at the Ryan Flying Company operation at Dutch Flats in San Diego, another Ryan-Standard, the "El Condor Del Rio Mayo". ***(Canadian National Aviation Museum)***

In the summer of 1921 Ryan was assigned to a detachment at Corning, just south of Red Bluff, California and soon gained valuable experience flying patrols in the DH-4 over mountainous and forested areas at altitudes of 10,000 feet. This proved to be valuable training for surveying an airmail route later in his career.

Claude recalled many years later that—"There were some accidents, and the patrol lost several airplanes and pilots we shouldn't have. The planes were well maintained; the fault didn't lie there. I never had any trouble, despite the number thirteen painted on the fuselage, but I did do a few unnecessary things because the flights were getting pretty routine." [2]

In January 1922 Ryan left the Army and went on the inactive reserve list with the idea of getting into civilian flying. One way for an aviator to break in was by flying the mail; the U.S. Post Office used de Havillands, and he figured he had a good chance. There were far more pilots than jobs available. To support himself financially Ryan went into the automobile parts business and then shifted over to the laundry business. But he soon tired of dirty linen and his mind went back into the sky.

At a nearby airport he met a young engineer and aviator, Millard Boyd, who as a schoolboy had built and flown his own airplane in 1915. Claude figured if Boyd could do this, he could too.

So Ryan packed up all his belongings, bought a used Ford, and with $100. in his pocket, headed for San Diego. He planned to do some flying on his Army Reserve commission at Rockwell Field. He also decided to buy his own airplane and go barnstorming. He was an experienced and good aviator, he was young, and he knew he was in on the beginning of a great industry.

Major Hap Arnold was commander of Rockwell Field on North Island. A number of old airplanes in fair condition left over from the war were based there. Ryan would buy one of them, fix it up and look for a field to operate from

At the foot of Broadway near the waterfront of San Diego there was a field formerly operated by another flyer, Jim Hennessey. Ryan approached J. W. Brennan, who represented the Harbor Department as the Harbor Master and was in charge of the property. Joe Brennan encouraged Ryan and told him not to worry about the required $50. per month rental fee until he was well under way and making money.

With that, Claude went to see Arnold about the purchase of an airplane. Ryan had sold his Ford for $300 and collected $150 from his savings account, shelling out $400 for a war-surplus JN4-D Jenny. He had $50 left over to start business. He paid a mechanic $25 for helping him assemble the still crated Jenny, which left him with $25 for operating expenses. An old piano box and wood from the Jenny crate were remodeled into both office and tool shed.

In September, 1922 Claude Ryan was in his own business as a combined aerial taxi service, flight training school, and daily excursion service, officially known as The Ryan Flying Company.

THE RYAN FLYING COMPANY

Business for this new company for those first few months was poor. There was not much activity at the improvised airport along the San Diego bay front. What money Ryan had just about paid for fuel and oil for the Jenny.

After several visits to the old family homestead up in Orange and other landing sites in the area to drum up business, he was approached by a barnstorming expedition. He was hired for $35 a week plus expenses to fly with three other pilots and four Jennies down the west coast of Mexico to build up publicity for the Mexican city of Tijuana, Baja California. The planes were purchased by the Mayor of Tijuana as war surplus in the U.S. But when it came time to export them to Mexico, the mayor ran into difficulties. Ryan found himself back in San Diego trying to get another start in the flying business.

A carnival moved up to San Bernardino and Claude, at their invitation, went along too. The carnival business philosophy was that they and Ryan could help each other attract customers to their individual businesses. It worked out okay for a while, but eventually Claude returned to San Diego. He continued to fly passengers, teach students to fly, and buy and sell airplanes. His business was slowly building up with some profit beginning to show.

Claude Ryan, the aviator, shown in the cockpit of one of the Standard J-1s with some attractive passengers. ***(Ryan Aeronautical Company)***

Now another problem faced him. He found that taking off under high voltage electric wires, going between two poles which had recently been erected at the end of the runway, and making a sharp turn to avoid the mast on a dredge was much too hazardous and felt he should consider moving his growing operation. At this time he owned two Jennies and had several other tenants on the field so the place always looked busy. Eight or nine airplanes on the field were impressive to passersby.

Eventually Claude found a location on a salt flat adjacent to the Marine Corps Recruit Depot, known as "Dutch Flats", at $15 per month. He moved the operation in the spring of 1923. He built a hangar and office and hired his first employee, his old friend Hawley Bowlus, to be the mechanic at $35. a week. Soon he hired another mechanic, Jon Harm van der Linde, a Dutchman from the Netherlands East Indies, who was to stay with him for many years.

Still buying and selling airplanes at a modest profit, instructing, and hopping passengers, he continued to set his sights on greater things. The year was 1924 and Ryan was now twenty-six years old, dashing and still single, and full of adventure. He made a deal with some local Los Angeles sightseeing bus drivers to bring their passengers to "Ryan Field", thereby gaining more passengers to take up over San Diego.

THE RYAN STANDARD

In 1923, when the government disposed of its wartime flying equipment, Claude had put in a bid of a few hundred dollars for six Standard J-1 biplanes and spare parts to be shipped from Texas. The Standard was a World War I wood-and-fabric trainer powered by a four-cylinder 100 hp Hall-Scott engine. Because it was larger than the Jenny, it had a two passenger forward compartment or open cockpit. When the planes arrived from Texas he found them in deplorable condition, but with the help of his mechanics and with the design expertise of both himself and Bowlus, Ryan converted them into "mini-airliners". When the Ryan crew completed the modification, the old Standards had a forward cabin capable of carrying four passengers inside, and they replaced the Hall-Scott engine with a 150 hp Hispano-Suiza water-cooled engine.

These conversions depended largely upon the ingenuity of Hawley Bowlus, who devised his own system of engineering design—called "fingertip aerodynamics." One of Ryan's early pilots, Frank W. Wiley described it. "We rode in the cabin and put one hand out each window until our fingertips reached the slipstream. That's the way we determined how wide we could make the cabin."

After the modifications the Ryan-Standards had a very impressive performance. With a full load of passengers including the pilot, full fuel and oil, grossing at 1000 pounds, they could top out at 90 mph, cruise at 80 and land at a comfortable 40. They could climb to 1000 feet in just 90 seconds. Service ceiling was 10,000 feet.

ENTER BENJAMIN FRANKLIN MAHONEY

The romance of flying an airplane was very enticing to any young man of that era, and if one was well-heeled, he could enjoy this new sport and satisfy his ego. One such man who happened upon the scene was twenty-three year old Benjamin Franklin Mahoney. Little did the world realize how important a part this man would play financially in the company which was to build the world's most famous airplane.

Mahoney had moved west in the early 1920's from Wilkes-Barre, Pennsylvania with his widowed mother. Settling in San Diego, he eventually met and married Helen Ann Post, daughter of a prominent San Diego family. Mahoney became more and more lured by the high adventure of aviation as the days went by. As a flying student of Ryan, he developed a keen interest in the business side of flying, and it was not long before he proposed a business partnership. After several days of deep thought, Ryan agreed. That was in April of 1925.

Since Ryan was already making frequent flights to the Los Angeles area, Mahoney's first idea was to start a Los Angeles—San Diego Airline. Ryan supplied the aircraft, pilots, and necessary equipment; Mahoney underwrote the operation, and they split the profits, whenever there were any.

BIRTH OF RYAN AIRLINES

The service was successful and the partners opened a Los Angeles terminal. Mahoney moved there and ran that terminal, located on a small grass field at Western Avenue and 99th Street. They hired a former automobile salesman, J. B. Alexander, whose first job was to locate a piece of land that would be closer to the downtown area of the growing Western city. He found it at Angeles Mesa Drive, now Crenshaw Boulevard in the Baldwin Hills area.

It wasn't long before the company hired a soft-spoken and shy Irish mechanic named Douglas Corrigan. Years later he became well known as "Wrong Way Corrigan" for his flight to Ireland in a Curtiss Robin.

"From the beginning of time, advancement of civilization has been marked by improvement in methods of transportation. The inauguration of airway service reveals the most perfect form of travel known to man", read a Ryan brochure of the period.

On March 1, 1925, big names from the motion picture industry were invited for the first flight from Los Angeles to San Diego. Director Robert Vignola and actress Vera Reynolds added color and prestige to this new venture.

The Ryan-Airlines, Inc. made aviation history as it became the nation's first year-round regularly scheduled passenger airline, later christened the "Los Angeles-San Diego Air Line".

One day when Charlie Widmer, one of the newly hired pilots, was practicing landings and take-offs, he felt a jolt just as he was ready to flare for the landing. When he had landed, passengers Tom Mathews, company publicist, and Frank Wiley ran back to investigate and found a farmer sitting in a model "T" his hat knocked on the ground, hands in a death grip on the wheel, feet jammed between the foot pedals, and staring straight ahead in shock. Wiley immediately untangled the farmer's feet, cranked up the engine, put the man's hat back on his head, put the car into high gear and jumped off. With that the "T" went sailing off the airport.

Fascinating and funny tales, the proverbial "hangar stories" of those lean years, were building up among the people running the Los Angeles-San Diego Air Line, but they were losing more money as each day passed. Mathews could see the handwriting on the wall and tried every trick in the book to get more business for the line. He arranged for radio commercials, attractive women spokespersons,, travel bureau connections and 30-day round-trip fares. Nothing seemed to work. By the end of the summer of 1926 the situation looked bleak.

Ryan and Mahoney decided to come up with something really new, something that no one else could equal; a new airplane. But what kind, where would they find it, could they build one—and what would the cost be?

THE "CLOUDSTER"

Back in 1920 a wealthy sportsman, David R. Davis, became deeply interested in aviation. He wanted a plane in which he could fly the continent, coast-to-coast, non-stop.

At about the same time Donald Douglas, a dynamic young engineer who would build an empire of classic air transports in later years, was trying to get into the airplane manufacturing business. Douglas had several ideas for new airplanes on the drawing boards, but no hardware, and wanted to turn out airplanes on a mass-production basis.

Douglas learned of Davis through a sportswriter on the Los Angeles Times. Douglas was informed that Davis would finance the construction of one airplane built just for a coast-to-coast flight. To build one plane that could fly across the country and perhaps garner enough publicity to win support for new designs was at least a start.

Thus was formed the Davis-Douglas Company. Construction was done in the old Koll Lumber Mill in Los Angeles. Douglas's only machinery was a crude hand drill press. All the plane's wood parts were fashioned in the planning mill.

One year and $40,000. later the plane was completed and ready for flight. It was the first airplane designed to carry the equivalent of its own weight. Eric Springer, former test pilot at Martin, took one look at it and said to Douglas, "You've got a real cloud duster there, Doug." The phrase caught on; thus the name "Cloudster".

Modified Davis-Douglas "Cloudster" rebuilt and modified by Ryan to carry 10 passengers in enclosed comfort, and powered by a 400 hp Liberty V12 water-cooled engine. ***(Ryan Aeronautical Company)***

The public paid little attention to these men who were about to fly a monster airplane across the nation nonstop. On June 27, 1921 the Cloudster was loaded in sections on a truck and driven to the take-off point, a large field abandoned by the Army in Riverside. Springer and Davis took off around sunrise. Douglas was not present, still bent over his drafting board at the plant working on another design.

Over Fort Bliss, near El Paso, Texas, a mechanical failure caused Springer to make a forced landing. That was the end of the venture, and in 1925 they put the Cloudster up for sale. With passenger seats installed the airplane was sold to a group of promoters in Venice, California, who set up business at Clover Field near Santa Monica. But people would just not ride in the Cloudster, so it was again put up for sale.

By now Mahoney and Ryan learned of the impending sale of the Cloudster. A deal was made, and after the price of $6,000. was agreed upon, Ryan Airlines, Inc. was the new owner. Sitting next to the Standards back at home field, it looked like a 747 parked next to DC-3s.

With the help and expertise of Hawley Bowlus again, it was decided to completely modify the cockpit and passenger sections to give the big bird a plush face-lifting.

They moved the rear open cockpit just forward of the passenger compartment with open side-by-side seating for the pilot and copilot. The bench seats were removed and passengers were seated along a center aisle, five in tandem on each side. The seats were

Early Ryan M-1 used for the Pacific Air Transport (PAT) early air mail run, CAM #8, and powered by a Wright J-4 "Whirlwind" air-cooled radial engine. **(Ryan Aeronautical Company)**

like those in a Pullman car, as comfortable as anything the railroad could offer at the time. They even carpeted the floor, mounted ash trays, and installed dome lights for the night flights. The fuselage was painted black with silver wings and tail, with Yale blue trim.

George Allen was checked out as the second pilot to command the plane. From then on he and Claude, with Jon van der Linde as backup copilot and chief mechanic, did most of the flying. J. J. "Red" Harrigan was another pilot checked out as a backup pilot on the big Cloudster.

Ryan Airlines would run on a regular schedule if enough passengers showed up at the field. They used the Cloudster for charter as well as hauling real estate people with hot prospects over land developments on the southern California coastline. As the flagship, the Cloudster was a luxury item ahead of its time. One of its regular flights was to San Clemente, where it landed in an open field just south of the town near the Cotton home, later the western White House of former President Richard Nixon.

Even though Claude Ryan had initiated one of the first airlines in the country and business was holding its own, people were still leery of flying. After a year and a half, Ryan made the decision to discontinue all operations because the airline was

Another Ryan M-1 powered with a Ryan-Siemens engine showing the first use of the trade-mark Damascene decorative finish on the sheet metal surfaces. ***(Title Insurance and Trust Company, San Diego, California)***

slowly losing money and because he wanted to get into aircraft manufacturing.

M-1 & M-2 SERIES

In February 1925 Congress passed the Kelly Air Mail Bill. Up to that time the Post Office had flown the airmail, mostly in de Havilland DH-4s, but now the Kelly Bill would permit commercial operators to bid for routes. These were known as CAM (Contract Air Mail) routes. Successful bidders would receive a specified rate by the pound for mail carried, and later a percentage of the revenue from airmail stamps. On May 15, 1918, the Post Office inaugurated an experimental airmail service between New York and Washington, with a stop in Philadelphia.

Ryan learned of the airmail contract situation with considerable interest. From their modification of the Standards and later the Cloudster, he and Frank Mahoney and Hawley Bowlus had gained some experience in airplane manufacturing," and so in 1925 he began to think of building a special plane to fly the mail. This new machine would be a new mail/passenger monoplane to be built in their own shops. Ryan walked into Mahoney's office one day in the fall of 1925 and handed his partner a freehand sketch.

It was of a unique airplane featuring an odd mixture of old and new design concepts—a high-wing monoplane with the wing mounted on the upper longerons. It was a logical location of the wing for a cabin design, yet the sketch showed two open cockpits. This was made possible by running secondary longerons aft from the firewall at the top of the removable engine mount. The area between these longerons and the wing was left open to create a parasol monoplane configuration. Access to the cockpits was made by separate doors on the left side.

This arrangement provided unobstructed visibility. The pilot sat in the rear cockpit, while two passengers rode up front side by side. Sometime later Ryan patented his "parasol" design and assigned rights to Ryan Airlines, Inc., without receiving any payment.

Ryan proposed that the new plane, officially designated the M-1 (first Ryan monoplane) would cruise at 115 mph with a 600-lb payload, which would be just about perfect for the air mail of that time. After some discussion, Mahoney went along with the idea.

Claude Ryan attacked this project with gusto. Here was a chance for a new departure in airplanes. Everyone else was still thinking in terms of biplanes, but Ryan wanted to develop the monoplane concept.

The M-1 went from dream to reality in a very short period. Ryan had sketched out an airplane with a high safety factor, plenty of reserve power, and good performance. Airmail routes in various parts of the country called for all varieties of flying performance, and this ship was intended to fill the bill everywhere.

Gradually the tail surfaces—rather square at first—took

Pilot Jerry Jones, who later became Chief Pilot for Pan American in Alaska, with Peaches Wallace at Ryan Field. Engine is a Wright J-4B. ***(William Wagner)***

shape, and a conventional landing gear configuration was mounted on the steel tube fuselage. Dimensions allowed for a front cockpit that could accommodate two passengers side by side, or one passenger and a sack of mail, or just mail sacks and no passenger. Dual controls were provided, so a passenger flying up front could get in some "stick time" if he required.

The M-1 cowling had a feature that was to become a trademark on all subsequent Ryan models up to but not including the ST. This was the distinctive "engine-turning" or "jeweling" effect, also known as Damascene when used on machine tools. It was basically a decorative finish on lathes, mills etc. It had been used in Europe as well as the U.S. as an accepted machine tool practice for at least 150 years. On the M-1 and M-2s this type of surface finish also appeared on the wheel disc covers and the panel around the cockpits on top of the fuselage.

The first M-1 had a Hispano-Suiza 150 hp water-cooled engine to power its maiden flight, but the ship's engine anchor points were also designed to accommodate a number of war-surplus engines, including the Curtiss OX-5, the 200 hp Wright J-4 "Whirlwind" radial, and the Hispano-Suiza 180 hp engines.

Under the skilled hands of Bowlus and van der Linde, every piece of wood and metal for the first M-1 was fashioned by hand. The work went on between Christmas 1925 and the middle of February 1926.

By Valentine's Day, the all silver M-1 prototype, the first real production airplane to come out of the Ryan shops on Dutch Flats, stood shining in the Southern California sun. Above the hangar doors The Ryan Company sign said "Operators of Los Angeles-San Diego Air Line," "School of Aviation" and shortly, "Builders of Air Craft" was added.

In his leather jacket, helmet and goggles, Claude Ryan climbed into the rear cockpit, as Hawley Bowlus called out "Contact", and the new Hisso engine roared to life. Ryan taxied to the other end of the field, lined up the M-1, gave it full throttle, and after less than 100 feet of runway, the new plane was in the air.

After the test flight a certain amount of further design engineering was deemed necessary. As some of this was beyond the ability of Ryan and his staff, he called upon John K. Northrop. Northrop was then working for Donald Douglas in Los Angeles, but he agreed to come down on weekends to help redesign the M-1, bringing along Art Mankey, a Douglas draftsman.

With Northrop's help the required airframe changes were made, and then the Ryan group began to experiment with various engines to obtain performance figures for various potential uses of the ship. Beside the OX-5, the J-4, and the Hispano-Suiza engines, they worked with the 120 hp Super Rhone, the Siemens-Halske RS-9, and the Salmson-Menasco power plants.

The Hispano-Suiza and OX-5 engines had an advantage in that they were readily available from war-surplus stock at nearby Rockwell Field. The Wright J-4 and Hisso were finally selected.

The new Ryan model M-1 was ready to take on the tough job of flying the mail for Uncle Sam.

RYAN FLIES THE MAIL

It was January 26, 1926, and Vernon Centennial Gorst of North Bend, Oregon had just been awarded the Pacific Coast night airmail contract. He owned six struggling bus lines which had operated over short routes all the way from Medford, Oregon to Santa Monica, California. His only exposure to flying had been as a passenger.

Gorst had heard of Claude Ryan and had been observing his Los Angeles-San Diego Air Line. He went to San Diego to look over the Ryan operation and to take flying lessons. He considered using the M-1, then under development, for his recently acquired night airmail run, which was between Los Angeles and Seattle.

Ryan had seen the need for a medium-weight aircraft which could fly faster and have a greater carrying capacity than the de Havilland airplanes being used on other routes by the Post Office.

Shown on the left is Vern C. Gorst, President of Pacific Air Transport, standing next to a Ryan M-1 with T. Claude Ryan. Location is Sand Point Field near Seattle after a flight from San Francisco on March 18, 1926. ***(United Air Lines)***

While Gorst was learning to fly, he kept a close watch on the development of the M-1, and he thought the ship might be suitable for his airmail business.

However, Gorst lacked the finances to purchase the M-1. One day a retired Eastern banker, C.M. Comstock, dropped in to see Ryan and said that he would like to buy into any company which might be considering starting a local airmail route.

Ryan didn't waste any time arranging a meeting between himself, Gorst, and Comstock, out of which grew the formation of a new company, Pacific Air Transport, (PAT). PAT would eventually become a part of United Air Lines. PAT won an airmail contract, the new Contract Airmail Route 8 (CAM #8,) up to that time the longest route awarded by the government.

Although Gorst was convinced of the projected capabilities of the M-1, he wanted to check out other manufacturers in the country. Upon return from a survey trip around the U. S., he found himself on hand the day the M-1 went through test paces requested by Comstock. The ship carried a 600-pound load of sandbags, equalling the payload for the airmail service. The performance was so impressive that Gorst requested Ryan to demonstrate the M-1 with a Wright J-4 "Whirlwind" 200 hp engine instead of the 150 hp Hispano-Suiza. He also asked Ryan to fly the plane on a survey trip over the Los Angeles-Seattle route to prove its superiority.

With Gorst and Comstock as passengers, their baggage, and a very small amount of airmail, Ryan set out in March 1926 from Los Angeles and headed for Seattle. The airway became socked in with clouds over the Tehachapi Mountains southeast of Bakersfield, and Claude elected to land for fuel on a Mojave Desert lake bed. Comstock decided to return to Los Angeles. Later that night Gorst and Ryan made it on to Fresno, where they spent the night. Their next stop was Crissy Field at San Francisco, then on to Seattle.

Inter-city records had been broken as the Los Angeles-Seattle trip was made in seven hours and three minutes. Enthusiastic postmasters, trying to promote the new airmail route, were on hand at nearly every stop.

The first six M-1s had gone to PAT and a seventh was ordered for them, others went back East to various operators. Later that year Ryan sold several of the refined M-1s (redesignated as the M-2 with an improved wing engineered by Northrop,) to Colorado Airways of Denver.

By 1928 the M-1s were phased out by attrition. The mortality rate was high. Boeing Air Transport, operators of the Chicago-Salt Lake City airmail route, purchased PAT early in 1928. Eventually both became part of the United Air Lines system. Not only did the little M-1s pioneer the early mail routes over the rugged West Coast but played a part in the development of one of the nation's largest air lines of today.

Up to this time all Ryan-produced aircraft were painted overall silver, with black registration numbers.

200 hp Hispano-Suiza water-cooled engine powered and re-worked Ryan M-2 "Bluebird" in flight over San Diego about 1926. *(William Wagner)*

THE BLUEBIRD

Lessons learned flying the M-1 airmail ships in the cold winter months convinced the Ryan people it was time to design and build a closed-in airplane, one that could carry passengers in comfort.

With Hawley Bowlus, Walter Locke (a recent MIT graduate), and Jack Northrop handling engineering, a new enclosed cabin plane began to take shape in the Ryan shops in mid-1926. They took an existing M-1, factory number 10. which remained at Dutch Flats for use in Ryan flight operations, and began reworking its structure into an enclosed airplane. First an "I" beam spar was installed, as designed by Northrop instead of the standard box spar in the earlier M-1. This new wing had a span of thirty-six feet.

In the M-1 the pilot had flown from the rear cockpit, but with this new design the pilot would fly from the front. With this arrangement, seats for four passengers would be provided behind the pilot in the aft part of the cockpit, with a baggage compartment behind the passenger seats.

The fuselage was widened and heightened to accommodate the passengers. Its bracing was changed to reshape the old wedge door on the right side of the M-2 to a semisquare. The bottom of the door was angled off on each side. The old firewall was moved forward about ten inches, but the engine sat in the same relative position as in the M-2. This gave the plane a nose-heavy condition and, when flown solo, weight had to be added to the rear baggage compartment in order to compensate. Two passengers in the rear seats, however, would balance things out.

Power was provided by the Hispano-Suiza engine, a water-cooled V-8 type, the 200 hp E model built under license in this country by Wright, who also built the "Whirlwind" radial engine.

The original narrow-tread landing gear of the M-1 series was retained, in which landing impact loads were carried by struts attached to the lower fuselage structure.

This unique airplane came out of the shop in November 1926, was reassigned s/n 27, and painted in a two-tone blue color scheme, and given the name "Bluebird." The colors were light blue on the fuselage and darker blue on the wings. The cowling was burnished (damascene) like the other M-1s. The new airplane was assigned registration number 3219.

The Bluebird became the first "corporate" ship of Ryan Air Lines and was often flown on business trips. Other than the fact it was a bit hotter on take-offs and landings, it was a smooth flying airplane.

This new cabin airplane was a step in the right direction for the Ryan organization, none of whom realized it was a steppingstone to another cabin airplane, similar in configuration, destined to win "The Prize" for a young aviator in the spring of the following year.

On the day that Charles Lindbergh landed in Paris, Doug Kelly, A.J. Edwards, and some passengers flew the Bluebird up to Rogers Field in Los Angeles. Just before Kelly was about to land, Edwards decided to open the right-hand door and lean out to wave at friends below. This upset the aerodynamic balance causing the plane to go into a violent sideslip. Doug lost control and crashed on the airport injuring several of the passengers including Edwards. The remains were trucked back to San Diego, where the plane was rebuilt. Rumor has it that it was rebuilt back into an M-2 configuration and sold.

RYAN—MAHONEY SPLIT

Meanwhile, all was not well between Claude Ryan and B. F. Mahoney. Ryan the businessman and Mahoney the fashionable sportsman were not working out as partners. Ryan wanted to strengthen the company's weak financial base by incorporating and raising capital through the sale of stock. Mahoney never came

Early poster used by Ryan Airlines, Inc. advertising their airline services between Los Angeles and San Diego, in a modified Standard J-1. ***(Ryan Aeronautical Company)***

around to signing the papers. Ryan reached the end of his patience in November 1926. He confronted Mahoney and suggested that one of them buy out the other. Mahoney was not the least bit interested in getting out of the business, so Ryan sold Ryan Airlines, including Ryan Flying Company and Los Angeles-San Diego Air Line, for the price of $25,000 and one new M-2 airplane.

With contrasting emotions of relief and disappointment, Claude Ryan said good-bye to the company he had started. Mahoney did suggest that Ryan stay on as manager to run the operation for an agreed salary of $200. a month. On November 30, 1926 the legal documents were drawn up that ended the Ryan-Mahoney partnership. Said Tom Mathews in later years, "That was the winter of the big rains; we sloshed around between the office and hangar in two feet of water and business was at a standstill."

Articles of incorporation of the reorganized company under the name of B. F. Mahoney Aircraft Corporation were filed on July 15, 1927. The firm, capitalized at $500,000, announced it would continue the manufacture of monoplanes, to be known hence forth as Mahoney monoplanes, instead of the former name of Ryan Monoplanes.

As a result of this transition of ownership, much discussion in aviation history circles over the years centered on the fact that the name Ryan was not only painted on the *Spirit of St. Louis* rudder, but always associated with the manufacture of that airplane. The name Mahoney does not appear anywhere on the Spirit, and means nothing to the average aviation enthusiast or the general public.

Claude Ryan has always stated over the years, that he quite honestly only "founded" the company that bears his name. Many years later Lindbergh presented a copy of his book "*Spirit of St. Louis*" to Claude, and on the title page wrote the following—"To Claude Ryan, who built the company that built the '*Spirit of St. Louis*'. With best wishes, Charles A. Lindbergh." In this author's opinion, that says it all.

TRANSITION TO FAME

After the success of the M-1, their first production airplane, the Ryan people were convinced that any future aircraft should be of the enclosed type. The Bluebird became a transition between the M series and what was to come. All they needed to do then was rework the Bluebird and the M-1 into what became another transition, a transition to fame.

Credit belongs to the unschooled but practical draftsman/designer Ed Morrow for the initial design of this next new airplane, to be designated the B-1. The "B" was to stand for "Brougham."

In any corporation, naming a new product usually falls into the hands of its public relations people. Thus Tom Mathews, thinking back to the Bluebird, a name he thought was popular with lovesick youth and old ladies, but not one for making high sales, felt a new name should have an airplane/automobile tie-in to be more acceptable to a large number of potential customers. Mathews further thought that a new name should give people confidence because of the automobile association.

Named after Lord Henry Peter Brougham, British barrister and philosopher, the designation "brougham" for a vehicle was first used in 1838. It described the "closed down carriage with seats inside for two or four persons", which Lord Brougham designed and had built for his own use.

Sixty-five years passed between Lord Brougham's machine and that of the 9 hp vapor (gasoline) engine powered Oldsmobile "Brougham". A quarter of a century later this same name was applied to a vehicle in the aerial age, the new Ryan Airlines, Inc., (B. F. Mahoney Aircraft Corp.) "B-1 Brougham".

Morrow sketched out a three-view drawing that resembled the Bluebird, but with a larger forty-two foot wingspan. He made the fuselage wider and longer and suggested either a Hisso E or the Wright J-4 engine for power. The landing gear of the M series

Sale of Business to B. Franklin Mahoney. ***(Missouri Historical Society)***

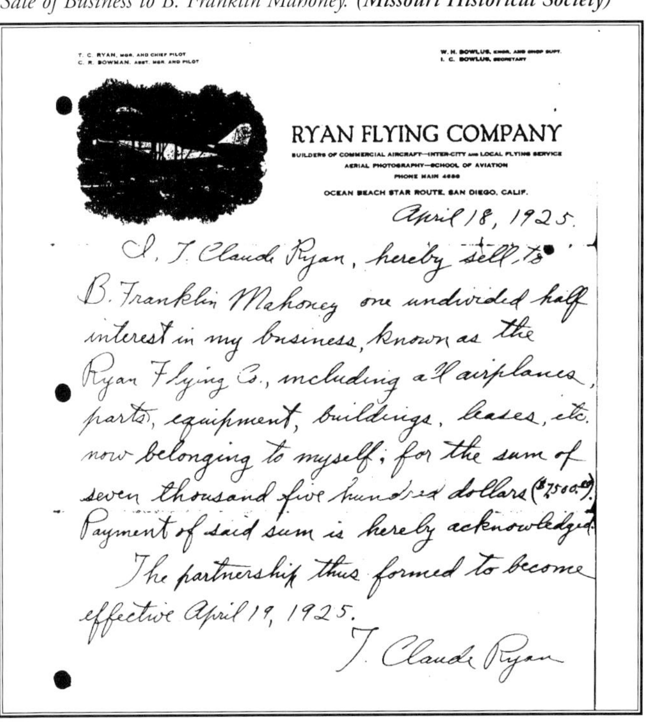

T. C. RYAN, MGR. AND CHIEF PILOT
C. R. BOWMAN, ASST. MGR. AND PILOT

W. H. BOWLUS, ENGR. AND SHOP SUPT.
I. C. BOWLUS, SECRETARY

RYAN FLYING COMPANY

BUILDERS OF COMMERCIAL AIRCRAFT—INTER-CITY AND LOCAL FLYING SERVICE
AERIAL PHOTOGRAPHY—SCHOOL OF AVIATION
PHONE MAIN 4680
OCEAN BEACH STAR ROUTE, SAN DIEGO, CALIF.

April 18, 1925.

I, T. Claude Ryan, hereby sell to B. Franklin Mahoney one undivided half interest in my business, known as the Ryan Flying Co., including all airplanes, parts, equipment, buildings, leases, etc. now belonging to myself; for the sum of seven thousand five hundred dollars ($7500.00). Payment of said sum is hereby acknowledged.

The partnership thus formed to become effective April 19, 1925.

T. Claude Ryan

caused structural problems on the airframe in hard landings, so a new design, outwardly braced through the wing struts, was conceived.

The final design had been firmed up, enthusiasm was high, and all the company needed was a buyer. Richard T. "Dick" Robinson, builder of the El Cortez Hotel in San Diego, placed his order for the first ship off the line. He specified that it be painted in a gold color scheme, except the engine cowling which was burnished aluminum, and it was named the "Gold Bug." (It appears that Robinson never did take the delivery of the Gold Bug). In the meantime the consensus around the Ryan plant was that if they were to advance ahead into the aviation industry, it would be advantageous to hire a full-time engineer.

DONALD A. HALL

It was in January 1927 that Donald Albert Hall approached the Ryan firm seeking employment. Mahoney was rather impressed with the twenty-eight year old engineer, and so Hall was hired and began work on Monday, January 31, 1927. [3]

Donald Hall was born on December 7, 1898, the son of Harland M. and Louise K. Hall, of Brooklyn, New York.

Don, as he preferred to be called, attended public and high school in Brooklyn, and on September 19, 1917 entered Pratt Institute School of Science and Technology, a student in the Industrial Mechanical Engineering program, and graduated June 20, 1919 with a Mechanical Engineering Certificate. [4]

Eventually he met and married Elizabeth Walker of San Diego, California.

After graduating from Pratt he obtained his first job as a junior draftsman, checker, and designer at the Curtiss Aeroplane & Motor Corp., in Garden City, Long Island, New York. That company was founded by prominent aviation pioneer, Glenn H. Curtiss. In 1922 Hall went with the Elias Brothers, in Buffalo, New York, and from there to the L. W. F. Engineering Company, at College Point, Long Island, New York.

Hall did primary design work for a while with the Ford Motor Company, Airplane Division, in Dearborn, Michigan. He worked on the 4-AT-1, & -2, the earlier versions of the famous Ford Tri-Motor airliners.

In 1924-1925 Hall worked for the Douglas Company in Santa Monica, California, doing preliminary aircraft design under Art Mankey and Donald Douglas, gaining invaluable experience in aircraft production.

Unknown to most people is the fact that Lindbergh and Hall's trails crossed before either was aware of the other's existence, as Army Air Service cadets. This fact bears the mark of destiny. Taking a leave of absence from Douglas, Hall enlisted in the Army Air Service, at Brooks Field, San Antonio, Texas in the fall of 1926. As a pilot he wished to get a pilot's viewpoint of an airplane's performance and control.

He was issued a copy of Training Regulations Number 190-5, a paper bound pamphlet titled Topography and Surveying, subtitle, Map Reading. Because the United States Army was notoriously frugal in the issuance of material to "rookies", this pamphlet was not new, and had seen service in the hands of other cadets. Hall found the copy issued to him had a name scrawled in the upper left hand corner, the name prefixed by the owner's rating.

Hall noticed the name and casually ran his pen through it, and wrote his own name below the other name. That other name was Cadet C. A. Lindbergh—25 (class of 1925.)

Cadet Lindbergh after graduating from Brooks in 1925, went on to become an airmail pilot, and eventually journeyed to San Diego to have an airplane built.

Cadet Hall did not graduate in his class of 1926-27, but eventually made it to San Diego, too, just a short time before Lindbergh, to design airplanes for a local company operating out of a fish cannery.

Charles A. Lindbergh standing by a Ryan M-1 with his friend and new owner of the Ryan company, B. Franklin Mahoney. Note fuselage has side stringers like later M-2. Possibly a modified M-1. Picture was taken prior to Lindbergh's first flight in an M-1, February 23, 1927, his first day in San Diego. ***(Ryan Aeronautical Company)***

Like Lindbergh, Donald Hall was also an outdoor person, spending much of his spare time canoeing, hiking, mountain climbing, swimming, traveling and exploring, in addition to photography (unlike Lindbergh). Lindbergh and Hall became friends, after the NYP project, and in fact carried on considerable correspondence over the years.

As Hall settled into his upstairs office, he recalled how the new factory was sandwiched between two fish canneries at the foot of Juniper Street. The smell of fish blended with the pungent fragrance of airplane dope. The firm had moved into the spacious building in late 1926.

Hall's first assignment was to work on the Gold Bug. He did the preliminary general and structural design work between February 7th and 24th as construction was started. On Thursday, February 3, 1927, the fuselage and tail surfaces were underway when an unexpected telegram which was to change plans for not only the Gold Bug, but the Ryan Airlines as well, was received at the plant.

Hall reminisced, "When I read the telegram I was a little doubtful. But I said yes, anyway, and we sent off a reply."

The little company was about to face their biggest challenge and begin a transition to fame that was completely unexpected.

Engineering and further production work on the Gold Bug was dropped. On Friday, February 25th a contract was signed, and Hall began the preliminary design of the NYP. Lindbergh arrived on Wednesday, February 23rd and work started on Monday, the 28th.

In recent years some historians have suspected that the Gold Bug fuselage might have been used in its steel tube structural state to build up the NYP. However, when the question was presented to Hall, he clearly stated that any fuselage under construction, either the Gold Bug or possibly a B-1 Brougham, before starting the NYP could only have been started to keep the shop busy. It would not have been used for the NYP. (It is unclear what the reasoning was.)

In Hall's first impression, he recalled a lanky young man with a reticent manner. "He spoke only a sentence or two, and I realized he had something behind him. He had that quality we recognize in those who have their eyes set beyond self." That Lindbergh was a very serious there was no doubt in the engineer's mind.

At this first meeting of two similar individuals, an airplane capable of flying from New York to Paris, France did not exist. Not even two components of such a craft existed. It only existed within the mind of Donald A. Hall's imagination. Each man,

This is the first true Ryan "Brougham" built. Customer was race pilot Frank Hawks, and the ship was known as the "Gold Bug". Summer 1927. ***(Bunnel Photo Shop)***

Lindbergh and Hall, had faith in the other, as the planning got underway.

Hall said, "Lindbergh had his own ideas, most of which I accepted, some I disagreed with, but we came to a mutual agreement. I was all alone during the design except for two nights when the purchasing agent Walter Locke helped me with weight analysis. Locke had two years of engineering in college. From the Ryan M-2 we took the wing ribs and tail surfaces, everything else was different. We laid some stuff down full size on plywood and worked from that."

Lindbergh was the only test pilot. That was one of his original requirements. Hall had a ride in the NYP, and sat on the right-hand arm rest of the wicker chair. He took the controls with his left hand. It wasn't a very stable airplane, he said. He also took several pictures with his own camera during that flight.

According to Hall, "Lindbergh wasn't a bit nervous about the flight, the most composed man I ever ran across. Physically very good, had excellent vision, maybe better than normal. He was an excellent cross-country navigator by dead-reckoning, and here he spent a lot of time working on his own maps."

There followed a phenomenal complementing of two brains and spirits, in Lindbergh and Hall, with the backing of Mahoney, and the Ryan workers in producing the NYP. The devotion of all those people who worked for the struggling Ryan Airlines was an important factor in the success of the ultimate product.

The success of the design and development and construction of the NYP can be attributed not only to Lindbergh, Mahoney and the Ryan workers, but in just as important a part to Donald A. Hall. Lindbergh and Hall were the key to a unique combination of two men who worked well together, personally as well as intellectually. Lindbergh became a household word, an American hero, and still admired around the world, even up to the present time. Donald A. Hall, however, never did receive the acclaim he most certainly deserved, for the part he played in the success of the flight.

Hall stated one time, "I wasn't really worried about the trip from New York to Paris," he confessed. "My chief concern was the trip from North Island to St. Louis. You see, I'd designed the NYP for long range, for flying the ocean. Well, between here and St. Louis there are some high mountain peaks—13,000 feet altitude near Flagstaff, Arizona. I'd made no calculations for altitude flying. My worry was—what if the weather turned bad when he headed over those peaks? Well, the moon was shining at Flagstaff and he made it safely to St. Louis, then on to New York and Paris."

The story of Lindbergh the aviator, Hall the engineer/designer, and the men and women of Ryan who built the NYP is a story of San Diego. It might well have begun in this manner!

"Once upon a time two eager, serious young men sat on a bench in the sunshine of the Coronado Beach. They did not leave cares behind as beach haunting usually connotes. Instead they talked of wing span and wing-loading. They spoke of the first flight, nonstop, across a lonely ocean."

A combination of factors associated with the development and building of the NYP made it possible to complete the project in such a short time, according to Hall.

Due to the constant availability of Lindbergh on site, his presence with such a keen knowledge of flying, understanding of engineering problems, his implicit faith in the success of the flight, and his untiring devotion to the project, was an important factor in tying together the entire factory organization into one smooth and efficient running team. The Ryan staff and its officers had been unusually conscientious, cooperative, and extremely hard working.

FOOTNOTES

1. *First Transcontinental Flight,* Charles S. Wiggin, The Bookmailer, Inc. New York, 1961.
2. *Ryan the Aviator,* William Wagner in collaboration with Lee Dye, McGraw-Hill Book Company, New York, NY, 1971, page 6.
3. Notes written in longhand by Donald Hall shortly before his death, later transcribed and typed by his son Donald Hall, Jr. about 1971.
4. Pratt Institute, Jeffrey C. Campbell, Director, Alumni Office, Alumni Office Biographical Record, obtained from Pratt Institute, Brooklyn, NY. Includes other forms and applications filled out by Donald A. Hall upon entering as a student in 1917. (Graduated 1919.)

ENDNOTES

For three weeks in May, 1968, the author spent vacation time in San Diego and Los Angeles visiting with many former employees and other associates of the Ryan Company, most of whom were retired at the time. They include the following persons: Vance Breese, Edwin Morrow, "Dapper" Dan Burnett, O.R. McNeel, Art Mankey, Jon van der Linde, Douglas Kelly, Douglas Corrigan, Adelaide Prudden, Ruth Kennough Clemens, Helen Hendrix, Carl Hatfield, Millard C. Boyd, Tom Mathews, T. Claude Ryan, and Clair Rand.

In the Spring of 1998, the author had the pleasure of visiting Donald Hall, Jr. and his son, Nova, at their home. They were happy to share family memorabilia, original negatives of pictures taken during the construction of the NYP by the senior Hall. Included in the collection were a few original drawings, one of the initial wing design on a laundered and pressed shirt cardboard, a formal drawing of the six panels of the engine cowling, and the original inked drawing of the first three-views of the airplane. Letters between Lindbergh and Doinald Hall and other miscellaneous documentation were included in the collection. Copies of all of the above were used for detailed research and are in the author's collection.

The Spirit of Ryan, Ev Cassagneres, TAB Books, Inc. Blue Ridge Summit, PA, 1982.

Ryan the Aviator, William Wagner in collaboration with Lee Dye, McGraw-Hill Book Company, New York, NY, 1971.

Flying the Mail, Donald Dale Jackson and the editors of Time-Life Books, 1982, Time Life Books, Inc., Alexandria, VA.

Bonfires to Beacons, Nick A. Komons, Smithsonian Institution Press, Washington, DC, in association with Airlife Publishing, England, 1989.

Vern C. Gorst, Pioneer and Grandad of United Airlines, Wilbur H. Gorst (son of Vern,) Gorst Publications, Coos Bay, OR, 1979.

Interview with Donald A Hall by John Dudley Phelps, 1932. "The Building of The Ship." Copy of which was given to the author by Donald Hall, Jr., 1998. This document has many notes of editing by Donald A. Hall in his handwriting.

The Spirit of St. Louis, Charles A. Lindbergh, Charles Scribner's Sons, New York, NY, 1953.

The Spirit of St. Louis and Its Designer, for immediate release. Release No. 57-3, 8 March 1957, North Islander, NAS San Diego, CA.

CHAPTER 5

NYP Development & Construction

From the very start, Lindbergh made it clear that the NYP was to be built for one purpose, and one purpose only, to fly successfully from New York to Paris, and that was it.

He had no thought or plans for its use after that flight, although he did think it would be fun to fly around Europe after the Paris hop. But what to do with the NYP after that barely entered his mind, as it was not the mission, not important, not part of the overall plan.

It was the first airplane in history that was developed to accomplish one goal, one flight. Each and every part of the NYP was designed with that purpose in mind. Nothing was to be wasted on luxuries or non-essential items that would be dead weight, or not function to meet the goal or accomplish the mission.

Through the craftsmanship and artistry of the Ryan people, together with the input of Lindbergh's own philosophy of design, he and his sponsors would have the most carefully crafted piece of flying machinery, with the highest efficiency of its time, and soon be ready to conquer the mighty Atlantic Ocean.

One important consideration from the start had to do with the selection of a power plant. There was no question at the time that the Wright Aeronautical Corporation in Paterson, New Jersey, was manufacturing the best internal combustion aircraft engine in the industry, except for Pratt & Whitney's 9 cylinder 410 hp "Wasp", built in East Hartford, Connecticut. (The "Wasp" was not available for commercial or private use yet). The Wright engine was known as the "Whirlwind" and became a legend over many years in the aircraft industry.

By the end of World War I, no dependable American-designed and built air-cooled engine producing more than 100 hp had been successfully constructed, and it was felt that the expense of developing such an engine, together with the difficulties to be met, would not be worth it. Fortunately, however, a few farsighted men had faith enough in the air cooling principle to devote their time and finances to further development of such a type of engine.

Charles Lanier Lawrance was one of those men. Initially he built the Model A 'water cooled' Lawrance-Moulton auto engine in France. Lawrance's first air-cooled engine, under the name of the Lawrance Aero Engine Corporation, was a two cylinder horizontally opposed Model A-3 engine of 28 hp at 1400 rpm. designed in 1916. His next two cylinder horizontally opposed air-cooled engine was known as the N-2 and produced 40 hp at 1900 rpm.

The first Lawrance radial air-cooled type was the Model B, 3 cylinder, of 35 to 60 hp, built also in 1916. After further engineering and with the success of the "B," the "L" air-cooled radial engine, with 3 cylinders, was marketed by the company, then located in New York City, known as the L-2.

After the L-2 came the L-3 and L-4. In 1923 the Lawrance Aero Engine Company was merged with the Wright Aeronautical Corporation, located in Paterson, New Jersey. Charles Lawrance became Vice President of Engineering at Wright, eventually becoming President in 1925.

Under the Wright name the L-4 was produced and named the "Gale". They also built the L-5 and with success, trials, and further engineering, the company went on to the famous "J" series nine cylinder, radial, air-cooled engines, beginning with the J-1, and following successively by the J-3, J-4 and J-4A, J-4B, all in the 200 hp class, leading up to the J-5C, "Whirlwind."

These engines eventually superseded all other American built engines in their power range and up to the end of 1925 were the only American-built air-cooled radial engines to successfully complete a standard fifty-hour endurance test.

This success was the result of seven years of development, which began on February 28, 1920. Up to 1927 seven successive models of air-cooled engines had been developed and over 1000 engines sold. The practical experience and technical data resulting from the tests of each model formed the groundwork for further improvement in detailed design.

Lindbergh definitely wanted a Wright "Whirlwind" engine, but the actual model was still to be selected. Claude Ryan was convinced of the reliability of the J-4 flown by Pacific Air Transport (PAT) in their Ryan M-1's. But the new J-5 developed 220 hp, twenty more horsepower than the J-4. Lindbergh wanted the extra power of the J-5.

By the time Lindbergh and Hall began the assembly phase of the NYP development, the Wright Company was producing the J-5C (commercial) model. The J-5C was built for commercial purposes and was identical with the model J-5 engine except that

A young engineer, Donald Hall, working on drawings for the NYP at his drafting table in the loft of the fish cannery. ***(Donald Albert Hall family)***

Lindbergh working on the navigation charts for the planned flight to Paris. This is in the office on the second floor of the fish cannery. ***(Donald Albert Hall family)***

it was not equipped with fuel pump and machine-gun synchronizer drives. The compression ratio was slightly less than that of the J-5 and was designed to make possible the use of a wider range of commercial fuels.

As it turned out, the basic dimensions were the same as the earlier "J" series engines. The cylinders had a bore of 4.5 inches and a stroke of 5.5 inches, giving a displacement of 788 cubic inches with a 5.2 to 1 compression ratio. Guaranteed output at sea level was 200 hp with normal output of 220 hp at 1800 rpm. Outside diameter was 45 inches; length excluding the starter, was 40 5/32 inches.

Lindbergh liked the J-5C because it had enclosed and shielded rocker arms, very important for a long distance flight. This same engine powered many endurance flights, including those which used the mid-air refueling technique. The very first aircraft to fly over the North Pole, was a Fokker F.VIIa-3M, named the "Josephine Ford", and powered with three Wright J-4 "Whirlwind" engines, and flown by Lt. Cmdr. Richard E. Byrd and Floyd Bennett on May 9, 1926. Because of its use during the publicity and "stunt" era of aviation, the J-5C became especially famous.

So the final decision by Lindbergh and Hall was to use the 9 cylinder, air-cooled J-5C. An order was placed with the Paterson, New Jersey firm about the end of February 1927.

The engine ordered was one of about ten (Byrd, Chamberlin, Fonck etc.) "super inspected" models carrying serial number 7331 and was shipped from the factory at Paterson about April 2, 1927, and arrived April 8. It represented Wright Aeronautical Corporation sales order #11958 to Ryan Airlines, Inc., 3200 Barnett Avenue, San Diego, California. It appears as though the price was around 4000 to 5000 dollars, but no official document showing the original price has been found. [1]

Lindbergh's J-5C was modified from the standard production model. On his engine were provided special grease fittings on the rocker arm covers. These Alemite grease fittings had reservoirs and a tiny spring loaded piston, whose job was to gradually force lubrication into the rocker arm bearings during the flight to Paris. They were designed to do the job for a thirty to forty hour period. His engine was also equipped with a fuel pump (serial #1692.)

When it arrived at the Ryan plant on April 8, 1927, Lindbergh recalled, they gathered around the wooden crate as if

February 2, 1933. Scene shows the main entrance of the fish cannery, which is the small door in front of the car. Engineering department and drafting room is on the 2nd floor in the corner with two windows on right and one on the left. ***(Donald Albert Hall family)***

some statue were to be unveiled. It was like a large jewel set in its wrappings.

With any good engine a propeller selection would be the next priority. This depends on airframe design and other miscellaneous requirements.

PROPELLER SELECTION

Based on reputation, it was not surprising that Lindbergh and Hall selected a top propeller of the day, the dural-blade ground adjustable model made by Standard Steel Propeller Company of Homestead (near Pittsburgh,) Pennsylvania.

This company and the Hamilton Aero Mfg. Company of Milwaukee, Wisconsin became the world famous Hamilton-Standard Division of United Aircraft Corporation, predecessor of United Technologies Corporation of Hartford, Connecticut. They (UTC) formed the Hamilton-Standard Propeller Company in 1929 by acquiring Hamilton Aero and Standard Steel.

THE AIRFRAME

Development of the NYP airframe was next and began with the idea of using components from the standard model Ryan M-2, then in production, together with B-1 "Brougham" components, then under development. Ryan would then make modifications to suit the special purpose of the Paris flight. However, after further consideration and study, they found that this was less practical than re-engineering certain components. Lindbergh laid out the following basic criteria: use a single Wright engine, 400 gallons of fuel, and have the pilot located in the rear of all fuel tanks for safety in a forced landing, and that the airplane be of a monoplane configuration. [2]

The Brougham design, under development at that time, called for a forty-two foot wing span, but the NYP would have to

Welded up fuselage, with vertical fin temporarily mounted on the tail post/spar. The rudder pedals, control stick, and trim lever can be clearly seen in the picture. ***(Donald Albert Hall family)***

have a long wing of forty-six feet to reduce the wing loading for take off and increase the aspect ratio for range. The fuselage would have to be about two feet longer in order to support the fuel weight. The decision was made to use the standard Ryan fuselage truss type structural configuration as a basis. The tail surfaces would have to be moved aft to maintain satisfactory stability and control, which would result in moving the engine forward eighteen inches.

Even with the increased wing span, the struts were left in the same location. There was just that much more overhang, which was acceptable for a one purpose flight. This brought the wing loading down to where it could handle the heavy load.

As Lindbergh reasoned, additional fuel tanks could be provided in the space which would have been used for a copilot. This idea took Hall by complete surprise, as it was the first he had heard that Lindbergh planned to fly alone. But he soon realized the merits of this theory; this extra storage space would provide reserve fuel, something that had been worrying Hall since the initial order for the airplane was received.

Hall asked Lindbergh if he could stay awake for forty hours or so, which he felt the flight would take. Actually Lindbergh did not really know how much time it would take. Neither of them knew what the actual distance was. To find out they drove over to the public library and stretched a piece of string over a globe. The distance turned out to be about 3600 statute miles. [3]

So the order was placed with Ryan Airlines, Inc. on February 25, 1927 for the airplane to be equipped with a Wright J-5 engine. A check in the amount of $1000 was given to Ryan Airlines as a down payment on the total price of $10,580.00. On that day Donald Hall began the preliminary design of the NYP.

On the 28th Lindbergh was driven out to Dutch Flats by Franklin Mahoney, where an M-1 demonstrator was put at his disposal. Harm Jon van der Linde, chief mechanic on the flight line, talked years later about the time he was told to warm up the M-1. "But instead of one of our pilots getting in, this young boy got aboard and I wondered if it was all right for him to fly the airplane. So I walked over to John J. "Red" Harrigan who was chief pilot at the time and asked if the 'kid' was supposed to fly it. Harrigan said 'yeah' and proceeded to tell me who he was. He flew that ship for about an hour, wrung it out like nothing I'd ever seen. He could fly it, all right."

Also on February 28th Carl Schory of the National Aeronautics Association in Washington announced receipt of a formal entry to the competition for the Orteig Prize from a St. Louis mail pilot named C.A. Lindbergh. "I sent him a routine letter that his application was received and properly noted." This was the second formal entry received, the first being that of Lt. Commander Noel Davis.

Tail skid assembly at the aft end of the fuselage and connected to the bungee cords. **(Donald Albert Hall family)**

Another view of the fuselage showing the instrument panel, earth inductor compass generator and tail skid assembly installed. **(Donald Albert Hall family)**

The little Ryan Company, operating out of the defunct and abandoned fish cannery at the foot of Juniper Street near the San Diego water front, was given sixty days to build the NYP, a most formidable challenge. Ryan Airlines, Inc. personnel immediately became enthusiastic about this project. They would work day and night, seven days a week, for sixty days until they had constructed one of the most efficient airplanes of its day.

Much creative tension pervaded the atmosphere at the plant. Some of the men worked twenty-four hours without rest. On one occasion Donald Hall worked over his drafting board for thirty-six hours. They all knew that this young aviator from the Midwest wanted a flawless airplane. Lindbergh spurred the enthusiasm of the employees. In their admiration for him they would do just about anything he suggested.

Rudder post mechanism clearly showing how the stabilizer (trailing edge) trim is actuated with cables and sliding couplings etc. **(Donald Albert Hall family)**

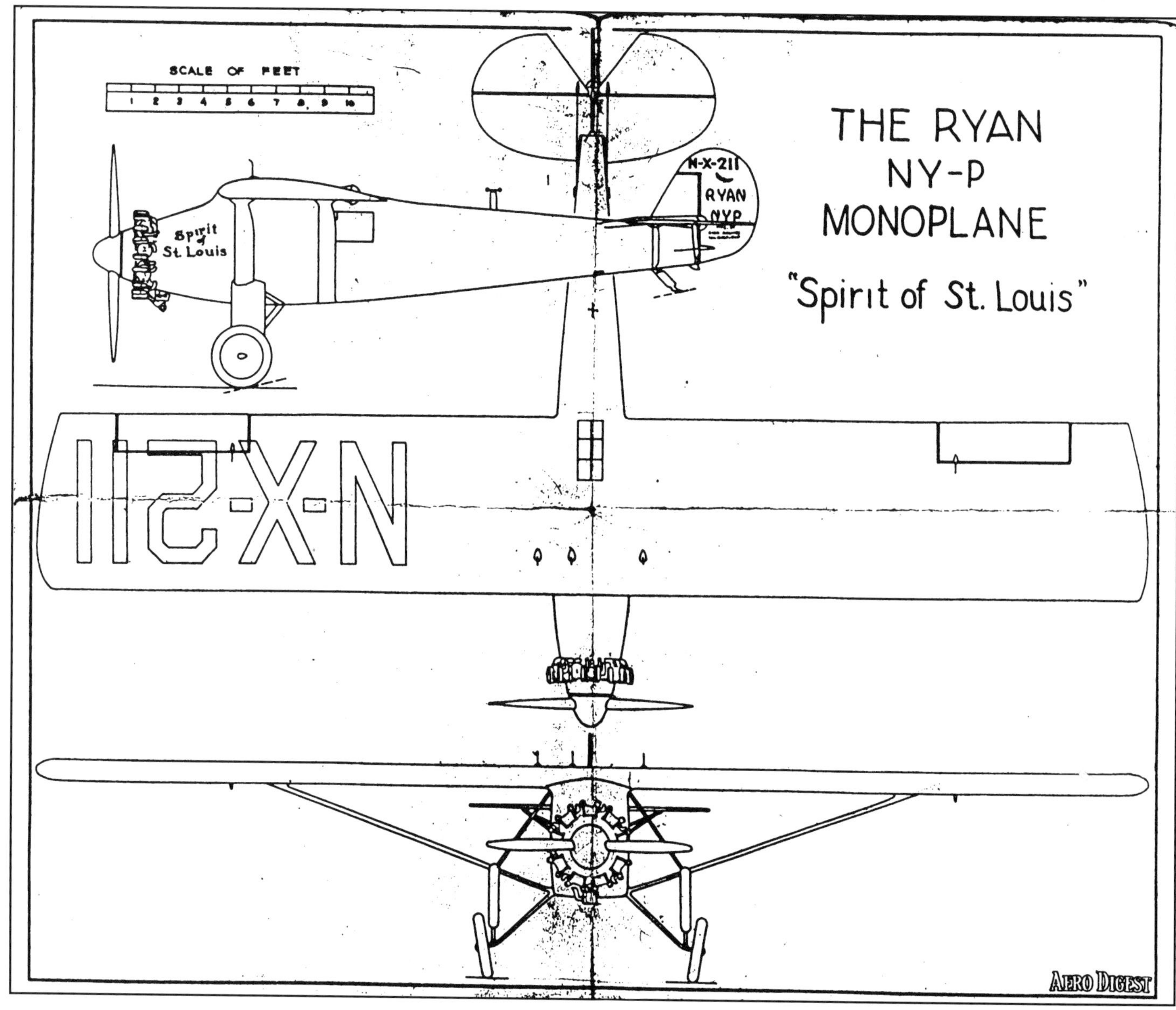

Reproduction of 3-view drawing by Donald A. Hall, 1927 ***(Donald Albert Hall family)***

First photo taken of the brand new instrument panel and instruments, including the Lindbergh designed fuel econometer. Notice the fuel selection valves just below the panel. ***(Donald Albert Hall family)***

A good view of the main fuel tank, showing the baffles arrangements. ***(Donald Albert Hall family)***

Most of the male employees worked for about sixty-five cents an hour and overtime pay was just out of the question. There were a few women, working either in the office or the fabric department earning thirty-five to forty cents an hour. Even at these low wages by today's standards, it was not always easy for the company to meet the payroll.

Douglas "Wrong Way to Ireland" Corrigan started working in the fitting department filing metal fittings four hours a day. Eventually he became a welder and helped make up the fuel tanks and the one oil tank for the NYP. [4] One worker, Ed Crosby, recalled that "We didn't have much equipment in those days. I remember we had an old lathe and drill press and a couple nibbling machines. We worked hard and long hours to turn out the 'Spirit.'" [5]

Ruth Kennough (now Ruth Clemens of Ohio) started working for the Ryan group in July 1926. "I was hired by the Ryan Company at a starting salary of $12. a week, with $9.00 of that going for room and board. I worked under Fred Ayers,, who was in charge of the fabric and painting department, learning to measure the airplane parts and get the covers ready for Mrs. Lillian Bray to sew up on a regular home sewing machine, the type a woman would use for making clothes." [6]

Mrs. Clemens went on to say , "We all worked very hard and long hours to get the NYP finished on time. Mr. Lindbergh would walk around to see how things were progressing, but he never bothered us. In fact, he very seldom spoke to any of us unless we spoke to him first."

The Ryan workers were very proud of the reputation they had built up from the production of the M-1 and M-2. At the start of the NYP project, some of them resented this lanky pilot hovering over them like a shepherd, but the project was shrouded in secrecy.

Fred Rohr, with his assistant Fred Magula, hand crafted all of the metal fuel tanks, cowlings and fairings. Rohr was considered a wizard in metal forming. He was years later held in high regard for inventions that tumbled from his creative, mechanical genius.

Left side view of the cockpit and main tank area of the fuselage. The earth inductor compass "controller" and the connecting rods and universal joints can be clearly seen in the photo, just aft of the throttle and trim handles. ***(Donald Albert Hall family)***

He pioneered drop-hammer forming and invented a ball-socket exhaust manifold, way ahead of competition, eventually forming his own company—Rohr Aircraft Corporation, in 1940. [7]

Fred Magula, sheet metal worker, remembered, "We were working out at the mud flat airport but we didn't even know what we were working on. All at once we were told to build a great big old gas tank out there, and we didn't even know what for. I thought it was a gas tank for a doggone fishing boat. It was a mammoth thing. They didn't want a scratch on it because they figured vibration would set in and create a leak. Talking to the other fellows while we were building it, we wondered why we should take so much care with a gas tank for a fishing boat. Then it finally leaked out what the tank was for." [8]

Appears to be the first basic airframe assembly on horses on the floor of the fish cannery. Not confirmed, but this could also have been the NYP-2 Japanese NYP replica. Notice M-1 fuselage partially covered in the background. ***(Donald Albert Hall family)***

View of the forward fuselage section showing the engine installation, forward fuel and oil tanks and the landing gear bungee cord, etc. ***(Donald Albert Hall family)***

Helen Tharp (now Helen Hendrix of San Diego) came to work at the Ryan plant at age sixteen from Lincoln, Nebraska. She made ribs, did some fabric work, and painted engines and inside cabins and cockpits of the M-1s. She worked with Ruth Corbett Sasalla and Peggy Dewitt. To this day she has never been up in an airplane, although she worked many times on crashed ships "fixing them up." [9]

O. R. McNeel took care of fuel tank installations, controls, instrumentation and fuel valves, of which there were many. He was also final assembly foreman. [10]

Factory layout consisted of the fuselage department and fittings department downstairs along with the main business office, stock room, and sheet metal department. Upstairs, the full span at the front of the building housed the engineering office and the wood shop which produced rib jigs, and wing assemblies, (about three at a time on the production line), monorails to carry the wings to the last stage for fabric covering, and then on to the dope shop and finishing.

Fuselages were built on the first floor and then brought upstairs for covering and finishing.

As the story became known about this "mystery airplane," the workers began to develop an early respect for Lindbergh, especially as they began to understand what was at stake. The normal eight hour day became longer, hours running into midnight—and this was every night. However, they all agreed that no one worked harder than Hall and Lindbergh. Hall showed his dedication by arriving several hours early so that the other workers could carry out his instructions without time lost. He showed engineering foresight in his careful attention to weight limits and wind drag on the NYP.

During discussions on saving weight and cutting down on aerodynamic drag, the subject of a landing gear that could be dropped was considered. Hall said it could be done, but it would be heavier and would cause a crack-up in the landing.

Lindbergh felt that if he were to land on sod in a lightly loaded condition that it might get the propeller with little or no other damage except scraping on the bottom of the fuselage and perhaps a wing tip. If the margins were close, it might make the difference between success and failure. It might even save the airplane.

Hall further felt the weight savings would give them a lot of extra range. However, he cautioned that if Lindbergh had to turn back after cutting loose the gear, with that full load of fuel, it could be disastrous.

They went on discussing methods of dropping the gear from the air so that it would break cleanly without danger of injuring any part of the airplane. Neither one of them was too happy about the idea. They finally decided to keep the idea in the back of their minds as an emergency reserve in case more accurate performance calculations proved disappointing. They also discussed the use of a droppable streamlined fuel tank.

In later years comments from the general public as well as the general aviation community on the location of the cockpit in the NYP have often indicated a complete misunderstanding of its rather logical location. People seem to wonder and/or question the lack of forward visibility. In actuality it was not overlooked, but was not of priority such as was Lindbergh's well being and longevity. He was capable of flying an airplane with minimal forward visibility from his experiences of flying "blind" type of aircraft in the U.S. Mail services, for instance. After all, he and Hall *did* put a window on each side of the cockpit. Therefore Lindbergh could simply 'side slip' the NYP in order to see forward for navigating or landing.

This arrangement of the windows with no windshield also cut down considerably on drag and proved to be aerodynamically efficient. It protected the pilot in case of an accident so he would not be sandwiched between the engine and the large and heavy main fuel tank.

When Hall mentioned that no forward vision in normal cruise attitude would make navigation difficult, Lindbergh reminded him that it would make little difference as he would be flying by instruments most of the time anyway. In fact there would be no one to run into out over the Atlantic. He further reasoned that when he was near an airport he could make shallow banks to line up for final approach, and for landing he could side-slip, a common maneuver in those days. He felt strongly that first consideration should be given to efficiency in flight, second to protection in a crash and third, to pilot comfort. The rearward cockpit location would permit mounting the compass far enough from the engine to eliminate much deviation—so beneficial on such a flight.

Soon Hall asked Lindbergh what he was planning to use the airplane for after the flight. Lindbergh said he had not given any thought to that question, and would not consider such until he successfully landed in Paris.

Hall raised the question of what night flying equipment he would like to install in the airplane. None were planned by Lindbergh, who felt that such things would be nice to have, but they could not afford the extra weight. When asked about using a parachute Lindbergh gave the same reply. With that Hall felt it would make his job much easier.

When the subject of designing the tail surfaces arose, Hall said he was not satisfied with the size of the M-2 tail and suggested they design a larger version to handle a maximum efficiency take-off and obtain better stability in cruise flight. According to a letter dated April 7, 1968 to the author from Lindbergh, "time was lacking, and I was not much concerned about stability for the New York—Paris flight. Most of the planes I had flown up to that time were unstable." [11]

Lindbergh was only concerned that the smaller M-2 tail surfaces might cause a dangerous situation. Hall assured him it would not. When Lindbergh questioned the possibility of larger surfaces cutting down on range, Hall felt it would be minimal.

Further reasoning by Lindbergh indicated he would have to be watching the compass all the time so a stable airplane was not necessary. He did not plan on sleeping during the flight. The plane's instability was to help Lindbergh stay awake during the long hours of the flight.

As they discussed the NYP's range, the final agreement was to eliminate from their calculations the uncertainties of wind along the route and to plan their reserves on the basis that it would nei-

Good view of the left landing gear assembly and the newly mounted wheel and tire assembly. Notice the clean job of fairing the V strut with balsa wood and fabric. ***(Donald Albert Hall family)***

ther hinder them nor help. They concluded that the minimum requirement for fuel would be enough to fly between New York and Paris over the great circle route in still air. Of course, to do that in actual practice required a theoretical reserve. They decided that the airplane should be designed around a theoretical range of 4000 statute miles.

PROPELLER DESIGN

During this design stage Lindbergh made a careful study of the propeller setting, compromising between a low blade angle for good take-off performance and a high angle for economical cruising. The pitch setting, after consultation with the Standard Steel Propeller Company was 16.25 degrees. This favored cruising and fuel economy, but cut down on take-off performance. In a conversation with Lindbergh in later years, he explained the choice to this author; "We felt edgy about the range. We did not dare to use optimistic figures because time was short and we lacked the benefit of a lot of tests. After conferences we elected to set the blades for cruising. I decided to 'feel' the plane off the ground just as I had often done in underpowered planes while barnstorming. If I felt I was not going to get off the ground, my plan was simply to cut the throttle."

When Lindbergh selected his propeller blade setting, he was following a suggestion contained in a telegram from the propeller company. In recent years a discussion with George Rosen, propeller aerodynamicist at Hamilton, now retired, resulted in the following comments: "At take-off, with a blade setting of 16.25 degrees, the Wright J-5C engine could deliver about 190 hp at 1545 rpm for a propeller static thrust of 700 pounds."

Take-off problems would have been greatly reduced and fuel economy improved if a controllable pitch propeller, which came a few years later, had been available in 1927. "With a two-position controllable," Rosen said, "the blade angle could have been set at 14.5 degrees for take-off and 18 degrees for cruising. That would have given 210 hp at 1720 rpm and a propeller thrust of 905 pounds for take-off, and considerable better fuel consumption at cruise. The later constant speed controllable would have enabled blade pitch to be set at 13.5 degrees for take-off and that would have given the full rated 220 hp at 1800 rpm and propeller thrust of 960 pounds. Such a situation would have left no room for doubt on take-off even with the muddy field."

In an interview at the Hamilton-Standards production plant Alex F. Mannella, general factory superintendent recalled those historical days. Mannella was then an assembly foreman and also served as an inspector, which is why his initials (AFM) made the long flight to Paris and remained embedded in the blades and hub

Clear photo of the left nose area and newly painted "Spirit of St. Louis" on the damascene cowling. Also notice the blunt spinner assembly cap. This is the one that was to develop a crack as the airplane was flown across the country to New York. ***(Donald Albert Hall family)***

of the propeller. Also stamped on the blades were the following: "Drawing. No. 1519." (Mr. Mannella still has the two small metal cylinders which are the stamps used when he checked that propeller as OK. They are his souvenirs of that flight.)

The propeller was sometimes advertised as the Sport "Senior" model. The hub was of the two piece split type, made of a high grade chrome steel. Blade type was #5B1-0 from drawing no. 1519, and the diameter was 8 ft 9 in. The blades were made of a specially forged and hardened aluminum metal alloy. [12]

Man (Hall ?) holding the landing gear shock strut assembly, clearly showing the bungees in place. ***(Donald Albert Hall family)***

Appears to be the right wing rear spar, showing the pulleys and cable for the aileron control and the right rear strut support fitting. ***(Donald Albert Hall family)***

The propeller forging was made in the ALCOA (Aluminum Company of America) Cleveland, Ohio, plant before being finished by Standard Steel Company in Pennsylvania.

The Hamilton propeller was then ordered at a cost of $350.00. Lindbergh wrote out check #3 for this amount, payable to the Ryan Airlines on March 3, 1927.

Soon after Hall and Lindbergh's design concept had been firmed up, Hall felt they could freeze the decision and said he would proceed with a preliminary layout of the general arrangement. He felt at that time there would not be much left of the M-2 design. Only two parts were the same, for convenience, the tail surfaces—since Lindbergh wanted an unstable airplane—and the wing rib Clark Y airfoil similar to that on the Douglas Army O-2 Observation airplane, and the Curtiss Hawk, for instance, and commonly used on many aircraft of the era.

Top view of the right side wing assembly. ***(Donald Albert Hall family)***

His plan was to begin a weight and balance analysis, followed by the fuselage and wing stress analysis. Then he would produce fuselage and wing construction and detail drawings so the plant could begin fabrication.

Due to the time element to get the airplane out, there was only time to make shop sketches for fabricating the various parts and assemblies. Of these sketches and drawings, only the wing assembly, cowling, and the initial three view drawing of the NYP exist today. They were drawn by Donald A. Hall, in ink, on linen drawing media, and belong to his son, Donald A. Hall, Jr.

During this design stage Lindbergh and Hall kept the center of gravity of the fuel load close to the NYP's center of gravity, resulting in improved longitudinal stability for the critical start of the New York to Paris flight.

NYP CONSTRUCTION

FUSELAGE

The fuselage was primarily the same basic welded truss type tube configuration as the M-2/B-1 except where the main fuel tank was installed and for the "V" cut-out for the cockpit door on the right side. The door was located on the right side because just about all airplanes of that era (except the M-1) had the throttle and mixture controls, trim etc. on the left wall. The control stick was in the standard center position and rudder pedals in their usual location. The fuselage was about 2 ft longer than the M-2.

The tubing used was seamless SAE 1020 mild carbon steel supplied by the Service Steel Company of Detroit.

According to one worker there were no jigs or fixtures to determine main points. Steel backed wooden frames of 4 x 4's were made and the tubing was laid into them and heated up to contour into the frame, measured, and then welded up. Much of this work was done by sight with an "artistic eye."

Due to the dimensions being new, they could not use the previously developed Brougham jig. So the NYP fuselage became a sort of free hand operation. Walt Crawford used a center-line wire, plumb bobs and a great deal of measuring. His helpers were Guss Eoff and Lon Wheeler.

After the main side frames were welded, cross members were added from top to bottom and dove-tailed into the side tubing. No photos have ever been found that show this operation.

Lifting handles, one on each side, were welded to the lower longerons just forward of the tail post to assist in moving the airplane around.

All fuselage tubes and fittings were coated with Nitro-Valspar outside and the inside of all tubing was probably coated with Lion oil, part linseed and part turpentine.

Spruce was likely used for all the stringers; three on top, three on the bottom, and three on each side of the fuselage. No bulkheads or formers were used except for one small thin one on each side of and at the bottom of Station 1, at the forward part of the main fuel tank.

One bulkhead/former strip is mounted on top at Station 3 to support the top three stringers and butt against the skylight trailing edge frame. All wood was coated with Nitro-Valspar.

Two ⅝" o.d. tubular type frames circling the engine mount frame; one at the engine mount ring and one at about halfway to

Here is the Studebaker Light Six EM touring car, about April 26th, towing the NYP out to Dutch Flats. Notice that the periscope has not been installed yet in the upper left corner of the left cockpit window. Ed Morrow can be seen in the front right seat checking back at situation. ***(Donald Albert Hall family)***

Station 1, were welded to the engine mount (1½" o.d.) structure via struts. These tubular rings actually support the six sided aluminum engine cowl panels. They clearly allow space for carry through fuel lines, oil lines, electrical wire, and push-pull tubes for the throttle, mixture and carburetor heater and spark advance controls, in addition to instrument lead lines.

The bottom aft portion of the fuselage tail section was fitted with an aluminum cover plate to be used for inspection and servicing of the tail skid and other internal mechanism. By March 9th, the fuselage framework was completed. [13]

COWLING

The aluminum cowling was built in six sections and fastened with studs and aircraft safety pins. The interesting swirling pattern is actually an old type of finish known as Damascene. It is basically a decorative finish and was often used on machinery in Europe as well as the U.S. It has been an accepted practice for at least 150 years.

It would therefore be a natural extension of shop practice to extend that technique to aircraft finishes. It is customary to overlap the swirled circle by one-half inch horizontally and one-half inch vertically so only one-half of the circle is showing. One starts the procedure on the lower left corner, like the scales on a fish. The scales should turn the wind when the airplane flies and turn the water when it rains whether the airplane is flying or at rest, so the saying goes.

Ryan had been using the Damascene process for some time on its M-1 and M-2 airplanes and later continued on the Brougham series. Fred Magula said at one time that Ryan adopted this process in order to hide the imperfections of the hammered out sheet metal, not knowing it would become a trade-mark for Ryan and other aircraft manufacturers.

The six sections of the cowling and other fairings and fillets were cut and fitted by hand by Fred H. Rohr, foreman, together with Fred Magula. No cooling louvers were cut into any part of the engine cowling at this time, except in the bump dishpan section.

One of the toughest jobs for Fred Magula was to build the 'dishpan' section of the cowling. This is the circular piece that runs back from the spinner backing plate, then between the cylinders to the forward edge of the side cowling. He pounded it into shape over his sandbag. To reinforce the unit he formed a circular piece of ⅛" wire, then crimped the edge of the dishpan around the wire with pliers. "It was 'cut and tried' all the way," said Jon van der Linde many years later. Magula had to judge distance and contours by eye.

In addition to the main body of the dishpan, Magula had to make up two 'bump' pieces to fit over each of the Magnetos. That was no easy job considering the compound curves involved.

Four main fittings to secure the wing in place were welded to the top longerons at Stations 1 and 2.

SPINNER

The spinner was designed in two main sections; a shroud/collar that fastened to a propeller backing plate and slanted forward to just ahead of the prop hub area and which provided propeller openings located at the 0 degree and 180 degree locations. Attached to the shroud was the spinner cap itself, sometimes in later years incorrectly referred to as a "nose cone." The term nose cone did not surface until created by the builders of space vehicles. A spinner is actually a fairing of approximately conical or paraboloidal form fitted coaxially with the propeller boss, all of which revolves with the propeller.

The spinner (and it is not clear if the whole assembly was included) was 'spun' by a firm in the Los Angeles area, name unknown. According to Fred Magula it was a rather rough job which he in turn had to smooth out before it was installed. The cowling and spinner were of soft aluminum. As seen in photos, the spinner had a very definite blunt nose. The spinner assembly carried the Damascene finish matching the cowling.

FUSELAGE FUEL TANKS

Fred Magula, the man in charge of sheet metal work, under foreman Fred Rohr, in a letter to the author indicated the five fuel tanks were built of terneplate, a soft steel covered with lead. He said the solder would flow into it quite well.

The tanks were hand built. They were told not to get a mark in where they drive the rivets because it could result in fatigue cracks and create a leak. The tanks were hand seamed and rolled and soldered. Weight was extremely important. It took so many pounds of solder for so many inches of seam. In the top of the fuselage between stations 1 & 2 there was a rectangular opening with no diagonal members for the main 210 gallon fuel tank. The tank sat on two fittings and had wood saddles on the floor section that it sat on. It was a very tight fit, with barely ⅛th inch clearance on either side of the fuselage frame structure. It was secured with straps and other hardware and was a custom fit.

The forward 88 gallon fuel tank was mounted just forward of the main tank and secured in place with straps and other appropriate hardware.

The filler neck on the forward tank was at the top aft position

The wing was just maneuvered out of the second floor opening onto the freight car, where the workmen are holding it for security, as the contractor's derrick is put into position. ***(Donald Albert Hall family)***

and was the same type of filler neck as the one for the main tank. On the forward tank the neck came straight up. The filler neck on the main tank came straight forward from the top of the front bulkhead of the tank with a 90 degree elbow to come up along side the forward tank filler neck. The two filler necks were accessible via an access plate in the wing.

All of the fuel tanks were vented with a ¼ inch tubing and egressed just forward of the fuel tanks' filler necks.

OIL TANK

The 25 gallon oil tank was built up of terneplate also and mounted and secured just behind the engine and forward of the forward fuel tank. Its filler neck was mounted at the top rear of the tank. The outlet for the supply oil to feed to the engine was on the bottom center of the tank. The oil return line runs from the rear of the engine, (engine oil outlet) up and over to dump into the top of the tank, between the leading edge (or front) of the tank and the oil filler neck.

COCKPIT

The cockpit was designed strictly as a 'control center' and nothing more with only controls and instruments necessary to do the job and a place for the pilot to sit, operate and observe these controls and instruments.

Stick and rudder pedals were located in their normal positions. The trim lever with the large varnished wooden handle is located on the left wall just below the window. The lever operated the aft portion of the stabilizer for pitch trim.

Just aft of the trim lever and a bit below was the throttle lever, also with a wood handle on top. Integrated with the throttle was the spark advance lever, with a wood handle and slightly below and in the center between the trim and throttle was the wobble pump for the fuel system.

On the left side of the instrument panel, probably the most advanced there was in 1927, was the mixture lever, which operated up and down to a graded scale. Rich mixture was at the top of the scale.

Instruments mounted on the panel included the following as manufactured or supplied by Pioneer Instrument Company of Brooklyn, New York:

Air Speed (0-140 mph)	Type #179, s/n 499 (documented by invoice)
Pitot static tube	P5C
Bank and Turn	Model 103C-563
Venturi	Pioneer V74
Inclinometer (degrees)	#P-3217 (lateral & longitudinal, liquid type) W. C. Rieker (maker) Philadelphia, PA
Earth Inductor Compass	Type 301B
Earth Inductor Compass Controller	301B—78
Liquid Magnetic Compass	Type 145 s/n 509
Magneto Switch	Splitdorf Model A 232
Tachometer-Victometer	Joseph V. Jones U. S. Navy Type B Consolidated Instrument Company of America, Inc.
Altimeter	Neko, Newark, NJ Type G. No. 2044 U. S. Army Signal Corp.
Oil Pressure Gauge	Moto Meter Company, Inc. (War Stock)
Oil Temperature Gauge	Moto Meter Company, Inc. Type C, U. S. Air Service
Fuel Pressure Gauge	U. S. Navy Type B
Waltham 8 Day Clock	Number XA, 15J, (15 jewels) 37 size 3⅛", with mount #314. Made for Pioneer by Waltham
Primer	Lunkenheimer
Fuel tank distributor valve	Lunkenheimer
Speed and Drift Meter, with carrying case and base plate	#54, s/n 259

Six dry batteries were installed on the left wall just aft of the window. They were for the instrument eyebrow lights, top of instrument panel. Lindbergh did not use them on the Paris flight.

A wood map case was built and mounted on the fuselage frame just behind the pilot seat on the right side. This case held the removable windows, maps, and drift meter.

Lindbergh refused to put any type of fuel gauges in the airplane. He reasoned that he could measure fuel consumption with time on his watch. Fuel gauges would add extra weight, and he felt they were unreliable anyway.

Just below the instrument panel were the fuel control valves for all five fuel tanks. This was a crucial consideration for the fuel distribution system. This system was designed and hand built by Fred Rohr, an uncanny wizard of sheet metal work and other details.

WALTHAM EIGHT DAY CLOCK MODEL XA

The Waltham 8 Day Clock, model XA, mounted on the instrument panel, appears to be a model XP but with the outside turning knob. The knob shown is actually a knob to take off the small plate, in order to put the pilot's fingers in the opening in the wood panel. This turned the clock controls to set the time and wind the spring.

LINDBERGH INVENTED ECONOMETER

Lindbergh invented an econometer to keep track of fuel flow/consumption. No such instrument was available at that time. Actually it was a calibrated flowmeter. It was built by the Ryan shop and mounted on the right side of the panel, a clear vertical glass tube. All the fuel tanks were connected below the panel to a manifold and had fifteen fuel cocks. If the two center ones were shut off, fuel would go through the glass and the rate it bubbled up and down in the glass would give the pilot an idea how much was being used. The NYP had one of the first cross-feed fuel systems for aircraft. The flowmeter did not do the job so it was removed at Curtiss Field in New York, but can be seen in photos taken at San Diego.

PERISCOPE

Albert Clyde Randolph, who had considerable submarine experience, worked for Dan Burnett in the rib department. Randolph had suggested to Lindbergh that a periscope be fabricated to give the aviator better visibility straight ahead in certain or difficult flight situations. He showed Lindbergh a drawing of his idea. Lindbergh agreed to have it made on a trial basis. If it was not satisfactory or was of any disadvantage aerodynamically, it would be discarded at New York.

The periscope consisted of a telescoping set of boxes mounted on and behind the left side of the instrument panel and projecting out the left side of the fuselage. This afforded a direct front view on the left side of the fuselage toward the engine. He used two angular mirrors having a frontal size of about three by five inches. The whole assembly was retractable. The periscope was installed during assembly of the NYP at Dutch Flats.

The device proved of little or no disadvantage aerodynamically, and in fact, proved useful.

During the first hour of the flight to Paris, Lindbergh realized he could take off his goggles, lean back in his seat and sit quietly in the center of the cockpit to avoid fatigue and steer with the periscope. He did not have to keep leaning to either side for a clearer view. He could look directly ahead and spot a higher hill, a chimney or radio tower, especially during the early part of the flight with that full fuel load and lower altitude. It did stay in the airplane and is still in there today.

SEAT

The pilot seat was hand made by Harold Von Breisen and was of woven wicker. It was made to Lindbergh's dimensions, after several sittings and fittings to ensure as comfortable and safe an anchor point as possible.

The arms were padded and covered with brown velveteen. The seat was secured in the cockpit to two cross members of the tubular fuselage frame. The complete seat was varnished.

WINDOWS AND SKYLIGHT

The windows and skylight were made of .060 Pyralin, a nitro-Cellulose, (Celluloid), produced at that time by the Dupont Viscoloid Company of San Francisco, California.

Windows were mounted loosely in frames provided in the fuselage structure and when not in use were stored in the map case just behind the pilot on the right side.

SPEED AND DRIFT METER

As can be seen in the equipment list, a Speed and Drift Meter

The wing has just been lowered by derrick from the top of the freight car to a waiting solid tired flatbed cart. ***(Donald Albert Hall family)***

Excellent view of the nose, the Damascene swirling, and the Standard Steel propeller. ***(Donald Albert Hall family)***

was installed. A drift meter is used for measurement of angular deviation of an aircraft from a set course.

With a drift indicator Lindbergh could determine the difference between the heading and actual course. The indicator would show the difference in degrees, so he could calculate the heading and speed and steer the NYP accordingly.

Such an indicator was usually mounted in a hole in the floor of the airplane for easy reading. However, Lindbergh mentioned in his book (pg. 401) that it was stored in the wood case on the side of the fuselage behind his seat and taken out and clipped to the windowsill, probably on the left side. The scale on such an indicator was graduated 0 degrees to 50 degrees, both sides of zero.

After much research, photographs and other documentation have not shown where the indicator was finally mounted, if at all. However, one photograph does show a drift indicator temporarily mounted on the fuselage frame just outside and below the left window at the time of construction but before any fabric was applied. Apparently Ryan technicians were checking the possibility of its being mounted in an appropriate and convenient location to be used in flight. No other photos show the indicator mounted in that position at any time during its flying life.

During the Paris flight Lindbergh's initial plan was to take drift sights at dawn and each succeeding hour during the day. There were brackets provided on the window sill to hold the device so he could read the parallel hairs to determine his exact angle of drift and then offset it on his compass. He could line up the hairs with the sea foam's apparent path.

However, on the planned flight to Paris he realized how difficult it would be to lean out over the instrument and do all that while still trying to fly the unstable airplane. It was not worth its weight, equivalent to a half gallon of fuel. He did, however, have it aboard the NYP, stored in a rack behind his seat.

INCLINOMETER

A lateral and longitudinal liquid inclinometer was installed in the lower center of the instrument panel and worked to Lindbergh's satisfaction. Wouldn't it be fun for many of us modern day instrument pilots to fly with such an instrument and see how well it would help us to keep the airplane straight and level, or just level, in two planes?

RAFT HAND PUMP

Lindbergh purchased a raft in San Diego which was inflated with a hand pump. This pump was located and mounted low and next to his wicker seat on the right side of the cockpit. It was held in place with the use of heavy cord or cloth tape of some kind, as can be seen in photographs taken in France. As of 1997, it was not in the NYP.

EARTH INDUCTOR COMPASS

A new design in navigation compasses, known as the Earth Inductor Compass (EIC), was a revolutionary breakthrough in aerial navigation for its time.

At least two instrument design & manufacturing companies were actively & contemporaneously developing EIC technology in the early 1920's. Working models of compasses employing this technology were available as early as 1921.

Aeronautical Instrument Company of Pittsburgh, PA received patent rights to one style of EIC which was invented by Dr. Paul R. Heyl and Dr. Lyman J. Briggs of Washington, DC. In addition, Pioneer Instrument Company, Inc. of Brooklyn, NY received patent rights to another style of EIC which was invented by its Chief Engineer, Morris M. Titterington, also of Brooklyn, NY.

Lindbergh selected a Pioneer EIC for use in the NYP. This particular unit was installed by "Dapper" Dan Burnett, the first one ever installed by The Ryan Company. [14]

In order for one to understand the importance of this latest in navigation technology, one needs to understand and consider the characteristics of the ordinary magnetic compass as used on aircraft. The force which causes the magnetic compass to point out directions is the reaction between the compass magnets and the earth's magnetic field.

As long as the magnetic element, the compass card with its magnets and pivot, is constrained to rotate in a horizontal plane and the magnets tend to line up with the horizontal force of the earth's magnetism, the compass points out directions in relation to magnetic north.

Considering the magnetic force to be separated into horizontal and vertical components we find that the vertical component is about three times as strong as the horizontal component. When the compass is mounted on a fixed support where the magnetic element is held horizontal by the force of gravity, its magnets react with the horizontal component of the earth's magnetism. Under these conditions the compass is very accurate. However, on aircraft the conditions are much different. The fore-and-aft acceleration forces and the centrifugal forces act on the pendulous magnetic element to tilt it out of the horizontal and cause it to act as if constrained to rotate about some axis inclined to the vertical. This may result in errors of as much as 180 degrees.

The second source of error is the angular movement of the aircraft in yawing, rolling and pitching. These movements are transmitted to the magnetic element via the liquid. While the liquid tends to reduce the first type of error, it is responsible for the errors of the second type.

A third variety of error is caused by the vibration of the aircraft. These vibrations usually have rotary components which act on the magnetic element through the liquid and the pivot point causing erratic indications.

A fourth type of error is caused by magnetic materials in the vicinity of the compass, such as the engine and its ignition system and even the movable parts of the control system. Structural parts of the airplane, if of ferrous material and not magnetized, still produce errors due to distortion of the flux lines. Much of these magnetic errors can be reduce to some extent by compensation but not totally eliminated.

With the installation of the Pioneer EIC, the defects of the ordinary magnetic compass were obviated or greatly reduced. The outstanding feature of this new design was the separation of the magnetic element from the direction indicating element.

This new compass consisted of three principal units; a generator, a controller and an indicator. The generator contained the armature which was suspended in gimbal rings and driven by an anemometer or windmill outside the airplane. The generator brushes were mounted so that they could be rotated. The stability of the armature was maintained by the action of its own gyroscopic force.

The indicator was a sensitive zero center galvanometer, electrically connected to the brushes of the generator.

The controller was a mechanical device for setting the angle of the generator brushes to correspond to the desired heading. It was connected to the generator by a flexible shaft.

The dial on the face of the controller indicated the angle through which the brushes had been oriented in relation to the airplane.

The generator was mounted in the top rear of the fuselage of the NYP with the anemometer driving it projecting above the fuselage into the air stream. In this position, the instrument was not affected by metallic portions of the aircraft structure.

The meter/indicator was mounted in the top center of the NYP instrument panel, directly in front of Lindbergh. All Lindbergh had to do was merely steer to keep the indicator needle on zero. The indicator was wired directly from the generator, as is clearly seen in photos.

Any error resulting from a lack of horizontal stability was overcome by the stabilizing of the earth inductor generator. Since there was no pivotal suspension, no inertia (in the magnetic-responsive element) and no liquid to cause trouble by its viscosity, the generator was not affected by any movements of the NYP except while turning, which it was designed to discover and indicate. For the same reason, vibrations were without effect, there being no delicate moving part in which rotation might be induced.

This type of compass had the further advantage that its characteristics could be independently adjusted. This would not have been possible in a magnetic compass where the period, inertia and damping were inseparably inter-related. Much more accurate reading was possible with the inductor compass than with the magnetic type. The heading could be set to one-half degree and departures of less than one-half degree from this heading were easily noted on the meter.

HOW THE EIC WAS USED

After selecting his course the pilot simply kept the indicator/meter needle centered on zero. For long distance navigation/flying, the angle of deviation needed to be changed progressively. Lindbergh made this slight adjustment roughly each 100 statute miles as he crossed the Atlantic.

Without question, it was an unmatched tribute to the new compass combined with Lindbergh's mastery of the instrument that he was less than five miles off his plotted course as he passed over the Irish coastline.

The course to be followed was set on the controller dial; this moved the brushes to a certain position around the armature; the airplane was then steered one way or the other until the hand of the compass meter read zero. A deviation of the needle to the left indicated that the airplane was to the left of the course and must be brought back to zero by heading more to the right. Once the course was set, the pilot had only to keep the plane so headed that the hand of the compass always remained on zero.

MAST TUBE AIR DRIVEN MECHANISM FOR THE GENERATOR.

It appears in photographs that the original Pioneer EIC wind driven mechanism, or anemometer, was a vane type of air driven unit, or windwheel. This was probably the unit, or its shaft, that developed a bearing problem before Lindbergh left San Diego for New York. During some of the test flights at San Diego the bad bearing was discovered and the air driven vane was removed for his flight across the country, probably so it would not burn up the bearing and cause a fire.

According to Douglas Corrigan, a terrible flutter developed in the rear of the fuselage during a test flight. After Lindbergh landed they found that the universal joint on the EIC drive shaft was stuck. Mr. Balderston of the Pacific Scientific Company in Los Angeles came to San Diego to repair the EIC. Corrigan was selected to climb behind the seat and remove the generator. When it was dismantled, they found that someone had put castor oil in the bearing about a year earlier, and the oil caked up, causing the universal joint to stick. [15]

The generator assembly was mounted on the inside upper portion of the fuselage, just aft of the cockpit area. The shaft housing was covered with balsa and fabric or some other form of aerodynamic fairing.

LIQUID MAGNETIC COMPASS

In addition to the Earth Inductor Compass, Ryan technicians installed a liquid filled magnetic damped compass, one that was made for mounting upon the ceiling of a cabin aircraft, or elsewhere that would be far enough from the engine but near the pilot. In this instance, the liquid magnetic compass was installed on the floor, to the left of the control stick torque tube, as can be seen in one photograph.

The one mounted in San Diego (Pioneer type 145) had excessive deviation, but it would be OK for the trip to New York where Pioneer said they would replace it with a newer model. It was replaced at Curtiss Field in New York.

EMPENNAGE

The tail surfaces consisted of the standard stabilizer and elevators, vertical fin and balanced rudder. All of these components were built up of welded steel and fabric covered. They were similar to those of the M-2 but were installed two feet farther aft on the already lengthened fuselage.

The fin was ground adjustable for directional correction for torque. This mechanism consisted of a tube attached to the forward spar of the stabilizer and the lower forward part of the fin. It appears Lindbergh only adjusted the fin location during the initial test flights and left it that way throughout the NYP's flying life.

The horizontal stabilizer trailing edge is designed to move vertically about three or four inches for pitch trim. The mechanism was a hoist arrangement, allowing a connecting tube to slide up and down on the tail post tube. Control of the trim was through cables attached to the trim lever in the cockpit, which in turn was connected via pulleys to a fitting on the sliding tube. Pulling back on the trim lever caused the rear of the stabilizer to rise for nose up trim, and the opposite for nose down trim.

The stabilizer lift struts were designed so they too move in order to allow for the trim adjustment but still support the stabilizer in flight. They were made of 1 11/16 inches SAE 1020 mild carbon steel streamline tubes.

A tear-drop shaped fairing about seven or eight inches long was fastened around the attach point where the forward lift strut connects to the stabilizer for aerodynamic efficiency. It appears to be made of balsa wood and painted silver.

Drain grommets were provided and spaced along the trailing edge of the stabilizer and elevators.

WING

The single one piece wing had a span of forty-six feet and a seven foot cord with a zero degree dihedral. Airfoil section was the common Clark Y, mentioned earlier.

The wing was built up of Sitka Spruce wood with metal fittings and drag wires and fabric covered with drain grommets at the trailing edge.

The wing was mounted on the NYP fuselage with a zero degree incidence.

The front and rear spars were built up I sections with reinforcing spacers varying in separation from about eighteen inches. Blocks were mounted at points where fittings, aileron hinges and pulleys were located. Wood for the spars was of spruce and two ply Haskelite mahogany plywood with the grain running at forty-five degrees.

Ribs were of the Warren truss type, made up of Sitka spruce. Each rib was built in a block box on a form jig. Gusset plates were glued with Hercules Glue. Some of the cap strip steam bending was done at the Campbell Boat Company No. 2 plant, which had steam box facilities and when the boat company was not running wood for boats they would work in Ryan ribs. The Ryan people would work at the boat place for the first two hours of each morning. They would let the piece being steam-formed remain overnight until it was dried. Then the material could be sliced into upper and lower cap strips.

The ribs were secured to the spars in the usual manner and braced by the use of bias tape criss-crossed over and under each rib span wise. These tapes were to simply stiffen the ribs in their locations. Ribs were located on eleven inch centers.

The leading edge was of Haskelite mahogany ⅛th inch thick plywood. The leading edge wrapped around from the top of the front spar to the bottom of the same spar.

Compression ribs for the drag trussing were wood members that appear to be about one inch to two inches square.

The drag and anti-drag wires were of double configuration and of ⅛th inch round steel wire. Turnbuckles were provided at one end of each wire.

Trailing edge of the wing is V shaped aluminum nailed to each rib, typical construction practice for many years.

The skylight was integrally built into the wing structure with the forward part of the frame being attached to the rear of the rear spar. It tapered from the aft spar to an extension of the trailing edge and lined up with the top fuselage stringers.

Space was provided for the center wing tank and the two outer tanks, one left and one right, for a total capacity of 152 gallons.

The wing tips were unique in that they were built to an airfoil shape in plan view. Lindbergh wanted the least drag possible so they formed the tip out of balsa with fabric covering, using strips of balsa and leaving the tip hollow like a boat.

All of the wood in the wing was coated with Bass-Hueter Versatile & Valentine spar varnish.

A ventilator air scoop was built into the underside of the right wing between the fourth and fifth ribs out from the fuselage, centered twenty-eight inches forward of the trailing edge. Air was then ducted into the cockpit to direct fresh air to the pilot, entering the cockpit at the upper right position. The vent was controlled by a hand turned butterfly valve from the cockpit.

Quick drains were provided for each of the wing outer fuel tanks (not known where the center tank had a quick drain) on the underside of each wing and can clearly be seen in most photographs. They were covered over with a fairing made of balsa wood of tear drop shape. These quick drains were to remove water condensation, not as emergency fuel dumps.

By the end of March the wing was almost completed.

AILERONS:

Due to the increased moment arm, the ailerons were designed smaller than those on the early M-1 and M-2 and located approximately 38 inches inboard of the wing tips. The reason was to reduce wing tip deflection and structural loads to give better aerodynamic efficiency. This design philosophy proved to do the job well in cruise flight. However, lateral stability suffered as can be seen in many photos of Lindbergh landing the NYP clearly showing excessive aileron deflection. Some photos show the NYP in an apparent side-slip with cross controls again with ailerons in the full deflection position. At slow speeds large lateral stick movement was necessary to keep the airplane wing somewhat level. This was acceptable to Lindbergh because cruise flight efficiency was more important than easy lateral control if he were to fly from New York to Paris successfully.

The ailerons were built up from welded steel and fabric covered. They are operated by cable from the control stick in the cockpit in the conventional manner.

WING FUEL TANKS

Three fuel tanks were installed in the wing; one thirty-six gallon in the center over the fuselage and one each on the left and right of fifty-eight gallons each for a total of 152 gallons.

An access plate was provided just back from the leading edge to fill the center and forward fuselage tanks. The filler necks from the tanks were hidden and out of the slipstream as a result of this arrangement in the initial design.

MAIN LIFT STRUTS

The main wing lifting struts were built up from SAE 1020 mild carbon steel tubes, two inches o.d. They were streamlined to a tear-drop shape with balsa wood and fabric covered to a chord of 6⅜ inch for the rear strut and 7¾ inches for the front strut. The rear tube may have been 1¾ inches or 1⅞ inches.

FABRIC COVERING OF THE NYP

The entire airplane was covered with Flightex Grade A cotton fabric and finished with Titanine aluminum pigmented cellulose acetate dope in a silver color with black registration numbers on the upper right wing and lower left wing. All other markings on the nose cowl and rudder were in black. It is not known how many total coats of silver dope were applied, possibly six coats.

Looking carefully at photographs, one will notice the individual letters of "THE SPIRIT OF ST. LOUIS" on the right side of the nose cowl are not exactly the same as on the left side cowl.

Likewise, the black markings on the rudder are not exactly the same on both sides. This would be of special importance to model builders and full size reproductions of the NYP, if they wish to be accurate. Albert B. Crygier did all the silver painting.

According to Ruth M. Kennaugh Clemens, who did much of the fabric work, the tail surfaces and ailerons were covered with the pillow case method, or slip-on fabric, with either one side or one end open so the cover could then be slipped on and the open end closed with a baseball stitch.

The wing covers were made up of as many pieces as were needed for the entire wing. Each was measured to go from the trailing edge, around the leading edge and back to the trailing edge. The cover was then pinned on and hand sewn with the baseball stitch. The pieces were sewn together and then another seam would flatten both edges down. "We always had to be careful that the fabric of all the covers was pulled very snugly. After the covers were sewn on the parts, and where they were needed, they had to be rib stitched. This was done with linen thread and long needles. The needle was run alongside the rib, straight out to the other side of the rib, around it and the fabric, and back to the side of the rib. There it was tied with a special knot," said Clemens.

Just before covering of the wing was commenced all of the workers decided to sign their names onto the front side of the front spar in the center of the wing, just behind the filler necks for the two fuselage fuel tanks.

They considered this to be their 'good luck' token

Left side view of the NYP shortly after assembly at Dutch Flats. ***(Donald Albert Hall family)***

CRACKED WING RIBS

Everyone at Ryan was feeling so slap-happy from so many hours working they began celebrating. Bowlus picked up Peggy DeWitt , the fabric sewer and set her up on the wing and cracked three ribs in the wing. The wing was apparently on saw horses at the time. She was petite. It was late at night. They undid the base-ball stitching and glued a couple of gussets on the cap strips and repainted the fabric. Lindbergh never did know about the incident.

ENGINE INSTALLATION

It is interesting to note that the engine was bolted directly to the 1½ " o.d. steel engine mount ring made of seamless SAE 1020 mild carbon steel tubing with eight ⅜" through bolts from the engine rear flange onto the engine mount. There were no shock mounts of any kind.

There was no provision for a carburetor heater, either controlled or uncontrolled, from the cockpit. The carb air heater was added later at New York.

The engine did have a throttle, mixture and spark control mechanism, all controlled from the cockpit.

When Lindbergh noticed the workers installing fuel and oil lines by using a single long tube, he became quite concerned about vibration. Perhaps he wondered about no shock mounts too, although nothing is mentioned to that effect in his book *The Spirit of St. Louis.* He suggested they cut each tube at eighteen inch intervals and connect the pieces at the joints with appropriate hose and clamps. He told them that a single tube could break or develop cracks and that with his air mail flying and barnstorming experience he found the problem could be solved by such a fix and it would prevent engine failure and a forced landing. This method was later used throughout the aircraft industry.

Right side view of the NYP showing a man sitting in the cockpit, who appears to be either Lindbergh or possibly Ed Morrow, who looked somewhat like the flyer. ***(Donald Albert Hall family)***

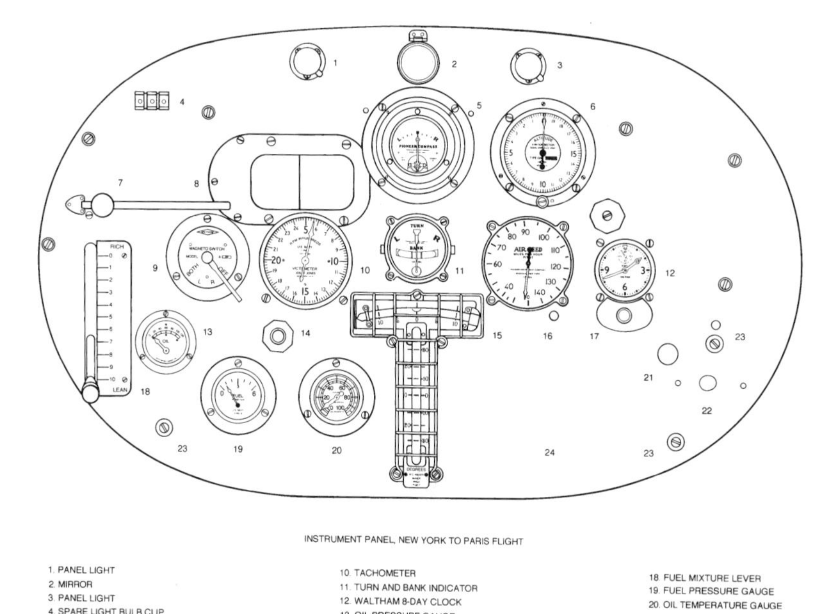

The NYP instrument panel on the day of takeoff for Paris ***(Dale Caldwell illustration 2002)***

INSURANCE

One of Lindbergh's advisors and legal representatives, Harry Hall Knight, made arrangements with the brokerage firm of Cornwall & Stevens (New York) to arrange for insurance coverage for the NYP.

This was done through Mr. Mark I. Ashley of the National Insurance Agency, Pierce Building in St. Louis, Missouri. It was written in the name of Harry Hall Knight, Trustee, later endorsed to add The Spirit of St. Louis, Inc.

The policy was written to cover it from San Diego and across the country to New York prior to the ocean flight. Continuance of the coverage hinged on an inspection by the Underwriters at either Curtiss or Mitchel Fields in New York, to determine if they would cover it to Paris.

The insuring company was the Independence Companies, based in Philadelphia, Pennsylvania. It was a "Combination Aviation Policies", number AC1107. However, it only covered for fire and lightning damage (liability, accidental damage and theft were excluded), from May 4, 1927 through May 4, 1928. The premium was $720.00.

In addition, arrangements were made for the NYP to be insured from Paris, (or Europe) to England, and from England to St. Louis, Missouri, USA. This part of his journey was covered by Lloyd's Fire Policy (Lloyd's of London.) It appears that the NYP was covered for $18,000.00. The policy number was J112912, covering from May 21, 1927 to June 21, 1927 with a premium of $60.75. It was for loss or damage by fire and/or lightning. It included coverage while in the crate aboard ship back to the USA. There was a hundred dollar deductible compensation clause feature.

NYP REGISTRATION NUMBER AND CAL AVIATOR'S LICENSE

It was about this time that the U.S. government began giving aviation some of the attention it deserved and the Department of Commerce began issuing licenses to pilots, beginning the practice on the West coast. A team of examiners set up shop at Rockwell Field, San Diego, and one of their customers was Lindbergh. He took time off from the construction of the NYP to take the test.

Major Clarence M. Young (Private pilot, License #2) was in San Diego for this purpose and stopped by the Ryan factory to see Lindbergh. Young commanded Lindbergh's reserve squadron at Richards Field, Raytown, Missouri, in 1925, where Lindbergh had given him some instruction in the Air Service's latest techniques. From that day they formed a personal and lasting friendship. Young had now been appointed Chief of the Air Regulations Division of the government's new Aeronautics Branch of the Department of Commerce under William P. MacCracken, Jr., (Private pilot License #1) Assistant Secretary for Aeronautics.

Lindbergh asked Young some questions about the new regu-

Another three-quarter right front view of the airplane. ***(Donald Albert Hall family)***

Left rear view clearly showing the re-painted "Ryan NYP" on the rudder. ***(Donald Albert Hall family)***

lations for civil aircraft. Previously, all a man needed in order to fly was an airplane and the ability to get it into the air. But now one needed an aviator's license, and the airplane had to be registered. The Spirit of St. Louis needed a registration to be legal for flight.

"I'll see that your applications are acted on right away, Charlie. We want to get a number on your wings before you take off for Paris, and we certainly want you to be a licensed pilot when you land in Europe," said Young. After inspecting the cockpit and generally looking over the NYP he said, "We'll give you an N-X license that will let you do about anything you want to."

"What's an N-X license?" Lindbergh asked.

"N is the international code letter assigned to the United States. Airplanes flying outside the country have to carry it for identification. X stands for experimental and authorizes you to make modifications without getting government approval. Of course, you can't carry passengers with an X license, but I guess you won't want to do that anyway." After he glanced at the huge fuel tank bolted in where passenger seats would ordinarily be, he said, "You won't have any trouble about licenses."

A telegram arrived sometime later and it read:

YOUR LICENSE NUMBER EXPERIMENTAL TRANS-ATLANTIC SHIP IS N DASH X TWO HUNDRED ELEVEN STOP TRANSPORT LICENSE WILL BE MAILED TOMOTTOW CARE ROBERTSON AIRCRAFT ANGLUM MISSOURI. [16]

E. Kintz

Fred Ayers painted NX-211 on the tail of the NYP and *Spirit of St. Louis* on both sides of the nose cowl.

EMERGENCY SURVIVAL EQUIPMENT PURCHASED IN SAN DIEGO

During the construction of the NYP, Lindbergh purchased the following items to be carried on the New York to Paris flight:

Item	Location today
2 flashlights,	MHS
1 ball of heavy string with two fish hooks,	NASM
1 ball of cord,	NASM
1 hunting knife,	?
4 red flares sealed in rubber (bicycle) tubes,	NASM (only 3)
1 match safe with matches,	NASM
1 large needle,	NASM
1 canteen – 4 quarts,	
1 canteen – 1 quart,	
1 Armbrust Cup,	MHS
1 Air Raft with pump and repair kit,	MHS minus pump
5 cans of Army emergency rations (from Abercrombie & Fitch Co. NYC $1.50 each)	MHS (3 missing)
2 Air Cushions,	NASM (one)
1 hack saw blade,	NASM

- NASM—National Air & Space Museum
- MHS — Missouri Historical Society

Good view clearly showing the newly installed periscope in the left window of the cockpit. ***(Donald Albert Hall family)***

FLYING SUIT

Two payments were made, one on March 25 and the other on April 18th, for a flying suit, for a total price of $51.00. Lindbergh apparently purchased it from the Hogard Gould Sport Company. [17]

The suit was quite similar to the Lee "Whizit" which was also popular at that time. The suit was of cloth with sheep wool lining, was waterproof, and had a fur collar. It and the puttees or breeches Lindbergh wore at that time presently belong to the Missouri Historical Society in St. Louis. Lindbergh wrote in black ink on the back of the flying suit collar—"Worn on the following flights, San Diego—St. Louis—St. Louis—New York, New York—Paris", with his signature Charles A. Lindbergh. [18]

COMPLETION AT FISH CANNERY AND OUT TO DUTCH FLATS

Factory work was completed toward the end of April. When the multitude of finishing touches were finally done, the fuselage was rolled out of the building on April 27th. To do that, they had to take off the right half of the landing gear to get it through the narrow doors. This was done through the quick thinking of Ed Morrow, was most likely via a dolly of some sort, and re-assembled outside.

Once outside, the complete empennage assembly was installed on the fuselage. The black markings had already been applied to the rudder at this point. The markings, however, were to last only for the trip to Dutch Flats.

The NYP carried a small logo "RYAN NYP mfg. by Ryan Airlines, S.D., California" on the rudder when leaving the Ryan factory. According to Doug Kelley, Ryan test pilot, Lindbergh suggested to Mahoney he increase the dimensions of the company name. "If we're successful, people will want to see the pedigree," Lindbergh persuaded Mahoney. So Mahoney had the logo repainted triple size.

So the "RYAN NYP and Mfg. By Ryan Airlines, San Diego,

Close up view of right side of fuselage showing the cockpit entry door. ***(Donald Albert Hall family)***

Nice portrait of the NYP on Dutch Flats after assembly. ***(Donald Albert Hall family)***

California" were painted out with silver dope and repainted as can be seen in all later photographs up to the present time. This was done at Dutch Flats.

Three photos show those original markings, one as the fuselage was being towed tail first from the Juniper Street factory/office to the flying field at Dutch Flats, about April 26th. The tail skid was lashed to a 1922 black Studebaker Light Six EM touring car. [19] It carried California license number 1-715-343. It appears the car was purchased by Donald Hall in Fort Worth, Texas, on his way to California in September 1926. He had a two hour driving lesson right after purchase and then continued on his way to Los Angeles. [20]

The other two photos show the wing being 'walked' up over the back of the fuselage to be fastened into place.

Moving the wing, which had been built on the second floor of the factory, also required ingenuity. It was too large in both span and chord to get it down the stairs and out the door, which they would normally have done. So they took it back to the dope room, cocked it up at an angle and, taking the hinges off a second floor outside door, eased the wing out. There happened to be a box car sitting on a railroad track running alongside the building. At the suggestion of Ed Morrow, the workers pushed the box car under the large double doors in the outer wall. They held the wing on top of the box car until the rest of the workers got out on the street and brought a contractor's derrick into position. The hoist then lowered the wing to a waiting flatbed truck and placed it in a wing cradle. The cart was just a frame on four automobile wheels pulled by a truck.

The box car, #63365 of the Santa Fe or A.T.S.F. line, was

Good view of rudder showing the details of the final markings, which was finalized at Dutch Flats, and is still on the airplane. ***(Donald Albert Hall family)***

traced by this writer in 1995. When this author inquired of a railroad history buff what might have happened to that particular box car, he was informed that it continued in service up to sometime after 1948 (21 years later) when it was apparently scrapped.

During the remainder of that day and into the night, the NYP was assembled in the hangar out at Dutch Flats, about two and a half miles from the fish cannery.

The wing had to be walked by about seventeen men, up and over the tail section and forward to its final location and bolted in.

Fuel lines from the wing tanks were connected and checked, along with the aileron cables being connected to the cockpit control stick yoke. The main wing struts were attached and hand formed aluminum fairings fitted to the contour of the balsa wood fairing around the struts where they attach to the wing. Ailerons were installed and connected.

The landing gear shock strut fairings were not fitted yet at this point in the assembly, as all wanted to be certain the design would be successful.

The cockpit access or pilot's door was installed at Dutch Flats.

LANDING GEAR

A different landing gear design was required in order to handle the projected heavy take-off weight of the fuel laden airplane. Hall designed a new type with a wide tread. This design paralleled that of the J-5 powered single engine 1925 American Fokker "Universal" and some German aircraft. It was known as the 'outrigger' design.

Therefore, the bearing loads could be carried to the lower fuselage and through struts to the upper fuselage and wing. It was designed to be both functional and streamlined to cut down on parasite drag. Wheel location was moved outside the slipstream to accomplish this goal.

The landing gear strutting was of 2" o. d. SAE 4130 mild carbon steel tubing, faired to a tear drop shape with balsa wood (leading and trailing edge) and wrapped with linen pinked edge tape and then doped and painted in silver. All subsequent Ryan Broughams were built by this same method.

Shock absorption was accomplished by using ⅝" dia. Shock cord, then known as Banjos, and referred to today as elastic bungee cords. The shock assembly was mounted vertically between the axle and the forward wing strut. The upper end of the shock absorber mechanism was braced to the upper and lower longerons, forming a tripod bracing. The shock absorber units were of the trombone type with a six and a half inch rise using shock absorber cord of individual links. The entire assembly is wrapped with a streamlined aluminum cover or fairing.

The dual axles (front and rear integral) were built of chrome molybdenum SAE 4130 steel tube and heat treated to 180,000 psi. There were no brakes on the main wheels and for this reason a tail skid was mounted to facilitate stopping, common in many airplanes of that era.

The landing gear was welded up at the factory and attached to the fuselage lower longerons, but none of the balsa fairings and pinked edge fabric tape had been installed yet. That was done later at Dutch Flats.

The turn and bank indicator was connected to a Venturi Tube mounted on the right side landing gear upper "V" strut.

TAIL SKID

The tail skid was made of heat-treated chrome molybdenum steel tubing of the same quality as the axles.

The shock system consisted of a "U" type fitting welded up in the fuselage, which was connected to the top of the skid with shock cord. Dan Burnett made a balsa wood fairing for the skid shaft, noticeable in early photographs of the NYP.

WHEELS

During the construction phase and before the final pair of wheels and tires were mounted, it appears that two sets of "shop wheels" were used. The spoke type wheels had conical wheel covers on the outside and a flat wheel cover on the inside. Both were metal and had the Damascene design. The wheels were the same as those used on the M-1 and M-2 of that period.

These shop wheels were used for moving the airplane around the shop and outside. One of these pairs was on when the wing was mounted out at Dutch Flats. They were definitely not the wheels used for the initial test flights or succeeding flights.

Finally a set of spoked wheels, 32" X 4" (Dayton Wire Wheel Company,) together with the B.F. Goodrich Company "Silvertown Airplane Cord" tires were mounted for the test flights. [21]

Goodrich Streamline Wind Shield panels were supplied as wheel covers. They were manufactured exclusively by the B. F. Goodrich Rubber Company in Akron, Ohio. [22] Lighter than metal covers, from six to eight pounds per wheel. They reduced wind resistance, and so increased the air speed of the airplane, which in turn lengthened the flight duration.

They were made of rubberized fabric, grommeted and laced to a vulcanized skirt on the Goodrich Airplane tire. The tire valve stems were accessible from the inside of each wheel.

Wood plugs were inserted in the outer ends of the two axles with a screw on type outer bearing nut with a bolt and nut through the axle to hold the wheel in place. Over that were tear drop shaped balsa wood fairings mounted to the axle as a sort of hub cap. This was done after the first test flight.

APRIL 28TH

On this day the NYP was ready, exactly sixty days after the order was placed, for her first test flight. This was a big event, and all the Ryan employees showed up to observe that flight. Donald Hall had this to say, "We had only about twelve days for testing, and Lindbergh flew every day he could except when we made little changes here and there." [23]

Fuel was Red Crown supplied by the Richmond Refinery of the Standard Oil Company of California on San Francisco Bay. Five gallons of Mobiloil B was put in the oil tank and about fifty gallons in the fuel tank for the first test flight. All was put in by hand from five gallon cans.

Aviation fuel, as it is designated today, is of a fairly recent (1944) origin. In the beginning days of aviation, 1903 to 1918, almost anything was used in an airplane engine that would enable it to operate. The quality of those fuels was generally the same as that of the regular fuel for automobiles and in some cases inferior to it. At that time no generally accepted specifications were established for aviation fuel.

After World War I and the somewhat expanded use of airplanes, a definite interest in aviation fuel developed. The government set up specifications for a suitable aviation fuel that would differentiate it from auto fuel. The next phase in that development was the recognition of antiknock value and a suitable rating method to determine it. But that did not take place until the early thirties, when the industry came up with the 87, 92 and finally 100 octane numbers for general use.

However, in 1927 with the blending of several chemicals in the manufacturing process, the straight-run gasolines from naphthenic and aromatic crude oils (60 to 80 octane number) were found from experience to give satisfactory performance. Thus, although apparently unaware of detonation effects and knocking, the users of aviation fuels were beginning to recognize differences in the effects of the different hydrocarbon types on engine performance.

It is interesting to note that in 1926 the average octane number of the fuel was around 65 to 70. Stability, volatility, corrosion, sulfur standards and other specifications ensured a fuel of reasonable quality especially adapted to aviation use. [24]

After fueling for the first test flight, Lindbergh climbed into the cockpit, as mechanics and others walked around the airplane checking all details of their handiwork.

The factory workers cheered as Jon Harm van der Linde stepped up to the propeller to pull her through a few times as a prime.

According to Douglas Corrigan in an interview in 1968 by this writer, it was hand propped by Jon van der Linde, next by Corrigan himself, and then by small Frank Saye, who got it started on the command of "Contact". It was about three o'clock in the afternoon.

Lindbergh ran the engine up all the way to 1400 rpm, and checked each individual magneto. The J-5 ran smoothly. Oil pressure, fuel pressure and tachometer were working fine and the pressures were where they should be. Lindbergh gave the signal to remove the wheel chocks. Corrigan quickly ran under the wing and pulled them free. Lindbergh taxied out and took off to the west, spiraling up to 2000 feet where he leveled off and checked all instruments, control movements and the inclinometer, which worked perfectly. Soon he headed out over San Diego Bay and North Island where he further checked the flight controls and noticed that the ailerons were riding a bit on the high side and that the fin needed a bit of adjustment, all of this being noted on his clip board. He also noted that the ailerons were not too

Left rear view of low tail area, showing the faired—in tail skid and stabilizer strutting. ***(Donald Albert Hall family)***

View from the cockpit as the NYP flew over San Diego on one of its many test flights. Notice that the periscope is in the out position. ***(Donald Albert Hall family)***

responsive, but rather sluggish. Donald Hall had made them small so as not to overstrain the wings under full load conditions. Lindbergh felt the response was O.K. for a long distance airplane.

Soon he pulled the NYP up into a stall configuration and let go of the stick. Immediately the nose dropped below the horizon and the right wing dropped slightly. He then pulled back on the stick to return to level flight. His next test was to take his feet off the rudder pedals and proceed to steer only with the stick. He found that the fuselage veered the opposite way to the stick, clearly indicating that the NYP was not a very stable airplane. This indicated adverse yaw and is why a long tail was needed.

He next wondered what kind of high speed he could get. So he descended to 1000 feet altitude, leveled off, and slowly advanced the throttle until the airspeed indicated 128 mph. He felt this was fine and headed back to Dutch Flats.

At about this point a Navy Hawk fighter came alongside from above and the two chased each other over the San Diego sky for a couple of minutes. I am sure it gave Lindbergh a bit more confidence in the NYP and he had some fun at the same time. After that episode, he headed once again for Dutch Flats doing a couple more stalls to prepare for the landing.

It appears he made a three-point landing and taxied in, much to the pleasure of the Ryan workers. After letting the engine idle for a few minutes, he shut it down. The flight according to his log lasted only twenty minutes.

The ground crew told him that he had taken off in only a hundred and sixty-five feet—six and one eighth seconds. Everyone was delighted with the performance.

Another view showing closely the fairing work by the Ryan workers, while on the May 3rd flight over San Diego. ***(Donald Albert Hall family)***

Another view from the right side of the cockpit, taken by Donald Hall on his flight as a passenger on May 3, 1927. Hall was the first passenger carried in the NYP ***(Donald Albert Hall family)***

Lindbergh mentioned to the mechanics that the left wing was a bit heavy. So they took up one quarter turn on the left rear strut and half a turn on the right strut. They had to move the ailerons up to where they projected a quarter of an inch above the trailing edge of the wing in level flight in order to give more effect from the ailerons.

After the aileron and fin were adjusted, Lindbergh made another test flight lasting only five minutes. The adjustments did the trick.

Before the next test flights on April 29th, mechanics installed the shock absorber aluminum fairings.

On the twenty-ninth Lindbergh made three test flights for a total time of twenty minutes. Then on May 3rd he made three more flights, the first one for ten minutes carrying Donald Hall. (Hall took several photographs with his camera of the San Diego

An especially nice portrait of Lindbergh with his New York to Paris airplane shortly after completion. ***(Donald Albert Hall family)***

area. Prints from the original negatives are in the author's possession.) The second flight was also for ten minutes, and he had photographer Major H. A. 'Jimmy' Erickson as his passenger. The last flight, lasting for fifteen minutes, was for the first air-to-air pictures with Erickson shooting from another airplane. On these flights the balsa wood axle fairings or 'hub caps' were not yet installed, but on all subsequent flight photos the caps are shown in place. It is assumed the wood plugs were also installed in the ends of each axle.

Lindbergh left the field one morning about five a.m. to make a run over the Silver Strand where nautical miles were laid out so he could check the top speed and cruising speed of the NYP. It was a little before seven a.m. when the morning fog came rolling in and the NYP did not come back.

Red Harrigan said, "Let's fire up an airplane and go chase him." So they set out across the bay but did not get half way across before they also got stopped by the fog. As they made their way back, fifteen feet off the water, they approached what is now the Marine Base and Barnett Avenue. They had to pull up over telephone wires. Just as they came over the wires they spotted the NYP about fifteen feet past their wing tip. Lindbergh never saw them. That's how close Lindbergh came to not making the flight to Paris.

Generally speaking, the construction of the NYP was not marked by bitterness or feuds, as was happening in New York between Clarence Chamberlin, Levine and others who were also planning the Atlantic trip. Some specific qualities which permeated the entire project were dedication, hard work, careful planning, and humor!

Lindbergh delighted in practical jokes and horseplay. One of his favorites was to connect a booster magnet to a wire fence that circled the flying field. When anyone touched the fence while he was around, Lindbergh would crank up the mag with shocking results.

Some of the factory workers reciprocated when they dreamed up an alarm clock rig to keep Lindbergh awake during his long flight to Paris. The rig was supposed to jab him in the seat of the pants with a sharp needle every fifteen minutes. It never went along on his flights.

HOSE IN TANK STORY

The incident of the hose that fell in the main tank took place at Camp Kearney late one night. Everyone was very tired by then and it would be easy to make a mistake on some part of the operation.

The young Charles Lindbergh in the NYP cockpit, showing clearly the fuel econometer on the panel as designed by the flyer. ***(United Technologies Archive)***

B. Franklin Mahoney and Charles Lindbergh standing in front of "The Spirit of St. Louis" at Dutch Flats. ***(Donald Albert Hall family)***

George Hammond, O. R. McNeel, Lon Wheeler, Jon van der Linde, and Fred Rohr were taking turns filling the fuel tanks with the use of five gallon cans and a funnel. Due to the need to vent the tank as the fuel was poured in, they decided to use a rubber hose, wire it in a position down the side of the funnel in order to displace the inside air from the fuel tank more quickly.

For the first several hours the rig worked OK. But then the hose got slippery from the fuel splashing over it. Eventually it slipped through the wire and fell into the tank.

The test flights the next day continued as the men tried to figure out how they would get the hose out. Lindbergh was never informed of the problem. This author did tell him the story in a meeting in Connecticut in February of 1968. Needless to say, he was surprised, but somewhat amused.

The men felt the hose would probably disintegrate, but Fred Rohr insisted that the hose be removed as it could eventually clog the drain hole or fuel lines.

So that night they drained all remaining fuel from that tank. Rohr and van der Linde worked into the wee hours of the night. It is not certain where they cut the hole large enough to get a man's hand and arm through, but possibly on top or on one of the lower sides. There were conflicting stories when this author interviewed some of these men in 1968.

They did use a piece of wire like a coat hangar and finally fished it out. They found that the hose had swollen up from the fuel soaking. They patched the hole with a piece of metal and 6/32 screws and with some sort of sealer. It could be stated that this

One of the first photos taken of the NYP in flight over San Diego, possibly May 3rd. ***(Air Photo by Erickson)***

might well be another 'secret' of the success of the flight.

Mechanics remembered that the hole was about six inches in diameter. One source said it was on the left side about a foot from the bottom of the tank. Van der Linde seemed to think they cut the hole in the top rear of the main tank behind the instrument panel.

In analyzing the situation in later years, it would be apparent to this researcher that they could not have cut a hole in the top of the tank because the wing was right over it. So accessibility would be impossible. To cut a hole near the bottom on either side would also be difficult because of the proximity of fuel lines, wires and control rods etc. and the fact that fabric would have to be cut and patched. There is no visible patch on either side of those areas. The only other possibility would be to go in from the cockpit on the right side near the fuel control manifold or just to the right of that location.

But in checking photos that clearly show that area, no patch can be seen. It is possibly there, but out of sight to the camera lens. Old timers at Ryan repeated the story many times.

NAVIGATIONAL PLANNING

Based on careful research, Lindbergh would have had access to the following charts, maps, and navigational aids that were available in 1927. [25]

Rand-McNally maps were the maps of choice for pilots for routes for which aeronautical maps were not available. The Rand McNally Company provided detailed railroad, road, and standard maps for individual states and regions. Moreover, the publication of Rand-McNally's popular "Auto Trails Map" series coincided with the Army's post-World War I cross-country flying programs. First issued as sectional maps in 1917 and then as state maps, this series covered the entire country by 1922.

Army Air Service/Post Office Blueline Strip Maps. In addition to Rand-McNally maps, Army Air Service and U. S. Air Mail Service pilots used Post Office Department postal route maps. These maps were generally cut into strips or "belts" corresponding to airway routes. Later, the postal route maps were used as the basis for preparing blueline strip maps that connected or linked most of the major cities in the East. They were issued by the Air Service and Post Office on an on-demand basis. These "belt" maps may still have been available in 1927, and as a former air-mail pilot, one would expect Lindbergh to be aware of them.

U. S. Army Air Corps Air Navigation Maps. The Army Air Service began issuing air navigation maps in 1923. These were prepared at a scale of 1.500,000 and covered a segment of an airway approximately 220 miles in length and 80 miles in width. By 1927 most of the Army's airway (forerunner of the national airways system) was mapped.

NYP being fine tuned at Dutch Flats, probably taken during final assembly ***(Smithsonian Institution).***

One of only two photographs taken when the long wing was humanly walked up and over the fuselage for its mating to the fuselage (Dutch Flats). ***(Ryan Aeronautical Company)***

U. S. Navy Aviation Charts. By 1927, the Navy had completed a series of charts connecting major coastal cities along the East Coast.

Army Air Corps "Aeronautical Bulletins. Two other cartographic navigation aids available to pilots during this period were "Airport Diagrams" and "Route Information" itineraries. They were published by the Army Air Service under the title "Aeronautical Bulletin." beginning in 1923. An airport diagram included an A-N range approach chart, a runway diagram and information on airport facilities. The route bulletins provided a verbal description of the airway route. Copies of most of these maps are in the National Archives or the Library of Congress.

During the NYP construction, Lindbergh began planning for the navigation part of the New York to Paris flight. He realized that he had never flown over water before, nor done any long-distance flying. Aerial navigation charts for the North Atlantic did not exist at the time. He would therefore have to obtain Marine charts, as used by ocean going vessels.

SAN PEDRO CHARTS

About March 8th Lindbergh, in a borrowed Ryan M-1, flew up to San Pedro, near Los Angeles, to arrange for the purchase of navigation charts. While the NYP was being constructed he would have time to engage in the detailed navigational planning for the New York to Paris flight.

It appears that someone suggested he make contact with Mr. Billy Wickersham, a man familiar with the source for the purchase of such charts. Wickersham, as it turns out, was the 'customs broker' for the Port of Los Angeles. [26] Lindbergh then went to the Southwest Instrument Company, then at 244-246 W 7th Street in San Pedro. This store sold marine charts in addition to buying, selling, and servicing marine compasses and instruments. Albert Webber was at that time the owner/proprietor of the firm which he had started in 1925 as the Southwestern Instrument Company. It became Southwest Instrument Company in 1926. Webber is the man who sold the charts to Lindbergh that day. The store still exists, now at 235 West Seventh Street in San Pedro. It is owned by Steve Moisen and Norbert Cupp, who in 1976 bought the business from Dewey France, son-in-law of Albert Webber.

NAVIGATION CHARTS

Marine Type Navigation Charts Used By Charles A. Lindbergh *For His Initial New York to Paris Flight Planning at San Diego*

Gnomic Chart No. 1280 Price 40 cents
Great Circle Sailing Chart Of The North Atlantic Ocean (Includes Supplementary Method For Finding Courses)
EDITION: 41st December 1920

Mercator's Chart No. 955 Price 50 cents
North Atlantic Ocean—Northwestern Sheet (America)
EDITION 40th May 1925 "Stamped"
(corrected to) No. 5 January 29, 1927.

Mercator's Chart No. 956 Price 50 cents
North Atlantic Ocean—Northeastern Sheet (Europe)
EDITION 31st March 1926 "Stamped"
No. 10 March 5, 1927

Charles Lawrence standing by a Wright J-5 "Whirlwind" engine, probably taken at the factory. ***(Alison O. Gray)***

Original charts noted above exist and formerly belonged to Donald A. Hall, Jr., son of Donald A. Hall, designer of the NYP. (Copies are in the possession of the author.)

The duplicate copies had been used for research, to check courses, times, and distances.

Each chart was "stamped" with "CORRECTED THROUGH NOTICE TO MARINERS-HYDROGRAPHIC OFFICE—Navy Department", and as noted above.

While the activity at the fish cannery and Dutch Flats was going on, the local San Diego people did not notice or pay much attention if they did see any of it. Not even the Chamber of Commerce was aware. There was no realization locally of the significance of what was happening at the Ryan plant. There had been no significant publicity. Dapper Dan Burnett took Lindbergh to a church dinner, and the people there took little notice.

Sometime after Lindbergh left for St. Louis and New York there was an auto show at the foot of Broadway, across from the railroad depot. Tents were erected for the show and Ryan's crew had two M-1's all shined up and on display. Burnett stood there for five nights telling the public about the NYP they built for Lindbergh and that he was going to make it to Paris. No one paid any attention to Burnett. A couple of weeks later everybody in the world would know who Lindbergh was!

THE CANNON STORY

To celebrate Lindbergh's successful flight according to mechanic Edward K. "Bing" Crosby, in San Diego the workers had a jubilant celebration. They drove old trucks through the center of town setting off homemade cannons of two and a half inch tubing loaded with acetylene and oxygen. The city of San Diego joined the party. By the time the trucks began their second round of the city, flags were out, confetti filled the air, and people passed jugs of good cheer to each other. Law enforcement officials studiously failed to notice this phase of the celebration despite the fact that prohibition was the law of the land at the time. [27]

The workers made a cannon out of their acetylene tank and welding outfit. The welding foreman welded a tube onto the floor board of the old Studebaker and put a little spout on it so he could fill it with acetylene for each big bang.

Before Lindbergh left for Paris everyone arranged a small pool. Each put in a dollar and guessed the time it would take Lindbergh to fly to Paris. [Gordy Boyd would be the closest. He only missed by 3½ minutes. He took the money and gave it to the Red Cross.]

FUEL LOAD TEST FLIGHTS

All of the fuel load test flights were made on May 4th at Camp Kearny Parade Grounds, sometimes referred to as Kearny Mesa, about ten miles north-north east of Dutch Flats, which is today the Miramar Naval Air Station.

Everyone involved worked on a tight schedule beginning at five in the morning. They had regular fifty-five gallon drums of gasoline and five gallon buckets and they kept up a bucket brigade, adding five gallons at a time. Test flights were made with 38, 71, 111, 151, 201, 251 and finally 301 gallons of fuel. Each flight averaged between five and ten minutes.

Lindbergh flew with these different loads to get the feel of the NYP and see what the balance was like. He carefully watched the gear and shock strut area as well as take-off performance.

The stony surface at Kearny caused trouble at the three hundred gallon phase. The stones were the size of eggs. At this heavy weight the wheel bearings overheated, the tail skid broke and the shock absorbers bottomed out. The skid assembly was quickly rebuilt and heavier shock cords added at the top of the skid. The workers did not replace the balsa wood fairing. Due to the main shock struts bottoming out, Lindbergh suggested they install even more shock cord segments. So Jon van der Linde welded on two more legs to wrap the additional shock cord segment around.

Lindbergh evaluated the situation quite carefully and decided he was satisfied with the results of the tests up to that point. The final maximum fuel load test would be the take-off in New York.

Somewhat rare diagrammatic photo of Lindbergh and the NYP with detailed information. ***(Leo B. Kimball collection)***

Some of the Ryan workers proudly standing in front of their beautiful creation, at Dutch Flats. ***(Ryan Aeronautical Company)***

In all, twenty-three test hops were flown in the San Diego area, on or off Dutch Flats, Rockwell Field on North Island, and Camp Kearny.

All 250 gallons of Red Crown fuel was put in by Jon van der Linde. He once said that the key to the success of the flight to Paris lay in the fact that they increased the span of the wing to carry the fuel load and a beefed up landing gear so it could handle it on the New York take-off and not collapse like many others that ended up in a fire, etc.

After these flight tests the airplane was either tied down or hangared and on May 5th with Major Erickson as his passenger Lindbergh made a flight of fifteen minutes back to Dutch Flats.

After more fine tuning of the airplane, on May 8th with A.J. Edwards, Sales Manager for Ryan, as his passenger, he flew for ten minutes over the local area.

All was in order now and he could concentrate on the long flight to New York.

The first leg would be a non-stop flight from San Diego to St. Louis, a feat in itself that would prove the feasibility of transcontinental air travel. If he had never attempted the oceanic solo, Lindbergh would have been commended for this accomplishment alone.

CLAUDE RYAN NOT PRESENT DURING CONSTRUCTION

The question has often been asked as to where Claude Ryan was during the building of the NYP.

In a letter from Lindbergh to Donald Hall, dated December 4, 1939, (Lindbergh was living in Englewood, NJ at the time,) he wrote; in part -

"To the best of my knowledge, Ryan had no part in building the "*Spirit of St. Louis*" except in the sense that the part he took in developing the Ryan Company and its monoplane was an essential factor in creating the organization which eventually built the plane. Obviously, Ryan is fully justified in claiming a connection with the "*Spirit of St. Louis*" to this extent and I do not believe anyone would challenge this claim. If the Ryan organization had not existed, there would have been no "*Spirit of St. Louis*" built in San Diego in 1927. However, Ryan took no part in the discussions I had concerning the purchase and construction of the plane.

Gus, the Sign Painter's, invoice for lettering NX211 on the Spirit's wings. ***(Missouri Historical Society)***

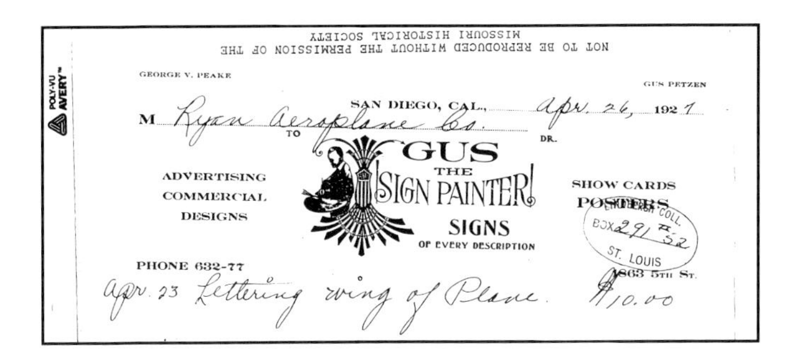

NOT TO BE REPRODUCED WITHOUT THE PERMISSION OF THE MISSOURI HISTORICAL SOCIETY

GEORGE V. PEAKE — GUS PETZEN

SAN DIEGO, CAL., Apr. 26, 1927

M Ryan Aeroplane Co. TO DR.

GUS THE SIGN PAINTER! SIGNS OF EVERY DESCRIPTION

ADVERTISING COMMERCIAL DESIGNS

SHOW CARDS POSTERS

863 5TH ST.

PHONE 632-77

Apr. 23 Lettering wing of Plane. $10.00

I do not know whether or not Ryan was in the factory at the time I arrived from the train. I do know that my negotiations were with Mahoney and Edwards but at no time with Ryan.

To the best of my knowledge, Ryan had nothing whatever to do with the operation of the factory at the time the "*Spirit of St. Louis*" was being built, or with the design or construction of the plane.

I do not know when Ryan "definitely wound up his affairs" with the Company.

With Best regards,

Charles A. Lindbergh

One photo does exist showing Mr. Ryan standing in front of the NYP at San Diego, taken in September 1927, when Lindbergh stopped there during his goodwill tour of the country.

During that visit Lindbergh only took up one passenger, B. Franklin Mahoney. Why not Ryan?

It appears that Claude Ryan was possibly off on another aviation business related venture, regarding sales of the German produced Siemens-Halske radial aircraft engine.

It's a pity that Mr. Ryan never got a ride, since he was responsible for organizing the company and its personnel that built the NYP.

Artist's cutaway sketch of the NYP showing details of the fuel tank arrangements ***(Ryan Aeronautical Company)***

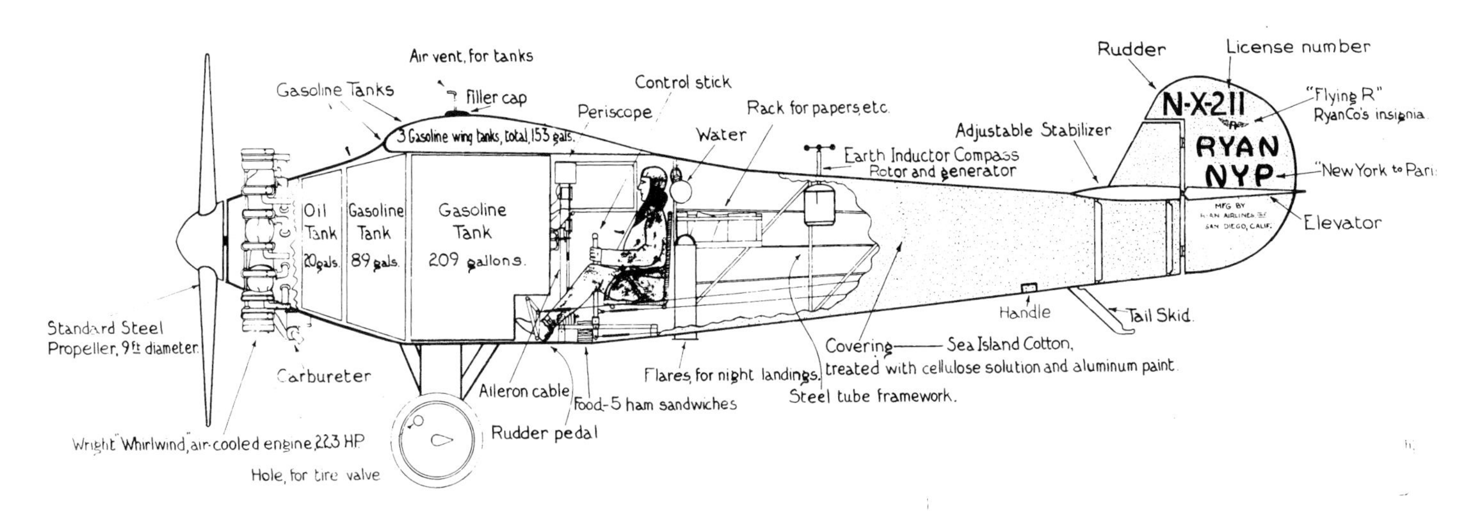

NOTICE OF DISSOLUTION OF PARTNERSHIP.

Notice is hereby given that the copartnership heretofore existing between the undersigned B. Franklin Mahoney and T. Claude Ryan, under the firm names of "Ryan Airlines", "Ryan Flying Co." and "Los Angeles-San Diego Airline", and doing business at San Diego, California, and at Los Angeles, California, and elsewhere in said State, has been this day dissolved by mutual consent. Said T. Claude Ryan has retired from said firm and business and has sold all his interest therein and in the assets thereof to said B. Franklin Mahoney, and said B. Franklin Mahoney will continue the business at the same place and under the same firm names. All debts due and owing to said partnership are to be paid to and received by said B. Franklin Mahoney, and all lawful demands on the said partnership are to be presented to him.

Dated at San Diego, California, this 23rd day of November, 1926.

B. FRANKLIN MAHONEY.
T. CLAUDE RYAN.

Date of first publication, Nov. 29, 1926.
(19109)

*Document of "Notice of Dissolution of Partnership" between B. Franklin Mahoney and T. Claude Ryan. **(Tom Mathews collection)***

MEN AND WOMEN AT SAN DIEGO WHO BUILT THE NYP

Benjamin Franklin Mahoney, Owner-President; William Hawley Bowlus, Superintendent in charge (factory manager); Gordon L. Boyd, Stock Room Clerk and Wood Shop apprentice; George F. Hammond, Draftsman, Student Pilot, Mechanic; Bert Tindale, Wood Shop Superintendent and in charge of wing department; Jesse Locke, Plant office; Orville R. McNeel, Final Assembly Foreman; Walter O. Locke, Office Manager, Production Manager, Draftsman/Engineering/Purchasing, Georgia Mathias, (who became Mrs. Anderson Borthwick), Field office—Secretary—Sales; Lawrance Muehleisen, Welder; Frank Saye, Final Assembly and Engine Mechanic; Edward "K" (Krauczyk) "Bing" Crosby, Machine shop and fittings; June Eddy, Plant office—Secretary; A. J. Edwards, Sales Manager; Daniel B. Burnett ("Dapper Dan"), Wood shop—rib maker—Wing Dept.—Miscellaneous Duties; Peggy DeWitt (Mrs. Edwin Schober), Fabric sewer—rib maker—Wing Dept.; Frederick H. Rohr, Sheet metal Foreman, fuel tanks & cowlings; Fred Magula, Sheet metal; Ruth M. Kennough Clemens, Fabric shop—seamstress; Mrs. Lillian Bray, Fabric shop—seamstress; Shirley Morrison, Final assembly (fuselage & engine); William Van Den Akker, Chief Carpenter—Wing Department; John Van Den Akker, Chief Mechanic, field flight test; Jon Harm van der Linde, Chief Mechanic, flight line; Melvin (Andy) Anderson, Welding; Patrick Davenport, Wood milling & shaping—Wing Dept.; Edward Terry, Painter—fuselage tubing; Albert Clyde Randolph, Wood shop—Wing Department; Elmer Dye, Welder—student field mechanic; Guss Willard Eoff, Welder; Walt A. Crawford, Welder- fuselage; Charles Miller, Fabric Shop; Jessie Cooper, Secretary; Claire C. Rand, Student Field Mechanic; Douglas Corrigan ("Wrong Way"), Welder—apprentice mechanic; Dale Powers, Wood shop—Office clerk; Donald A. Hall, Chief Engineer; John "Red" J. Harrigan, Chief Pilot—Test; Douglas T. Kelley, Test Pilot; H. Edwin Morrow, Welder—Metal fittings expert & inspector; Frederick C. Ayers, Fabric and dope Foreman; John Stoner, Office annex—clerk; Maj. H. A. "Jimmy" Erickson, Photographer; Albert B. Crygier, Painter of names and numbers, (tail and nose); George V. Peake & Gus Petzen, Painters of wing registration numbers ("Gus, the sign painter"); Paul Berbeck, Sheet metal; John Lester , Sheet metal—Office clerk; George Mathews, Sheet metal; Helen Tharpe, Rib maker—Wing Department; Harold Hunold, Welding shop Foreman; Edward A. Sherburn, Accountant—Time Keeper; William "Bill" Bodie, Field ticket sales/Wing Department; Jimmy James, Dope and paint department; Fred Young, Wire splicer; Mr. White, Wood shop; Mr. Sherman, Wood shop; Bob Young, Wood shop; Steven Varni, Dope and fabric worker; Harold Von Breisen, Seat Maker; Cecil B. Jones, Wood shop; G. Friedman, Wing Department; Lon E. Wheeler, Welder; O. L. Gray, Engine installation mechanic; Ruth Corbett Sasalla, Fabric Shop

NYP VENDORS

Steel tubing—Ohio Seamless Tube Co., Shelby, OH; Steel tubing, Chrome Moly—Summerill Tube Co. Bridgeport, CT, Montgomery Co. PA; Steel tubing—Service Steel Co., Los Angeles, CA; Alloy Steels—Crucible Steel Co. of America, NYC; Aluminum sheet metal and alum tubing—Aluminum Company of America, San Francisco, CA; Sheet metal—Dickerson Steel Co., Dayton, OH; Fabrics, tape, etc. (Flightex)—E. S. Twining & Co. NYC (Mr. Gaffney); Dope, dope thinner—Brown-Luithold

*Another good view of the instrument panel and plumbing for fuel tank selection. **(Erickson photograph, courtesy of Donald A. Hall)***

Good aerial view of Dutch Flats, showing Barnett Avenue in the foreground across from the Marine Base, and the hangar where the NYP was assembled. ***(Erickson photo via Ryan Aeronautical Company***

Co. Los Angeles, CA & Titanine, Inc. Union, NJ; Varnish (Nitro-Valspar)—Valentine & Co. NYC; Metal primer, varnish—Bass-Hueter Paint Co., San Francisco and Los Angeles, CA; Lacquer, enamel, bronze, etc.—W. P. Fuller Co. San Diego, CA; Wing registration numbers—"Gus The Sign Painter", San Diego, CA; Spruce, ash, black walnut—Sullivan Harwood Co., San Diego, CA; Spruce—J. V. G. Posey & Co. Portland, OR; Mahogany plywood—California Panel & Veneer Co., Los Angeles, CA; Plywood—Haskelite Mfg. Corp. Chicago, IL; Balsa wood—Fleischmann Transport Co., NYC; Cottonwood plywood—White Brothers, San Francisco, CA; Upholstering (seat arm rest)—Henry B. Day Co., Los Angeles, CA; Waterproof glue—Hercules Glue Co., San Francisco, CA; Lift-the-dot fasteners—Carr Fastener Co., Cambridge, MA; Pyralin celluloid—DuPont Viscoloid Company, San Francisco, CA; Tires and tubes—Silvertown Cords, B. F. Goodrich, San Diego, CA; Wheels—Dayton Wire Wheel Co., Dayton, OH; Wheel Covers—B. F. Goodrich Rubber Co., Akron, OH; Bolts, nuts, instruments and accessories—Nicholas-Beazley Airplane Co.; Accessories—Johnson Airplane & Supply Co., Dayton, OH; Wires and fittings—Roeblings & Sons, Los Angeles, CA; Hand fuel pump, Type D-1—Pioneer Instrument Co., Brooklyn, NY, Part no. 39394, Contract #23654; Gasoline line, fittings, etc.—Lunkenheimer Co., Cincinnati, OH; Gasoline and oil tanks and aluminum cowling—Standard Sheet Metal Works, San Diego, CA; Hose clamps—Ideal Clamp Mfg. Co. Inc. Brooklyn, NY; Propeller—Standard Steel Propeller Co., Pittsburgh, PA; Wright Whirlwind engine—Wright Aeronautical Corp., Paterson, NJ;

(Below) Four of the most important people in the development of the NYP. Left to right they are: William Hawley Bowlus, factory manager; B. Franklin Mahoney, president of Ryan Airlines, Inc.; Charles Lindbergh; and Donald Hall, engineer and designer. ***(Air Photo by Erickson)***

Form R7

UNITED STATES OF AMERICA
DEPARTMENT OF COMMERCE
AERONAUTICS BRANCH

Official No.
E-X211

Special Airplane License

This certifies that the airplane described below, of the property of Charles A. Lindbergh is a specially licensed aircraft of the United States of America, subject to the following conditions:

Plane to be used in the New York-Paris Non Stop Flight contest; property or passengers not be carried for hire or reward.

Description of aircraft:

TYPE - Ryan Monoplane

WEIGHT EMPTY - 1930 lbs. WING AREA - 320 sq. ft.

USEFUL LOAD - 3020 lbs. ENGINE TYPE - Wright Whirlwind J5C

GROSS WEIGHT - 4950 lbs. MFG'S NO. - 7331

SPAN OVER ALL - 46'

LENGTH OVER ALL - 27'

Dated April 27, 1927

W. P. MacCracken Jr.
Assistant Secretary of Commerce

FORM 198A

PACKING SHEET

SALES ORDER 11958

WRIGHT AERONAUTICAL CORPORATION
PATERSON, N. J.

DATE April 2, 1927.

SHIP TO
Ryan Airlines Inc.
3200 Barnett Ave.
San Diego, Cal.

QUANTITY	NAME OF PART
1	Wright Whirlwind J-5C Engine Mfg. #7331
2	Mags. Scintilla R.H.63237 L.H.50292
1	Carburetor Stromberg #3402293
	ATTACHED PARTS
1	Propeller Hub
1	" " Nut-Inner
1	" " " -Outer
1	Fuel Pump-#1692
1	Set Exhaust Flanges, Gaskets, Plates, Nuts and Lockwashers
	UNATTACHED PARTS
1	WA-258 Tool Kit
1	Ignition Switch
1	Reducing Tee
1	Oil Suction Pipe
1	Priming Pump
1	Carburetor Feed Pipe
	Short-1 Instruction Book.

Documents from the archives of the Missouri Historical Society.

Magnetos—Scintilla Aircraft Magnetos, Sidney, NY; Carburetor—Stromberg Motor Devises Co., Chicago, IL; Spark Plugs, metric Type N—A. C. Spark Plug Co., Flint, MI; Aircraft and oars ("Boat-in-a-Bag")—Airships, Inc., Hammondsport, NY; Armbrust life saving water making cup—C. W. Armbrust, Washington, DC; Bearings—Norman-Hoffman Bearings Corp., Stamford, CT

INSTRUMENTS (Flight and Engine)

Air Speed—Pioneer Instrument Co., Brooklyn, NY; Bank & Turn—Pioneer Instrument Co., Brooklyn, NY; Inclinometer—(supplied by) Pioneer Instrument Co., Brooklyn, NY; Earth Inductor Compass—Pioneer Instrument Co., Brooklyn, NY; Liquid Magnetic Compass—Pioneer Instrument Co., Brooklyn, NY; Magneto Switch;—Splitdorf Electrical Company, Newark, NJ; Tachometer—Consolidated Instrument Company of America, Inc. NYC; Altimeter—Neko, Newark, NJ; Oil Pressure Gauge—Moto Meter Co., Long Island City, NY; Oil Temperature Gauge—Moto Meter Co., Long Island City, NY; Fuel Pressure Gauge—Moto Meter Co., Long Island City, NY; Waltham 8 Day Clock—Waltham Watch Co., Waltham, MA; Primer—Lunkenheimer Co., Cincinnati, OH; Econometer—Lindbergh; Inclinometer—(mfg. by) W. C. Rieker, Philadelphia, PA; Speed & Drift Meter—Pioneer Instrument Co., Brooklyn, NY

FOOTNOTES

1. *Lindbergh,* A. Scott Berg, G.P. Putnam's Sons, New York, NY, 1998, pages 102, 578.

2. *Technical Notes National Advisory Committee For Aeronautics,* No. 257, Technical Preparation of the Airplane "Spirit of St. Louis," by Donald A. Hall, Chief Engineer, Ryan Airlines, Inc., Washington, DC, July 1927, page 1.

3. Interview with Harm Jon Van Der Linde, June 6, 1968, San Diego, CA.

4. Interview with Douglas Corrigan, Santa Ana, CA, May 30, 1968.

5. Letter to the author dated September 25, 1968 from Ed Crosby, Wauwatosa, WI.

6. Letter to the author dated August 1, 1970 from Ruth Kennough Clemens, Covington, OH.

7. *Air Capitol of the West,* Mary L. Scott, The Donning Company Publishers, Virginia Beach, VA, 1991, pages 111-112.

8. *Ryan the Aviator,* William Wagner in collaboration with Lee Dye, McGraw-Hill Book Company, New York, 1971, p.124.

9. Interview with Helen Tharp Hendrix, San Diego, CA, May 31, 1968.

10. Interview with O.R. McNeel, Twenty-Nine Palms, CA, June 3, 1968

11. *Lindbergh,* Ibid. pages 88-89.

12. *Hamilton-Standard Adjustable Propellers,* Hamilton-Standard Propeller Corporation, original brochure, Pittsburgh, PA.

13. Letter from Charles A. Lindbergh to Harry Knight, dated March 9, 1927 on U.S. Grant Hotel, San Diego, CA stationery, handwritten and signed by C.A.L.

14. Interview with Dan Burnett, La Mesa, CA, May 27, 1968.

15. *That's My Story,* Douglas Corrigan, E.P. Dutton & Co., Inc., 1938, New York, NY, page 94.

16. *Lindbergh,* Ibid, page 112.

17. Yale University Archives, Checks number 6 and 12.

18. Original flying suit found in the Lindbergh Collection at the Missouri Historical Society, St. Louis, MO. Statement in quotes written on the label inside the suit.

19. Letter to the author, dated November 19, 1998, from Richard T. Quinn of Mokena, IL, expert on Studebaker automobile history. Also, letter to the author dated December 3, 1998 from Mrs. Kim M. Miller, Librarian, American Automobile Club of America, AACA Library and Research Center, Hershey, PA.

20. Statement from Donald A. Hall, Jr. sent to the author in 1998.

21. Inspection of original NYP artifacts by the author at the Paul Edward Garber Restoration Facility, National Air & Space Museum, Silver Hill, MD, 1997.

22. *Aero Digest* (magazine,) Aero Digest Publishing Company, New York, March 1929, page 67.

23. *The New York Times,* newspaper Saturday, June 11, 1927, page 9. Large format advertisement by the Standard Oil Company of California.

24. *Aviation Gasoline Manufacture* (Mineral Industries Series,) Matthew Van Winkle, First Edition, McGraw-Hill Book Company, Inc. New York and London, 1944, pages 1 through 11.

25. Letter to the author dated December 7, 1999 from Ralph Ehrenberg, Falls Church, VA, expert on the history of navigation charts, former Director of the Center for Cartographic and Architectural Archives, National Archives and Records Administration. Chief Emeritus, Geography and Map Division, Library of Congress.

26. Interview with Steve Moisen, Norbert Cupp and Dewey France, June 9, 2000, San Pedro, CA.

27. Letter from Edward K. "Bing" Crosby. Ibid.

ENDNOTES

Physical details of the NYP structure were determined via close examination of original photographs taken during construction in San Diego, CA from the end of February to May 10, 1927.

Personal interviews with Ryan Airlines, Inc. employees who worked on NYP construction were done in May, 1968. The author continued to be in contact with these people while they were still living and were able to recall the early days with considerable accuracy.

Technical data such as model number, serial number, costs and manufacturer's name and location were gleaned from sales invoices, packing sheets, telegrams, and other legal documentation from manufacturers, miscellaneous aviation supplies and vendor catalogs of the period, copies in the author's collection.

Regarding the installation of instruments at San Diego, information was determined through use of photos of the instrument panel taken at the Ryan plant during construction and other documents. Where technical data was not available via documents and photos, correct information was gleaned from other photos taken at Curtiss Field, NY, and Paris, France.

Technical and legal information pertaining to the earth Inductor Compass was reviewed by Alice A. Brewer, Esq., and Doctor Alek P. Szecsy, Esq.

Other sources including general aeronautical, technical and historical sources available to the general public, including libraries and individual collections from all over the world were reviewed with experts in each field.

Aerosphere 1939, edited by Glenn D. Angle, Consulting Engineer/Technical Editor, Aero Digest (magazine,) Aircraft Publications, New York, 1940.

Letter from Francis C. Lawrance (son of Charles L. Lawrance) Tucson, AZ to the author, dated April 16, 1998.

Letter to the author dated march 12, 1998 from August Zoll, Aviation Hall of Fame of New Jersey, Wright Aeronautical Corporation archivist.

Modern Aircraft, Major Victor W. Page, Air Corps Reserve, U.S.A., The Norman W. Henley Publishing Company, New York, 1928.

Dyke's Aircraft Engine Instructor, A.L. Dyke, The Goodheart-Wilcox Company, Inc., Publishers, Chicago, 1928.

Aviation Magazine, McGraw-Hill Publishing Co., Inc., Albany, NY, June 1927.

Ryan the Aviator, William Wagner in collaboration with Lee Dye, McGraw-Hill Book Company, New York, 1971.

The Spirit of St. Louis, Charles A. Lindbergh, Charles Scribner's Sons, New York, NY 1953.

Polar Aviation, Edited by Lt. Col. C.V. Glines, USAF, written by Richard E. Byrd, Franklin Watts, Inc. New York, 1964.

Packing sheets, Wright Aeronautical Corporation, Paterson, NJ, Sales Order 11958, April 2, 1927 to Ryan Airlines, Inc. San Diego, CA.

Notes written in longhand by Donald Hall shortly before his death, transcribed by his son Donald Hall Jr. about 1971.

Charles A. Lindbergh's personal logbook. Copy at Yale University, Sterling Memorial Library, Manuscripts and Archives Department, New Haven, CT. Log dated from November 11, 1926 to July 7, 1928.

American Aircraft Directory, Supplement to First Edition, 1927, published April 1928, Aviation Publishing Corporation, NYC.

Valley News Dispatch (newspaper) Reporter's Notebook (column) by John Gibson, "Alcoa Played Key Role in Lindbergh Flight," May 19, 1977. Location of newspaper is not known.

Aero Digest (magazine,) Aero Digest Publishing Company, New York, June 1927.

Letter from Albert Clyde Randolph, San Diego, CA to General William E. Gillmore, Chief of Material Department, McCook Field, Dayton, OH, May 26, 1927.

Interviews with Harold Von Briesen and Doug Kelley by Stanley E. Jones, 1950s, San Diego, CA and quoted in a letter from Jones to the author on June 2, 1997.

Conservation, Condition and Treatment Report, Spirit of St. Louis airplane, Washington, DC, April 1992, National Air & Space Museum, by Edward McManus, Chief Conservator, A.I.C. Fellow. The National Air & Space Museum, report by Patricia Williams and John Cusack.

Letter from Ryan Airlines, Inc. to Du Pont Viscoloid Company, San Francisco, CA, June 16, 1927, and signed by Walter O. Locke, Production Manager of Ryan Airlines, Inc. included was a "History of DuPont's Plastics department." Accession 1410 Box 142, Du Pont Public Relations, Wilmington, DE.

U.S. Patent No. 1,660,751. See also P.R. Heyl, et al. "The Earth Inductor Compass," Proceedings American Philosophical Society, Vol. 1xi, No. 1, 1922, August 10, 1922.

US Patent Nos. 1,770,243; 1,770,244; 1,770,245; 1,770,246; 1,770,247; 1,770,328.

Flight, An Illustrated Weekly Journal, Vol. XIX. January to December, 1927, "Earth Inductor Compass," St. Martin's Publishing Co., Ltd., London, England.

1930 Catalog, *Pioneer Instruments and Equipment,* Pioneer Aircraft Instruments, Brooklyn, NY.

Invoice from "Gus the Sign Painter," April 26, 1927 for work accomplished on April 23, 1927. Charge $10.00.

Letter from Charles A. Lindbergh to Harry Hall Knight, dated March 26, 1927 on Ryan Airlines, Inc., San Diego, CA stationery, hand-written and signed by C.A.L.

Letter to the author from Clarence M. Young (then of Sedona, AZ,) November 20, 1968.

Aircraft Yearbook, 1927, Aeronautical Chamber of Commerce of America, Inc., New York City.

The New York Times (newspaper), Saturday, June 11, 1927. Large format advertisement by the Standard Oil Company of California.

CHAPTER 6

San Diego: St. Louis - New York

Tuesday, May 10 to Friday, May 13, 1927

Due to a general storm area covering much of the country, Lindbergh delayed his departure from San Diego for four days. He did not wish to jeopardize the success of an overnight flight over desolate and mountainous terrain on his way to St. Louis, Missouri.

On the afternoon of the day before his departure he consulted with Dean Blake, Chief of the San Diego Weather Bureau. Mr. Blake predicted good flying conditions over most of the country. So the decision was made to leave on May 10th.

During the morning of the 10th Lindbergh carefully packed a small suitcase, which he strapped inside the left side of the fuselage next to his wicker seat. In addition to other personal items, he needed a business suit for St. Louis and New York, but planned to leave all of it in New York for his flight to Paris.

The NYP on North Island, near San Diego, shortly before leaving for the flight to St. Louis and New York. In the photo John van der Linde is up on the wing doing the fueling. On left is O. R. McNeel holding banner and on right holding banner is George Hammond, then Lindbergh, Donald Hall and A. J. Edwards, who was then sales manager at Ryan. ***(Ryan Aeronautical Company)***

He then drove to the Ryan factory to visit briefly with the men and women who helped build the NYP and thank them for their help and compliment the crew for doing such a fine job.

From the factory he drove over to Dutch Flats and after a brief pre-flight, climbed into the NYP with O. R. McNeel as his passenger. Then he took off for the five minute flight to Rockwell Field on North Island.

While the Spirit was being fueled at Rockwell by Jon van der Linde and others, he had lunch with some of the officers and Donald Hall. Then they all toured the station inspecting the airplanes and facilities. He was given the opportunity to fly one of the Navy's new Curtiss Hawk fighters for about twenty minutes doing some aerobatics.

His plan was to leave for St. Louis late in the afternoon in order to be over Kansas at daybreak. This would give the sun a chance to burn the early morning mists away and give him better visibility for navigating.

It was 3:15 p.m. when he made his way to the airplane to give it one more pre-flight inspection as the final gallons of fuel were being poured into the tanks. He had instructed the mechanics to only fill the tanks half way, for a total of about 250 gallons.

The NYP about ready to go for the flight to St. Louis and New York. Site is in front of Hangar #4 at North Island, across the bay from presently Lindbergh Field. ***(Leo B. Kimball collection)***

He was rather concerned about the Pioneer Earth Inductor Compass which had a bearing freeze up on one of the test flights, but he felt that because the Pioneer Company was located in Brooklyn, New York it could be repaired and serviced before he left for Paris. Parts were scarce on the West Coast for such a specialized instrument. After a brief telephone conversation with Pioneer he was assured they would have a new compass available for him when he got to New York. They said they would also put in a new type of liquid compass for his Paris trip. The present one had excessive deviation but would be satisfactory for his flight across the country.

At 3:40 p.m. Lindbergh put on his cloth and fur-lined flying suit over his "Ike" flying jacket and put-tees (britches) and found this a bit uncomfortable due to the California heat. It would be much easier to put on now rather than later while in flight he reasoned.

Hall asked Lindbergh to report his fuel consumption at the end of the trip so that Hall could recalculate the fuel burn curves before the flight to Paris.

Soon the engine was started, Lindbergh waved to the people on North Island, taxied into position and took off at 3:55 p.m. Pacific time. He made a wide climbing turn to the left as two Army observation aircraft and a Ryan M-2 monoplane took off after him to escort the pair for a few miles. In the Ryan were Donald Hall, A.J. Edwards, Hawley Bowlus and "Red" Harrigan, the pilot.

Lindbergh made a graceful circle over North Island, the little Ryan factory, the city of San Diego, and then headed east. This would be a test of man and machine over desolate mountain ranges and desert, good preparation for what lay ahead over the Atlantic. Red Harrigan and the others in the Bluebird M-2 followed him as far as the mountains. Then about 4:30 they dipped their wings in farewell and returned home, satisfied that the Ryan part of the saga was over.

Work almost halted at the factory. The workers felt they deserved some relaxation after the rough, hectic tempo they'd kept up. Requests to get back to work were met with humor.

Meanwhile Lindbergh was over rough country. "What a hopeless place for a forced landing," he thought as he peered down on the rugged terrain strewn with boulders on the mountainsides. There was not a level area in sight to which he could glide in an emergency.

Lindbergh's course took him over the coastal range of mountains. He passed Superstition Mountain on his right and the San Jacinto peaks on his left.

As he headed over the Chocolate range, at about 4000 feet he passed over the Salton Sea. The sun was fast setting behind him while the moon was well above the eastern horizon.

Due to the moon's glow he was able to distinguish the contour of the countryside or terrain the entire night. As he held his compass course of about 55 degrees, he flew alternately over snow-capped mountains and ridges, deserts and fertile valleys. He cleared one range by about 500 feet.

May 11th, the morning he arrived from San Diego, Lindbergh is shown by the NYP. This photo has been duplicated many times and printed often over the years. ***(Louis M. Lowry)***

Lindbergh himself with a can of Mobiloil "B", to be put into the oil tank soon after arriving at Lambert Field in St. Louis, May 11, 1927. ***(courtesy Exxon Mobil Corporation)***

He passed the winding Colorado River at 5:45, right on course. As Dean Blake also predicted, he had a nice tail wind.

At 4900 feet msl he re-checked his instruments -all normal- and then the magnetos—both running smoothly. He put on his boots and mittens as the temperature was dropping at the higher altitude with the sun setting over the mountains and desert. At three hours and fifteen minutes into the flight he climbed to 8000 feet msl and continued upward in order to stay well clear of the mountain ridges. The moon was almost overhead.

As the darkness fell into the cockpit, Lindbergh switched on his flashlight to scan the instrument panel. Some of the instruments were luminous, others were not and needed to be checked. As he made a log entry and settled back in the seat—it happened!

Without warning the engine started to vibrate and sputter. The NYP began to descend. Anxiety gripped him. Had a part broken in the engine? A fuel mixture problem? Moving the fuel mixture control didn't immediately help the trouble. Altitude loss was slow, affording time to analyze the problem. Lindbergh figured he could stay in the air by gliding for perhaps another fifteen minutes. He scanned the terrain, which did not indicate many suitable landing areas. He wondered which way the wind was blowing, although earlier he knew he had a tail wind. He would have to land to the west or northwest.

Fuel pressure was up at 3 psi, considered normal. That was not the problem. In spite of its coughing and sputtering, the engine was still putting out some power. He even tried wobbling the hand pump, which did not help the situation either. He wondered if he had water in the carburetor, even though he knew they had drained all the fuel low points including the Lunkenheimer trap very carefully before he left San Diego. As all this was going on he was down to 7000 msl feet, putting him within two or three thousand feet off the ground. He finally climbed up to 7500 feet.

He concluded after moving the throttle and mixture controls that high humidity was causing ice to form in the carburetor. He continued to adjust the throttle and mixture levers, ever so slowly, ever so carefully. Finally the missing and roughness ceased. The Whirlwind ran smoothly once more. With the engine turning at 1750 rpm, he started to regain the altitude lost in this first crisis. He climbed to over 13,000 feet and at 10:00 p.m. cleared the summit of the Continental Divide by only 500 feet.

He looked at his clock—8:07 p.m. It had been fifteen minutes since the missing began.

With the engine running much smoother, he contemplated his next move. Should he stay in the area in case of a forced landing or head back to San Diego, five hours away, or should he stay on his eastward course. He elected to continue eastward.

Soon the flyer was over the foothills and plains of the panhandle of Oklahoma, where a forced landing would present less of a problem. It was midnight and he was about half way to St. Louis. He had been flying for eight hours. This was the longest flight he had ever made. At this point he decided to have a carburetor heater installed when he reached New York. This could make the difference between failure and success on the way to Paris.

Lindbergh saw this long flight not only as a test of equipment but of his navigation abilities as well. As he flew into the dawn he figured that he was somewhere over Kansas. After observing terrain check-points, he found he was east of Wichita and about fifty miles south of his originally planned route. He was in the vicinity of Parsons, Kansas, birthplace of T. Claude Ryan!

At 6:00 p.m. Pacific time (8:00 Central time) he passed over Lambert Field, northwest of the city of St. Louis. After buzzing the field and downtown St. Louis in celebration, he landed the Spirit at 8:20 a.m. Central Standard Time, May 11, 1927, fourteen hours and twenty-five minutes after leaving San Diego. He had set a new record for a nonstop flight over this distance and course. Bill and Frank Robertson and a half dozen other aviators, mechanics and friends were there to meet him and admire the

The boyish looking Lindbergh with a rare and slight grin on his face, probably taken shortly after his arrival at Curtiss Field. ***(Leo B. Kimball collection)***

Another photo produced by the hundreds over the years, shows Lindbergh just after he arrived at Curtiss Field, on Long Island, on May 12th, 1927. ***(Library of Congress)***

NYP. Shortly he taxied up to the black hangars of his National Guard squadron.

A few minutes later Lindbergh and his friends were having breakfast at Louis Dehatre's shack next to the hangar. At that point Bill Robertson handed Lindbergh a Bureau of Aeronautics envelope that had Lindbergh's transport-pilot's license in it. He was given number 69.

One of Lindbergh's friends informed him that the U.S. Embassy in Paris sent a cable saying it might be misunderstood if an American plane landed in France before receiving definite word about Nungesser and Coli. Lindbergh remarked, "I'll have to find out exactly what the situation is. I'll go through to New York at least. If Nungesser and Coli are lost it seems to me it's up to the rest of us to carry on what they attempted."

The partners in the Spirit of St. Louis organization (We) came to the field to see the airplane and the flyer and Lindbergh briefed them on the technical details. They generously released him from dinner and speaking engagements so he could get his sleep for the trip to New York. He was grateful for their thoughtfulness and understanding.

After refueling and with an overnight rest, Lindbergh lifted the NYP off Lambert Field at 8:13 a.m. Central Standard Time the next morning, May 12th, and headed east under a clear sky. This would be a short flight after the previous trip. Seven hours later, at 5:15 p.m. EDT , he was over New York City.

It would be just a few more minutes to Roosevelt Field. As he flew over Manhattan he wondered just which field he would use for the actual take-off for Paris. Would it by Roosevelt or Mitchel or Curtiss Field? It all depended on conditions he would have to face at the time, obstacles to clear, length of take-off available, wind, and weather.

Lindbergh was not sure which field was which until he circled over the area. The best maintained airport had olive painted airplanes, so it had to be the military strip, Mitchel Field. Curtiss was perhaps too small for a heavily-loaded take-off.

Roosevelt looked good with a long east-west runway, even if it was a bit narrow. So it was decided even before he had landed that it would probably be Roosevelt. However, he did want to walk over each one and inspect the surface several times. And there was the problem of getting permission to use any of them.

He circled Curtiss, sizing up the field. He checked the windsock and noticed the crowd, two or three hundred perhaps, looking up at him in anticipation of his landing. He banked steeply around, throttled back and checked his watch—3:31 Central Standard Time. Photographers fanned out on the field, some right where he wanted to touch down. He banked out of the way and then slipped down to land, hard on the tail skid at an angle to the wind. As soon as the Spirit stopped rolling, it was surrounded by news and camera men. To Lindbergh's dismay the spectators were pushing and shoving each other, some dangerously near the still-revolving propeller. Charles Sherman "Casey" Jones, airport manager and prominent race pilot, came up to the cockpit window in greeting. He had already readied a hangar for the Spirit, most likely hangar #16.

Dick Blythe, PR man for Wright Aeronautical, introduced himself and informed Lindbergh that a team of Wright mechanics would be at his disposal. Once Lindbergh was out of the cockpit and his plane safely roped off in the hangar, he was set upon by the press, many of whom asked trivial and sensationalistic questions. His initial impression of New York journalism was not good and with a few exceptions would not improve.

CONCLUSION

The distance from San Diego to St. Louis was 1480 statute miles. From St. Louis to New York it was 940 miles for a total of 2420 statute miles.

Average speed for the trip was 102.7 mph the first leg and 112.8 mph on the second leg and an overall average speed of 106.4 mph.

Two hundred and fifty gallons of Red Crown gasoline were put in at San Diego and 150 more gallons at St. Louis. Of the 400 gallons placed in the tanks, 118 gallons remained upon the arrival at New York. This shows a consumption of 282 gallons. The average fuel consumption would be 12.4 gph. The Mobiloil "B" (Vacuum Oil Company) oil was drained at Curtiss. It was found that exactly three gallons had been used in the twenty-two hours of flying, or an average of 1.1 pints per hour.

ENDNOTES

The Spirit of St. Louis, Charles A. Lindbergh, Charles Scribner's Sons, New York, 1953.

Hand printed log by Charles A. Lindbergh dated May 9, 10, 11, "Flight San Diego-St. Louis-New York, Log of Wright Whirlwind." Log was published in *Aviation* magazine, June 6, 1927.

Aviation (magazine,) "Fuel and Oil Consumption Important Factors on Long Distance Flights," R.V. Cautley, Wright Aeronautical Corporation, June 1927.

CHAPTER 7

New York - Curtiss Field Preparations

Just twenty miles east of New York City, at a place known as Garden City, Long Island, two legendary airfields existed in 1927; Curtiss Field, and right next door, Roosevelt Field, both in Nassau County. The area was once known as Hempstead Plains due to the immense area of flat acreage.

Curtiss Field was named for early aviation pioneer Glenn Hammond Curtiss, and was established as such in about 1909. Military operations dominated the field's use during the First World War, but was operated in a civilian mode for another twenty years until about 1939.

Roosevelt Field, adjacent to Curtiss on the east side, and twelve feet higher, was named after Quentin Roosevelt, who was killed in France in World War I at the age of twenty (July 14, 1918.) Interestingly enough, very near these two pioneering airfields, there also existed two other prominent airports, Mitchel Field and Floyd Bennett Field.

Today Curtiss and Roosevelt Fields do not exist. There is not even a hangar, only a small plaque in the Roosevelt Plaza Shopping Mall.

Floyd Bennett is still there but is used by the US Coast Guard as a heliport for air-sea rescue operations in the area.

Mitchel exists in the form of a few of the old original hangars, now housing the Cradle of Aviation History Museum.

It's a pity that Curtiss and Roosevelt were not given the distinction of a National Historic Site, and put on the National Register as such. The saving of even one hangar, as a museum, would have greatly enhanced the modern development of the area and paid tribute and respect to the many pioneer aviators and airplanes that flew out of there, each in their own right contributing to our American aviation heritage and the development of air travel. All of this, however, has lead to further development of La Guardia Airport, John F. Kennedy Airport, Newark International Airport and Teterboro Airport.

Aerial view of Curtiss Field at Garden City, Long Island, showing the Curtiss plant and the flying field beyond. Notice house being moved down Clinton Road. View is looking north. This was once known as Hazelhurst Field. ***(Leo B. Kimball collection)***

Only the people associated with the Mitchel museum have had the foresight to preserve this wonderful heritage. They are to be commended.

Curtiss, at the time of Lindbergh's arrival, was buzzing with activity, as other flyers sought the Orteig prize. Navy Commander Richard Evelyn Byrd and Clarence D. Chamberlin were serious contenders.

It would be a close contest, and at Lindbergh's arrival the competition became keen and pressured. Each camp had its problems, mechanical and political, and it was only the weather that would control any departure attempt. Any one of the three contenders could be successful in reaching Paris. Very careful planning and preparation would be the secret ingredient for success, as Lindbergh was to prove.

According to the American Oil Company of Atlanta, Georgia, the office of which has the original bill of lading, No. 17554, dated April 20, 1927, showing that ten drums of "Amoco Gasoline" (octane not shown) were delivered to Lindbergh's take-off point on that date.

The actual location of delivery was shown on the bill as being Hempstead, Long Island. It was transported via the Baltimore and Ohio Railroad from Baltimore, Maryland, from the Baltimore office of the American Oil Company.

It is not clear from the document if the final delivery was to Curtiss Field or Roosevelt, but due to the date of April 20, it can be assumed that it was Curtiss. The weight is listed as 4500 lbs which would translate into 750 gallons at six lbs per gallon, or 45 gallons per drum.

It appears that from the very start of Lindbergh's arrival, that the NYP was housed in a hangar apparently owned and operated by the Curtiss Flying Service. It was hangar # 16. Curtiss at that time consisted of a chain of fixed base operators, as well as dealers and manufacturers of aircraft, and also propellers such as the well known Curtiss-Reed one piece metal propeller.

All three contenders' airplanes were powered with the Wright J-5 "Whirlwind" engine, so the Wright company had much to gain in future sales if and when any of these flyers was successful in reaching Paris. However, the company had to maintain a strictly neutral position and show no partiality toward either of the three aviators.

The Paterson, New Jersey based Wright Aeronautical Company assigned several men to Curtiss Field to assist the J-5 owners. They were engine expert Ed Mulligan (from the Howard DGA "Mr. Mulligan" fame); Kenneth J. Boedecker, another engine expert and field service rep; Kenneth M. Lane, who was the engineer in charge of structural design, weight control and performance, eventually becoming Chief Designer, and Thomas "Doc" Kincaid, mechanic. The Wright Company also hired two partners in a public relations firm to cover the activity at Curtiss; Dick Blythe and Harry Bruno. Wright was one of their first clients in the new business. Blythe and Bruno were both Canadian trained pilots and were probably the first to form an aviation public relations firm in the US.

Pioneer Instrument Company of Brooklyn, New York had Brice H. Goldsborough, instrument expert, in their employ. L. B. Umlauf of the Vacuum Oil Company was there also to assist with oil and fuel requirements. Casey Jones, airport manager and famous Curtiss test pilot, arranged for a hangar for the NYP.

Recollections of some of these people involved with the Curtiss Field activities follow.

EDWARD J. MULLIGAN

When word reached the Wright Company that Lindbergh had just departed from California, I was assigned to look after him and the ship upon its arrival at Curtiss. In view of the fact that he had made his schedule across the continent and because some of those present knew the man, it was suggested that he be officially welcomed and the keys of the field be given to him. A set of keys of several varieties were dug up and Casey Jones was appointed "Mayor" to make the speech and presentation. This was done and the plane rolled into the hangar."

"After going over with Colonel Lindbergh his readings made during the transcontinental flight, general performance of engine, etc. and the possible chance of a quick continuation, an immediate check-up of the engine was made. Due to the assistance of Boedecker it was possible to complete this before morning. I believe everything we could think of and which was possible was done by Boedecker and me during this check, not only to the engine but also to the NYP.

"As things turned out it was possible, due to bad weather, to become better acquainted with Lindbergh. In the days that followed everything, including instruments, gas and oil tanks, were checked and measured and several check flights made until finally everything was deemed satisfactory.

"Lindbergh's personality, finesse, ability and awareness of what he intended to do and his preparedness for the job so impressed itself on those with whom he came in contact, particularly 'hard-boiled' newspapermen, that I believe seventy-five percent of the people of the country were not only wishing him success but were more than half-sure he would make it. To me, considering man, engine, plane and all, it seemed impossible to fail.

"In all the time of waiting, it was never possible to leave his ship alone in the hangar, and a police guard was necessary to keep innocent curiosity of his well wishers from possibly damaging some part of his plane. It was quite the accepted thing for parties of people dropping in at the hangar at two or three o'clock in the morning, after theatre or dance, on the possible chance of seeing Lindbergh or perhaps being there when he took off.

"When you consider that only two hangars away, another transatlantic flight airplane was "standing by" waiting for clear weather, and over at Roosevelt Field still another in the same condition, it seemed remarkable that everyone who came to the field wished to see and speak with Lindbergh and see his engine and airplane. Even the local kitten, 'Patsy,' which the papers played up as his mascot, was in great demand by not only all the children but by many others. He needed all nine of his lives to survive the food showered on him.

"Many times Mr. Lawrance dropped in around midnight to check up on the possibility of an early morning take off.

"The afternoon before the flight, while Lindbergh was visiting the Wright plant and the weather seemed rather worse than usual, I ran home, not having been there for about three weeks, when the word came that the weather was clearing and looked good over the ocean. I made the fastest run to the field I ever made with the help of a couple of cops!" [1]

Lindbergh standing by the NYP soon after arrival at Curtiss Field and NYP was placed in hangar #5 on May 12. Notice blunt original propeller spinner. ***(Cassagneres collection)***

KENNETH J. BOEDECKER

In a 1973 interview, Ken Boedecker, affectionately known as "Boady", had the following to say about his part in preparing for the epic flight.

"Looking back through these years to the days immediately preceding the flight to Paris, there comes a profound feeling of gratitude for the privilege accorded several of us of the Wright Company of being closely connected with the final touches and flight tests of the J-5C Whirlwind engine. Our coworkers in the plant, too, could be justly proud of their parts in this historical

NYP being placed in Hangar #5 for that first night after his arrival on May 12th. ***(Joe Christy***

Probably being moved from Hangar #5 over to Hangar #16 at Curtiss Field. Notice the NYP still has the blunt spinner. ***(Bernard Millot Archives, France)***

flight, for without their enthusiasm and their tradition in building every engine as perfect as is humanly possible, there could have been an entirely different story.

"Mulligan was officially assigned to check and tune up Lindbergh's engine, and I had been officially assigned to check and tune up the Whirlwind in Chamberlin's airplane.

"Upon Lindbergh's arrival, Chamberlin's ship and engine had their final checks and were all ready to go. Early in the evening of May 12th it looked as though the weather might be satisfactory for an early morning take-off, and knowing that Mulligan had only a limited amount of time in which to get Lindbergh's engine checked, I pitched in and helped him into the wee hours of the morning. This really proved unnecessary, as the weather turned bad over various parts of the route and actual departure was delayed for about two weeks. This gave us the opportunity of making some flight tests, the recollections of which can never be erased. If a little vanity can enter here, these test flights made Mulligan and myself two of the very few who have had the privilege of flying in the Spirit." [2]

Boedecker, in addition to working on Lindbergh's engine, inspected Clarence Chamberlin, Maitland, Hegenberger, Smith, and Bronte, and all of the Dole flyers' engines prior to their respective epochal flights. From 1915 to 1922, he was chief inspector for the Lawrance Aero Engine Corp., New York City, and assistant manager from 1922 to the merger of this company with the Wright Aeronautical Corp. in 1923, when he was made field service engineer of the new organization until October 1927, at which time he was promoted to service manager.

KENNETH M. LANE

Lane had this to say about those very important days in aviation history.

"The passing of many years may dull the memory of many of the events of that hectic week which was climaxed by that flight. But the impressions of the man who made the trip, however—particularly upon those who were privileged to be more or less intimately associated with him in the enterprise—will last as long as life itself."

"Before his arrival in New York, Lindbergh was practically unknown in the East—merely a 'dark horse' entry in the New York-Paris race. The general attitude toward one who had the temerity to think that he had even an outside chance of succeeding in such a hazardous undertaking is fairly well exemplified by the utterance of one skeptic who, upon learning that this young chap had hopped from San Diego to St. Louis and was now on his way to New York, remarked, 'Flying all alone, eh? Must have got away from his keeper.' But what a different story after he arrived. In no time at all, the profound impression which he made upon the representatives of the press flowed through the pens to make itself felt by the general public. Almost overnight he was promoted from dark horse to outstanding favorite.

"It is gratifying to realize that it was to Wright Aero personnel that he entrusted full responsibility for the proper preparation of both airplane and engine, and history tells us that this confidence

This is the Hangar #16 in which the NYP spent most of the time before the flight, being fine tuned. The building no longer exists. ***(Cradle of Aviation Museum)***

was not misplaced. Mr. Mulligan and Mr. Boedecker went over the engine repeatedly with a fine-tooth comb as though it were something taken out of a secondhand Model T Ford. Heifitz before his most important concert never tuned his violin more carefully than they tuned that engine.

"As is rarely the case, further contact with him only served to increase this feeling of certainty. His maturity of judgment, unusual in one of his years, his freedom from swank or bombast, his equable disposition, his tireless energy and above all his grim determination to come through could not but instill a like spirit in his co-workers. He proved to be an ideal executive, delegating responsibility and commensurate authority to those whom he judged worthy of it." [3]

It was at Curtiss that the NYP's first of three clearly noticeable changes took place—the spinner assembly, tail skid, carburetor air intake heater and the Earth Inductor Compass mast and drive mechanism. Because of these outside visible changes, identification of locations and dates of photographs has been closely pinpointed and confirmed.

To better understand that early life of the NYP, let us go back to those nine days at Curtiss, day by day, and study those first changes and modifications to ready the airplane for its incredible mission and lasting fame.

THURSDAY, MAY 12, 1927

Lindbergh had landed at 5:33 EDT. The very first pictures taken of the airplane and Lindbergh show him just minutes after his landing, standing in front of the airplane, hand on prop, and still in the winter flying suit which he had purchased in San Diego.

The original blunt nose spinner cap can clearly be seen in the photo. The battery of professional photographers was apparently many, as the pictures were taken from more than one angle and prints can still be found in publications and elsewhere.

Other pictures were taken of the NYP, showing the tail skid on a spoked wheel dolly being moved into the #16 Curtiss hangar.

Lindbergh, after settling into his room at the Garden City Hotel and freshening up had supper with Blythe and Boady and some of the other people associated with operations. They briefed him on what was happening on the field with regard to preparations by Byrd and Chamberlin and others. He was informed of Byrd's having a lease on Roosevelt Field, which had the longest runway in the area—nearly a mile long, suggesting it as the best runway to be used for the take-off for Paris.

Details of other flyers' camps and the problems they were encountering were explained and are well covered in Lindbergh's book, *The Spirit of St. Louis.*

Eventually they made their way over to Curtiss Field to check on the NYP and found that Ed Mulligan of the Wright Company had already been working on the airplane since it was first put into the hangar. Mulligan had already removed the cowling around the engine. As it turned out, and while Lindbergh and his friends were having supper, Mulligan had discovered a crack in the spinner shroud/collar.

While Mulligan and Boedecker worked on the engine and other details, Lindbergh himself began to check things over. Always having weight in mind, he decided to remove the six dry batteries located in the cockpit, on the left side even with the window sill aft of the left window. The batteries were installed at San Diego, and he had found during the night portion of his flight from San Diego to St. Louis that the lights that the batteries powered for the instrument panel were a bit bright and reasoned that with his flashlight he could read the gauges satisfactorily and save some weight at the same time. [4]

FRIDAY, MAY 13, 1927

This day turned out to be an extremely active one, with most of the modifications and repairs being taken care of, some of it rather exciting.

Local tech reps from the nearby vendors were there all day and into the night, assisting not only Lindbergh but others going for the Orteig prize as well.

The engine of the NYP being worked on by Wright technicians Ed Mulligan and Kenneth J. Boedecker (on work stool). Notice Lindbergh looking into the cockpit. There was much interest from the public as can be seen by the many people standing outside the roped off area. May 13th. ***(Leo B. Kimball collection)***

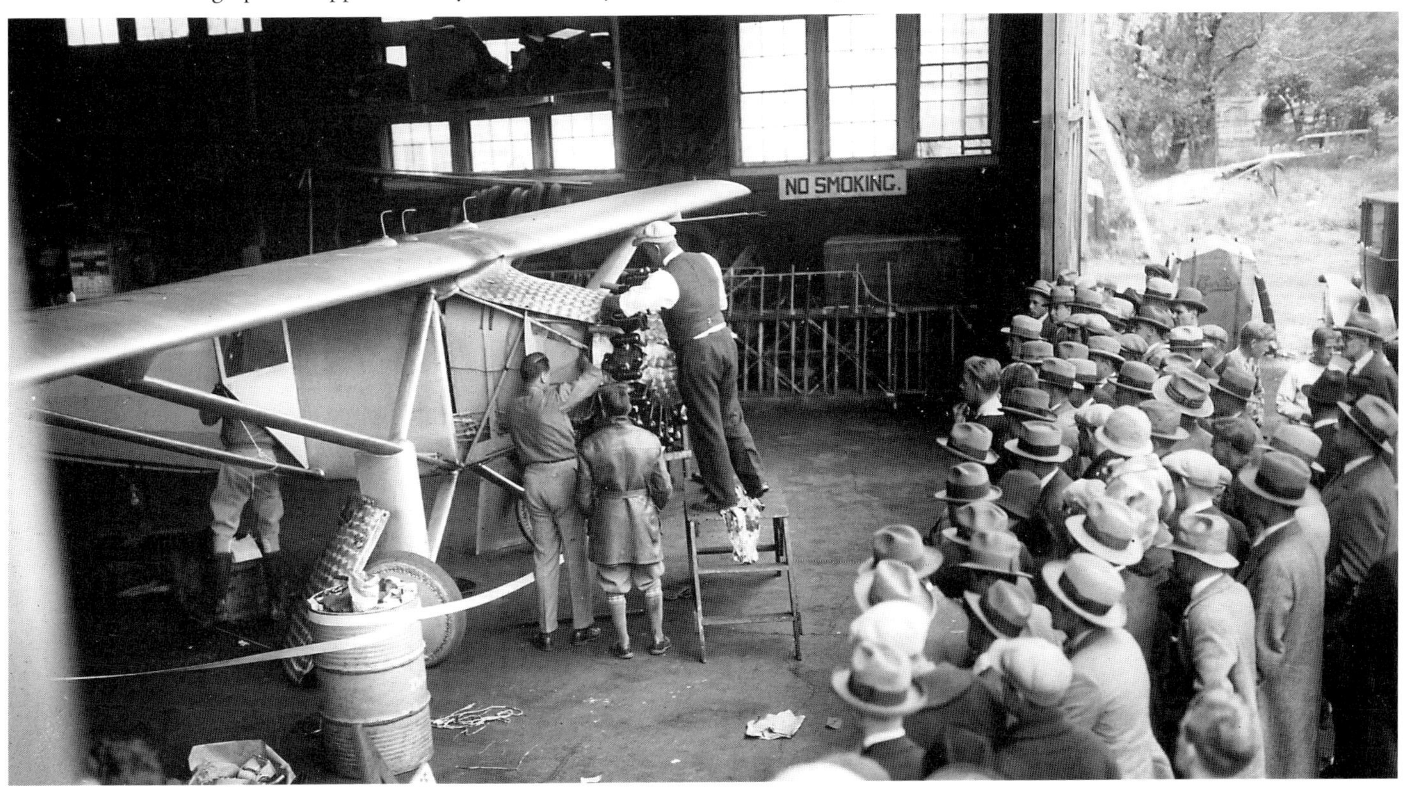

Another view of the crowds watching the activities at Hangar #16. ***(Library of Congress)***

Blythe picked up Lindbergh at the hotel, and they drove over to Curtiss after some breakfast. When they arrived at the hangar they found Mulligan and Boady, both of whom had been working on the NYP most of the night. The propeller and spinner assembly had already been removed. Mulligan informed Lindbergh that a new spinner was being fabricated at the Curtiss plant nearby, at no cost to Lindbergh.

Mulligan then introduced Lindbergh to Kenneth Lane, Chief Airframe Engineer of the Wright Company, who had just arrived that morning. Wright put Lane in charge of the company activities at the field.

Sometime that morning press photographers asked to take pictures of Lindbergh, together with Commander Byrd and Clarence B. Chamberlin. Photos show them standing in front of the NYP with the propeller and spinner assembly removed. Later they photographed Lindbergh while he was standing on a work stand checking the engine.

Because Lindbergh had mentioned to these engine experts his problems over the mountains on his flight to St. Louis, they decided to install a carburetor air intake heater, which they did that morning. Due to the obvious possibility that he would encounter severe and wet weather over the ocean, they wired the heater in the hot position. There may be pros and cons on this arrangement, but it may have been one of the secrets between success and failure. Mulligan did the installation of the carburetor air heater. It was Wright No. 13828 (presently stamped on rear side #20594). This heater was attached to the bottom of the

Friday, May 13, showing Lindbergh checking things over on the Wright J-5. The propeller and spinner assembly are removed for repair by the Curtiss people. Notice that the carburetor air heater just below the carburetor has already been installed. ***(United Technologies Archive)***

Stromberg NA-T4 carburetor, as clearly seen in photographs. [5]

Lindbergh helped out with the work being done all morning. In the meantime while other work was being done, Brice H. Goldsborough was supervising the compasses situation and the "swinging of the compass."

[Goldsborough, a former aeronautical engineer for The Sperry Gyroscope Company of Brooklyn, NY, helped found The Pioneer Instrument Company, becoming vice-president and treasurer. (Goldsborough held Industrial Pilot license # 1223.)

Goldsborough was later the navigator on the ill-fated airplane, "The Dawn" on another trans-Atlantic flight. On December 23, 1927, it left Roosevelt Field, and no trace of the occupants or the airplane have ever been found.] [6]

One test flight was made that day at 3:08 p. m., a ten minute flight. It is not absolutely clear as to what propeller was used for the flight, as the supposedly original one was at the Curtiss plant being fitted with the new spinner assembly. Photos of test flights show it with a Hamilton ground adjustable propeller. However, other photos (none of which is dated) show a Curtiss-Reed metal propeller, popular at the time, mounted on the NYP, on the ground. Possibly the Hamilton was used that day and the Curtiss-Reed the next day (14th). On the above mentioned test flight

Lindbergh in the hangar affectionately petting the hangar mascot, "Patsy" the kitten, who appears to have taken over Lindbergh's hat. ***(Library of Congress)***

Here is Lindbergh accepting the compact mirror from Mrs. Loma Oliver, Jr.—the "Mirror Girl". This is the mirror that he used to read the 'reverse reading' liquid magnetic compass. ***(Library of Congress)***

View shows someone "swinging the compass" on the NYP at Curtiss Field. Notice Curtiss Reed propeller on the nose. **(Donald Hall, Jr.)**

Lindbergh carried Brice Goldsborough, as a passenger to check out the NYP instruments and compasses, and newly installed carburetor air heater.

Because Byrd had offered the use of Roosevelt Field to Lindbergh, the latter decided to go over after lunch and personally walk the field, to check the ground surface and get a feel for what he might expect or encounter at take-off for Paris.

One of the most important instruments required in an aircraft and especially for such a flight as this is the compass or compasses. Because such accurate guidance and dependability was needed, the Pioneer Instrument Company was there to fine tune both the Earth Inductor Compass as well as the Liquid Magnetic Compass.

As is clearly seen in photographs, the EIC generator mast vane type drive mechanism was replaced with a cup type anemometer. It appears that the wind generator mast tube was changed a time or two at Curtiss, but the original as installed in San Diego was finally the very one that made the flight to Paris. New cups, however, were installed at Curtiss to turn the generator.

The anemometer for the generator, was a Type 301B with four hemispherical cups fastened on the ends of arms at right angles to each other and mounted on a vertical spindle.

Pioneer instrument people removed the rod and universal joint type drive mechanism, which ran from the generator down to the controller (Pioneer model 301B-78) at the lower right side of the pilot seat. This was replaced with a speedometer/tachometer type flexible cable. The generator was also replaced.

With regard to the liquid magnetic compass (LMC), it is not clear at this writing why Pioneer installed a "reverse reading" type, model C782, which is still in the airplane. Lindbergh was twenty-five years old, with 20-20 vision, and his eyes were about eighteen inches from that compass, so therefore could easily read a correct reading compass card. It is not clear for what application a reverse-reading compass would apply.

A gentleman by the name of Charles Henry, a service rep for the Pioneer Instrument Company, claims to have been at Curtiss, helping with work on the NYP. He remembered years later that he was apparently asked to return the compass to the Pioneer Company on Lexington Avenue in Brooklyn to have the card readings reversed. [7]

At any rate, the scenario was this—the Pioneer specialist, Louis J. Bollo was installing the compass via a bracket fastened to the center stringer of the overhead skylight, and remarked—"That's the best place I can find for it, but you'll have to read it through a mirror. It will give you a more accurate indication up there than any other place we can find. It will swing less in rough air—you sure haven't any extra room in here." [8]

THE MIRROR GIRL STORY

It appears, but is not confirmed, that it was on May 13th the mirror girl appeared on the scene. While all of the activity was going on in hangar 16, a sizable crowd of spectators had gathered

Ed Mulligan swinging the Curtiss Reed propeller as another test flight or engine run in is planned while the Curtiss plant makes a new spinner assembly. May 14th. **(Ellen W. Dioguardi)**

outside the hangar where they could overhear some of this conversation. When the specialist mentioned the need for a mirror, a young lady about twenty-two or twenty-three, well dressed and well groomed, said, "Will this do?" She had looked into her pocketbook, found a standard circular woman's powder/mirror compact, and offered it. They lifted the rope so she could come into the work area, and the mechanic took the mirror and stuck it up on the top center of the instrument panel temporarily with a piece of gum and suggested it would do the job.

Lucky for us historians, a press photographer took a picture of the girl handing the mirror to Lindbergh, and in the caption below, most of which was inaccurate, her name was given as Mrs. Loma Oliver, Jr. Photographer's name and newspaper are unknown.

Shortly thereafter the girl disappeared into the crowd and has never been found. Exhaustive effort has been spent attempting to locate and honor Mrs. Oliver, but she has never been found.

While Lindbergh was relaxing in his room that night at the Garden City Hotel, he received a telegram from his mother informing him of her plans to arrive the next morning, via train from Detroit, to be with him for a while.

Triggered by inaccuracies, sensationalism and constant phone calls from the press, Mrs. Evangeline Lindbergh decided to take a train to New York from Detroit, where she was living and teaching. She wished to consult and discuss the flight with her son and be assured that it was the right thing for him to do. She did not wish to spend much time with him, as she knew the importance of his concentration on the details and logistics of the planning for the flight, and she did not wish to detract from this in any way.

INSURANCE

Regarding the insurance for the NYP, and as mentioned in Chapter 5, it appears that coverage was confirmed for the flight across the ocean to Paris. [9]

On this date the following document was drawn up:

KNOW ALL MEN BY THESE PRESENTS:

THAT

I, CHARLES A. LINDBERGH, residing at St. Louis, in the State of Missouri, have made, constituted and appointed and by these presents do make, constitute and appoint HARRY H. KNIGHT, residing at No. 401 Olive Street, St. Louis, Missouri, my true and lawful attorney for me and in my name and stead to make with any person, a contract for the sale and disposal of any and all stories pertaining to my life and experiences in relation to my flight across the Atlantic or attempted flight across the

Atlantic, giving and granting to my said attorney by these presents, full power and authority to do and perform all and every act and thing whatsoever requisite and necessary to be done in and about the premises as fully and to all intents and purposes as I might or could do if personally present, hereby ratifying and confirming all that my said attorney shall lawfully do or cause to be done by virtue hereof.

The reason for the execution of this power of attorney is that I am about to attempt to fly an airplane from America to Europe and realize that the story of my life and of my experiences may have a commercial value and which commercial value cannot be determined at this moment but can be better determined after I have started on the flight, and that it is desirous that I should have some person in this country who can negotiate for me and on my behalf.

IN WITNESS WHEREOF, I have hereunto set my hand and seal this 13th day of May, 1927. [10]

Charles A. Lindbergh (L. S.)

SATURDAY, MAY 14, 1927

Mrs. Lindbergh spent much of the day with her son and departed for Detroit satisfied that her son was doing what he felt was important for the development of air travel and was confident he would be successful.

It is thought that this was the day that Lindbergh visited Dr. James H. Kimball at the weather bureau in New York City (probably late afternoon after his mother left for Detroit) to get an update on the meteorological situation in the North Atlantic.

Not confirmed or documented, it appears that also on this day technicians mounted a Curtiss-Reed metal propeller and a temporary spinner assembly on the Spirit. Only one photo exists showing this arrangement with Lindbergh and his mother standing in front of the right side of the nose area of the NYP. It is also not clear or known if this arrangement was used for the two test flights that day.

In the morning, Lindbergh made three test flights over Curtiss Field. The first one was for only 10 minutes.

On the second flight, which lasted 15 minutes, he carried Ken Boedecker apparently to have his input as to the operation of the engine in flight and to check both compasses.

On the third and last flight of the day, in late afternoon, he carried Ed Mulligan for the same reason. It was on this 20 minute flight that a spectator got in his way upon landing, and he had to do some fast stick and rudder work to avoid the person on the ground. In so doing he hit rather hard on the tail skid, breaking it and some of the aft fuselage structure.

According to Ken Lane, who did the repair—"Its ease of repair was demonstrated when on Saturday, May 14th, as Lindbergh landed from a test flight checking his compasses, a fool photographer ran out in front of the plane and Slim had to ground-loop to avoid hitting him. This was too much for the tail-skid swivel fitting trunion, which broke off allowing the tailskid to damage extensively the tubing in the rear end of the fuselage. It looked like a hopeless mess. But we managed, with tubing donated by Curtiss and the help of a very capable welder and two bright young mechanics (from the Curtiss Company,) to have the plane ready to make the flight to Paris and all the subsequent flights in this hemisphere until it came to a well earned rest in the Smithsonian." [11]

View shows the brand new and more pointed spinner assembly mounted and ready to go. It appears to be aerodynamically a much cleaner and efficient design. May 15th ***(Leo B. Kimball collection)***

SWINGING THE COMPASS

As can be seen in photographs, the airplane had the newly installed liquid magnetic compass swung, via a tripod mounted on top of the wing and fuselage. This particular compass was to be put to the severest trial or test, so particular attention to accuracy was necessary.

Because a compass is affected by the presence of the engine or aircraft steel structure etc., the process of accurately adjusting the compass is known as "swinging the compass", to allow for deviation. Any inaccuracy could effect the success or failure of a long distance flight such as this.

Swinging the compass is tedious work. The point toward which all magnetic compasses point is known as the magnetic pole, located about 800 miles south of the geographical pole, near Bathurst Island in northern Canada. It is therefore necessary to ascertain the exact angular relation between the fore and aft line of the ship or aircraft and the compass heading. The exact direction of the magnetic pole was located on the airport by transiting the sun to locate the true or geographical pole and thence determining the variation from the true north to the magnetic north. This first point being established, the NYP was rolled out to a location where the swinging process began. After the preliminary work was complete, it was a mere matter of pointing the NYP in several directions and noting the reading of the compasses.

SUNDAY, MAY 15, 1927

Lindbergh made two test flights this day with the newly installed spinner assembly and original Hamilton propeller.

Curtiss had apparently made a whole new assembly and either discarded the original or put it in the hands of Vaughn. The Curtiss shroud mounting screws are more numerous and are close to the trailing edge, whereas the original screws are about one to two inches forward of the trailing edge.

Also noticeable is the different design of the reinforcing plates around the base of each propeller blade at the shroud. The San Diego shroud had only three screws on each side, the middle one with a smaller head and the plate is squared at the trailing edge. The Curtiss one is curved around the base of the blade with more screws used. The overall design includes a more pointed spinner cap. The Curtiss assembly is still on the NYP. Curtiss did not Damascene the unit, but just roughed up the aluminum surface. Function rather than appearance was priority.

On the first flight he had carried Brice Goldsborough, instrument expert, and on the second flight Ken Boedecker, to give a last minute check of the J-5.

MONDAY, MAY 16, 1927

From this day on the NYP would be ready to go and was still kept in Hangar 16 at Curtiss Field. The decision to take off was not made however, due to poor or unsuitable weather over the Atlantic.

The NYP in Hangar #16 on May 15th, 1927. Lindbergh can be seen near the rear of the fuselage leaning on top of the fuselage. ***(Oscar Jenkins, courtesy of Neal L. Martin, DC)***

Lindbergh spent the time, while waiting out the weather reports, accepting several invitations to visit people in the area. He had lunch with Colonel Theodore Roosevelt, Jr. nearby. Roosevelt suggested that when Lindbergh reached Paris he would want to make friends with Ambassador Myron T. Herrick, a good friend of Roosevelt's.

While spending time at Curtiss and after his lunch with Roosevelt, he was approached by several interesting people.

Charles Lawrence introduced himself to Lindbergh and expressed his best wishes for a successful flight. Also Harry Guggenheim and his wife, Carol, came out to Curtiss and spoke to Lindbergh. This was their first meeting, but would not be their last.

And his old friend from San Diego, Franklin Mahoney, came to the field to be sure that all was well with the NYP and offered any other help that might be necessary from the Ryan Company.

A photo was taken with Lawrence, Mahoney, Lindbergh and Harry Guggenheim together. Guggenheim suggested that Lindbergh call on him when he returned from Paris, the beginning of a long lasting friendship of the two.

Al Williams, Rene Fonck and Tony Fokker came by to chat with the flyer, in addition to C. M. Keys and Frank Russell of the Curtiss Company. Grover Loening and Chance Vought also paid a visit to the Lindbergh camp. They were all very prominent aviation people in their own right.

Lindbergh had visitors from the press, one of whom had developed a high respect for. Lorin D. "Deak" Lyman of The *New York Times* was one. Their friendship developed and lasted for many years, with the two living near each other in Connecticut; Lyman in Southport and Lindbergh in Darien.

William P. MacCracken, Jr., at that time Assistant Secretary of Commerce for Aeronautics, an attorney and wartime Air Service Flying instructor and first head of the new agency, flew up from Washington to go over any last minute legal items that might need addressing. New federal regulations were written that required all aircraft intended to be flown at night to have appropriate navigation lighting. Lindbergh did not work such lighting into the initial design in order to save weight. When Lindbergh asked MacCracken about such lights, the latter, after some thought, felt that Lindbergh would not be running into 'much' night traffic where he was going and that special dispensation could be given at that time, and that settled the matter. Navigation lights never were installed on the NYP. And Lindbergh was never sited for a violation by the CAA.

This was also the day that Lindbergh journeyed into New York to have his passport picture taken. A photo exists in the author's collection that shows Lindbergh taking the oath for a passport, with two gentlemen from the passport office in New York City on either side of him.

While Curtiss Field was abuzz with activity, on the other side of the Atlantic preparations were being made for the arrival of any American flyer who might make it. Two letters have been found having to do with any official arrangements and permissions, etc. Both letters are quoted:

R. C. Wood (official capacity unknown: author)

Neuilly-sur-Seine, France, 16 May 1927
Monsieur General Fortant
Directeur General de L'Aeronautique
Monsieur le Directeur;

The American pilot, Capt. Lindbergh will be trying the New York Paris crossing shortly.

I kindly request for the evening of his arrival the lighting of -
The Paris London Airway
The Le Bourget Airport
The Mont Valerien light (house)

This shows the instrument panel as it appeared before and after the flight to Paris. Notice the econometer has been removed from the right side, but the mounting hole is still there. Notice mirror at top dead center. ***(courtesy Exxon Mobil Corporation)***

Lindbergh with his mother, taken on Saturday, May 14th in Hangar #16. Notice the Curtiss Reed propeller, with yet another, larger spinner mounted. **(Leo B. Kimball collection)**

and whatever other arrangements are necessary.

I would also be grateful if you could grant landing permission at Le Bourget.

The plane is a Ryan monoplane, equipped with a Wright "Whirlwind" 200 hp.

Hoping to receive a favorable reply, I am ....

Sincerely yours, [12]

R. C. Wood

The reply;

Monsieur,

It is my honor to inform you that the permission to land at Le Bourget for pilot Lindbergh, which you requested in your letter of 16th May 1927, has been granted.

Please be informed moreover that I have alerted my staff so that the necessary measures may be taken for his arrival.

Sincerely Yours,

General Fortant

TUESDAY, MAY 17, 1927

Lindbergh kept a close watch on the weather this day, but in the meantime he was loaned the Curtiss Wright "Iron Horse" Fokker S-3 (S.111), J-5 powered service plane. It was number 1085, and he flew it from Curtiss Field to Teterboro near Hasbrouck Heights and return.

WEDNESDAY, MAY 18, 1927

Lindbergh continued to keep a close watch on the weather over the Atlantic via Dr. Kimball in the city.

THURSDAY, MAY 19, 1927

Sometime during the day Lindbergh, Mahoney, Ken Lane, Dick Blythe, and Lieutenant George Stumpf (National Guardsman from St. Louis who represented Lindbergh's thirty-fifth division) made a visit to the Wright factory in Paterson, New Jersey, and later visited the home of Guy W. Vaughan, VP and General Manager of Wright. Lindbergh was again given the use of the company's Fokker S.111 which he flew from Curtiss to Teterboro Airport, not far from Paterson.

There was an overcast with light rain showers on this day and reports of dense fog along the coasts of Nova Scotia and Newfoundland. There was also a report of a storm just west of France.

Further checking with Dr. Kimball disclosed that the weather was clearing over the ocean and that low pressure over Newfoundland was dissipating with a high pressure area developing just behind it.

A photograph was taken of Lindbergh, Mahoney and Charles Lawrence in front of the NYP, showing the new spinner assembly on the NYP and in front of Hangar 16. The spinner is on the airplane to this day.

Later in the day Dr. Kimball relayed a message that there was a light rain and overcast over Long Island, but improvement continued over the ocean.

At this point Lindbergh and his crew sensed the possibility of an early morning take off on the 20th. After all, the NYP was ready, Lindbergh was ready, most of the last minute details had been taken care of , and all that remained was to fill the fuel tanks to maximum capacity.

Because Roosevelt Field, which would be used for the take off, was twelve feet higher than Curtis Field, and the NYP would have to be towed from Hangar 16 to Roosevelt in soft ground, it was decided to put only 100 gallons of fuel in the main tank while at Curtiss and do the final filling of fuel at Roosevelt in the early morning hours or during the night.

The other reason for not filling the tanks too full was that the weight would be too much on the tires and might subject them to unnecessary stress during the towing procedure.

The plan was to fill the tanks when the NYP was in the take off position at the western end of the Roosevelt runway.

Workers lifted the tail and secured it to a flat-bed truck, seen in some photographs, for the trip to Roosevelt Field. They then wrapped a tarpaulin over the engine.

During the night, when the airplane was in that position, the tires were greased by mechanic Raymond Brown in order to lessen the friction factor. Mechanics also put oil rather than grease in the wheel bearings to cut down on resistance and friction. [13]

CARL SCHORY AND THE BAROGRAPH

This flight had to be officially certified by the National Aeronautic Association of the United States of America and the Federation Aeronautique Internationale of Paris, France to claim the Orteig prize.

Since 1905 the NAA as representative of the FAI has been responsible for overseeing and certifying all official aviation records set in the United States or from its shores.

The method used to record a non-stop flight was by the use of an instrument called a barograph. The barograph would confirm that no intermediate landing was made between New York and Paris or out of sight of any official observers. It was first used for balloons and then for aircraft. The instrument could be wound and installed any time and only required movement of an outside lever to activate the drum and recording pen.

Lindbergh's initial application for certification was mailed to NAA and received in their Washington offices on February 28, 1927 by Carl F. Schory, who at that time was Secretary of the contest committee for NAA.

According to Schory, who was called out to Lindbergh's airplane to seal the barograph, he recalls mounting the instrument behind the pilot's seat (possibly in free suspension with the use of bungee cord to the airframe structure. No photos or other documentation exist to confirm the exact location or method of securing the instrument). Schory did not recall precisely how it was fastened or secured. He did think he did the mounting as the

NYP was being towed from Curtiss over to Roosevelt Field. [14]

In this case it was a lead-sealed six hour barograph made by Hue, Paris, and is no. 353. It was mounted in a wooden case, as can be seen in photographs.

Due to the thirty-three and a half hours of the New York to Paris flight, the drum revolved every six hours, so the continuous tracing occupies more than five lines.

In Paris a member of the Aero Club of France (representative of the FAI) would unseal the instrument and certify that the ship did not land anywhere along the route of flight. As it turned out, Chief Engineer L. Hirschauer, General Secretary of the contest committee of the Aero Club of France was the responsible officer and did the unsealing at Le Bourget. [15]

Schory had to also officially lead-seal the fuel tanks, which he did to the three wing tanks. They were sealed with lead strips which were squeezed with pincers but were without mark. The two fuel tanks and one oil tank in the fuselage were not lead-sealed.

When Lindbergh left the Garden City Hotel, he was driven to the airport by Frank A. Tichenor and Jessie Horsfall, Publisher and Editor of Aero Digest magazine.

WHAT LINDBERGH CARRIED ON HIS PERSON

In his pocket he had the following: [16]

PILOTS IDENTIFICATION CARD (with photo of him in his Army uniform.).

He was rated as a Transport Pilot.

License number 69
Issued on April 21, 1927.
Age 25
Weight: 160 — Color hair: light
Height: 6' 2½" — Color eyes: blue
License form: M 12
License expires October 21, 1927

PASSPORT CARD

Includes photo (white shirt, tie, and suit)
Height 6 foot 2 inches
Hair: light brown
Eyes: blue
Place of birth: Detroit, Michigan
Date of Birth: February 4, 1902
Occupation: Airplane Pilot

ROOSEVELT FIELD TAKE OFF

Photographs taken at both Curtiss and Roosevelt often show Sgt. Andrew C. Wilson of the Nassau County Police Department in Garden City. He carried badge no. 36 and often guarded the NYP in the hangar and was the man who closed the door of the NYP just before the take off for Paris.

Boedecker said, Ed Mulligan and Ken Lane loaded the fuel tanks with fuel from five gallon cans which was hand poured through a very fine mesh strainer. Mulligan handed most of the fuel up to Lane who did the pouring. Occasionally, I lent a hand to give Mulligan a rest."

"After CAL looked everything over thoroughly, he climbed into the cockpit and Mulligan and I started the engine. Ed pulled the prop through while I spun a booster magneto by hand. I then checked the RPM with "Slim" and found that the engine was turning only 1560 rpm. We cut the switch and I checked everything very carefully and could find nothing wrong. We started it up again with no better results.

"I said, Slim, I can't find anything wrong. However, we have never run it up before at this hour of the day nor under these weather conditions and that may account for the low RPMs. He said, "What do you say?—Let's try it. I said, Do you want the chocks removed? He said—yes. I kicked the chocks out and that 'try' ended up in Paris.

"Many of us pushed on struts and other firm spots to get the plane rolling through the mud, and it finally struggled off. My heart was in my throat, and when I saw the ship just barely miss the telephone wires and sink somewhat on the other side, I almost collapsed. I don't think I slept for the next thirty three hours as I had my ears glued to the radio to catch any messages that might be forthcoming on the progress of the flight."

As a matter of interest, Lindbergh's flight log clearly indicates that he had a total pilot flight time of 1790:10 at takeoff time. [17]

Left to right Lindbergh, Commander Richard E. Byrd, and Clarence Chamberlin, taken on May 13th. ***(Dale Thompson)***

Left to right: B. F. Mahoney, Harry Guggenheim, Lindbergh, and Charles Lawrence, president of the Wright Aeronautical Corporation. May 19th. ***(United Technologies Archive)***

PERSONAL RECOLLECTIONS OF TAKE OFF PEOPLE WHO WERE THERE

DOROTHY R. MEYER (Mrs. John W. Meyer), HUNTINGTON, NY

She was eight years old and lived next door to Igor Sikorsky and watched his airplane, the S-35, being built to be used for his proposed Paris flight.

"I was small for my age and remember at dawn on May 20th my mother, sister and I walked through the rain to Roosevelt Field. I remember my mother lifting me up so I could see. People nearby were kind enough to push my sister and me right to the front. I couldn't believe I was standing so close to this tall, handsome young man who was about to attempt a flight that would surely go down in history.

We watched as the plane took off and cleared the telephone wires. The crowd was still cheering as we took off for home. After breakfast we left for school which was two miles away, but all the way we talked of the great moment we had witnessed. [18]

GRACE E. DRYDEN, FORT LAUDERDALE, FLORIDA

Grace was seven years old, and it was her birthday on May 20. Her mother, aunt and uncle thought taking her to Roosevelt Field and watching Lindbergh take off would stay in her memory as a birthday present.

"It was a cloudy dark day and rain was threatening, and we left our home in Freeport, Long Island very early in the morning. We waited for what seemed like a long time for a seven year old but finally he walked to his plane with what looked like a parachute on his back (not so, author). My folks, being religious people, did a lot of praying that he would be safe and make his destination. He touched everyone's heart—everyone loved him.

"Finally he started down the field and the plane seemed so slow in rising, he hardly cleared the telephone wires and everyone was saying—get it up.

"When we got home I remember everyone glued to their radios to keep abreast of the news of his trip. When we finally heard he arrived safely at his destination, a prayer of thanksgiving was said by all." [19]

WILLIAM K. JOUNKE, UNIONDALE, NY

William was nine years old and attended the Garden City Public School near the Garden City Hotel. The excitement of the teachers and students in the school, stimulated by the nearby presence of Lindbergh, led him and other students to skip a few classes to spend time around the hotel or to ride their bicycles

Kenneth Lane filling the main fuel tank with a five gallon can and funnel. ***(Cassagneres collection)***

Lindbergh is shown at the New York Passport Agency Office, when he filed for the document. Left to right is James J. Hughes, Assistant Passport Agent; Lindbergh; Ira F. Hoyt, Passport Agent. May 16th. ***(Mrs. Frances G. Knight)***

over to Curtiss Field to share the thrill of the day and to observe the mechanics and helpers working on the NYP. They were also elated to watch the test flights of Lindbergh in the NYP.

"Shortly before midnight on the day of May 19th, my father received word from a friend of his at the Garden City Hotel that Lindbergh was planning to take off from Roosevelt Field early the next morning. My father woke me up in the dark hours before dawn. Riding in a light drizzle he drove us by car and parked in the muddy ground behind a wooden hangar alongside Old Country Road at the upper Roosevelt Field. I was dressed in a black, hooded raincoat that Mom had made me wear. We walked down toward the neighboring Curtiss Field in the gloom to see the Spirit of St. Louis being towed tail first toward the upper Roosevelt Field area. A small group of people followed the plane to help guide it around a rise in the ground while we joined a crowd of spectators and photographers who rushed up toward the runway to be near the take off location.

"When the plane was positioned at the west end of the field, they had to struggle to position the airplane in the soft earth. The morning had become light, although there was still an overcast, but not raining. A group of about six or seven men lined up behind the main wing struts. They began shoving the airplane and then running while pushing to help the plane get rolling through the soft earth. The airplane left them behind as it gathered speed. It seemed to bounce off a bump. Two more times the plane looked like it got off the ground for a moment but couldn't stay up. I remember squeezing my dad's hand hard and thinking Lindbergh would never get airborne when slowly the plane left the runway and very gradually rose until it cleared the electric wires at the road just east of Roosevelt Field.

"I remember my dad putting his hand on my shoulder, leaning down to me and saying—I think he'll make it now. Those words have stuck with me all these years."

As a result of this experience, Lindbergh became a role model and shaped a great deal of my life's ambitions and activities. I became fascinated with aviation." [20]

HELEN LOCKOWSKI, GARDEN CITY PARK, NY

Helen was eight years old at the time. Her uncle Simon was a mechanic at Curtiss Field and suggested to Helen's parents, immigrants to this country from Europe, that they should come to Roosevelt Field to watch the departure of a young man by the name of Lindbergh, who was going to fly to Europe.

"Uncle Simon brought along his daughter to accompany me. He picked us all up in his Model T Ford. It was a cold dreary misty morning. We walked across the field to where a group of people were gathered. It didn't seem like a large group. Perhaps fifty to seventy-five people. When Lindbergh finally lifted off the runway, everyone clapped and let out a loud moan like ooh my! I did not know it then what it was all about, till I heard it from the elders that he just missed the wires." [21]

ALISON D. GRAY, WESTON, CT

Alison Gray's mother, Edith, was a friend of Charles Lawrence back in 1927. and her husband were at a dinner party, also attended by Lawrence.

Because Edith was a curious and traveled woman, he said to her—"Edith, you should come with me to Roosevelt Field early this morning. I've designed an engine for an airplane that a young chap is going to fly solo across the Atlantic. The take off is planned for early morning."

Edith replied—"Good heavens—I can't wait to stay up till that hour for some crackpot scheme."

Lawrence said, "No, no I think, I'm sure, he's really going to make it and it'll be a very historic moment that you shouldn't miss."

"Charlie Lawrence, you must be drunk and I'm not going to Roosevelt Field with you at 4 am." [22]

LAST PHOTOS TAKEN OF NYP OVER LONG ISLAND ON HIS WAY TO PARIS

The last few pictures of Lindbergh flying low and leaving the north shore of Long Island were taken by George Wies from a Curtiss Oriole flown by Arthur L. Caperton. This was for Fox Movietone News. Weis dipped his wings in farewell to Lindbergh and headed back across Long Island Sound to Curtiss Field.

FOOTNOTES

1. Trade Winds, Vol. 3, May 1937, No. 7 Wright Aeronautical Corporation, Paterson, NJ.

2. Ibid.

3. Ibid.

4. The Spirit of St. Louis, Charles A. Lindbergh, Charles Scribner's Sons, New York, 1953.

5. Personal inspection of original *Spirit of St. Louis* at Smithsonian National Air & Space Museum, Washington, DC on several occasions.

6. *American Aircraft Directory, Supplement to First Edition,* 1927, (published April, 1928,) Aviation Publishing Corporation, NYC, page 22.

7. Letter to the author from Charles Henry, Slatington, PA, dated May 1994.

8. *Spirit of St. Louis*, Lindbergh, 1953, Scribners, page 225.

9. Publication: *The Insurance Field*, #55, January - June, 1927, 900 117, page 37, June, 1927, full page advertisement, The Independence Companies, Philadelphia, PA.

10. Publication: *The Aero Analyst*, May - June 1929, page 13, full page advertisement, The Independence Companies, Philadelphia, PA.

11. Copy in the collection of the Krone Pen Company, Buffalo Grove, IL. Copy in the author's collection.

12. Typed statement by Lenneth M. Lane, Chief Plane Engineer, Wright Aeronautical Corp. Date Unknown. Original in the archives of the Smithsonian Institution, Washington, DC.

13. Letter to the author dated September 2, 1975 from Frances G. Knight, Director, Passport Office, Department of State, Washington, DC.

14. Letter to the author dated February 7, 2000 from C.W. Sutton, Gaylord, MN, a friend of Raymond Brown.

Left to right—Nungesser and Coli, the two French flyers who left Le Bourget Aerodrome in Paris, France to fly to New York and were never seen again. ***(Cassagneres collection)***

15. Letter to Paul E. Garber, Smithsonian Institution, Washington, DC, from Carl F. Schory, Vero Beach, FL, former Directing Official of the National Aeronatique Association of USA, Washington, DC, dated November 4, 1977.

16. Ibid.

17. Originals at the Missouri Historical Society, St. Louis, MO.

18. Letter to the author dated December 4, 1972 from Boedecker. Boedecker was then living in Jamesburg, NJ.

19. Letter to the author dated June 29, 1993 from Dorothy R. Meyer, Huntington, NY.

20. Letter to the author dated August 6, 1993 from Grace E. Dryden.

21. Letter to the author date July 14, 1993 from William K. Jounke, Uniondale, NY.

22. Letter to the author dated September 5, 1993 from Helen T. Lockowski, Garden City Park, NY.

23. Letter to the author date 1990 from Allison D. Gray of Weston, CT.

24. *The Wartime Journals of Charles A. Lindbergh,* Harcourt Brace Jovanovich, Inc., New York, 1970, page 487.

ENDNOTES

Much of the information in this chapter was learned and confirmed by interview with "people who were there."

Careful study of photographs, Lindbergh's own notes in his logbooks and notebook answered many questions. The photographs, as seen through a magnifying glass, revealed details of the NYP structure and equipment and various mechanical changes to the airplane while at Curtiss Field.

Besides the personal interviews and other sources, photographs were probably the single most accurate means of determining sequence of events that took place up to the time of the takeoff for Paris.

Contact with highly qualified technical people who are experts in the aviation industry helped to clear up historical and technical questions.

Newspaper articles of the time were also consulted, but often were found to be inaccurate on various details of the time or period. Anything written by Lauren "Deak" Lyman of *The New York Times* was quite accurate, however.

Picture History of Aviation on Long Island 1908-1938, George C. Dade and Frand Strnad, Dover Publications, Inc. New York, 1989

Original Document—"Bill of Lading," No. 17554, Memorandum, dated April 20, 1927, Consigned to Captain Charles A. Lindbergh, Hempstead, Long Island, New York from the American Oil Company via the Baltimore & Ohio Railroad.

The Spirit of St. Louis, Charles A. Lindbergh, Charles Scribner's Sons, New York, 1953.

The Book of Aviation, 1932 edition, Edward P. Curtis, The Hoagland Company, Los Angeles, CA.

Charles Lindbergh, His Life, D. Appleton and Company, 1927.

Charles A. Lindbergh's personal pilot log, copy at Yale University, Sterling Memorial Library, Manuscripts and Archives Department, New Haven, CT. Log dated from November 11, 1926 to July 7, 1928.

National Aeronautic Association, Washington, DC, Official NAA documentation and reports on file at the NAA offices, copies of which are in the author's collection. These documents include official reports from the Aero Club de France, representatives of the Federation Aeronautique Internationale, Paris, France.

Personal inspection of original NYP artifacts at the Paul Edward Garber Restoration Facility, National Air & Space Museum, Silver Hill, Maryland.

CHAPTER 8

The Flight

INTRODUCTION TO LINDBERGH'S METHOD OF NAVIGATION

This is a basic description of how Lindbergh navigated to Paris using the only method of the time, a combination of *pilotage* and *dead reckoning.*

Pilotage over the land masses (Long Island, Connecticut, Rhode Island, Massachusetts, Nova Scotia, Cape Breton Island, Newfoundland, Ireland, England, France)

Dead Reckoning over the Atlantic Ocean.

PILOTAGE: Aerial navigation by visual reference to landmarks, especially with the use of maps or charts. Also known as "piloting". Navigation by observation of ground features and the use of charts.

Example: A native of Washington, DC gives these directions to a visitor: "To reach the Capitol from the Navy Yard, follow the car tracks up 8th Street to Pennsylvania Avenue, turn left on Pennsylvania Avenue, and follow the car tracks past the Library of Congress to the Capitol. (piloting reference to landmarks)

Lindbergh flew the NYP by hand, without an autopilot, which did not exist at the time, and in so doing he steered with the rudder pedals, in a straight line, by using a Liquid Magnetic Compass in combination with an Earth Inductor Compass.

DEAD RECKONING: The estimating or determining of position by advancing an earlier known position by the application of direction and speed data. Or—Finding a ship's position by an estimate based on data recorded in the log, as speed and the time spent on a certain course, rather than by more precise means, such as astronomical (Celestial) observations or Loran or the modern GPS method.

Example: Washington, DC directions—"To reach the Capitol from the Navy Yard, drive north on 8th Street for seven blocks; turn northwest on Pennsylvania Avenue and continue for eight blocks to the Capitol." (determining your position by distance and direction from a known starting point.)

In this situation Lindbergh used both the Liquid Magnetic Compass as well as the Earth Inductor Compass (EIC.) At his side, near the right knee in the cockpit, was a "controller", with a crank, that he could turn to set his course, say 090 degrees. On the upper center of the instrument panel was an "indicator", with a vertical needle. By steering so that needle was centered after the compass course of 090 degrees was set with the controller, he was on course. He would use the Liquid Magnetic Compass as a back-up.

He changed course once every hour as he crossed the ocean as can be read in his book—*The Spirit of St. Louis.*

The EIC was his primary instrument for over the ocean navigation. The EIC was electrically operated. There being a windvane mounted on the top of the fuselage just behind the cockpit, with four cups, much like an anemometer, which drove a generator. The generator was connected to the controller, mechanically. The controller was, in turn, connected to the indicator on the instrument panel via an electrical wire.

Early on the morning of May 20th, the NYP is shown being towed from Curtiss Field over to Roosevelt Field for take-off. ***(Kenneth Lane)***

MAPS versus CHARTS

A *map* is chiefly a representation of land area, such as a road map (Rand-McNally etc.)

A *chart* represents water area (marine navigation) or land masses with an overlay of aerial navigation routes (airway.) Charts are a working base for the plotting of navigational data and for the graphic solution of the navigator's problems.

For the modern pilot, the chart is known as the Aeronautical Chart. They are available in various scales and types, either for VFR (visual flight rules) or IFR (instrument flight rules.)

FIRST HOUR

On May 20, 1927 the wheels of the Spirit of St. Louis left the muddy and wet ground of Roosevelt Field, Long Island, just east of New York City, and Lindbergh and the NYP were on their way to incredible fame. Time—6:51:30.2 a.m. EST. (7:54 EDT.) [1]

More than likely the question most asked by the people standing on that same wet, muddy ground that misty morning was—"Will he make it?" But this same question had been asked before by many people when seeing aviators, on either side of the Atlantic Ocean, attempting to make the big crossing.

But here was a young lad of twenty-five, an unknown airmail aviator, with a single engine airplane, built by an obscure West Coast manufacturer, attempting to fly over the largest body of water he had ever seen, without a navigator or extra engine, and with little or virtually no sleep.

To understand this situation realistically, one has to read Lindbergh's book, THE SPIRIT OF ST. LOUIS, in which his theory, philosophy, and keen planning come across quite clearly. There is really no need nor is it appropriate to attempt to tell of the details or philosophy of the "great flight." Therefore I will basically dwell on the mechanics of what actually took place during those long thirty-three and a half hours. Lindbergh's writing was absolutely magnificent, describing his flight with exciting and intriguing clarity.

Lindbergh's route of flight over Long Island after he took off, and before departing the North Shore of Long Island to cross Long Island Sound, was later known amongst Air Traffic Controllers as "The Lindbergh Line." Airliners flying to Europe would file their flight plans to their destination via the L/L (Lindy Line). In December 1957, an order was put into effect stating that the term 'Lindy Line' would no longer be used, as the new terms became NA 101, NA 102 (North Atlantic Track 101, etc.)

So what was the "Lindy Line"? Just after take-off Lindbergh had to make a shallow-banked turn to the right to avoid a tree-covered hill on a golf course. He had planned on a magnetic heading of 66 degrees for the first one hundred miles. His route of flight actually took him over New Mill Pond, Blydenburgh Park, just north-west of Hauppauge where Richard Brush of Hauppauge recalled that morning clearly—"I was walking just west of the pond and saw him. He was low, just above the tops of the trees, as a Daily News airplane flew along side taking pictures.

A few minutes later he was spotted over Smithtown, by Charles E. Rockwell, a now retired United Airlines 747 Captain. Captain Rockwell said—"Lindbergh flew right over Smithtown on his way to Paris. In fact, right over a tree on my farm. The family has always called it the Lindbergh tree." [2]

The last photograph taken of the NYP by an aerial newsmen in a Curtiss Oriole was as Lindbergh left the north shore at a place known as Miller Place, just east of Port Jefferson. The photo shows the sand dune cliffs of Miller Place, which looks much the same today.

From the time he took off, and to the end of that first hour, he flew on the center wing tank, and at 8:07 switched to the nose tank. His plan was to fly fifteen minutes on each of the five fuel tanks. This was to leave enough air space in each tank to prevent any possibility of overflow from either rough air or steep banked turns etc. Each drop of fuel was precious.

Kenneth Lane shown filling the fuel tanks with five gallon can and funnel at Roosevelt Field, May 20th. ***(Raymond Billings, England)***

His compass heading at that time was 65 degrees, altitude 200 feet, at an air speed of about 100 mph. He left the shore of Long Island slightly east of Port Jefferson and headed out over Long Island Sound.

The air was smooth over the water and soon he crossed the Connecticut shoreline at the mouth of the Connecticut River near the town of Saybrook, with the engine running at 1750 rpm. He climbed to 500 feet and for the first time on this flight pushed out the periscope on the left side to try it out. It could come in handy if he had to check for some unforeseen obstacle, tower, mountain or hill, without leaning out the window, and he could take off his goggles and just sit in his seat relaxed to avoid fatigue.

He crossed the Thames River, just north of the submarine capital, New London, and just south of Norwich, Connecticut

SECOND HOUR

Over New England

8:52 a.m.Compass course 63 degrees, altitude 600 feet, 102 mph, engine at 1750 rpm, now on main fuselage tank.

He had already covered one hundred miles. The weather began to clear.

"WHAT KIND OF MAN WOULD LIVE WHERE THERE IS NO DARING? I DON'T BELIEVE IN TAKING FOOLISH CHANCES, BUT NOTHING CAN BE ACCOMPLISHED WITHOUT TAKING ANY CHANCE AT ALL."

Charles A. Lindbergh

Roosevelt Field, May 20th. Lindbergh shaking hands with Charles Lawrence, president of the Wright Aeronautical Corp. Policeman with hand on door is Andrew Wilson. Carl Shory is securing one of the fuel caps. ***(Kenneth Lane)***

The NYP in position on the west end of Roosevelt Field for the take-off for Paris. ***(Cradle of Aviation Museum)***

With Providence, Rhode Island under his left wing, Lindbergh held a compass heading of 63 degrees. His course took him just south-east of Boston with Cape Cod visible on his right, a considerable distance away.

There has been much speculation over the years as to where he left the shores of the United States with reports from many people who claim they actually spotted him over their town or beach. However, this author has not been able to determine, either through photographs or official documentation the exact point of departure from the U.S. shores. It is only speculation that he left at roughly Cohasset, continuing out over Massachusetts Bay and skirting both Glouster and Rockport, before heading out over the Atlantic toward Nova Scotia in Canada. A Brockton, MA newspaper reported that he was sighted over Bryantville at 9:40 a.m.. They claim to have seen the NX—211 registration marking under the wing.

Lindbergh at this point was looking at about 250 nautical miles of overwater flying before hitting the coast of Nova Scotia. At this most crucial point in the flight, his theory and carefully planned navigation efforts would prove him either correct or inaccurate to some degree. He was now heading out over a large expanse of water, with not a single land point to check his accuracy. He was now on dead reckoning!

THIRD HOUR

Over the Atlantic Ocean

Compass course 70 degrees, altitude 150 feet, 107 mph, engine at 1760 rpm, now on nose tank.

Out over the Atlantic Ocean, with a 4000 foot ceiling and unlimited visibility, all mechanical systems appear to be running very well.

It was at this part of the flight that Lindbergh flew down to just above the ocean, as low as twenty feet, with his wheels less than a man's height above the waves. This was his method of checking his altimeter, as there was no way of knowing the present barometric pressure. Also by flying so close to the sea he could take advantage of, as we term it today, "ground effect", that invisible cushion of air near the surface of the earth. He was actually flying by use of the periscope, and had to be careful of his stick movements in the pitch mode. This is rather tedious work. He had to keep a sharp eye on his wheels to not roll them in the

Last photograph taken of the NYP over the north shore of Long Island, from Curtiss "Oriole" flown by Arthur Caperton. ***(Library of Congress)***

water, so he climbed to 100 feet altitude where he could relax a bit more.

He was now coming into what appeared to be a breaking up of the weather system, with scattered to broken cumulus clouds all around and limitless blue sky ahead.

FOURTH HOUR

Over the Atlantic Ocean

Compass course 73 degrees, altitude 50 feet, 104 mph, engine at 1725 rpm, now on the right wing tank.

With an unlimited ceiling Lindbergh figured he had been consuming about sixteen gallons of fuel per hour, which is three hundred pounds of fuel he had used since leaving New York.

He sipped some water from the canteen, hanging at his side. Under his seat were five sandwiches in a brown paper bag, but he did not feel hungry enough to bother with them at this point in the flight. Easier to stay awake on an empty stomach, he reasoned.

At eleven a.m. he climbed higher so that the strain of flying close to the water without touching it was lessened. He needed to conserve as much energy as possible this early in the trip.

He spotted a clump of brown mud sticking to the underside of the right wing, thrown up there during the muddy take-off at Roosevelt Field. Just a few feet away, that will have to ride with him all the way to Paris, and there's nothing he can do about it even though it caused parasite drag and useless extra weight. Why did he tear leaves from his notebook to save weight and now have that mud out there just out of arm's reach. He soon found another band of mud on the left wing. He slid the periscope back inside.

FIFTH HOUR

Approaches Nova Scotia

11:52 a.m. Compass course 78 degrees, altitude 200 feet, 103 mph, engine at 1725 rpm, now on the left wing tank.

Ceiling unlimited, a north-west wind giving a bit of a boost, although a south-west wind would be better.

It was eight minutes past noon when he noticed land ahead—Nova Scotia—and although he was quite tired at this point, seeing that beautiful but rugged coast-line boosted his spirits, and he was suddenly wide awake. This was a key point in the flight, and he could again check on the accuracy of his navigation.

He climbed higher to be in a better position to check for landmarks. At 1000 feet he saw a peninsula on his left, a cape on the right, and figured he had made his landfall at the mouth of St. Mary Bay, on the western coast about six miles south-east of his original course.

At this point he worked out his average speed which was 102 mph. He had covered a distance of 440 statute miles. He had held his course within two degrees of his original great circle plotted course line. It was less than half of the error he had originally planned for.

SIXTH HOUR

Over Nova Scotia

12:52 p.m. Compass course 82 degrees, altitude 700 feet, 101 mph, engine at 1700 rpm, and now on the nose tank.

Still with an unlimited ceiling, and over Nova Scotia with a west-north-west following wind at about 30 mph.

Lindbergh had taken off from Roosevelt Field with open windows, the Pyralin ones neatly stowed in their racks behind his right shoulder, and he wondered why he had not put them in to keep the air flow around that area of the fuselage clean. They were actually figured in the performance curves at San Diego, proving

*This is the actual tie that Lindbergh wore with his white shirt on the flight from New York to Paris. The tie still exists at Yale University, New Haven, Connecticut. **(Charles Augustus Lindbergh Papers, Manuscripts and Archives, Yale University Library)***

their aerodynamic weight advantage. They were worth more than their weight in fuel. They would smooth out the flow of air along the side of the fuselage.

He spotted rain squalls ahead, and flew through some air turbulence, he throttled back to 1625 rpm and let the air speed drop to 90 mph. He was then at 1500 feet. He fought the storm, changed course to stay away from more rain and turbulence and loss of visibility, and eventually steered back on course.

SEVENTH HOUR

Over Nova Scotia

1:52 p.m. Compass course 84 degrees, altitude 900 feet, 100 mph, engine at 1675 rpm, fuel feeding from the main fuselage tank.

The wind calmed to 10 mph and from the south-south-east, a good omen and a good boost to Lindbergh's ground speed.

His initial weather report said it would be clearing along the North American coast—and it had, with patches of blue sky appearing ahead. He had forty hours of fuel remaining in the tanks.

EIGHTH HOUR

Over Nova Scotia

2:52 p.m. Compass course 89 degrees, altitude 600 feet, 96 mph, engine at 1650 rpm, fuel feeding still from the main fuselage tank.

Wind was out of the south-south-west now, at 15 mph, and he had unlimited visibility. Fog ahead on the horizon.

Lindbergh checked his magneto switches and all was O.K. He climbed to check his position with some landmarks on the ground, hoping they would be found on his chart. It was extremely critical to pinpoint his position before flying out over the largest expanse of ocean. The fog was only a narrow strip of clouds near the surface along the shore line.

He approached the coast of Cape Breton Island after leaving the main island of Nova Scotia at Chedabucto Bay. He was probably in the vicinity of what is today Petit de grat Island, just southeast of Port Hawkesbury.

He continued up the south-east coast line, and thought back to Curtiss Field and the girl who gave him the mirror as the earth-inductor compass needle leaned to the right. He checked his compass heading with the liquid compass and the mirror showed 94 degrees.

NINTH HOUR

Cape Breton Island

3:52 p.m. Compass course 91 degrees, altitude 500 feet, 94 mph, engine at 1625 rpm, fuel feeding from main fuselage tank.

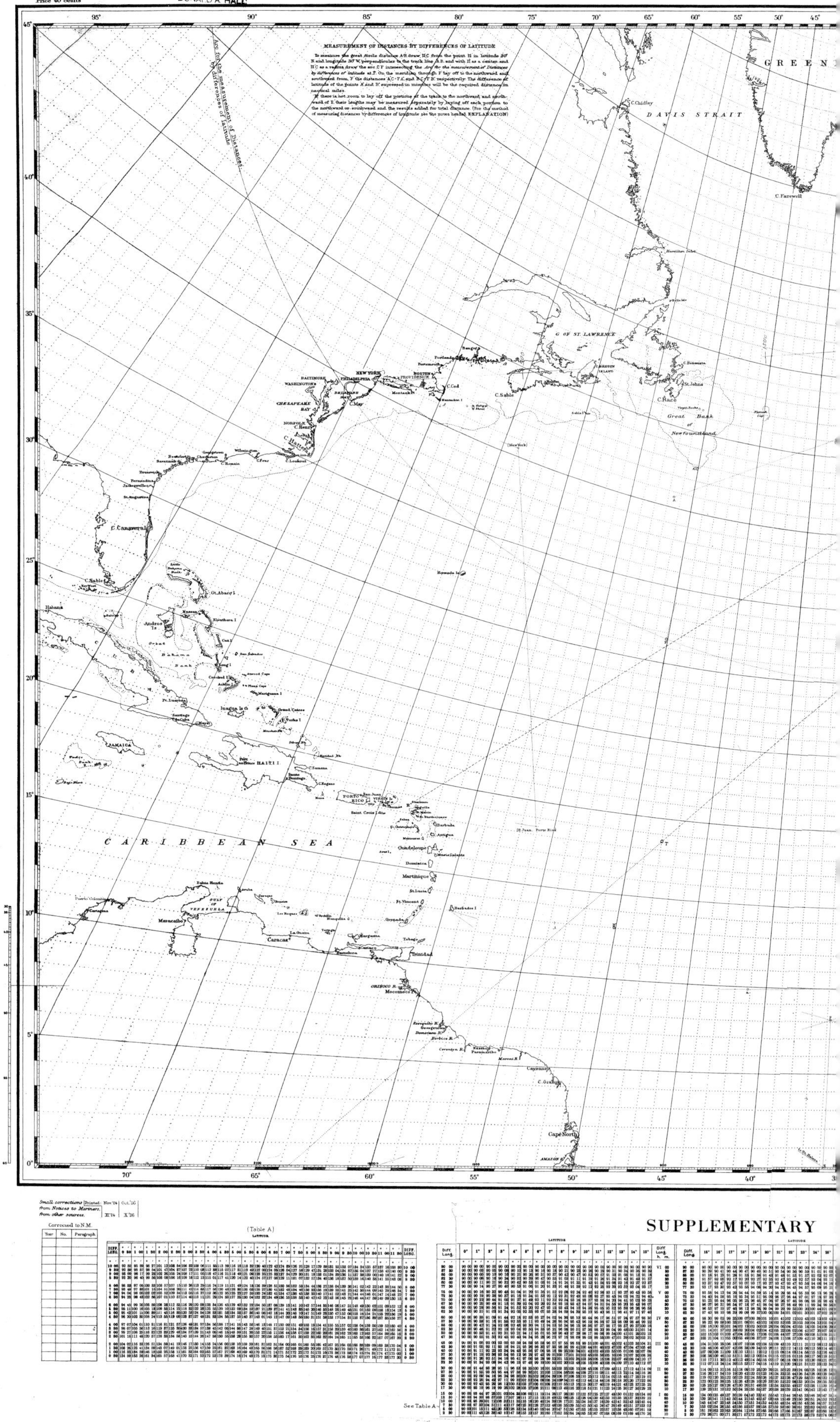

No. 1280
Price 40 cents
DONALD A. HALL
GREAT CIRCLE SAILING CHA
MEASUREMENT OF DISTANCES BY DIFFERENCES OF LATITUDE
To measure the great circle distance A'B draw H'C from the point H in latitude 30° N. and longitude 30° W. perpendicular to the track line A'B and with H as a center and H'C as a radius draw the arc C'F intersecting the Arc for the measurement of Distances by differences of latitude at F. On the meridian through F lay off to the northward and southward from F the distances A'C=FA' and B'C=FB' respectively. The difference of latitude of the points A' and B' expressed in minutes will be the required distance in nautical miles.
If there is not room to lay off the portions of the track to the northward and southward of F their lengths may be measured separately by laying off each portion to the northward or southward and the results added for total distance. (For the method of measuring distances by differences of longitude see the notes headed EXPLANATION)
Arc for the measurement of Distances by differences of latitude
DAVIS STRAIT
C. Chidley
C. Farewell
G OF ST. LAWRENCE
NEW YORK
PHILADELPHIA
BALTIMORE
WASHINGTON
BOSTON
PROVIDENCE
Portland
C. Cod
C. Sable
C. Race
St. Johns
Great Bank of Newfoundland
CHESAPEAKE BAY
DELAWARE BAY
C. May
NORFOLK
C. Henry
C. Hatteras
C. Lookout
Wilmington
Charleston
Savannah
Brunswick
Fernandina
Jacksonville
St. Augustine
C. Canaveral
C. Sable
Habana
Andros I.
Gt. Abaco I.
Nassau
Eleuthera I.
Great Bahama Bank
Inagua Is.
JAMAICA
HAITI I.
Santo Domingo
C. Samana
PORTO RICO
Saint Croix I.
Bermuda Is.
Guadeloupe
Dominica
Martinique
St. Lucia
St. Vincent
Barbados I.
Grenada
Tobago
Trinidad
CARIBBEAN SEA
GULF OF VENEZUELA
Maracaibo
Caracas
Margarita
Barcelona
ORINOCO R.
Georgetown
Cayenne
C. Orange
Cape North
AMAZON R.
95° 90° 85° 80° 75° 70° 65° 60° 55° 50° 45°
70° 65° 60° 55° 50° 45° 40°
45° 40° 35° 30° 25° 20° 15° 10° 5° 0°
Small corrections from Notices to Mariners, from other sources. Printed: Nov. '24, Oct. '26; II '24, X '26
Corrected to N.M.
Year | No. | Paragraph
(Table A)
LATITUDE
DIFF. LONG.
SUPPLEMENTARY
See Table A

'HE NORTH ATLANTIC OCEAN

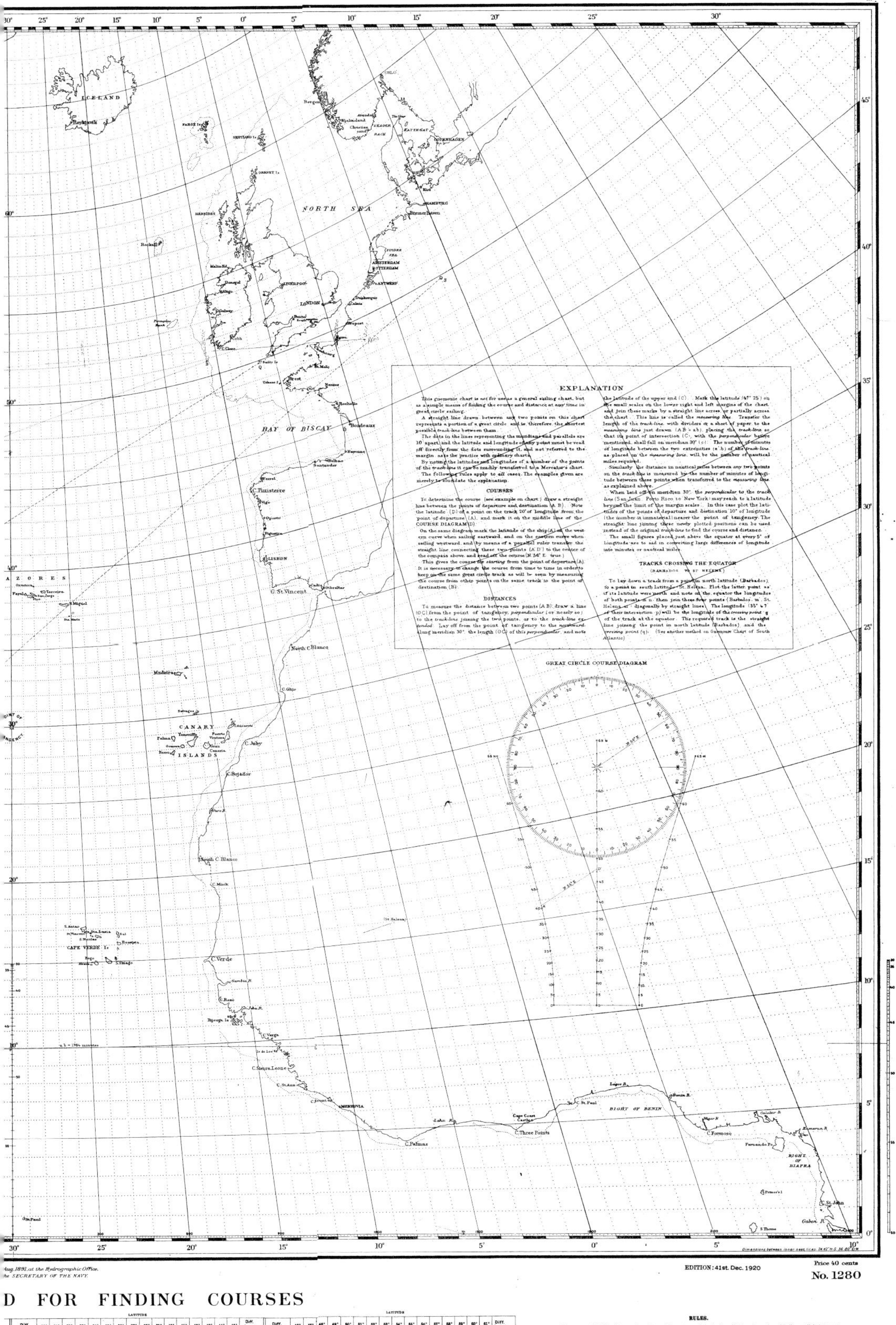

D FOR FINDING COURSES

Diff. Long. ° '	30°	31°	32°	33°	34°	35°	36°	37°	38°	39°	40°	41°	42°	43°	44°	45°	Diff. Long. h m
90 00	90 00	90 00	90 00	90 00	90 00	90 00	90 00	90 00	90 00	90 00	90 00	90 00	90 00	90 00	90 00	90 00	VI 00
87 30	91 15	91 17	91 20	91 22	91 24	91 26	91 28	91 30	91 32	91 34	91 36	91 38	91 40	91 42	91 44	91 46	50
85 00	92 30	92 35	92 39	92 44	92 48	92 52	92 57	93 01	93 05	93 09	93 13	93 17	93 21	93 25	93 29	93 32	40
82 30	93 46	93 53	93 59	94 06	94 13	94 19	94 25	94 32	94 38	94 44	94 50	94 56	95 02	95 08	95 14	95 19	30
80 00	95 02	95 11	95 20	95 29	95 38	95 47	95 55	96 03	96 12	96 20	96 28	96 36	96 44	96 51	96 59	97 06	20
77 30	96 19	96 31	96 42	96 53	97 04	97 15	97 25	97 36	97 46	97 57	98 07	98 17	98 26	98 36	98 45	98 55	10
75 00	97 38	97 51	98 05	98 18	98 31	98 44	98 57	99 10	99 22	99 34	99 46	99 58	100 10	100 21	100 33	100 44	V 00
72 30	98 58	99 14	99 29	99 45	100 00	100 16	100 30	100 45	100 59	101 13	101 27	101 41	101 55	102 08	102 21	102 34	50
70 00	100 19	100 37	100 56	101 13	101 30	101 48	102 05	102 21	102 38	102 54	103 10	103 26	103 41	103 56	104 11	104 26	40
67 30	101 42	102 02	102 23	102 43	103 02	103 22	103 41	104 00	104 18	104 37	104 55	105 12	105 30	105 46	106 03	106 20	30
65 00	103 07	103 30	103 53	104 15	104 37	104 58	105 20	105 41	106 01	106 21	106 41	107 01	107 20	107 39	107 57	108 15	20
62 30	104 35	105 01	105 25	105 50	106 14	106 37	107 01	107 24	107 46	108 08	108 30	108 51	109 12	109 33	109 53	110 13	10
60 00	106 06	106 34	107 01	107 27	107 53	108 19	108 45	109 10	109 34	109 58	110 22	110 45	111 07	111 29	111 51	112 12	IV 00
57 30	107 40	108 10	108 39	109 08	109 36	110 04	110 32	110 59	111 25	111 51	112 16	112 41	113 05	113 29	113 52	114 15	50
55 00	109 18	109 50	110 21	110 53	111 23	111 53	112 22	112 51	113 19	113 47	114 14	114 40	115 06	115 32	115 56	116 20	40
52 30	110 59	111 34	112 08	112 41	113 13	113 45	114 17	114 47	115 17	115 47	116 15	116 43	117 11	117 37	118 04	118 29	30
50 00	112 46	113 22	113 58	114 34	115 08	115 42	116 15	116 48	117 19	117 50	118 21	118 50	119 19	119 47	120 14	120 41	20
47 30	114 37	115 16	115 54	116 31	117 08	117 44	118 18	118 53	119 26	119 58	120 30	121 01	121 31	122 00	122 28	122 56	10
45 00	116 34	117 15	117 55	118 34	119 13	119 50	120 27	121 02	121 37	122 11	122 44	123 16	123 47	124 18	124 47	125 16	III 00
42 30	118 37	119 20	120 03	120 44	121 23	122 03	122 41	123 18	123 54	124 29	125 03	125 36	126 08	126 40	127 10	127 39	50
40 00	120 47	121 32	122 16	122 59	123 41	124 21	125 01	125 39	126 16	126 52	127 27	128 01	128 34	129 06	129 37	130 07	40
37 30	123 05	123 52	124 38	125 22	126 05	126 47	127 27	128 06	128 45	129 21	129 57	130 32	131 05	131 38	132 09	132 40	30
35 00	125 32	126 20	127 07	127 53	128 37	129 20	130 01	130 41	131 19	131 57	132 33	133 08	133 42	134 15	134 46	135 17	20
32 30	128 08	128 57	129 45	130 32	131 17	132 00	132 42	133 22	134 01	134 39	135 15	135 51	136 24	136 57	137 29	137 59	10
30 00	130 54	131 44	132 33	133 20	134 05	134 49	135 31	136 11	136 50	137 28	138 04	138 39	139 13	139 45	140 16	140 46	II 00
27 30	133 51	134 42	135 31	136 18	137 03	137 46	138 28	139 08	139 47	140 24	141 00	141 34	142 07	142 39	143 09	143 39	50
25 00	137 00	137 50	138 39	139 26	140 10	140 53	141 34	142 14	142 52	143 28	144 03	144 36	145 08	145 38	146 08	146 36	40
22 30	140 22	141 12	141 59	142 45	143 29	144 10	144 50	145 28	146 04	146 39	147 12	147 44	148 14	148 44	149 12	149 38	30
20 00	143 57	144 45	145 31	146 15	146 56	147 36	148 14	148 50	149 25	149 57	150 29	150 59	151 27	151 55	152 21	152 46	20
17 30	147 46	148 32	149 15	149 56	150 35	151 12	151 47	152 21	152 53	153 23	153 52	154 20	154 46	155 11	155 35	155 58	10
15 00	151 49	152 31	153 11	153 48	154 24	154 58	155 30	156 00	156 29	156 56	157 22	157 47	158 11	158 33	158 54	159 15	I 00
12 30	156 05	156 43	157 18	157 51	158 22	158 52	159 20	159 47	160 12	160 36	160 58	161 20	161 40	162 00	162 18	162 36	50
10 00	160 34	161 06	161 36	162 04	162 30	162 55	163 18	163 40	164 01	164 21	164 40	164 57	165 14	165 30	165 45	166 00	40
7 30	165 15	165 40	166 03	166 25	166 45	167 04	167 23	167 40	167 56	168 11	168 26	168 39	168 52	169 04	169 16	169 27	30
5 00	170 06	170 22	170 38	170 52	171 06	171 20	171 32	171 44	171 55	172 06	172 15	172 24	172 33	172 41	172 49	172 57	20
2 30	175 01	175 09	175 17	175 25	175 32	175 39	175 45	175 51	175 57	176 02	176 07	176 12	176 16	176 20	176 24	176 28	10

Diff. Long. ° '	46°	47°	48°	49°	50°	51°	52°	53°	54°	55°	56°	57°	58°	59°	60°	61°	Diff. Long. h m
90 00	90 00	90 00	90 00	90 00	90 00	90 00	90 00	90 00	90 00	90 00	90 00	90 00	90 00	90 00	90 00	90 00	VI 00
87 30	91 48	91 50	91 52	91 53	91 55	91 57	91 58	92 00	92 01	92 03	92 04	92 06	92 07	92 09	92 10	92 11	50
85 00	93 36	93 40	93 43	93 47	93 50	93 53	93 57	94 00	94 03	94 06	94 09	94 12	94 15	94 17	94 20	94 23	40
82 30	95 25	95 30	95 35	95 40	95 46	95 50	95 55	96 00	96 05	96 09	96 14	96 18	96 22	96 26	96 30	96 34	30
80 00	97 14	97 21	97 28	97 35	97 42	97 48	97 55	98 01	98 07	98 13	98 19	98 25	98 30	98 36	98 41	98 46	20
77 30	99 04	99 13	99 21	99 30	99 38	99 47	99 55	100 02	100 10	100 18	100 25	100 32	100 39	100 46	100 52	100 58	10
75 00	100 55	101 05	101 16	101 26	101 36	101 46	101 55	102 05	102 14	102 23	102 31	102 40	102 48	102 56	103 04	103 11	V 00
72 30	102 47	102 59	103 11	103 23	103 35	103 46	103 57	104 08	104 19	104 29	104 39	104 49	104 58	105 07	105 16	105 25	50
70 00	104 40	104 54	105 08	105 22	105 35	105 47	106 00	106 13	106 24	106 36	106 47	106 59	107 09	107 20	107 30	107 39	40
67 30	106 36	106 51	107 07	107 22	107 36	107 51	108 05	108 18	108 32	108 45	108 57	109 09	109 21	109 32	109 44	109 55	30
65 00	108 33	108 50	109 07	109 23	109 39	109 55	110 11	110 26	110 40	110 54	111 08	111 22	111 35	111 47	111 59	112 11	20
62 30	110 32	110 51	111 09	111 27	111 44	112 02	112 18	112 34	112 50	113 06	113 21	113 35	113 49	114 03	114 16	114 28	10
60 00	112 33	112 53	113 13	113 33	113 52	114 10	114 28	114 45	115 02	115 19	115 35	115 50	116 05	116 20	116 34	116 48	IV 00
57 30	114 37	114 59	115 20	115 41	116 01	116 20	116 39	116 58	117 16	117 33	117 51	118 07	118 23	118 38	118 53	119 08	50
55 00	116 44	117 07	117 29	117 51	118 12	118 33	118 53	119 13	119 32	119 50	120 08	120 25	120 42	120 58	121 14	121 29	40
52 30	118 54	119 18	119 42	120 05	120 27	120 49	121 10	121 30	121 50	122 09	122 28	122 46	123 03	123 20	123 36	123 52	30
50 00	121 07	121 32	121 57	122 21	122 44	123 07	123 28	123 50	124 10	124 30	124 49	125 08	125 26	125 44	126 00	126 17	20
47 30	123 23	123 50	124 15	124 40	125 04	125 27	125 50	126 12	126 33	126 54	127 13	127 33	127 51	128 09	128 26	128 43	10
45 00	125 44	126 11	126 37	127 03	127 27	127 51	128 14	128 37	128 58	129 19	129 40	129 59	130 18	130 36	130 54	131 10	III 00
42 30	128 08	128 36	129 03	129 29	129 54	130 18	130 42	131 04	131 27	131 48	132 08	132 28	132 47	133 05	133 23	133 40	50
40 00	130 36	131 04	131 32	131 58	132 24	132 48	133 12	133 35	133 57	134 19	134 39	134 59	135 18	135 37	135 54	136 11	40
37 30	133 09	133 38	134 05	134 32	134 57	135 22	135 46	136 09	136 31	136 52	137 13	137 33	137 52	138 10	138 28	138 44	30
35 00	135 46	136 15	136 42	137 09	137 34	137 59	138 23	138 45	139 07	139 29	139 49	140 08	140 27	140 45	141 03	141 19	20
32 30	138 28	138 57	139 24	139 50	140 15	140 39	141 03	141 25	141 47	142 08	142 28	142 47	143 05	143 22	143 40	143 56	10
30 00	141 15	141 43	142 09	142 35	143 00	143 24	143 46	144 08	144 29	144 49	145 09	145 27	145 45	146 02	146 19	146 34	II 00
27 30	144 06	144 34	144 59	145 24	145 48	146 11	146 33	146 54	147 14	147 34	147 53	148 10	148 27	148 44	148 59	149 14	50
25 00	147 03	147 29	147 54	148 17	148 40	149 02	149 23	149 43	150 02	150 21	150 39	150 55	151 12	151 27	151 42	151 56	40
22 30	150 04	150 28	150 52	151 14	151 36	151 57	152 16	152 35	152 53	153 11	153 27	153 43	153 58	154 13	154 25	154 39	30
20 00	153 10	153 33	153 54	154 15	154 35	154 54	155 13	155 30	155 47	156 03	156 18	156 32	156 46	157 00	157 12	157 24	20
17 30	156 20	156 41	157 01	157 20	157 38	157 55	158 12	158 27	158 42	158 57	159 11	159 24	159 36	159 48	160 00	160 11	10
15 00	159 34	159 53	160 10	160 27	160 43	160 58	161 13	161 27	161 41	161 53	162 05	162 17	162 28	162 38	162 49	162 58	I 00
12 30	162 52	163 08	163 23	163 38	163 52	164 05	164 17	164 29	164 41	164 51	165 02	165 12	165 21	165 30	165 38	165 47	50
10 00	166 14	166 27	166 39	166 51	167 02	167 13	167 23	167 33	167 42	167 51	168 00	168 08	168 15	168 23	168 29	168 36	40
7 30	169 38	169 48	169 57	170 06	170 15	170 23	170 31	170 38	170 45	170 52	170 59	171 05	171 11	171 16	171 21	171 26	30
5 00	173 04	173 10	173 17	173 23	173 29	173 35	173 40	173 45	173 50	173 54	173 58	174 03	174 07	174 10	174 14	174 17	20
2 30	176 32	176 35	176 38	176 41	176 44	176 47	176 50	176 53	176 55	176 57	176 59	177 01	177 03	177 05	177 07	177 09	10

RULES.

Draw a straight line between the points of departure and destination (QR), and produce this line until it intersects the Equator, or, if the line produced does not intersect the Equator within the limits of the chart, as in the case presented of the great-circle track between the Scilly Islands and Sombrero plot the latitude of the point of departure on any selected meridian (S) and the latitude of the point of destination on a meridian (T) whose difference of longitude from the selected meridian is equal to the difference of longitude between the points of departure and destination, and, having connected S and T by a straight line, produce this line until it intersects the Equator. Note the difference of longitude between the intersection thus found on the Equator and the selected meridian on which the latitude of the point of departure is plotted, and, in the marginal tables, opposite the difference of longitude, if less than 90°, and under the latitude of the point of departure, will be found the true bearing toward the intersection of the track with the Equator, reckoned from the North Pole in north latitude and from the South Pole in south latitude through 180° toward the eastward or westward according as the intersection of the track with the Equator lies to the eastward or westward of the meridian on which the latitude of the point of departure has been plotted. If the difference of longitude is greater than 90°, enter the marginal tables with the remainder obtained by subtracting it from 180° and the remainder obtained by subtracting the tabulated quantity from 180 will give the true bearing toward the intersection of the track with the Equator.

If the intersection with the Equator is on the same side of the point of departure as the destination, then the true bearing thus found from the tables will be the true course to be steered; but if the intersection with the Equator and the point of destination are on the opposite sides of the point of departure, this quantity subtracted from 180° will give the course to be steered.

If the point of departure is on the Equator, extend the track line until it passes tangent to a parallel of latitude, this will be the latitude of the vertex of the great-circle, and the remainder found by subtracting it from 90° will give the course to be steered.

(The selected meridian of S, instead of being chosen on this chart, may be taken on any one of the series of Great Circle Sailing Charts of the several oceans.)

Air was smooth as he neared the end of Cape Breton Island, about to fly out over the ocean again. Ceiling unlimited. Next landfall should be Newfoundland. Visibility was unlimited.

TENTH HOUR

Over the Atlantic Ocean

4:52 p.m. Compass course 102 degrees, altitude 150 feet, 95 mph, engine at 1600 rpm, fuel feeding from the nose tank.

Ceiling and visibility still unlimited, air smooth as he neared Newfoundland.

He centered the earth inductor compass needle and lowered his altitude to get a closer look at the ice fields that appeared in the ocean. He drained a few drops of fuel from the Lunkenheimer valve to check for dirt and water. The fuel was clear.

As fuel was burned from the tanks the nose became lighter, and Lindbergh wondered why the airplane had a tendency to gain altitude. He re-adjusted the stabilizer trim lever by one single notch. This relieved forward stick pressure.

He approached Newfoundland just south of the French islands of Miquelon and Saint Pierre and flew along the Burin peninsula coast on the southern side over Placentia Bay

ELEVENTH HOUR

Placentia Bay

5:52 p.m. Compass course 100 degrees, altitude 300 feet, 92 mph, engine at 1600 rpm, fuel feeding from the main fuselage tank.

Ceiling and visibility unlimited. Lindbergh was flying over the center of Placentia Bay and climbed higher as he approached Avalon Peninsula, just south of St. Johns.

TWELFTH HOUR

Over Newfoundland

6:52 p.m. Compass course 99 degrees, altitude 700 feet, 98 mph, engine at 1650 rpm, fuel feeding from the main fuselage tank.

Visibility ten miles, ceiling unlimited. Nearing sunset. Coming up on the nose was Conception Bay.

He took another check of his ground speed and found he was averaging 100 mph. The wind was out of the west at 30 mph.

He came over the city of St. Johns and soon headed out over the open sea. He checked both magnetos and all was well. Engine running smoothly.

Lindbergh realized at this point in the flight that he was ninety miles south of the original great circle route drawn on his chart. He would have to make up for this and began checking the waves on the ocean. He estimated the wind to be about thirty mph and the direction roughly out of the west. He decided to correct his compass heading ten degrees left or northward.

THIRTEENTH HOUR

Over the Atlantic Ocean

7:52 p.m. Compass course 97 degrees, altitude 800 feet, 90 mph, engine at 1625 rpm, fuel feeding from the fuselage tank.

Visibility five miles, above fog with ceiling unlimited.

He was at the one third point now, with two thirds to go, about 2400 miles. He had flown an hour and a quarter from each of the outer wing tanks, and a quarter hour from the center wing tank. He planned to run through the night on the fuselage and nose tanks, leaving fuel in the wing tanks for reserve. That way he could feed by gravity from the wing tanks in case the fuel pump for the fuselage tanks decided to quit or malfunction. He also reasoned that if a leak should develop in either of the fuselage tanks, every hour he used from those tanks would put him that much ahead. Logical thinking, though by the same reasoning leaks could develop in wing tanks too.

He climbed to 2000 feet to stay above the fog. His airspeed held at 95 mph as he continued into the dark night. At about 8:35 pm. he had climbed to 5000 feet and was still climbing above billowy clouds, but they seemed to climb also. His engine speed had been 1625 rpm, and he moved the throttle forward slightly to indicate 1650 rpm, pulling the nose up and re-setting the stabilizer to compensate for the fuel loss.

With the climb into thinner air he realized that this thin air had caused the air cushion that he sat on to expand, pushing him up to where his head touched the ribs of the sky-light. He opened the valve for a few seconds, so the cushion would not burst.

He climbed further to 7500 feet with a clear sky above and nearing the next hour check point.

Policeman Andrew Wilson, who helped Lindbergh close the door on the NYP before flight. (Mrs. Ellen W. Dioguardi)

FOURTEENTH HOUR

Over the Atlantic Ocean

8:52 p.m. Compass course 99 degrees, altitude 9300 feet, 85 mph, engine at 1700 rpm, fuel being fed from the fuselage nose tank.

Visibility rather hazy, ceiling unlimited above clouds.

He completed the log entry and turned off the light of his flashlight.

Lindbergh continued to climb, following the clouds as they rose and realized there must be a storm ahead.

At nine o'clock he had reached an altitude of 10,000 feet, yet the clouds were still rising. It was cold, and he had to zip up his flying suit. He put on his mittens and wool-lined helmet.

The clouds had become quite billowy, with mountains and valleys in all directions, and much of it higher than he. One cloud ahead appeared to be a thunderhead with a huge mushroom on top. The Spirit of St. Louis bounced around as he entered the clouds and the generated turbulence. This called for all the attention he could give to his instruments.

He had now climbed up to 10,500 feet, and he briefly put his bare hand outside and felt stinging pinpricks. When he checked the outside with his flashlight he discovered ice on the strut and thought about the rest of the airplane picking up this ice and that the air speed indicator pitot tube and venturi may clog as a result.

After about ten minutes he emerged from the cloud and decided it was a thunderhead after all. But now he was in the clear, but still carrying some ice on the leading edge of the struts and wing.

FIFTEENTH HOUR

Over the Atlantic Ocean

9:52 p.m. Compass course 99 degrees, altitude 10,500 feet, 87 mph, engine at 1700 rpm, fuel feeding from main fuselage tank.

Visibility still night haze, unlimited ceiling above the clouds.

It appeared the ice was beginning to dissipate and visibility ahead was clear.

He checked the earth inductor compass and found he had drifted south and took up a new heading to get back on the great circle route.

The earth inductor compass had begun to act unusual with fluctuating movements of the needle, overshooting the longitudinal axis indicator (lubber line) and continued to drop down on the other side.

It was the first time Lindbergh noticed the instrument acting other than normal. He wondered if the newly designed navigation instrument was beginning to fail, just when he needed it most, or if his flying was not up to par due to fatigue.

He projected his flashlight beam upward to the liquid compass and found it too was swinging more than usual, so he flew straight and level and held the airplane as steady as possible. The liquid compass continued to swing from side to side.

The liquid compass card was rocking through an arc of more than sixty degrees, sometimes more than ninety degrees. Lindbergh wondered if he was entering a magnetic storm of some kind. He gave up on the EIC and concentrated on the liquid compass, as it would remain fairly steady for several seconds between oscillations. He set his heading and concentrated on holding a steady heading.

The liquid compass luminous figures were not quite bright enough in the night to navigate by so he used his flashlight, which in turn made it difficult to see the stars outside and the other instruments within the cockpit all at the same time.

As he flew around thunderheads, in an unknown wind, with an erratic compass, he wondered what his chances were of making landfall on the southern Irish coast, if he found a coast at all. And on top of it all, could he stay awake.

As he stared out the left window he noticed the stars were dropping lower and valleys between the thunderheads were widening. He did not have to look straight up to see the stars in order to hold course or to find a more stable point in space. He noticed the clouds becoming much sharper in contrast to the background, and the sky generally a bit brighter. Perhaps it was time for the moon to come into view, and he looked out the south window on his right. There the night had a much deeper shade.

Because of the compass situation he still wondered if he was drifting off course and was heading for Africa rather than Europe. However, the North Star was in the approximate correct position high on his left, which was as it should be.

According to his chart, he had been heading more and more eastward as he followed the great-circle route, cutting each meridian at a greater angle than the last, changing course one or two degrees clockwise every hour through the previous day and that night.

SIXTEENTH HOUR

Over the Atlantic Ocean

10:52 p.m. Compass course 102 degrees, altitude 10,200 feet, 86 mph, engine at 1675 rpm, fuel feeding from main fuselage tank.

Visibility unlimited but clouds all around, and unlimited above clouds.

He was now halfway between New York and Ireland and had covered 1500 miles.

Arthur L. Caperton, the pilot of the Curtiss "Oriole" that carried the photographer, George Wies, to take the last pictures of the NYP as it headed for Paris. (Nat Quinn)

The compasses were still not acting normal, and he had steered off course slightly, as he noticed the moon a bit higher but too far to the north. Having to watch the stars more intently as a result of the compasses not doing the full job, his neck was a bit stiff and cramped and rest was highly needed.

He cupped his hands out the window, re-directing the cool air toward his face and breathed this fresh air into his mouth to stay awake and more alert.

SEVENTEENTH HOUR

Over the Atlantic Ocean

11:52 p.m. Compass course 103 degrees, altitude 10,000 feet, 90 mph, engine at 1675 rpm, fuel feeding from main fuselage tank.

Visibility unlimited beyond the clouds and ceiling unlimited above the clouds.

Two o'clock in the morning New York time, and he had changed course about thirty degrees longitude since leaving Roosevelt Field.

Outside there appeared to be cirrus, cumulus and stratus formations, separating into layers and isolated masses, with stars in between, to help with the navigation.

The liquid compass settled down to a more reasonable indication and steady reading. Also the EIC no longer wobbled but showed a steady indication.

He checked the wing struts with his flashlight and there was no ice. It was getting warmer in the cockpit, so he removed his mittens, and noticed the outside air felt tropical. He put his mittens on the floor and unzipped his flying suit. Perhaps he had crossed the Gulf Stream border and the Labrador current with its icebergs and cold arctic climate were well behind.

At this point his mixture control was well advanced into the rich position, and the engine was throttled back as far as possible.

EIGHTEENTH HOUR

Over the Atlantic Ocean

12:52 a.m. Compass course 106 degrees, altitude 9600 feet, 88 mph, engine at 1625 rpm, fuel feeding from fuselage main tank.

Visibility unlimited outside of clouds, and ceiling showed a high thin overcast above the clouds.

Lindbergh calculated that in another hour he would be halfway to Paris.

As he flew into the dawn he had an uncontrollable desire to sleep. This was his greatest test of endurance; to give in or continue on.

He pulled some cotton out of his ears, fluffed it out and replaced it in each ear again. He continued to try to fly the airplane and do little exercises to stay awake and alert. He removed his helmet, rubbed his head and drank some water from the canteen. He looked at the bag with the sandwiches in it, lying on the floor unopened since take-off.

It was at this point that he thought of his decision to keep the Spirit of St. Louis unstable-stable and build in a safety factor guarding against excessive errors.

He was so sleepy he could barely welcome the diversion of pulling out his pencil and putting the log sheet on his lap to enter the necessary information for the next hour's report.

NINETEENTH HOUR

Over the Atlantic Ocean

1:52 a.m. Compass heading 96 degrees, altitude 9000 feet, 87 mph, engine at 1625 rpm, fuel feeding from the fuselage nose tank.

Visibility unlimited beyond the clouds, and ceiling unlimited above clouds. Wind direction and velocity unknown.

This was the "half way point", which he planned to celebrate. He had been running a long time on the main fuselage tank and wondered if he should switch to another tank. He put another pencil mark on the instrument board to register the eighteenth hour of fuel consumed. He moved the valves to start fuel flowing from the nose tank and stop fuel from the main fuselage tank.

TWENTIETH HOUR

Over the Atlantic Ocean

2:52 a.m. Compass heading 96 degrees, altitude 8800 feet, 89 mph, engine at 1625 rpm, fuel feeding from fuselage nose tank.

Visibility variable, ceiling variable while flying between cloud layers.

He had last re-set his altimeter near the ocean at Newfoundland (eight hours ago), and now that dawn had broken and light had increased he needed to check the altimeter again. He descended and leveled out at 8000 feet, and noticed the ocean covered with ripples, which indicated a heavy sea.

He trimmed the stabilizer to nose up and continued to descend. His air speed indicator showed 110 - 120 - 140 mph, and he closed the mixture control to full rich and throttled back, just enough to keep the engine warm and clear. He spiraled down through the clouds. His air cushion became flat with the increase of outside pressure and he began to feel the wicker of the seat.

As he neared the ocean the waves appeared high; great waves, with streaks of foam indicating a gale wind from the northwest. A tail wind, about the same direction as he had off the coast of Newfoundland at dusk yesterday, was much stronger now.

He descended lower to check the wind speed and estimated it to be fifty or sixty mph. The ocean was covered in whitecaps and ragged strips of foam. He reset his altimeter to sea level zero altitude.

TWENTY-FIRST HOUR

Over the Atlantic Ocean

Hours of fuel consumed

Nose Tank
¼ + ~~////~~

Left Wing	Center Wing Tank	Right Wing
¼ + /	¼ +	¼ + /

Fuselage Tank
~~////~~ ~~////~~ /

TWENTY-SECOND HOUR

Over the Atlantic Ocean

Hours of fuel consumed

Nose Tank
¼ + ~~////~~ //

Left Wing	Center Wing Tank	Right Wing
¼ + /	¼ +	¼ + /

Fuselage Tank
~~////~~ ~~////~~ /

Time 4:52 a.m. He made a mark under the nose tank with his pencil and switched to the right wing tank.

He descended to the ocean again until his wheels were almost clipping the salt spray, and then he climbed once more to a safer altitude, above the bits of fog below.

TWENTY-THIRD HOUR

Over the Atlantic Ocean

Hours of fuel consumed

Nose Tank
¼ + ~~////~~ //

Left Wing	Center Wing Tank	Right Wing
¼ + /	¼ +	¼ + /

Fuselage Tank
~~////~~ ~~////~~ /

Time 6:05 a.m. Altitude about 500 feet.

Behind him somewhere in the fuselage a drift indicator was lying in its rack. But he could not use it as it would require his leaning back and loosing control of the airplane.

TWENTY-FOURTH HOUR

Over the Atlantic Ocean

Hours of fuel consumed

Nose Tank
¼ + ~~////~~ //

Left Wing	Center Wing Tank	Right Wing
¼ + //	¼ +	¼ + //

Fuselage Tank
~~////~~ ~~////~~ /

Air speed indicator showed a little over 90 mph. No readings were taken at this time, and he only marked one more score on the instrument board.

The sun was shining into the cockpit and making it quite warm now. He took deep sips of water from his canteen and had a whole gallon put away for emergency in another container. He zipped open his flying suit and cupped his hands again outside to bring in cool air to his face. It was then 7:20 a.m.

TWENTY-FIFTH HOUR

Over the Atlantic Ocean

Hours of fuel consumed

Nose Tank
¼ + ~~////~~ //

Left Wing
¼ + ///

Center Wing Tank
¼ +

Right Wing
¼ + ///

Fuselage Tank
~~////~~ ~~////~~ /

Time 7:52 a.m. on his watch.

At this point he shifted back to the right wing tank and marked another pencil line on the instrument panel paper.

He unfolded the chart on his lap to re-examine his course. He then concentrated on what had happened to his navigation, his course, during the previous night, with all the deviations to avoid storms, to check wind and direction. Where was he, he wondered. What were his chances of hitting the Irish coast?

TWENTY-SIXTH HOUR

Over the Atlantic Ocean

Hours of fuel consumed

Nose Tank
¼ + ~~////~~ //

Left Wing
¼ + ///

Center Wing Tank
¼ +

Right Wing
¼ + ///

Fuselage Tank
~~////~~ ~~////~~ /

Engine at 1575 rpm, no compass course or altitude reported. Cumulus clouds scattered to broken in the area. Airspeed 93 mph, mixture slightly back from full lean, in rather clear weather.

He figured he had consumed about three hundred gallons of fuel to this point. He also thought that if he were to throttle back to 1550 rpm or even 1525 rpm, he could conserve fuel and extend his range. But then he would be flying in the dark before reaching the European coast.

After much re-thinking, he chose the opposite plan and decided to set the throttle at 1650 rpm, gaining seven mph more air speed.

At this point he spotted a porpoise in the water below, the first living thing he had seen since Newfoundland. He was elated, and this sign of life gave him courage and confidence.

TWENTY-SEVENTH HOUR

Over the Atlantic Ocean

Hours of fuel consumed

Nose Tank
¼ + ~~////~~ //

Left Wing
¼ + ///

Center Wing Tank
¼ +

Right Wing
¼ + ///

Fuselage Tank
~~////~~ ~~////~~ //

Time 9:52 a.m. No compass course or altitude reported. No other data reported.

Lindbergh checked the chart case to be sure the European charts were there, and tucked his helmet and goggles neatly in the case. He then checked the first-aid kit and found the dark glasses that were given to him by a doctor on Long Island. He put them on for the first time on the flight. He had forgotten they were there. But the dark contrast made him a bit uneasy, a little too comfortable and pleasant, like it was evening. They made him sleepy, so he put them back in the bag.

He was now flying at less than ten feet above the water, keeping his senses sharpened in the control of the airplane.

A gull appeared out of nowhere, and he remarked to himself, that this was the second sign of life he'd noticed on the trip.

A little while later he spotted his first boat, about three miles to the southeast, then some more small fishing boats. He flew a little closer to one of the boats, and saw a man's face in one of the portholes. He circled the boat, finally throttling back, and yelling out of his own window—"Which way is Ireland?" He circled the boat again, seeing the same face, but there was no response. The man was more than likely so stunned to see an airplane way out over the ocean he was probably frozen in wonder. Meanwhile Lindbergh nearly lost control of the airplane, due to his fatigue and circling low around the boats. He decided he was only wasting time trying to make contact and climbed for altitude to continue his journey east.

Report of Start of Race. (Missouri Historical Society)

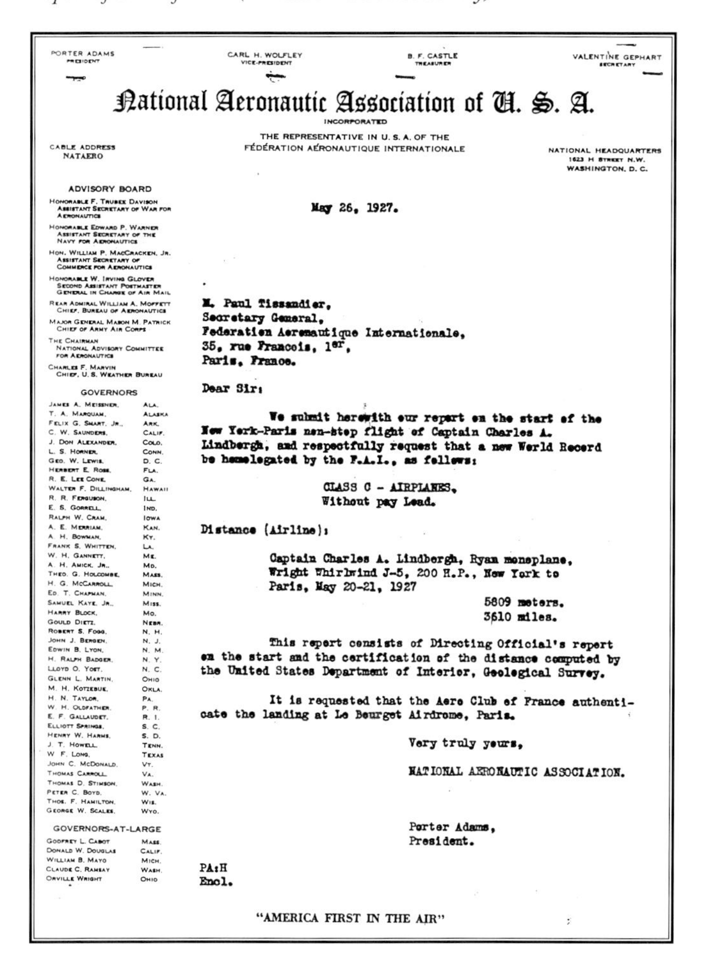

PORTER ADAMS, PRESIDENT — CARL H. WOLFLEY, VICE-PRESIDENT — B. F. CASTLE, TREASURER — VALENTINE GEPHART, SECRETARY

National Aeronautic Association of U. S. A.
INCORPORATED
THE REPRESENTATIVE IN U. S. A. OF THE FÉDÉRATION AÉRONAUTIQUE INTERNATIONALE

CABLE ADDRESS NATAERO

NATIONAL HEADQUARTERS
1623 H STREET N.W.
WASHINGTON, D. C.

ADVISORY BOARD
Honorable F. Trubee Davison, Assistant Secretary of War for Aeronautics
Honorable Edward P. Warner, Assistant Secretary of the Navy for Aeronautics
Hon. William P. MacCracken, Jr., Assistant Secretary of Commerce for Aeronautics
Honorable W. Irving Glover, Second Assistant Postmaster General in Charge of Air Mail
Rear Admiral William A. Moffett, Chief, Bureau of Aeronautics
Major General Mason M. Patrick, Chief of Army Air Corps
The Chairman, National Advisory Committee for Aeronautics
Charles F. Marvin, Chief, U. S. Weather Bureau

GOVERNORS
James A. Meissner, Ala.
T. A. Marquam, Alaska
Felix G. Smart, Jr., Ark.
C. W. Saunders, Calif.
J. Don Alexander, Colo.
L. S. Horner, Conn.
Geo. W. Lewis, D. C.
Herbert E. Ross, Fla.
R. E. Lee Cone, Ga.
Walter F. Dillingham, Hawaii
R. R. Ferguson, Ill.
E. S. Gorrell, Ind.
Ralph W. Cram, Iowa
A. E. Merriam, Kan.
A. H. Bowman, Ky.
Frank S. Whitten, La.
W. H. Gannett, Me.
A. H. Amick, Jr., Md.
Theo. G. Holcombe, Mass.
H. G. McCarroll, Mich.
Ed. T. Chapman, Minn.
Samuel Kaye, Jr., Miss.
Harry Block, Mo.
Gould Dietz, Nebr.
Robert S. Fogg, N. H.
John J. Bergen, N. J.
Edwin B. Lyon, N. M.
H. Ralph Badger, N. Y.
Lloyd O. Yost, N. C.
Glenn L. Martin, Ohio
M. H. Kotzebue, Okla.
H. N. Taylor, Pa.
W. H. Oldfather, P. R.
E. F. Gallaudet, R. I.
Elliott Springs, S. C.
Henry W. Harms, S. D.
J. T. Howell, Tenn.
W. F. Long, Texas
John C. McDonald, Vt.
Thomas Carroll, Va.
Thomas D. Stimson, Wash.
Peter C. Boyd, W. Va.
Thos. F. Hamilton, Wis.
George W. Scales, Wyo.

GOVERNORS-AT-LARGE
Godfrey L. Cabot, Mass.
Donald W. Douglas, Calif.
William B. Mayo, Mich.
Claude C. Ramsay, Wash.
Orville Wright, Ohio

May 26, 1927.

M. Paul Tissandier,
Secretary General,
Federation Aeronautique Internationale,
35, rue Francois, 1er,
Paris, France.

Dear Sir:

We submit herewith our report on the start of the New York-Paris non-stop flight of Captain Charles A. Lindbergh, and respectfully request that a new World Record be homologated by the F.A.I., as follows:

CLASS C - AIRPLANES,
Without pay Load.

Distance (Airline):

Captain Charles A. Lindbergh, Ryan monoplane, Wright Whirlwind J-5, 200 H.P., New York to Paris, May 20-21, 1927
5809 meters.
3610 miles.

This report consists of Directing Official's report on the start and the certification of the distance computed by the United States Department of Interior, Geological Survey.

It is requested that the Aero Club of France authenticate the landing at Le Bourget Airdrome, Paris.

Very truly yours,

NATIONAL AERONAUTIC ASSOCIATION.

Porter Adams,
President.

PA:H
Encl.

"AMERICA FIRST IN THE AIR"

TWENTY-EIGHTH HOUR

Over the Atlantic Ocean

Hours of fuel consumed

Nose Tank

¼ + ~~////~~ //

Left Wing	Center Wing Tank	Right Wing
¼ + ///	¼ +	¼ + ///

Fuselage Tank

~~////~~ ~~////~~ ///

Time 10:52 a.m. No compass course or altitude reported. No other data reported. Location, just west of Ireland, still over water.

Lindbergh was flying through some rain squalls, with shrinking patches of blue sky here and there. The air was clean and clear but turbulent. He flew 100 feet above the waves.

When he thought he saw a cloud on the northeastern horizon, or a strip of low fog. It turned out to be land, and he realized he was actually two and a half hours ahead of his schedule.

The coast line he saw was coming down from the north and bending toward the east, and he wondered if it could be England, France or Scotland. He climbed two thousand feet to get a better view to check with the lines on his chart, to compare and determine just what it was. It was Ireland, and it appeared he would cross the southwestern coast of the country, at about Clogher Head, near the village of Carhool, in County Kerry. It matched his chart perfectly. He was closer to his projected route than he ever believed would be possible, right on course.

As he flew over a farm in the village of Ventry, a young man, ten years of age, Ned Moriarty, was standing outside the farmhouse and heard the sounds of some kind of engine, the first he had ever heard, and saw his first airplane fly right over him. Ned was one of ten children, some of whom were out weeding in a potato field.

*Contest Committee, "Purpose of Trial.". **(Missouri Historical Society)***

CONTEST COMMITTEE

NATIONAL AERONAUTIC ASSOCIATION

1623 H Street, N. W. Washington, D. C.

Report on New York-Paris non-stop flight starting at Roosevelt Field, Long Island, New York, May 20, 1927.

Purpose of Trial: To establish a record for distance (airline) Class C Airplanes.

Pilot: Captain Charles A. Lindbergh.

Airplane: Ryan monoplane "Spirit of St. Louis".

Engine: Wright Whirlwind J 5 - 200 HP

Baragraph: The barograph (6 hr.) was sealed by the Directing Official prior to the start of the flight.

Gas Tanks: Gasoline tank filler caps were lead sealed by the Directing Official.

Officials.

Directing Official: Carl F. Schory.

Official Observers: G. S. Ireland, Kenneth M. Lane, B. Goldsborough, G. O. Noville.

REMARKS: The flight started at 6:51:30.2 A.M. eastern standard time, May 20, 1927. The plane started from the western end of Roosevelt Field, Long Island. The starting time being taken the plane crossed the starting line in full flight.

C. F. Schory

Directing Official

At first Ned thought it might be some phantom or pre-historic flying creature. He noticed that the cows acted scared as they looked up. He remembered it was late in the afternoon. His sixteen year old sister Mary was out in the field and recalled the incident years later, remembering that the airplane was gray with black markings of some kind. They had no idea what it was or who it might be until the news reached the little hamlet several days later, communication being what it was in those days.

As Lindbergh mentioned in his book, The Spirit of St. Louis, he flew out over Dingle Bay and toward Valentia Island, then back over the bay, apparently loosing his bearings for a few minutes.

The weather was clearing, the sun was warm and high as he circled the area to be sure this really was Ireland. People were running out into the streets, looking up at him and waving their arms frantically. He circled two more times and checked his chart. He figured it was only 600 miles to Paris. In all the excitement of finding land, then straightening out his flight path and checking the chart in his lap, he became momentarily confused when he spotted only water ahead, and wondered if the past few minutes were a fantasy or mirage. When he looked back about a mile or so, yes, it was true, and it was Ireland, and now he would leave that beautiful sight and head out over the water again toward the coast of England. [3]

He set his course southeastward. He decided it was safe to check the magnetos, and immediately switched over to left mag, then right mag, and checked all of the instruments, finding them reading normal.

TWENTY-NINTH HOUR

Over St. George's Channel

Hours of fuel consumed

Nose Tank

¼ + ~~////~~ //

Left Wing	Center Wing Tank	Right Wing
¼ + ///	¼ +	¼ + ///

Fuselage Tank

~~////~~ ~~////~~ ////

Time 11:50 a.m. on his clock. No compass course or altitude reported. No other data reported.

He checked his pocket watch, inherited from his Grandfather, and compared it with the clock on the instrument panel. They were within a few seconds of each other.

He again checked the instruments, put the twenty-seventh score on the board, and switched to the nose tank. He found that the tail wind was now increasing in speed. There were still cumulus clouds around, together with scattered squalls but a clearing sky.

He sighted four large ships as he crossed St. George's Channel, heading for England. As he soared along toward Paris he thought about the possibilities of air travel, and what the future could hold, and reasoned that someday passengers, mail and cargo would routinely fly between New York, Paris, and other major cities on either side of the Atlantic Ocean.

Suddenly, and without warning, and for the first time during the flight, the engine sputtered and sent a message to its pilot that it was about to quit. Lindbergh was quite startled but within a few seconds realized that the nose tank had run dry, and all he had to do was switch to another tank. He switched to the center wing tank, closed the throttle and mixture control, and began working the wobble pump. The jerking of the engine finally stopped. He eased the throttle forward and the engine picked up speed. His airspeed returned to normal and he continued on course at 2000 feet.

THIRTIETH HOUR

Over St. George's Channel

Hours of fuel consumed

Nose Tank
¼ + ~~////~~ ///

Left Wing	Center Wing Tank	Right Wing
¼ + ///	¼ +	¼ + ///

Fuselage Tank
~~////~~ ~~////~~ ~~////~~

Time 12:52 p.m. New York time 5:30 NYP time.

Lindbergh opened the throttle to 1725 rpm and the air speed increased to 110 mph. He estimated that the center wing tank had a 25 gallon reserve of fuel. He flew along at 1500 feet altitude during this period.

His next image was of the English coast at Cornwall and the Cornish cliffs, which rises so abruptly out of the sea.

THIRTY-FIRST HOUR

Over England

Hours of fuel consumed

Nose Tank
¼ + ~~////~~ ///

Left Wing	Center Wing Tank	Right Wing
¼ + ///	¼ +	¼ + ///

Fuselage Tank
~~////~~ ~~////~~ ~~////~~

Time 1:52 p.m. EDT at NY, 6:30 NYP time.

As he penciled in the twenty-ninth score, he was flying in basically VFR conditions over England and noticed people looking up at him. He had no idea that they knew who he was, where he came from, and where he was headed.

It appeared he crossed the English coast roughly between Newquay and Parranporth and crossed the peninsula just northeast of Lands End. Soon he passed just south of Plymouth and headed out over the English Channel, leaving the English coast at about Salcombe and Start Point, having about eighty-five statute miles to go to the French coast at Cape de la Hague.

He climbed to 1000 feet, then 2000 feet as the sun behind slowly dropped away to the horizon.

THIRTY-SECOND HOUR

Over the English Channel

Hours of fuel consumed

Nose Tank
¼ + ~~////~~ ///

Left Wing	Center Wing Tank	Right Wing
¼ + ///	¼ +	¼ + ///

Fuselage Tank
~~////~~ ~~////~~ ~~////~~ /

The coast of France appeared on the horizon at just about sunset and Lindbergh made landfall over the coast at the north side of Cape de la Hague. At 8:30 p.m. he was over Cherbourg, still at 2000 feet with 200 miles to go.

He put away his Mercator's projection chart and pulled out the map of France. In the deepening darkness, he flew on, over the Baie de la Seine, with the coast line of Normandy on his right. South of Le Havre he flew over the town of Deauville; he was almost three hours ahead of his planned schedule.

At this point Lindbergh began to think about his reception and that there may be a few people at the airport, probably only a few mechanics. He was concerned that he did not have a visa and wondered if it would cause any problems. He knew no French, but expected he might find someone who knew some English. He thought he would have to buy a new suit of clothes and a few other odds and ends, like a toothbrush and an extra shirt. He only had the shirt on his back and no toothbrush.

He thought about where he would go after Paris, perhaps fly on to many other countries, perhaps around the world, and why not? How would he return home? It would impress the world about the potential of aviation and air travel. It would be beneath the dignity of the NYP to put it aboard a boat for its return to America. So he imagined he would rather just fly the airplane all the way back, over the same route, with stop offs in England, Ireland, Newfoundland, Canada and so on.

THIRTY-THIRD HOUR

Over France

Hours of fuel consumed

Nose Tank
¼ + ~~////~~ ///

Left Wing	Center Wing Tank	Right Wing
¼ + ///	¼ +	¼ + ///

Fuselage Tank
~~////~~ ~~////~~ ~~////~~ //

He had broken the world's distance record for non-stop Class C airplanes.

He estimated his fuselage tank must be nearly empty, and there was no need to run it dry being so near to Paris. He turned on the right wing tank.

Ahead on his left was La Havre and the estuary of the Seine River.

People came running out from their homes at the sound of the airplane overhead. It was 4:20 p.m. on his clock, which was 9:20 pm. French time. He held the control stick between his knees and pulled a sandwich out of his lunch bag, the first he had eaten since leaving New York. As he pushed the stick forward, again clamping it between his knees, he drank from the canteen. He found the food rather dry and had to wash each mouthful down with water. He had one sandwich and thought about throwing the bag out of the window. He decided the fields were just too clean to dirty them with paper. He crumpled the wrapping and stuffed it back in the bag, as he did not want to make a poor impression upon his first visit to France.

The sky was clear, but quite dark. His instruments glowed because of their luminous paint. He was flying at only a few hundred feet, but decided to get a better view to find the city of Paris. At two thousand feet he saw a light flashing some distance ahead.

By the dim light he saw the Seine on his left as it twisted and turned on its way to Paris.

The Wright Whirlwind was running like a Swiss watch; he checked the magnetos and all was well.

He checked the engine instruments with his flashlight, and all the needles were in the right location. He had climbed to four thousand feet.

Lindbergh was in good physical as well as mental condition with no desire to sleep. He was nearing the goal he set so many months before. The engine could quit, and he could almost glide to Paris from this point. He felt it would be a shame if he had to land when the night was so clear and beautiful, and he had so much fuel left in the tanks.

He approached the Eiffel Tower, and he circled it once, then headed northeast toward Le Bourget.

THIRTY-FOURTH HOUR

Over France

Hours of fuel consumed

Nose Tank
¼ + ~~||||~~ |||

Left Wing	Center Wing Tank	Right Wing
¼ + |||	¼ +	¼ + ~~||||~~

Fuselage Tank
~~||||~~ ~~||||~~ ~~||||~~ ||

4:52 NYP time, 9:52 Paris time.

Lindbergh was not sure if he had seen Le Bourget and could not figure out why there were so many dim lights on only one side of the airport, if in fact that was the airport. He flew further northeast and only saw the lights of small villages. Then he turned back and began his descent to a lower latitude. He was at two thousand feet when he again approached Le Bourget. He circled the airport and tried to key out a message with his flashlight, but received no reply.

He switched his fuel valves to the center wing tank, rechecked the instrument panel with his flashlight and fastened his seat belt. He began the long descent in a spiral.

THE LANDING

Lindbergh spotted a wind sock on top of a building, and it appeared to be far from stiff, which would indicate a mild ten or fifteen mph wind from the north. He planned to land over the floodlights, at an angle away from the hangar line on the east side.

He was wide awake, but he could not feel the airplane, so he decided to keep a higher speed on the approach, so as not to stall and to keep the engine from loading up from too long a slide with the power off, and possibly quitting.

He suddenly felt his control movements were uncoordinated, like a student pilot on his first solo landing.

On final to the north he held a flat approach, with the engine half throttled. Then he opened the throttle and initiated a climbing turn to the right, and climbing to a thousand feet when he saw the lights of Paris again and returned to the down-wind leg for a second approach with airspeed at ninety, he pulled back on the stick, trimmed the stabilizer back a notch, and then closed the throttle to idle. During the glide, he opened the throttle briefly, but reconsidered when it seemed his approach was too fast.

He tested the rudder and pushed the stick back and forth to check response and was noted that his airspeed was now at eighty mph.

This was his first night landing in the NYP, so he was working pretty hard with heavy fatigue from a lack of sleep, with an airplane especially designed to be unstable so he would not fall asleep over the ocean. But at the end of the flight, the most critical time for any pilot, he faced a night landing at a place he had never seen before in his life, and with no landing light.

He touched down, and in what was basically a wheel landing, with the skid touching a bit late and the plane bounced one time. He could not see a thing ahead and had no idea there were thousands of people already out on the airfield in front of him as he rolled out on the landing. He finally and intentionally ground looped the NYP, gently, to get it stopped as soon as possible, still not knowing what was ahead. As he started to taxi toward the hangars and floodlights, he noticed mobs of people running out onto the field. The time was 10:22 p.m. Paris local time, May 21, 1927. (French Standard Time). It was 5:22 a.m. in New York.

His official time from New York to Paris was 33:30:29.8 sec. Official distance was 5850 km, 3635.2 statute miles, 3199 nautical miles. *(Official report from the National Aeronautic Association of USA, dated May 26, 1927, National Headquarters, Washington, DC.)*

FOOTNOTES

1. *The Spirit of St. Louis,* Charles A. Lindbergh, Charles Scribner's Sons, New York, NY, 1953, page 188.

2. *Long Island Forum,* published by The Friends of Long Island Heritage, May 1983 article "The Lindbergh Line," by Jack J. Marr, former air traffic controller for the CAA. Pages 84-89.

3. Interview by author with Ned and Mary Moriarity in South Windsor, CT, 1996.

ENDNOTES

The Spirit of St. Louis, Charles A. Lindbergh, Charles Scribner's Sons, New York, NY, 1953.

National Geographic maps of North America and other road maps by Rand-McNally and the American Automobile Association, were checked by the author for correct general compass headings over specific towns, cities and bodies of water. (Also current Sectional Aeronautical Charts—"New York," "Montreal," "Halifax," published by U.S. Department of Commerce, National Oceanic and Atmospheric Administration, National Ocean Service, Washington, DC.)

CHAPTER 9

Paris

Capsule History of the City

More than 2000 years old, Paris (from a Celtic tribe of fishermen known as the Parisi) is located on the Seine River, and is the largest city in France. In 52 B. C. Roman invaders established a colony there and called it Lutetia. The settlement soon spread out on both banks of the river. It became known as Paris about A. D. 300. It is a city of great culture, government and learning. As the capital of France, it is one of the most beautiful cities of the world, with lovely gardens, parks and historic squares throughout.

Capsule History of "Le Bourget"

There is an ancient road, leading from Paris to Senlis, and from there to Flanders, known as ru de Flandre. Where this main road crosses the river la Molette in a valley is where the small village of Le Bourget is located. The Latin origin of the name burgellum (diminutive of burgu, from which is derived the name Le Bourget) means "little city", or possibly "big village" or "little big village". [1]

It is thought the origin of the town was possibly a leper-house located on the site dating from the 11th century and existing up to the 13th century.

Le Bourget as an aerodrome came into being sometime before World War I as a military base of sorts consisting of several airplanes for a heterogeneous fighter squadron. Eventually commercial aviation was established, hoping for a worldwide market. One of the first major routes was to Croydon Aerodrome in London, England. For many years Le Bourget was the main airport for Paris. It is now a general aviation airport, over-shadowed by Charles-de-Gaulle Aeroport, just northeast of Le Bourget.

May 21 through May 28, 1927
(Saturday through Saturday)

It was late Saturday night on the 21st that Lindbergh surprised both the French and the rest of the world. Thirty thousand people had gathered at the Place de l'Opera and the Square du Harve, near St. Lazare station, where illuminated advertising signs flashed bulletins on the progress of the flight.

Although the entertainment business was in full swing in downtown Paris, it appeared the whole city was at Le Bourget when word came that the young American was on his way into town.

Lindbergh mentioned that he was completely unprepared for the welcome he received. He hadn't the slightest idea how often he had been spotted so accurately off Ireland, England and Cherbourg, France. In his tiredness he could not comprehend the reason for all the cars and people at Le Bourget as he circled while preparing to land. As far as he was concerned, he had just made a long flight, would do a normal landing as best he could under the circumstances, and sort of "play it by ear" from there. He was actually concerned that he might not have enough money in his pocket to cover the expense of a bus, train or taxi ride into the city and the hotel and food costs.

The NYP in the C.I.D.N.A. hangar at Le Bourget, under guard by French soldiers. This was apparently taken not long after he landed, and clearly shows the damage to the fabric and other parts by the enormous crowds that greeted him on the 21st. ***(Leo B. Kimball collection)***

Another view of the NYP in the hangar showing damage to the right aileron area. Notice that the Ryan wings logo is still visible on the rudder. Shortly after it was cut out with a knife and is still out there somewhere. ***(Leo B. Kimball collection)***

He had managed to keep track of his compass variations, the wind, his drift and speed for all those hours with almost no error. It was a masterpiece of air navigation.

From that flight, and over night he had become a world wide hero, the likes of which have not been repeated since. It was the start of a career like no other, filled with excitement, adventure, honor, fame, freedom, and tragedy.

Coincidentally, Louis IX (1214-1270) was one of the great kings of France (See Chapter 3, page 24)—a hero in every way. It is easy to imagine how the French felt seeing this silver airplane landing at night after crossing the ocean—bearing the words, "The Spirit of St. Louis".

To the warm-hearted French, the appearance of the young gallant of the skies in the winged NYP was the signal for one of the most overwhelming welcomes ever witnessed in the world.

Within minutes of his turning off the magneto switch, he was besieged in his small cockpit by people, speaking in French and repeating his name "Leenborg" over and over again asking questions, offering help. He could feel his beloved airplane move from the onrush and pressure of the people and the cracking of wood stringers on the side of the fuselage, the ripping of the fuselage fabric, the yelling and screaming. It's a wonder he could keep his composure considering his lack of sleep and the workload of the trip.

This view clearly shows the large piece of fabric that was cut out of the fuselage for souvenirs by someone. ***(Leo B. Kimball collection)***

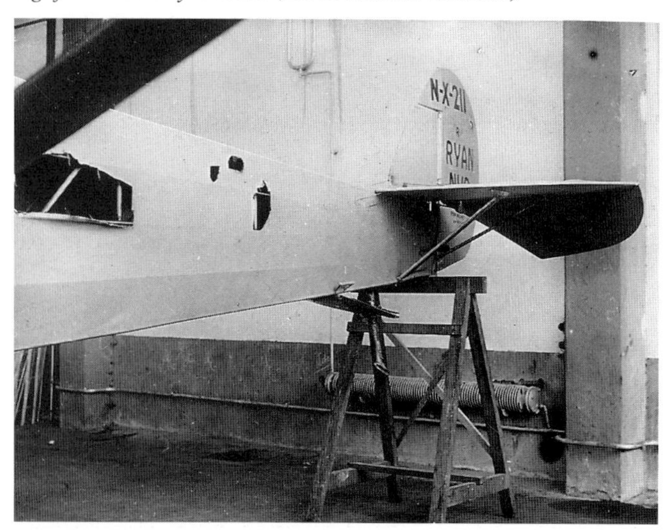

He tried in vain to communicate to the crowd, the French Gendarme police, guards and anyone in a uniform. But no one spoke English. The movement of the airplane was in a sidewise motion, left and right, at the tail skid putting tremendous strain on that part of the supporting structure.

When he finally opened the cockpit door and attempted to put his right foot down to the ground, he found himself being carried over the heads of the excited crowd. He felt that if for some reason they dropped him to the ground on his feet he would not have the strength to stand on his legs, and would collapse and be crushed, as he had been in the sitting position for so long a time and so tired. That would be it. He would be lost in the madness. [2]

"That reception was the most dangerous part of the trip. Never in my life have I seen anything like that human sea. It isn't clear to me yet just what happened. I saw one man tear away the switch (?) and another took something out of the cockpit. Then when they started cutting pieces from the wings, I struggled to get back to the plane, but it was impossible." [3]

Le Bourget was jammed with the Paris press corps. The largest contingent was from *The New York Times*, which had been given "exclusive rights" to Lindbergh's story by E. Lansing Ray, publisher of the *St. Louis Globe-Democrat*, and one of the financial backers of the flight. *The New York Herald Tribune* as well as *The Chicago Tribune* were there too, however.

With all of this going on, the Spirit of St. Louis was now at the mercy of the wild, stampeding crowd, and there was no telling what might happen to it physically. In some ways it's amazing it was not torn to pieces and left in shreds and bare bones in a pile on the field of Le Bourget that night.

As it turned out the French had prepared as best they could when word reached Paris that Lindbergh was on his way. They summoned up as many mechanics, guards and Gendarmes as possible to guard the airplane, which they did with much difficulty, finally pushing the plane into one of the large Air Union hangars on the east side of Le Bourget. Those hangars still stand today and are used to house the Musee de l'Air, one of the largest air museums in the world.

Another view of the fabric damage, taken in the C.I.D.N.A. hangar. ***(Bernard Millot Archive)***

In the meantime two prominent French aviators, Michel Detroyat, a military flyer, and Toto Delage, a civil pilot, were close to Lindbergh, who was carried by the crowd. Because of Detroyat's height and the wearing of a uniform which commanded some respect from the crowd, he took charge of the situation. As Lindbergh was lowered to the ground an American reporter grabbed his helmet and put it on. With that the crowd thought the reporter was Lindbergh and decoyed the attention in that direction allowing Lindbergh to "escape" with his two new flying friends. [4]

With the dark leather flying suit Lindbergh blended into the crowd in the dark night. The hero and his new friends were finally able to make their way to some safe location. With that in mind, Delage rushed off to retrieve his car, a Renault, as Detroyat escorted Lindbergh away from the mob. As he climbed into the car, Lindbergh continued to attempt to communicate his concern for the airplane. Once they understood his concern, they assured him that the Spirit of St. Louis would be well taken care of, and they should not attempt to go to the hangar.

They drove to another large hangar on the field. Lindbergh was taken to a small room where they offered him a comfortable chair and turned out the lights so he would not be discovered.

France was his now, and all he had to do was to order whatever he wanted; a bed, food, water, doctor. Again he expressed his concern about the airplane. Again they assured him of its safety. Lindbergh then mentioned his concern about his passport, customs and immigration formalities. And he had no Visa. The reply from his friends were laughter and smiles, a typical French response.

He then asked if there was any word of the fate of Nungesser and Coli. The French faces became serious and the reply was a sad no.

The NYP being pushed into a hangar to be the backdrop for the American Club luncheon on May 24th, Tuesday a.m. Notice temporary patches on fuselage. ***(Musee' de L'Air, Paris)***

Shortly Detroyat went searching for a high ranking French military officer. He finally found Commandant Tom Weiss of the Bombardment Group of the 34th Aviation Regiment Le Bourget. When Weiss spotted Lindbergh in the small room, he remarked, "It is impossible, Lindbergh has just been carried triumphantly to the official reception committee." Apparently Weiss had seen the American reporter wearing the helmet, who had been taken unwillingly to the American Ambassador before the mistaken identity had been discovered. [5]

Major Weiss insisted Lindbergh be taken across the field to his military office. They all climbed aboard Delage's Renault and drove the mile or so across Le Bouget to the military area on the west side of the field.

Shortly Weiss went off to find a higher ranking officer and soon came back with the American Ambassador, the Honorable Myron R. Herrick, accompanied by his son Parmely and daughter-in-law Agnes.

Herrick, from Cleveland, Ohio, was a kind, dignified and perceptive kind of person, and he and Lindbergh hit it off immediately.

Herrick suggested they go immediately to the Embassy, and again Lindbergh expressed his deep concern for the Spirit of St. Louis. After a discussion among the people there, Lindbergh was convinced it would not be necessary to see the airplane, but that they should get going to the embassy. However, they did say that

Notice patch on right side of fuselage and exhaust streaks on cowl and over wing center section. The tail is removed, possibly to get ready to rip off fabric and replace with new fabric on fuselage. Notice rudder on the floor that shows the patch over the Ryan wings logo that had been cut out earlier. ***(Bernard Millot Archive)***

A good view of the cockpit at Paris, after the fuselage fabric was removed, most likely on May 22nd. ***(Smithsonian Institution)***

the airplane was not too badly damaged, and it was placed in a locked hangar under military guard. They strongly suggested that he needed sleep, and there was no further protests from Lindbergh.

But Lindbergh could not forget the sounds of the crowd pressing against the airplane after he had landed. He was deeply concerned, and rightly so. The French wanted to fix the damages quickly before Lindbergh had a chance to see what had been done to it that night. He suggested that he wanted to retrieve some articles from the cockpit and to discuss with the French mechanics precisely how the Pyralin windows would or should be placed back in their proper place. It required a special technique he stressed.

So once more they climbed into Delage's Renault and drove back to the Air-Union hangar where the Spirit had been placed. Lindbergh was taken aback when he saw the damage.

As can be seen in the photographs, there were several gaping holes on both sides of the fuselage, and a lubrication fitting had been removed from one of the rocker arm housing covers on the Wright J-5 engine. As bad as it all looked initially though, Lindbergh felt it was not serious damage and could be repaired easily in a few hours.

With his mind settled he could concentrate on his stay in Paris. In the meantime Herrick had disappeared and after a brief unsuccessful search for Herrick, they decided to be off to the Embassy. The four of them—Weiss, Detroyat, Delage and Lindbergh climbed again into the Renault and headed out from Le Bourget, driving by way of the outskirts of Paris.

On their way they passed Dugny, Stains, Saint Denis, and entered via the Saint Ouen gate, Porte de St. Oven, arriving at the "Place de L'Opera." Then they made their way past the French Tomb of the Unknown Soldier, near the Arc De Triomphe and finally arrived at the Embassy.

While they were enroute, Herrick had searched all over Le Bourget for Lindbergh. Eventually he got into his own car and attempted to make his way to the Embassy, after much delay in the traffic jam between Le Bourget and the city. Neither he nor the escorting police officers on motorcycles knew about the detour Lindbergh and his friends had discovered. It was 3 a.m. when Herrick reached the Embassy at Avenue d'Iena.

In spite of the late hour Lindbergh was given a sumptuous supper by the Embassy staff. Soon the news people who had been patiently waiting outside for hours were invited in by Ambassador Herrick, and Lindbergh spent until 4:15 a.m. telling about his flight and then getting to bed. [6]

Later that afternoon (the 22nd) Lindbergh awoke a bit on the stiff side. He had been without sleep for sixty-three hours. As he stated in his book The Spirit of St. Louis "I awoke that afternoon, a little stiff but well rested, into a life which could hardly have been more amazing if I had landed on another planet instead of at Paris." And as has been documented so often over the years, his life would never be the same from here on.

ARRIVAL OF LINDBERGH AS TOLD BY MICHEL DETROYAT, FRENCH MILITARY AVIATOR

We, the military, were on the military (west) side of Bourget, in the canteen near the hangars about a kilometer from the civilian part of the airfield where Lindbergh was supposed to land. With an associate, we started walking briskly toward the civilian side as we did not want to miss the historic moment. At that time word came that he had been sighted over Cherbourg.

We were about half way there when suddenly the sound of an engine made us jump, a sound that strangely resembled the sound of an airplane engine but not one of ours. It was an apparatus trying to land and was groping about in the night.

I was informed of the historic moment by an immense shout. It was the cry of the crowd at breaking point, extremely happy to be able to shout out their admiration. At the same time the ground started to reverberate heavily under the steps of the thousands of charging men and women, pushing and shoving along the way towards Lindbergh's airplane.

In an instant I was separated or rather torn from my companions. I had almost arrived at the plane when I ran into Toto Delage, a pilot for the civilian company Air-Union. He shouted at me. "Look, 'HE' is there, fifty meters away. They are crazy. They are going to kill him! Come help me!

With Toto Delage who, like me, is in the heavyweight category, and thanks maybe also to my uniform we were somewhat imposing, in spite of the general hysteria. I reached for a man who was being carried on shoulders, being pulled at from all sides, and no longer reacting. His chin was on his chest and his eyes were half closed.

The strength of our punches must have awakened Lindbergh, who was finally able to put his feet on the French soil that he had so much difficulty reaching. When I shouted "Come on!" he followed at a run, Toto Delage in front while I followed behind. We succeeded in getting him into the Air-Union hangar.

He rubbed his face with his hand as if he wanted to wake himself up, come out of a dream. Then very calmly, in a gentle but firm voice he told me:

"Can I have some water, please?"

"What did he say?"

"He is asking me for water." I answered.

While my friend Toto generously offered his favorite beverage to Lindbergh, I went back into the crowd to find any personalities. The first that I found was the Commandant, Weiss. Very quietly, in the middle of the crowd, I slipped him the news.

"Oh no, that's it!" he exploded. "My dear Detroyat, you are a joker, that does not fit, they just told me twice that he was there. Besides, Lindbergh is over there."

He showed me a false Lindbergh wearing the cap (helmet) of the American ace and the excited crowd was carrying him triumphantly.

I finally succeeded in convincing him that Lindbergh was at Air-Union. He realized that I was not kidding and decided to follow me.

Thanks to the glass of water, Lindbergh regained his spirits and while waiting for the arrival of the authorities, we settled into Weiss's office, and it was Lindbergh who broke the silence. It was to ask me about news of Nungesser and Coli.

I explained to him that for ten days there had been total silence. A great sadness covered his face. He did not say anything, but got up. It was only then that I saw that he was very tall, blond and quite thin. His nose pressed against the glass, he remained there to ponder...

"It was almost 11 o'clock when the American ambassador, Myron T. Herrick, was able to arrive at Weiss's office to congratulate his countryman.

"Moreover, it was Myron T. Herrick who had the idea that was to end as a "gag" that historic evening.

"There is upheaval on the road to Paris; any official car risks being assaulted. So, since you have already saved Lindbergh from the crowd, I am counting on you to get him to the American Embassy.

"We decided to leave by Dugny and to take roads that were less crowded. Unfortunately, nothing resembles a little suburban back road more than another suburban back road, particularly when it is midnight, drizzling, and pitch black outside.

In short, after an hour zigzagging around, we had to face the facts. We were lost!

We looked like idiots! We seemed all the more stupid since Lindbergh did not realize any of it. I thought to myself, 'He didn't get lost over the Atlantic. He found the Bourget field in the middle of darkness. And us, we can't even find the darned way back to Paris.'" [7]

ARRIVAL AS TOLD BY MR. MARC GUILLARD

We arrive at Bourget around 7:00 p.m. On the Flandre route we see a flow of people going towards the civilian side of the airport. I head for the offices of the First Group (military) located on the east side of the airport near Dugny near the Moree where I have been posted since December 1926 as secretary to Commandant Weiss.

The end of the day is superb. The sky is a gentle blue; from time to time a commercial plane lands and rolls towards the civilian aviation located in front of our Group. I appear before Commandant Weiss. Also there is Captain Venson ("The Old Tiger").

From the civilian aviation side we note an enormous crowd. In order to calm the crowd Sergeant Detroyat takes off his Nieuport and executes all sorts of acrobatics.

Detroyat lands and a voice announces that all commercial airplanes have arrived and now if a plane lands, it will be the American aviator.

As night approaches, conversations soften, cut by prolonged silences. We are feeling tense; we represent the security services on guard. The firemen, civilians as well as military, are in a state of alert in their vehicles. We can't yet admit it..... and yet.....

*Rare photo of the first oil change after the famous flight, by French mechanics. **(courtesy Exxon Mobil Corporation)***

The civilian beacon turns regularly. One moment we heard the sound of a faraway engine.

Oh! If he arrives he will turn in full throttle around the field in triumph. Certainly that's natural. We don't yet know this tall, shy young man, so simple/modest...and yet he was approaching.

Suddenly a brief engine acceleration... the runway lights are lit and light up the runway. A faint white silhouette lands and rolls on the field. He is here!

With my friends we are hardly recovered from our surprise when we see a car make its way towards our group. It passes and heads towards the office. We run there.

What has happened? It's incredible! The American aviator is here, standing in Commandant Weiss's office. Pulled out of the

*New Mobiloil "B" going back into the oil tank at Paris. **(courtesy Exxon Mobil Corporation)***

In the hangar of the Compagnie Internationale de Navigation Aerienne, at Le Bourget. Picture shows chief mechanic M. Sarrazin, who was in charge of overhaul. Next to him are two mechanics and at right are two representatives of the Vacuum Oil Company S.A.F. Engineer H. H. Pagny (bowtie) and Mr. Villeval of the Vacuum Oil Company of Paris. **(courtesy Exxon Mobil Corporation)**

frenzied crowd that had turned over the metal barriers and surpassed the guards, the American aviator had been pulled out by Commandant Weiss, assisted by Michel Detroyat and two other civilian pilots and brought to the Commandant's office.

Right away Commandant Weiss gives us the order to call the civilian aviation and to ask for Director Renvoise. He asks for some cars to cross the field and Lindbergh, surrounded and congratulated by representatives of his country, heads towards Paris. [8]

ELIZABETH BELL, AN AMERICAN, WAS THERE TOO

Elizabeth Bell had always been fascinated as a young girl by "aeroplanes", and the people who flew them. She remembers that her friends were collecting pictures of movie stars, while she was pasting up scrap books of aviators and aviatrixes.

So it was not surprising when in the spring of 1927 and while a student in Paris, living with her parents, she became highly elated by the news that an American pilot was about to try to cross the Atlantic Ocean.

She and her parents were grieving with the French people who, it appeared, had lost their two hero flyers, Charles Nungesser and his co-pilot Pierre Coli, when they had attempted to fly the Atlantic from east to west. It was a devastating blow for the French people.

While attempting to subdue their excitement over the imminent Lindbergh venture, they were asked by a young French friend, Jean Bernier, if they would like to go to Le Bourget... "Just in case". He asked them if they thought he would actually make it. Elizabeth replied, "Of course," with more conviction than she actually felt.

"Then you must be there," he said firmly. I will pick you and your mother up at 6:30 this evening."

She bought a *Paris Herald* that noon to brief herself on the event and learned that there were several well known flyers preparing to take off from New York to win the Orteig prize. She read of Lindbergh who was anxious to get going in spite of the bad weather which was holding up the others.

She said that when they arrived at Le Bourget only a handful of people were there and that the mood was somber and quiet. Gradually the mood changed to one of mild anticipation as a contingent of gendarmes took their places in front of them. They were to be a living fence between the tarmac and the landing field area.

Soon the night was a black velvet, and the air was a bit on the chilly side. As the hours ticked by, it was almost unbearable as they waited.

Suddenly over the loudspeaker came the word: "Lindbergh has been sighted over Ireland. Ambassador Herrick is on his way to the field!" Then a rather hushed murmur went up from the crowd which had swollen to several thousand, as all of Paris, it seemed, was now spilling onto the tarmac. She said that her heart began to skip beats. It was really happening.

As the searchlights began scanning the clear evening sky, they heard the sounds of that Wright "Whirlwind" engine overhead. Elizabeth and Jean Bernier, her French friend, grabbed Elizabeth's mother's arms, practically lifting her off the ground as they ran with the crowd across the ground toward where everyone was sure he would land. The previous attempt of the gendarmes to subdue the people, a human chain, failed. The men were pushed aside like little toy solders, as a unit.

They were now part of an uncontrolled sea of racing, shouting and chanting people. "Vive Lindbergh, Vive L'american." Eventually they came to an abrupt stop as the Spirit of St. Louis touched down only a few hundred yards from where they were standing. She was able even in all the commotion to see Lindbergh as he was carried above the crowd. He appeared weary and bewildered. She said it looked as though Lindbergh and the NYP would be destroyed by the over-enthusiastic crowd.

That was all they saw of Lindbergh for the moment, and as they made their way back off the field they and the rest of the mob began to stamp and shout for one more glimpse of "l'american". But their shouting was to no avail. Ambassador Herrick appeared on the balcony of the airport building waving Lindbergh's goggles high over his head again and again. They knew this historical event was about over so they reluctantly headed toward their car and the long, bumper-to-bumper ride back to Paris. Elizabeth said that several hours later they were lifting glasses of cognac at the Cafe du Dome in a toast to the gallant young American. They had not yet realized that they had been part of such an important part of aviation history! [9]

TWO MAJOR HISTORICAL EVENTS

There was a newspaper headline that stated, "One Triumph of Science is Used to Tell of Another." And so it was that after Lindbergh successfully landed at Paris, France, the news had to find a way of reaching westward across that vast Atlantic Ocean to the American people. The transmission of pictures by radio, the most recent major triumph of science, was used to rush these pictures to the USA from Paris. They were sent by airplane from Paris to London on May 22nd, then by radio or Bartlane process (Western Union transmission) in one minute, then relayed westward over the telephone wires. This was the first such transmission across the Atlantic.

FIRST AND LAST KISS IN FRANCE

Another person at Le Bourget that evening was seven year old Francoise do Peyrelongue. (born May 1920) The story goes that Francoise lived in Cherbourg, France in 1927. Her father was a magistrate of the court and a man of some influence. Young Francoise and her father would not have been in Paris if it were not for the fact that she became ill. She needed the expertise of a doctor who happened to be practicing in Paris. The doctor had prescribed surgery.

Just as her parents were about to send Francoise to a hospital in Paris, the situation was delayed because of a death in the doctor's family. During this time her infection began to subside on its own, and the rapidly recovering child was there when her father was invited by an old friend in the French Air Force to wait for Lindbergh's arrival at Le Bourget. So Francois Dubun de Peyrelongue took his daughter along.

When Lindbergh landed on the military side of the airport,

the little girl and her father were fortunate enough to be in a building there. Francoise then handed Lindbergh a little bouquet of dandelions that she had picked from the field when she saw his airplane land. Lindbergh was touched by this kind gesture and kissed her on the cheek as her proud father and Air Force officials beamed.

This was far from their last meeting however. When Lindbergh flew into Lessay (Chapter 12) the de Peyrelongue family had returned from Paris and were staying at the home of Francoise's grandmother in Lessay. When her father learned that Lindbergh would land there, he drove over to the airfield and proceeded to invite him to lunch at his mother's home. Lindbergh accepted, it appears, but not confirmed. So again he met Francoise.

The family was invited to accompany Lindbergh in the motor launch or pilot boat to the Memphis anchored in the Cherbourg harbor. He gave her another kiss, so she became the first and last female to be kissed by Lindbergh in France after the historic flight.

Francoise eventually married, becoming Mrs. Kalognomos, and later moved to Hernando Beach, Florida. [10]

ROOSEVELT SENDS LETTER TO HERRICK

Colonel Theodore Roosevelt, shortly before Lindbergh left New York, wrote an introductory letter to Ambassador Myron T. Herrick in Paris. Lindbergh had requested that Roosevelt write a letter, or letters, of introduction to friends over there, as he feared that no one would know him when he arrived in Paris. He had hoped these "friends" could "show him around" during his stay.

The letter:

Dear Ambassador:

This will introduce to you Captain Charles A. Lindbergh, who is a real sportsman. I honestly hope he is successful in his flight and delivers it to you after having landed in Paris. He won't ask you to do anything for him. If I were you, however, I would insist upon seeing something of him, for I know you will like him.

Anyway, if you are able to help him, I will appreciate it deeply.

With kind regards. [11]
Theodore Roosevelt

The day after Lindbergh landed in Paris the Stars and Stripes and the Tricolour flags were flying from hundreds of windows in Paris and on the top of flag poles all over the area.

When the news was official that he had indeed landed, Parisians indulged in a spontaneous outburst of enthusiasm such as had not been witnessed for many years. In theaters and cafes the announcement was greeted by the rendering of *The Star Spangled Banner* and *The Marseilles,* while cheering crowds assembled in front of the newspaper offices and in the Place de l'Opera so densely that traffic was partially held up.

LINDBERGH'S MOTHER

While he was nearing Paris, Lindbergh's mother was still teaching chemistry in Cass Technical High School in Detroit. She taught her class in her usual manner and did not want to be disturbed with any news of her son's location as she had all the confidence in the world that he would be successful. She planned to listen to the radio later that day to learn of his position. "I am not worried. Charles is an excellent pilot and he will reach Paris," she stated. At one time she also said that he was the only pilot she would fly with. Obviously Mrs. Lindbergh was very proud of her son.

When word finally reached her that her son had landed safely in Paris, she said, "I am grateful. There is no use attempting to find words to express my happiness. He has accomplished the greatest undertaking of his life, and I am proud to be the mother of such a boy." [12]

Checking the oil filter by engineer H. H. Pagny (on the left) in charge of the aviation Division of the Vacuum Oil Company S.A.F. and Captain Cartier on the right from the 34th Air Regiment. ***(courtesy Exxon Mobil Corporation)***

PRESIDENT COOLIDGE

"The American people rejoice with me at the brilliant termination of your heroic flight. This flying record of American aviation brings the greetings of the American people to France. You likewise carry the assurance of our admiration of those intrepid Frenchmen, Nungesser and Coli, whose bold spirits first ventured on your exploit and likewise a message of our continued anxiety concerning their fate." [13]

On May 22, Sir Alan Cobham, prominent British long distance flyer flew over from Croydon, England, to congratulate Lindbergh on behalf of British airmen and to convey an invitation to him from the Royal Aero Club to visit London. Lindbergh accepted

UNITED STATES AMBASSADOR TO FRANCE MYRON T. HERRICK'S STORY

Frenchmen of all classes hailed Myron T. Herrick as an old and true friend. The fact that hard feelings over the war debts never lessened Herrick in the eyes of the French was a great tribute not only to his diplomacy but to the love they had for him.

On May 21st Herrick and several of his colleagues had been lunching with Mrs. Bernard Carter, and the subject of Lindbergh came up. After lunch they all went out to see Tilden play in a big tennis match then in progress in paris. Information came that morning that a young man had started from California to fly to

Photo shows that the original fabric on the fuselage is now removed to be replaced. ***(Smithsonian Institution)***

Paris. Herrick confessed that it did not mean much to him as he had been bombarded by Rodman Wanamaker saying that Byrd was planning his departure for Paris, diverting Herrick's attention from Lindbergh. Herrick felt that according to the newspapers if this young man was planning to fly from California to Paris, it seemed a long way from Paris for any kind of start.

"Nevertheless," Herrick said, "I had made up my mind to go out to Le Bourget and wait for his arrival as soon as I had some indication to go on.

During the tennis match a telegram was brought to me saying that Lindbergh had passed over Valencia in Ireland. It seemed too good to be true, but we all hurried home, had a quick dinner at half-past six, and started for the field. It was a good thing we did not delay another quarter of an hour, for crowds were already collecting along the road and in a short time passage was almost impossible. News had already reached Paris that Lindbergh had been surely sighted, and the whole population seemed bent upon being at Le Bourget to see him land. When we arrived there we were escorted to the big pavilion at one end of the field and found it full of people.

"We had been at our post of observation only a little while when a silvery plane circled the field and landed. Some thought it was the ship from Strasbourg, which was due about that time, but an official whispered to me that the color was not right and that it must be our man. It was, and in a moment pandemonium broke loose—not the pandemonium the newspaper always tells about at political conventions, but the real thing. I certainly never witnessed any occasion like it. Soldiers and police were swept away, the stout fence was demolished, and the crowd surged toward the airplane.

"A little man in white kid gloves, bearing a tiny "bokay" all fixed up in a white paper petticoat, came forward and presented his offering to me. He tried to make a speech, but of course not a word could be distinguished. He had brought the flowers for Lindbergh, but his emotion got the better of him and he gave them to me instead. I never knew who he was.

"Presently—I had no notion of time as far as that night was concerned—a man half torn to pieces managed to get up to the terrace where I was and handed me an aviator's helmet. This man turned out to be a *New York Herald* reporter, who was close by when the ship landed, and to whom Major Weiss had given the helmet with orders to take it to me. This was done to deceive the crowd and get them clear of Lindbergh and his airplane. The ruse succeeded, and it only goes to show how quickly aviators have to think and act. The crowd rushed off after him, believing it was Lindbergh, and they nearly annihilated him in their enthusiasm. I went out on the balcony, where a searchlight began to play on me, and waved the helmet to the crowd below. They went wild with enthusiasm.

"After about two hours one of the French officers put us in his car and drove us to Major Weiss's office across the field. Here we found Lindbergh in a little room with a few chairs and an army cot. They told him who I was. I shook hands with him, and he handed me some letters he had brought. Three of them were from Col. Theodore Roosevelt—one addressed to me, one to Mr. Houghton, and the third, I forget to whom. These three were letters of introduction; the others were from people who had asked him to take them, thinking it was an interesting idea to send mail across the ocean in a day's time.

"After shaking hands with Lindbergh and introducing him to my son and daughter-in-law, I said 'Young man, I am going to take you home with me and look after you.' He came up a little closer, saying 'I can't hear you very well; the sound of the motor is still in my ears.' I repeated my invitation to which he replied, 'I should like to sir; thank you very much. But I want to go over to my ship first and shut the windows; I left them open, and they will not know how to put them in.' I of course assented to this.

"Someone had suggested he see a doctor, but Lindbergh absolutely refused to be bothered with any doctor. He was calm and did not seem fatigued; his face was rosy and not at all drawn.

"Finally Lindbergh went to sleep about 4 a.m. and did not arise until 2 p.m. later that day (22nd). A dinner had been arranged for that evening at the Embassy. I hoped it would give Lindbergh some pleasure. He only had his flying clothes, so my son Parmalee and I obtained two suits from my valet, Blanchard.

A rare view of the 'naked' fuselage, showing a woman standing on a box working on preparing the fuselage for the new French fabric perhaps. Her name is unknown. Notice the removable windows stored in the rack fastened to the fuselage just behind the cockpit, right side. ***(Leo B. Kimball collection)***

Another view of the fabric removed from the fuselage. **(Leo B. Kimball collection)**

Lindbergh came to dinner looking perfectly normal and comfortable in his borrowed evening clothes." [14]

FERNAND SARRAZIN

Mssr. Fernand Sarrazin recalled a high point of his career as chief mechanic in the repair shop of the C.I.D.N.A. Company (Compagnie Internationale de Navigation Aerienne), based on Le Bourget in 1927.

"I learned that Lindbergh was on his way, but I had no idea where he would land on our grass field. I knew he was sighted over Cherbourg at 8:30 p.m., so about 10 p.m. I left the hanger and walked slowly onto the field. Fifteen minutes or so later I heard the noise of a motor. It was Lindbergh, circling the airport; I judged the wind, and the position of the lights across the field, and began to run toward the spot where I thought he would land.

"A few minutes after that, I heard him pass to my right, about 50 meters off the ground. Immediately I ran with all my strength, guided by the sparks coming from the exhaust of his motor. I reached the plane totally out of breath.

"Lindbergh lowered his window (it was probably open already in order for him to see to land). He looked completely exhausted and appeared nearly deaf from the engine noise. We shook hands, but I didn't speak any English, so I didn't know what to say to him. I finally yelled 'Ici Paris Le Bourget' to reassure him.

"I wanted to guide Lindbergh and his airplane toward the hanger of the C.I.D.N.A. company. But then I heard a tremendous noise and saw the crowd, which had overturned the barriers and was running toward the plane.

"The crowd almost kidnapped Lindbergh, and it began to tear souvenirs from the fabric covering the fuselage. I got punched a few times when I tried to keep them out of the cockpit.

"Finally, several of my mechanics and a few volunteers helped me get the plane back to the hangar.

"The day after that crazy night, we began to make repairs. The airplane had suffered a fair amount of damage to the fabric and to the engine.

"But when I checked over the engine, I realized just how Lindbergh's sensational success had hung by a hair. When I looked at the upper part of the oil reservoir, I found a hole about 20 centimeters long. (*) If that hole had been in the lower part of the reservoir, it's certain that Lindbergh would never have arrived at Le Bourget and that his effort would have ended as a catastrophe." [15]

*The hole was probably only 2 cm. A hole of 20 centimeters would be nearly 8".

NYP CONDITION AND REPAIRS

When the French authorities inspected the damage, they were both appalled and embarrassed at the same time and felt responsible as well as determined to get it back into flying condition.

As can be clearly seen in photographs, the oil was changed by Vacuum Oil Company representatives. The oil screen was removed and cleaned and no metal chips or any other contamination was found. It appears that other general servicing was done on the Wright "Whirlwind" and all components were in fine condition. Damage consisted of rips and holes on top and on both sides of the fuselage aft of the cockpit. It included fabric and metal damage at the leading edge of both ailerons, removal of a rocker arm grease fitting from the engine, a wings logo on the right side of the rudder, and removal from the cockpit of a few items from his survival equipment. The theft consisted of two of the cans of Army emergency rations, one flashlight, one hunting knife, one Armbrust cup and one canteen of water. The engine log and navigation log had been stolen as well.

Sometime after the airplane was placed in the hangar, either Mary 21, 22 or 23, someone took a pen knife and very neatly cut out the wings logo on the top right side of the rudder. One wonders if it was one of the mechanics or Gendarmes on duty to protect the Spirit. That logo emblem has never turned up in all these years, and it is any wonder where it might be today. The French did patch it however, and that patch is still on the aircraft.

Checking all of the photographs taken at Le Bourget, not one shows the right side of the airplane after the rudder logo was removed and before it was patched.

At this same time the Pyralin windows were put in their proper place, apparently to keep prodding hands from going inside the cockpit to pick up additional souvenirs.

The French temporarily patched all of the rips and open holes in the fuselage sometime before the 24th. The airplane is shown in a hangar during the luncheon of the American Club on that

Left to right: Lindbergh, French President Gaston Doumergue (elected 1924 to 1931) and U.S. Ambassador to France, Myron T. Herrick. ***(Air and Space Collections, Nassau County Museum)***

date, clearly showing the patches. Sometime after that it was decided to completely recover the fuselage with new fabric.

When repairs were started on May 25, mechanics first removed the rudder, stabilizer and elevators, leaving the vertical fin in place. The tail skid was removed at this time. The work was done in the back of the hangar with the tail placed on top of a saw horse support structure.

All four sides of the fuselage fabric back to the tail post was removed. The top portion was removed from just aft of the wing trailing edge. The left side was removed from about half way along the left window back and the right side from about where the rear wing strut attaches to the lower longeron and the trailing edge of the door back. From about that same location and back, the belly fabric was also replaced.

It appears that some form of heavy linen used commonly in France at that time was applied with the normal doping process being used in the re-covering up to the final coat of silver dope.

It was at this time mechanics cleaned the airplane of all the dirt and oil it accumulated during the flight. They also temporarily removed the forward portion of the spinner assembly. Did a crack develop on the flight that needed repair? It is not known. Perhaps they wished to check the propeller mounting for security.

PHOTO STUDY ON PARIS DAMAGE

The very first photo taken of the airplane after it landed at Le Bourget shows a group of Gendarmes and other people in a human chain surrounding the airplane. The general public can be seen in the background. Quite noticeable is the ripped fabric at what appears to be just forward of each aileron leading edge. The photo is not clear.

The next picture taken was after the NYP was placed inside the hangar of the C.I.D.N.A. (Internationale de Navigation Aerienne) or Air Union. As can clearly be seen, the fabric ripped near the aileron is the fabric on the wing just forward of the aileron.

Also in this same photo can be seen the "wings" logo on the upper portion of the right side of the rudder. Also noted is the right hand of a civilian gentleman, apparently spinning the cups on the wind driven generator of the Earth Inductor Compass on the upper portion of the fuselage just aft of the cockpit.

Space between people at the midway point of the right side of the fuselage shows a triangular rip in the fabric near the lower longeron. It is interesting to note also that no further photographs were taken of the right side of the airplane that show other fabric damage to the fuselage.

The next photo shows the extensive ripping of fabric on the left side of the aft part of the fuselage. This picture was taken in the same hangar mentioned above.

One photograph, taken from the rafters of the hangar showing the NYP next to two French Salmson 2A2 biplanes, is the only one that shows a small hole in the fabric on top of the fuselage just forward of the stabilizer on the left side of the center stringer. Not one of the photos shows damage to the bottom fabric of the fuselage. The overhead photo clearly shows the black exhaust traces over the top of the fuselage and wing center section. Other photos show the black exhaust along the side cowling.

It is assumed that in the next couple of days Perhaps May 25 or 26, the airplane and engine were serviced. One photo shows engineer H. H. Pagney in charge of the Aviation Division of the Vacuum Oil Company S.A.F. and Captain Cartier of the 34th Air Regiment inspecting the oil pump and screen, which is dismantled and placed on a makeshift ladder-bench. The Vacuum Company took care of draining the oil and refilling with new Mobiloil Gargoyle Grade B, as can be seen by the containers on the floor. The possibly cracked oil reservoir was also replaced or repaired. Chief mechanic M. Fernand Sarrazin was in charge of these services.

One photo shows the left landing gear strut fairing at the shock absorber removed for some reason. It was probably to check the general condition of the bungee shock cords.

No official documentation in the way of log books, statements or other reports have been found that would give further details of the servicing and repair work done at Paris. The only Lindbergh report can be found on page 504 of his book, *The Spirit of St. Louis,* in which he states that the fabric was torn by souvenir hunters, a fairing strip or strips broken, and a grease reservoir was torn off the engine. The fuselage was repaired and re-covered at Paris.

LINDBERGH'S STAY IN PARIS

While his airplane was being worked on, Lindbergh was entertained royally by the French. Much notoriety for the young man followed. He was recognized as an audacious pioneer flyer. He would be continually feted and decorated.

His success excited the admiration of the American people as well as the world, such that it would ignite the long lacking development of aviation and air travel.

As one writer put it many years ago, the "phenomenon of Lindbergh" was just beginning. Thus began the greatest torrent of mass emotion ever witnessed in human history. Lindbergh's modesty, his good looks, his winning smile, the brilliance of his achievement, and his refusal to be tempted by money or fame won him the admiration of almost everyone. Some said that his sudden appearance from obscurity was an act of Providence.

Sunday, May 22

After his landing that night of May 21, he went to bed and awakened the next day, the 22nd, after about ten hours of sleep. He ate a solid breakfast and was requested to appear on the balcony of the American Embassy to address the throngs of people in the streets below. There was a burst of applause and the people just kept on cheering and clapping and waving their hats or handkerchiefs. His personality radiated out to the French people like a magnet.

Later it was arranged for him to have a radio-telephone conversation with his mother in Detroit, over four thousand miles away.

Due to Nungesser and Coli's loss, Lindbergh made a point of calling on Madame Nungesser, mother of the lost flyer. His visit in her humble sixth floor flat endeared him still more in the hearts of the French people.

With tear-dimmed eyes and sobs choking her voice, Madame Nungesser described Captain Lindbergh's visit.

"I had to speak to him through an interpreter. Throughout the conversation he held my hand, squeezing it tightly, wishing to console me. He kissed me three times. I kissed him too, with all my heart, but while I kissed him my glance fell on a photograph of my son and there was a cruel stab at my heart. You will permit a mother to say that in that moment I would have preferred to enfold my own child in my arms.

"Mr. Lindbergh was very gentle. He spoke to me of hoping some day to meet my son. Oh, I shall be happy that he meet him. Mr. Lindbergh told me he wanted to see me because he loves his mother, and he thought his visit would make me happy. I hope to see the beautiful boy again before he leaves Paris." [16]

"I wanted to make my first call on the mother of my valiant friend, Capt. Nungesser," Lindbergh said to the sorrowing mother. Then they embraced.

Mrs. Nungesser said how sorry she was that she could not be at Le Bourget last night to welcome and see her boy's comrade of the air descend in triumph. When Lindbergh left his blue eyes, still tired from the trip, were dimmed with tears. He suggested that she not give up hope.

He then visited veterans of World War I in a local Paris hospital. It is said his presence gave them hope, and it lifted their spirits to be able to meet and visit with such a heroic world figure.

Monday, May 23

After arising early Monday morning, he was taken to a tailor to be fitted with some new clothes. He needed to be more presentable to meet so many dignitaries.

From there he went out to Le Bourget to give a more detailed inspection of the NYP. Arrangements, which Lindbergh accepted, were made by the French firm to repair the airplane and get it in airworthy condition.

While Mr. Sheldon Whitehouse of the U.S. Embassy acted as interpreter, Lindbergh visited with the President of France, Gaston Doumergue, at his private headquarters in Elysee Palace. Also present was Premier Poincaire. The President pinned the Cross of the Legion of Honor on the lapel of Lindbergh's suit, warmly kissing him on both cheeks.

Lindbergh gave his first speech at the Aero Club of France in the evening. With a packed house, including P. E. Flandrin, President of the Aero Club, the French Minister of War Paul Painleve, and fifty of the leading aviators of France, they made him the guest of honor. In a statement Flandrin said, "Lindbergh, you have set back the limits of the impossible." Painleve added, " Lindbergh, you have added to the sum of human heroism." Myron Herrick whispered to Lindbergh that he should respond to France's welcome. With that Lindbergh told them, "Nungesser and Coli had attempted a far greater flight or challenge than himself when they left Paris to fly to New York, and their difficulties far exceeded mine." He went on to say tactfully, "France should not give up hope." [17]

A speech by Ambassador Herrick emphasized the strengthened good will between France and America. He went on to point out the importance of Lindbergh's flight in cementing international warmth and friendliness from the people of America toward the people of France. As one writer put it, "Lindbergh was an 'ambassador without portfolio."

Tuesday, May 24

Lindbergh received a cabled invitation from President Coolidge via Secretary of Navy, Wilbur to return to the United States aboard one of the vessels of Destroyer Division 25 or the cruiser Memphis, at that time docked in Cadiz, Spain. [18]

It was also on this day that he began receiving hundreds of congratulatory messages from governmental heads throughout the world.

He was a luncheon guest at the American Club. Six hundred American citizens living in Paris joined him. The luncheon was held in one of the hangars with the NYP in its place of honor decked out in French and American flags. The patches being

Rare photo showing the NYP with the engine running while inside the hangar, for some reason. ***(Archives of the Royal Palace, Brussels, Belgium)***

Photo of original tablet which says—"Charles Lindbergh after having crossed the Atlantic landed here on the 21st of May, 1927." Lower left it says—"International League of Aviators. President, Clifford B. Harmon" Lower right it says—"Les Vieilles Tiges President; Leon Bathiat'. The tablet was set up as a landmark by the International League of Aviators in France and imbedded and flush with the concrete on the apron in front of the main terminal at Le Bourget, Paris, approximately 80 feet from the building. It is of granite material. ***(Photo by Ev Cassagneres)***

applied to the left side of the fuselage, can be seen in one of the photos taken May 24th.

Wednesday, May 24

On this day Lindbergh visited the French Chamber of Deputies at the President's residence. It was here that the increased cordiality between America and France became clear in a speech by France's adored General Gouraud when he said, "It is not only two continents that you have united, but the hearts of all men everywhere in admiration of the simple courage of a man who does great things....You and your youth belong to that glorious band of which M. Bleriot standing here beside you was one, and which has opened the great spaces. We greet you also in the name of those others of your countrymen who, in the Lafayette Escadrille, died here for France, who like you, helped to frame that unalterable fraternity, that indissoluble friendship which unites our two peoples. [19]

Lindbergh's reply: "Gentlemen, one hundred thirty-two years ago Benjamin Franklin was asked: 'What good is your balloon? What will it accomplish?' He replied, 'What good is a newborn child?' Less than twenty years ago when I was not far advanced from infancy, M. Bleriot flew across the English Channel and was asked 'What good is your aeroplane? What will it accomplish?' Today those same skeptics might ask me what good has been my flight from New York to Paris. My answer is that I believe it is the forerunner of a great air service from America to France, America to Europe, to bring our peoples nearer together in understanding and in friendship than they have ever been." In true Lindbergh style, he said a lot in a few words. [20]

Lindbergh had lunch this day with Louis Bleriot, who presented Lindbergh with a piece of the propeller of that famous aeroplane in which he first flew the English Channel in 1909.

Lindbergh had a brief visit with Marshal Ferdinand Foch, former Commander-in-Chief of the Allied Armies, and then went to Les Invalides to pay respects to disabled French and Belgium veterans of World War I.

Later he attended an official reception at the Hotel de Ville and received the Gold Medal of Paris. He visited at the home of Marshal Joffre, Father of the French Army and hero of the Marne, lunched with Foreign Minister Briand and other diplomatic celebrities at the Quai d'Orsay.

Thursday, May 26 "Lindbergh Day"

On this day Lindbergh attended the official reception by the City of Paris. By this time he was at the pinnacle of popularity with the Parisians and all of France. He received the Gold Medal of Paris in a ceremony that took place at the Hotel de Ville.

Ambassador Herrick was a guest speaker, delivering his most widely quoted and well delivered idea. "I am not a religious man, but I believe there are certain things that happen in life which can only be described as the interpretation of a Divine Act. I would not be surprised if this flight marks the beginning of a return of that sympathy and affection which lasted one hundred and fifty years between France and America. Lindbergh brought you the spirit of America in a manner in which it could never be brought in a diplomatic sack." [21]

Friday, May 27

At daybreak he made his way to Le Bourget where he was offered the opportunity to fly a 300 hp French built fighter airplane. Two Nieuport 29C Pursuit airplanes were taken out of the Chasse group's hanger. One was all black, with a white stork on the fuselage. It was Commandant Pinsard's airplane. Lindbergh, dressed in a flying suit with a fur collar, settled in at the controls, of Pinsard's Nieuport.

On board the second airplane a tall, smiling young man took his place. It was Michel Detroyat.

The engines roared into action. Soon they were in the air, putting on a show of aerobatics and a stunning air battle, demonstrating their skill and expertise, much to the delight of the local populace as well as the French flyers.

While at the airport he took another look at the NYP to check on repairs and servicing and later that morning it appeared he made a brief visit to the large military aviation field at Villa Coublay.

At noon he attended a luncheon with Paul Painleve, Minister of War, Marshal Foch, General Pershing of the United States and several French ministers.

In the afternoon he went to the Luxembourg Palace, where he was received by the French Senate. After that he attended a garden party at the Ministry of Commerce and a reception at the Airmen's Club in the Bois de Boulogne.

In the evening Lindbergh attended a gala performance at the Champs Elysees Theatre, a benefit for the Airmen's Relief Fund.

Saturday, May 28

In his usual manner of rising early, Lindbergh had breakfast at the Embassy and at about 8 a.m. was driven out to Le Bourget. Once there he spent a good three hours preparing and pre-flighting the NYP for his flight to Belgium. It is not known exactly what he did to groom the airplane during that time, but in addition to an extensive pre-flight because of the major repairs and servicing, he must have gone over in detail his routing, consulting with French flyers as to navigation and checkpoints.

An arrangement had been made so that Lindbergh give his farewell to Paris in a message wrapped in a French flag dropped at the base of Cleopatra's Needle, the obelisk brought from Egypt by Napoleon, located in the historic Place de la Concorde. The package was prepared as he ate his lunch sandwiches at 10:45 a.m. in the hangar.

After an emotional moment with those who had been closest to him during the week of his stay, they all expressed their farewells.

Every precaution had been taken to be sure the field was clear and there were no masses of people on the field, as happened during the May 21st landing.

At Lindbergh's apparent request, there would be no formal escort of aircraft as he left Le Bourget for Brussels. However, the French government did detail several of their military airplanes to follow him at some distance. Commandant Weiss did command a three plane V formation in tribute.

As he climbed out of Bourget, the many friends he had made stood there with moist eyes, lost in their emotions of the past week , a time that not one of them would ever forget for the rest of their lives.

The city of Paris again expressed her sentiments with whistles and horns until Lindbergh disappeared in a north-north east direction. He had circled twice around the Eiffel Tower and the Arc de Triomphe, and released his flag-enclosed farewell at Cleopatra's Needle in the Place de la Concorde.

Again, as with the New York to Paris flight, he traveled with a minimum of personal belongings. Whatever he had showered upon him during his Paris stay was sent ahead by regular passenger airplane so that he would not be obliged to borrow clothing from the King of Belgium.

In his final address to the French people, which was published sometime before his departure, he had this to say, "All the kindness the French people have shown me, and the many honors they have bestowed, are doubly dear to me as an aviator because France has been a leader in the development of aviation and has filled the pages of history with the names of her glorious heroes." When he referred to Nungesser and Coli he said, "Theirs was the hardest way to cross the Atlantic, and although they did not succeed, their names are immortal." [22]

MYRON T. HERRICK OPINION

Myron T. Herrick gave his opinion of the whole situation of Lindbergh coming to France as follows:

"How is it, then, that under these unpropitious conditions Lindbergh's arrival created such instant enthusiasm and sympathetic acclaim in all of France? I leave the scientific analysis of this question to the experts in mass psychology. For me the explanation lies, first, in the immediate response which Frenchmen make to any brave act. A gallant race themselves, courage excites their instant admiration and sweeps away all prejudices. But apart from this, I find a deeper reason in the latent feeling of admiration which exists in the hearts of the French for us Americans. Many of them had read the abuse of us and had joined in the criticism, but inside they really did not believe it; the instinct of the race was on our side. Therefore, in the presence of the decisive and amazing fact of Lindbergh's landing, this sentiment burst the bonds of an artificially excited prejudice, and in acclaiming this boy the people of France knew they were also expressing their innate love for their old friend, America. And they were glad of an excuse to do so." [23]

Herrick also once said, "Lindbergh was a perfectly mature man, for all his youthful appearance; that he knew exactly what he was about, and that nothing short of death would stop him."i

WEISS FAREWELL

Commander Weiss, in typical French sympathetic artistry had the following to say about his own impressions of the past week. The profoundly human and fraternal spirit was not lost in this translation. [24]

"Why farewell?

"Because this moment of union and joy which we have just lived through you, has flown with you...Your exploit is eternal, Lindbergh, but the fever of that night of waiting is not! Who will ever give it back to us?

"What is most delicious in these memories is that you have opened our eyes upon ourselves. We thought ourselves miserly in spirit, incapable of enthusiasm, rather blasé about everything, indifferent or worried. Your white apparition was sufficient—as in 1914 a call to arms was sufficient—to make the people of France again find that deep in its heart abides a constant longing for the infinite.

In 1977, the fiftieth anniversary of Lindbergh's flight, this photo was taken of (on left) Fernand Sarrazin, the chief mechanic, and Andre Braconnier who heard the pulsating engine of Lindbergh as he came overhead that night and ran to turn on the airport lights. He was the airport electrician. ***(Leo B. Kimball collection)***

"That crowd which on May 21 covered the plain of Le Bourget certainly desired your success, but without conviction and without fervor. When your air eddies had passed, everything changed. At the sound of the unusual motor a gravity without equal seized the conscience. People stopped thinking and held their breath to hear the sound of that historic second, and the throng for a lightning moment, was an immense prayer.

"We bless you, Lindbergh, for having thus brought us together, for having shown us the pride of living, for making us shed tears at a beautiful deed.

"And then the following days you ascended higher, if it is possible! You passed sentence on that familiar error which opposes muscle against brain, action against spirit. The victor, the air athlete, the scaler of the ocean, was also a young sage.

"Having terminated your task, you mounted the tribune in the assemblies, and as simple, as modest, as free among the statesmen as at your pilot's post, you spoke in short, precise phrases, articulated very quietly-real lessons in measure, tact and judgement-in the midst of the delirium.

"You have power, Lindbergh, but you also have soul...

"And it is your soul which conquered the French soul that is dispersed in all of us-the French soul which has saved us so many times. For, know it well, you have set us in a state of grace. Those civilians who raised you on their shoulders were the red and blue soldier of the Marne, the horizon-blue soldiers of Rheims and Douaumont. Those women who thrust their children toward you were the mothers and widows of the war, all the Calvary of the mother country. It was not Paris alone, but all our provinces; it was Alsace! And you had become suddenly, America drawing the sword, flying to the battlefield.

"Farewell, Lindbergh! The void frightens us as your fine profile disappears, but the spell is not broken. You remain for us the small ray of hope which makes the work lighter, the effort more voluntary, and life more like the dawn." *(Aircraft Year Book, 1928, Aeronautical Chamber of Commerce of America, Inc. New York City, p. 10)*

Information on Lindbergh's itinerary while in Paris before he left for Belgium was gleaned from several different sources and publications, some of which were Aviation magazine, Aero-Digest magazine, World's Work for January, The New York Times, The New York Herald Tribune, The Daily Telegraph (England).

This information was carefully studied for accuracy and consistency and compared with any other documentation available.

FOOTNOTES

1. French publications—"The Dawn of Aeronautical Vocation" Chapter III; "Head of Line for Commercial Aviation" Chapter V, supplied by Stefan Nicolaou, Musee de l'air, archives at Le Bourget Aeroport, France. Translation by Eileen Brown, MSEd, teacher of French.

2. *The Spirit of St. Louis,* Charles A. Lindbergh, Charles Scribner's Sons, New York, NY, page 495.

3. *Globe-Democrat,* a St. Louis newspaper, May 23, 1927.

4. *Spirit,* Ibid. page 497.

5. Ibid. page 498.

6. Ibid. page 501.

7. Aved les compliments du centre Culturel Americain, Priere de bien vouloir adresser un justificatif a; Press Section U.S.I.S., 4 Avenue Gabriel, paris, France, No 422 detroyat. Translation from French into English by French instructor laura Longacre of the Cheshire Academy, Cheshire, CT, October 1994.

8. Ibid.

9. Interview with Elizabeth Bell of Gill, Massachusetts. Also letter to the author dated July 19, 1992, August 6, 1992, and October 1, 1992.

10. Letters and interviews, winter of 1998 with Francoise de Peyrelongue, now Mrs. F. Kalognomos of Bantam, CT and Lessay, France.

11. *The New York Times* newspaper, New York City, Monday, May 23, 1927, page 4.

12. *The New York Herald Tribune* newspaper, New York City. Data compiled from the European Edition of May 21, 22, 23, 1927.

13. Ibid.

14. *World's Work for January,* pages 67-69 "Herrick and Lindbergh" author, publisher, and date of publication unknown. Copy in possession of author.

15. "Rendezvous with a memory of landing" publication unknown, interview with Fernand Sarrazin, somewhere in France, Date unknown. Copy in possession of author.

16. *St. Louis Star* newspaper, May 23, 1927, page 2.

17. *We,* Charles A. Lindbergh, G.P. Putnam's Sons, New York and London, The Knickerbocker Press, 1928, with a Foreword by Myron T. Herrick, U.S. Ambassador to France, and an Epilogue by Fitzhugh Green, first edition, page 240.

18. *U.S.S. Memphis,* a pamphlet edited by Roy E. Bishop, Chaplain, U.S. Navy, from material compiled by *All Hands, Log of U.S.S. Memphis,* page 7. Date and location of publication unknown. Copy in possession of author.

19. Ibid. page 242.

20. Ibid. page 243.

21. Ibid. page 246

22. Ibid. page 247.

23. *World's Work.* Ibid. page 72.

24. *Aircraft Yearbook,* 1928, Aeronautical Chamber of Commerce of America, inc. New York City, page 9.

ENDNOTES

Careful study of photographs in the author's collection as seen through a magnifying glass, revealed details of the NYP structure showing damage to particular airframe areas and equipment, while at Le Bourget Aerodrome, Paris, France, from May 21 through May 28, 1927.

CHAPTER 10

NYP in Belgium

Capsule History of the City

Bruxelles (Brussels) is the capital and second largest city in Belgium. Often called "Little Paris" because of its beautiful ancient and modern buildings, wide boulevards and world trade.

The city was founded sometime in the 500's. It became the capital of the Austrian Netherlands in 1477 and was known as one of the most pleasant and prosperous cities in Europe. It was a part of the kingdom of The Netherlands until 1830 when Belgium separated from Holland and made Brussels its capital.

In 1927 the only airfield for Brussels was known as Evere Aerodrome. It was northeast of the city, south of Leopold Laan Avenue and north of Leuvensesteenweg and just east of the General Wahis Laan, near St. Stevens-Woluwe. It was on the grounds of two communities, Haeren and Evere. (Haeren today is known as Haren.) The field was established after the Great War as a military aerodrome, and closed sometime after World War II. On that site today one can find the military cemetery and the Belgian military archives. [1]

May 28, 1927 to May 29, 1927
(Saturday & Sunday)

The flight to Paris from New York aroused so much interest around the world, especially in Europe, it was not surprising that Lindbergh received invitations to visit and be honored at that time throughout Europe. After all, he was already on the continent. Although I have not researched such requests, I would imagine that Ambassador Herrick's office in Paris was inundated with such invitations.

One that did come in, and which Lindbergh worked into his schedule, was from Brussels, Belgium via the American Embassy. Belgian state officials actually felt it would be impossible to invite him as a personal guest of the Embassy, but when Mr. Morrow, president of the American Club of Brussels, suggested inviting him to be a guest of honor at a luncheon or dinner to be given by the Club, the desired opportunity presented itself.

Therefore, on Monday morning, Mary 23rd, The Honorable James Clement Dunn, American charge d'affaires, sent the following telegram to Mr. Herrick at the American Embassy in Paris:

"FOR THE AMBASSADOR. AMERICAN CLUB OF BRUSSELS HAS ASKED TO HAVE TRANSMITTED THROUGH YOUR GOOD OFFICES AN INVITATION TO LINDBERGH TO COME TO BRUSSELS ANY TIME AFTER NEXT SUNDAY. AMERICAN CLUB WOULD LIKE TO HAVE LUNCHEON IN HIS HONOR. KING HAS CONVEYED CONGRATULATIONS TO EMBASSY AND HAS RECEIVED FROM ALL SIDES ENTHUSIASTIC EXPRESSIONS OF FELICITATIONS AT MAGNIFICENT PERFORMANCE. I DO HOPE LINDBERGH CAN ARRANGE TO COME AS EVERYONE HERE IS EAGER TO RECEIVE HIM.

DUNN"

Because of the damage to the NYP at Paris, the Belgians did not want the same to happen there, so placed the airplane on this platform under armed guard. ***(Archives of the Royal Palace, Brussels, Belgium***

On Wednesday morning, May 25, Mr. Whitehouse telephoned from Paris announcing that Lindbergh would come to Brussels on Saturday, May 28th, and he would leave Monday, May 30th for London, England. A special meeting of the American Club Board of Governors was quickly called for the afternoon of the 25th. A tentative program was drawn up and plans were made for Lindbergh's visit. The plan was as follows:

Lindbergh and James Clement Dunn, American Charge d'affaires, just after landing at Evere. ***(Image courtesy of BETTMANN/CORBIS)***

May 28, 1927 ***(Saturday)***

3:00a.m.	Arrival at Evere Aviation Field, on northern outskirts of Brussels. Short reception by officials, then to American Embassy.
4:30	Reception for representatives of the Press at Embassy
5:15	Visit to Tomb of Unknown Soldier, to lay wreath upon the cenotaph.
5:20	Audience with the King at Palais de Bruzelles.
5:55	Lay wreath at foot of Monument to Belgian Aviators, Port Louise.
6:00	Reception by Royal Aero Club of Belgium (Royal Aeroclub de Belgique) at the Club House on Avenue Louise.
8:00	Dinner given by the American Club of Brussels, which was honored by presence of H.R.H. (His Royal Highness) also Z.K.H. Zijne Koninklijke Hoogheid) the Duke of Brabant (Prince Leopold III)
12:00	Noon, May 28 (Saturday) Reception at the Hotel de Ville 2(City Hall) by Burgomaster , Adolphe Max, on the part of the city of Brussels.
1:30 p.m.	Small luncheon given by Mr. & Mrs. Dunn at Embassy.
3:30	Departure from Evere for London, England. [2]

In actuality he took off from Paris (Le Bourget) on Saturday, May 28th at about 1:00 p.m. and headed in a north-north-east direction, after circling Paris. Enroute he circled the little town of Senlis, and further north he circled the city of Valenciennes, at about 2:30 p.m. before crossing the border into Belgium.

Plans for his arrival at Evere were coordinated by Major Smeyers, chief of the Military Aviation of the Belgian Army. King Albert I had given orders—"At all costs, Lindbergh must come off the field (Evere) untouched." [3]

From about noon the local police and the troops of the garrison took their positions to form a gigantic square around the airport, in which Lindbergh could land. The wind was rather strong and blowing out of the west, while sunshine and blue sky prevailed.

Music was provided, beginning at 1:30, by the Aeronautique Militaire (Air Force) to calm the large throngs of people already assembling in the area. Around 2:00 a flight of Belgian aircraft went aloft to greet Lindbergh and escort him to Evere.

At 3:08 Lindbergh and the NYP appeared overhead and the crowd went wild—"It's he, it's Lindbergh." According to one report their emotions were overcoming them. Lindbergh made a low pass across the field to check out the landing surface, followed by a large military airplane. He landed at precisely 3:15 p.m. [4]

After his arrival the "Spirit of St. Louis" was placed on a raised platform to prevent people from getting too close and doing damage. They did not want the same problem that took place in Paris on the night of his landing.

According to reports there were no less than 75,000 people at the airport when he arrived. A small reception was held at the officers' mess at the field. At that time Prime Minister Mr. H. Jaspar greeted him in the name of Belgium, and he received many Belgian high officials and officers of the American Club of Brussels. He was then motored through the streets lined with cheering crowds to the American Embassy.

He was taken immediately to his room in the Embassy, where he changed from his flying clothes into street clothes. He said that he had always wanted to visit Brussels and had a sympathetic feeling toward Belgium since the war. He made a great hit by announcing at several of the receptions that while in New York he had hoped he could visit Belgium after his Paris visit. [5]

Lindbergh remarked that he had not been subjected to customs examination at Evere and asked if airplanes arriving at the field did not have to pass customs. It was explained to him that he had been permitted to land on the military side of the field and that the customs examination had been waived in this case.

While he was changing, enormous crowds collected in front of the Embassy building, yelling out "Au balcon—Au balcon," (on the balcony.) The reason for his delay in getting out on the balcony was that he could not find his collar button. When finally reaching the balcony, he displayed a Belgian flag, which he waved to the crowd below. This gesture brought a tremendous burst of enthusiasm from the people standing in the square.

Lindbergh had never prepared beforehand, due to lack of time, for any of his speeches at the various receptions and most of the time did not know whether or not he would be expected to speak until asked by his host. At the American Club banquet he asked, "What shall I talk about?" He was told that everyone would be tremendously interested to hear about his flight. As a result he gave a most captivating account of the crossing. The Belgians were impressed to realize that he was actually making history and describing the event in real time. [6]

One of the thousand messages which interested him most was a telegram from a Boy Scout group in Antwerp. They were taking him as a model of inspiration to youth for his courage and for his principles of devotion to his work. [7]

On the way to the Palace where he would be presented to the King, Lindbergh asked Mr. Dunn if there were anything which he could be particularly told regarding his presentation. Dunn said there was nothing whatever to tell him. The King was quite eager to receive him because he too was a pilot and very keen on aviation in general. Lindbergh was pleased because it would be much easier for both of them to talk airplanes. [8]

Now it was time for Lindbergh to meet his first real King. At 5:30 pm. Lindbergh was received at the Palace by the King and

Queen, surrounded by the Duke and Duchess of Brabant. The first thing King Albert I (nephew of King Leopold II) said to him was that he had calculated Lindbergh's speed and direction, and that the "Spirit of St. Louis" had passed over Ireland very close to the point which the King himself had marked, but that Lindbergh was slightly in advance of the time calculated. This interested Lindbergh very much indeed and immediately put him at ease with Their Majesties. The King and Queen were most informal throughout the audience, the King even insisting that they all sit down himself, bringing up chairs for the group of four. [9]

The Queen inquired about Lindbergh's mother, and it was learned after the audience that she had sent a telegram to Mrs. Lindbergh in Detroit, Michigan.

During the audience the King expressed a desire to inspect the "Spirit of St. Louis" and asked if Lindbergh would be free on Sunday morning. Lindbergh turned to Dunn who did not believe he had anything which would prevent him from placing himself at the service of the King. Dunn thereupon took the liberty of observing that if the King so desired they might all meet at Evere Sunday morning, where if no announcement of the visit had been made the King could quietly make a thorough inspection of the "Spirit of St. Louis." The King said that nothing would give him greater pleasure and asked them to keep the secret between the four. He would tell no one, not even his own household. [10]

Dunn asked permission to inform Major Smyers, chief of the Military Aviation and also to have present the two Belgian aces, Georges Medaets and Jean Verhaegen. He felt that Lindbergh would be interested to talk with them and see the airplane in which they had flown to the Belgian Congo. It was agreed, therefore, that they would all meet Sunday morning, the 29th, at 10 o'clock, at Evere.

At the termination of his audience with the King and Queen, the King graciously conferred upon Lindbergh the rank of Chevalier of the Royal Order of Leopold. The decoration was pinned upon Lindbergh's breast by His Majesty himself.

Shortly thereafter the King said, "And now Captain Lindbergh, my children would like very much to meet you, if you do not mind." And with that the King immediately sent for Princess Marie-Jose and the Count of Flanders Prince Charles, who both came down with Lindbergh to the door where the motorcar was waiting. [11]

The next stop for Lindbergh was to lay a wreath at the foot of a Monument to Belgian Aviators, Porte Louise. This monument was erected in the memory of fallen aviators during the campaign of 1914-1918.

During the reception by the Royal Aero Club of Belgium, one of the oldest aviation clubs in the world, presided over by Mr. M. Adelin d'Oultremont, president, and Mr. Jean Wolff, general secretary of the club, Lindbergh received the great gold medal of the Aero Club and an engraved parchment upon which was recorded his election as Honorary Member of the Club. Also at this reception, Victor Boin, a former champion fencer representing the Sporting Press, in his enthusiasm kissed Lindbergh on both cheeks. In speaking of it afterward someone asked him if he had become accustomed to this form of embrace in France. He said that he had been kissed a great many times and had become quite accustomed to it by now, but he wished that Parisian girls would not use fresh lipstick just before kissing him. [12]

Several remarks were made at this time by Mr. Anseele, Minister of Aviation. "What you have done is more than a feat, it is an "ouvre" (work) that will always exist in the history of man, that will permit mankind not to doubt neither the genius nor the audacity and that crown gloriously the conquest of the air. You have undone the proverb: "A l'impossible nul n'est tenu." (When impossible, nothing is kept.) When we see your calm and your smile, we feel that you are hiding behind us all the science of your art, experience, audacity and the supreme quality between them: faith in oneself and all that makes you truly superb. As Minister of Aviation, I thank you with all of my heart . I am convinced that you will have transformed the mentality of our people on the subject of the art of aviation and that in a few hours you will have done more for the success of my department than hundreds of conferences. I am now certain that when I ask for several millions to have an airport at Evere built, the works of markers and others for air transportation, when I ask that Brussels be made an international center of aviation in response to its geographic location, I am convinced that all this will be accorded to me without difficulty, with joy, while thinking of you and while honoring you. Now, I no longer doubt that all the friends of aviation in Belgium will be doubly appreciative of you having heroically flown over the ocean and having come to greet us in Brussels."

In reply, Lindbergh said, "I thought that I had felt all my emotions after my landing at Bourget where I was greeted triumphantly. I thought that such a reception could not be created again. I was mistaken because Brussels has just equaled Paris. I thank you profoundly." [14]

On that same evening Lindbergh was honored at a banquet at the American Club of Brussels. Lindbergh was formally welcomed by Mr. Dunn, in the name of King Albert I. After a toast to Lindbergh, Prime Minister Jaspar arose and said, "The Belgian government is happy to be able to salute the young hero who, several days after his arrival in France, had agreed to come to Belgium. He had dreamed of this trip before his departure from America, he told us this afternoon. We see in this gesture proof of the friendship that unites America and our country." He went on to say, "He owes his success to the calm, to the serenity that did not leave him. He celebrates the simple man, the man of action, who remains himself. Admiration because he comes from America, from that people that leaned on us during the war. The bringing together of the continents is the symbol of the joining of the hearts. Lindbergh is future, hope and progress. He symbolizes in his gesture, besides the unprecedented feat, man's victory over the elements."

Mr. Hadelin of Oultremont, president of the Royal Aero Club of Belgium, was the next speaker. "As I had said over an hour ago, it is the method, linked to science and to courage, that van-

Photo taken on Sunday morning, May 29th. Lindbergh gave a special showing to the King and Queen . L to R: Queen Elizabeth of Belgium, Lindbergh, King Albert I, and The Honorable James Clement Dunn, American Charge d'affaires. ***(Archives of the Royal Palace, Brussels, Belgium)***

Her Majesty Queen Elizabeth of Belgium, thrilled to be sitting in the cockpit of the famous airplane. Sunday, May 29th. ***(courtesy Exxon Mobil Corporation)***

quished and conquered space. Charles Lindbergh has given us a wonderful lesson in energy, endurance and savoir faire. He constitutes a living example for present and future aviators." [15]

After the dinner Lindbergh visited the new club house of the Cercle Gaulois, which had been opened for the first time that day.

May 29 ***(Sunday morning)***

At 9:00 a.m. on Sunday morning, Lindbergh arrived at Evere to check on the NYP. The morning was a pleasant one, with brilliant sunshine and warm temperatures.

Shortly a car from the Court stopped just outside the hangar where the NYP was kept during the night. King Albert and Queen Elisabeth, accompanied by Major Hennin of Boussu Walcourt got out to meet with Lindbergh as planned. Due to the tight security and secrecy of this royal visit, there were no curious on-lookers or people from the press on the field.

Lindbergh demonstrated how he entered and sat in the tight cockpit. The Queen's eyes sparkled like a small child's when she was told she could mount into the seat of this famous airplane. Both she and the King took turns in the cockpit. The King had many detailed questions to present to Lindbergh: how the airplane handled, how it worked in general. Lindbergh, with a smile on his pink face and in his usual relaxed mood, answered every question clearly, and the conversation lasted over a half hour.

The Queen herself had her own camera and took several pictures of Lindbergh and their little group. Efforts to locate these photographs have not been successful, and it is a mystery where they could be today.

Even though the meeting was kept entirely secret and escaped all journalists, two wide-awake Americans with one photographer managed to follow the party from the Embassy.

At precisely noon Lindbergh accompanied by Mr. Dunn and Major MacDonald, arrived at the Hotel de Ville, which was actually the City Hall of Brussels. It was at this reception that Burgomaster Max conferred upon Lindbergh the medal of the City of Brussels.

After a luncheon given by Mr. & Mrs. Dunn at the American Embassy, Lindbergh went up to his room to change his clothes and when he came down to the living room he said, "Well, what about this trip to London?" At that point he pulled out of the pocket of his leather flying jacket two or three maps which were on the scale usually used in school room maps. Among these maps was the one he had used in crossing the Atlantic, upon which his course was marked out taking him directly to Paris. He laid his small map of Belgium with the Channel, northern France and part of England, up to just west of London, upon the top of the Dunn's gramaphone and asked if they had a ruler and pencil. Someone found a long tortoise shell paper cutter straight edge and Mr. Mitchell loaned him his pencil. Lindbergh then laid out his course in a direct line, due west from Brussels. Paul Mayo, thinking of the Memorial Day ceremony at the Waereghem Cemetery and seeing that Lindbergh's course passed very near Waereghem, (now Waregem) suggested that he might be able to fly over the town on his way. When the Memorial Day celebration was explained to Lindbergh, he was immediately enthusiastic about the idea and suggested that he write a note which could be attached to a bouquet of flowers which he would drop at the cemetery as he passed over. A large bouquet of flowers was immediately made up. Lindbergh sat down and wrote the note and a telephone message was sent to the Burgomaster at Waereghem announcing Lindbergh's passage at about four o'clock.

His whole attitude in laying out his course from Brussels to London was most nonchalant, and he did not seem to have given any thought to it until he started with the paper cutter and pencil to lay out his course on his small scale map.

In watching the line being drawn from Brussels to London, Dunn happened to see that it passed a few miles to the south of North Foreland point, on the coast of England. Dunn remarked that Lindbergh was passing very close to the place where their daughter was at school in England. Upon hearing this Lindbergh immediately asked where she was and whether there would be any means of identifying the school. Dunn was terrified, as he did not want to be responsible for any accident to Lindbergh on his way to England. He felt a certain responsibility for Lindbergh while he was in Belgium until he arrived in London safely.

But Dunn already had said the school was near the North Foreland light, but refused to tell him anything further about it and insisted that he should not pay any attention to it on his way over as he had enough to think about.

Lindbergh said nothing further, but sometime later Dunn received a letter from his daughter Marianne explaining that on Sunday afternoon she had been playing in the garden and that suddenly someone said that Lindbergh was coming. She described him flying quite low, past the North Foreland light, and described the airplane as having "one wing", whereas the two aircraft accompanying had "two wings". Curiously enough he had flown right over the garden of her school, without knowing exactly that it was her school. [16]

As Dunn and Lindbergh were driving to Evere for his departure for London, Dunn asked him if they could have some signed photographs as a souvenir for the Embassy. In reply, tapping his breast pocket, Lindbergh said that he had already written a memorandum to remind him to send just such photographs for Their Majesties and the Royal family as well as some for the members of the Embassy.

Lindbergh standing with King Albert I. ***(Musee Royal de L'armee, Brussels, Belgium)***

NYP *in flight on its way to Brussels, Belgium, May 28, 1927. This is either near or outside Paris.* ***(Leo B. Kimball collection)***

Lindbergh took off from Evere at 3:30 p.m. Sunday afternoon and shortly flew low over the white crosses in a cemetery near Ghent, where he dropped a wreath.

He had flown west-north-west to reach Ghent. After dropping the flowers he changed course to a south-west direction, toward Waereghem, where he dropped another wreath of flowers on the local American cemetery.

From Waereghem he headed more or less westerly and approached the Belgian coast at about Dunkirk (Dunkerque), and thereafter headed across the English Channel toward the coast of England, at approximately Margate, at the northern end of the Strait of Dover, and the southern part of the North Sea. There is some speculation that he may have left the shores of Belgium at the coastal town of Nieuwpoort (Nieuport, in French), north of Dunkirk

The NYP on Evere Aerodrome on May 29th, as Lindbergh prepared for his flight to London with the local military standing by. ***(Musee Royal de L'Armee, Brussels, Belgium)***

FOOTNOTES

1. Letter to the author, July 16, 2000 from belgiam aviation historian, Jean Dillen, Duerne, Belgium.
2. Official report by Mr. James Clement Dunn, American charge d'affaires, 9 pages. report found in the Archives de Palais Royal, brussels, belgium, July 1994. The report covers the complete itinerary of Lindbergh's visit to Belgium from Saturday, May 28, 1927 to May 30, 1927.
3. Ibid.
4. Ibid.
5. Ibid.
6. Ibid.
7. Ibid.
8. Ibid.
9. Ibid.
10. Ibid.
11. *The New York Times*, Sunday, May 29, 1927, "King Albert Decorates Lindbergh, Who Flies from Paris to Brussels: He Writes of His Busy Weekend Abroad," New York City, page 1.
12. James Dunn, Ibid.
13. Lindbergh in Brussels. Ibid.
14. Ibid.
15. Ibis.
16. Ibid.

ENDNOTES

National Geographic maps of Belgium, and France, in addition to appropriate road maps by Rand-McNally, The American Automobile Association, and maps as published by RAC Publlications, South Croydon, England, Dressee par la manufacture Francaise de Pnaumatiques Michelin, France, were checked by the author for correct general compass headings over specific towns, cities and bodies of water, in addition to correct distances between specific points.

Careful study of photographs in the author's collection revealed details of NYP structure, etc. while in Belgium from Saturday, May 28, to Sunday, May 29, 1927.

Personal research visits with Gustaaf Janssens, Dr. Philosophy & Letters (Histoire,) Chef de section aux Archives Generales du Royaume, Archiviste au Palais Royal, Bruxelles, Belgium (Belgique,) Wednesday, July 13, 1994.

Letter to the author from Jean Dillen, Duerne, Belgium, January 1, 1994, with explanation of names, places, people, and correct spelling of same. Includes other historical facts and translations.

Charles A. Lindbergh's personal pilot log. Copy at Yale University, Sterling memorial Library, manuscripts and Archives department, New Haven, CT. Log dated from November 11, 1926 to July 7, 1928.

Lindbergh A Bruxelles (Lindbergh in Brussels) Printed in French. Author not known, from Aero Club of Royal de Belgiuge, translated by Laura Longacre, Professor of French, Cheshire Academy, Chesire, CT, December, 1994.

CHAPTER 11

England-Croydon

Capsule History of the City

When the Romans conquered Britain in A. D. 43, they built a bridge near Westminster on the River Thames. They gave the name Londinium to the settlement near the bridge.

It is the capital of the United Kingdom of Great Britain and Northern Ireland. Not only is it the largest city in England, but also one of the largest in the world. It lies on the River Thames near the southeastern coast of England.

Capsule History of Croydon

In the year A. D. 960 the will of Beorhtric and Aelfswyth was found in which the witness is "Elfsies the Priest of Croydon." This was apparently the first time the word Croydon was written, but spelled Crogdaene, from the Anglo-Saxon Parish Church. It was most likely the very center of the settlement south of London in Anglo-Saxon times. It was also spelled Croindene in the time of King Edward. The village was also known as Croydon Manor, Croydon House, Croydon Archiepiscopal Palace or the Old Palace. The old churchmen had a keen eye for a good site; they loved natural beauty before people really discussed or sought for it as they do now.

In 1915 German Zeppelin raids reached Croydon. Because of these raids, which included London, a small number of airfields were selected for fighters to operate and oppose these invaders. Croydon was selected (then called Waddon Aerodrome) and later enlarged, and on January 1st 1928 it became the just rebuilt aerodrome with wireless in order to be in direct contact with the airlines of the time. [1]

Sunday, May 29, 1927

Lindbergh's original plan was to approach the English coast at about Dover, but he actually made landfall after crossing the English Channel at North Foreland Point, north of Ramsgate, just about over the town of Margate. This is where the Straits of Dover meet the southern part of the North Sea.

Headed westerly over the Isle of Sheppey, he approached the mouth of the River Thames.

An hour or so before Lindbergh was due, a large contingent of aircraft took off from Croydon to meet him some place along his expected air route from the Straits of Dover. This "armada" included R.H. McIntosh, former RAF Wing Commander, working as a civil pilot for Imperial Airways, Ltd., in a 230 hp Siddeley-Puma powered De Havilland DH 50A. McIntosh was commissioned by the *London Daily Sketch* to get photographs of the NYP in the air. [2]

Another DH 50, (G-EBFP) was flown by A.L. Robinson; Neville Stack was flying a DH 9. Jimmie Youell was flying a W.8b full of sight seers and photographers. Also flying was Capt. Wally Hope in a DH 50. Among the other planes were a Handley Page

If you look very closely, you will see the NYP as it approached the coast of England, north of the town of Ramsgate, over the town of Margate ***(Missouri Historical Society, St. Louis)***

NYP being escorted by three British aircraft, near Croydon, on May 28th. ***(Leo B. Kimball collection)***

W10 (G-EBMR), "City of Pretoria," another Handley Page W9 (G-EBLE), "City of New York" piloted by Col. F.F. Minchin, another DH 50 "City of Ottawa," DH 50 "City of Melbourne," an Avro 504J or K (G-EBFM,) and an assortment of Avros and DH Moths and various other types.

Four of the aircraft were owned by Imperial Airways, Ltd., each chartered by wealthy parties to see the fun from aloft.

According to McIntosh, known in flying circles as "All Weather Mac," Lindbergh was in a playful mood and flew at tree-top level. Due to the high wing of the NYP Lindbergh could not know about the photo plane which meant the photographer just could not do his job. Then McIntosh came level with the NYP on the starboard side and with sign language was able to convey the problem. Lindbergh leaned out of the cabin window, displaying a broad grin. One might question where the photos are today, as none have turned up. [3]

Lindbergh proceeded to follow the Thames past Tilbury and Dartford. Several of the "escorting" aircraft joined him over Dartford. McIntosh held his close position next to Lindbergh.

As Lindbergh approached the Croydon Aerodrome (formerly the Beddington and Waddon Aerodrome 1915—1920) he noticed throngs of people and automobiles all around the airport. It was a mass of cars and humans, just like at Paris and later Brussels. Only this looked even worse.

He proceeded to circle the field, eventually lining up from the southwest. With McIntosh following closely, for a final approach over Plough Lane in the direction of the A.D.C hangars, he landed into a northeast wind.

Immediately the fences went down with the pressure of the crowds as people came onto the field from all directions. As he throttled back and did the flare and a 3-point landing, some of the people came within inches of the propeller. Imagine being in the cockpit and seeing this. So he did what any other sensible pilot would do, he full throttled it for a quick get away and "go-around" and was in the air again. The throngs of people were in complete defiance of warnings that an airplane must have a large area of ground to land on.

On his second approach from the same direction he was finally able to touch down and complete the landing to an almost full stop, touching down at precisely 6:05 pm. without hitting anyone. Flight time was two hours and thirty-five minutes. As one English journalist wrote, "In some ways it's unfortunate that he actually missed them and did land safely. If a few had been killed, no one would have been sorry unless the NYP had been damaged." [4]

Arrangements for handling the crowd were non-existent. No arrangements of any kind had been made. Flimsy stick-and-wire barriers were put along the side of the Aerodrome. Any one could have either pushed them down or just walked through or over, which of course they did.

Croydon Aerodrome authorities provided about seventy policemen and it was not long before they recognized their helplessness. The crowd was utterly out of control and behaved "just like a bunch of foreigners," as one reporter stated. [5]

The NYP was almost damaged upon initial landing, as one man tried to enter the cockpit and another climbed over the after portion of the fuselage and tore some fabric. Lindbergh later said it was almost worse than Paris.

The whole of the carefully planned program for Lindbergh was literally swept away by the large crowd.

The official welcoming party, consisting of The Air Minister Sir Samuel Hoare and Lady Maud Hoare, chiefs of the Royal Air Force, American Ambassador Alanson B. Houghton, American Charge d' Affairs Mr. Frederick A. Sterling, and many of the top-hatted compatriots, the Swedish Minister (Baron Palmstierna), the American Military and Naval Air Attaches, and a few privileged ladies stood waiting by an enormous American flag, which was laid on the ground to make him feel welcome.

With many of these dignitaries wearing top hats and all types of uniforms, the whole scene together with the flag suggested a burial party rather than a welcoming party. The closest resemblance to such a sight was when, unfortunately, the official party was completely buried by the crowd as they stormed over the airport. The group went down very gallantly with the big American flag draped over them.

A reporter for the *Wallington & Carshalton Times* wrote, "Scenes of wild enthusiasm the likes of which have never been known in the history of British aviation." It was estimated that well over 120,000 people attended. [6]

When Lindbergh finally turned off the magneto switches and the engine stopped, it was feared that if he were to climb out of the airplane immediately he more than likely would have been torn into souvenirs.

Lindbergh slips the NYP into Croydon Aerodrome as the thousands of people watch his every move. ***(Cradle of Aviation Museum)***

While all this was taking place many of the escorting aircraft were still up there and in a 'hold' over the field, concerned for their fuel supply, awaiting the order that the landing area was now available. Jimmie Youell went down to surface level with his airplane and with the strong slip-stream and prop wash created a dust storm along the landing area, convincing some of the crowd that he and the others needed to land sometime.

Some funny incidents happened and deeds of valor were plenty. Mr. Gordon Olley was gesticulating at the suicide-intent mobs and went down fighting gallantly. When some people screamed at the crowds and called them darn-fools, a very tiny man with an enormous wife said almost hopefully, "Were you speaking to my wife?" [7]

There is a report that a particularly beautiful air-cooled Franklin automobile was intended as a gift to Lindbergh but was damaged so much it had to be touched up all over before its official presentation. No further information as to its demise is known.

A battered car with Aero Club officials and police made their way to the airplane. Commander Harold C. Perrin, Secretary of the Royal Aero Club, and his megaphone were mounted on the hood of the car as a mascot. Lindbergh was placed on the floor of the auto and with the aid of Perrin's megaphone, it was announced to the frenzied crowd, "We've got a badly injured woman here. Let us through." With that the throngs stepped aside and quieted down a bit, a strong contrast to the frenzy of a moment earlier. [8]

As the car moved along, men could be seen bending over the "woman" who was Lindbergh lying on the floor. The crowd did not discover the clever move until Lindbergh was safely behind the bricks and mortar at the control tower building.

After things settled down, Commander Perrin, introduced Lindbergh with his megaphone. He said a few words about the development of aviation and was shortly whisked away to a recently completed, though not officially opened, new terminal building on the Purley Way.

Croydon Aerodrome was in the process of reconstruction to become London's official airport and was due to open in May of 1928.

So while all of the fanfare was going on Lindbergh got out of the airplane and headed for the tower. The NYP was hauled across the field, rescued from the clutches of the mobs, and brought to the new buildings on the other side. Fortunately, the people were by then more interested in seeing Lindbergh than his airplane, so this movement was allowed to proceed comparatively unhampered.

So the NYP was wheeled into a large and very new hangar to keep it from being vandalized by souvenir hunters. This hangar was on the Purley Way side of the aerodrome, which had just

Lindbergh is shown up on the balcony of the control tower building. In the background can be seen Handley Page W10 "City of Pretoria" EMBR and the Avro 504J or K registered as G-EBFM. ***(Phil Munson, England)***

Here is the NYP in a new hangar at Croydon Aerodrome. Photographer was a Mr. Satchell. ***(The R. J. Mitchell Memorial Museum, Southampton, England)***

been completed for Imperial Airways, but not yet brought into use. The airplane was the first one to be sheltered in that hangar, which is still standing today. [9]

In the evening Lindbergh slept in the Croydon Aerodrome Hotel which still exists and where many famous flyers stayed over the years.

ENGLAND ITINERARY
NYP TO GOSPORT

Monday, May 30

In the morning Lindbergh was awake shortly after daybreak, as he was quite anxious about the condition of the NYP, and made his way over to the new hangar where it was housed. Despite his fears, very little harm was found except for some damage to the stabilizer from the pressure of the crowd the night before and a small hole in one wing. Also, supposedly, two bolts were missing from the landing gear struts, although this has never been confirmed or proven by photos or other documentation. This accusation is rather doubtful as all of the main landing gear attach points were faired over with fabric. The only bolt readily accessible would be the one at the bottom of the vertical shock strut, where it attaches to the "V" strut near the axle.

Lunch was at the American Embassy, where Lindbergh met prominent World War I hero, Lieut. Col. W. A. (Billy) Bishop, the Canadian ace who had brought down seventy-two German aircraft.

In the afternoon Lindbergh attended a Memorial Day service honoring the war dead of England, which was held at St. Margaret's Church at Westminster.

Lindbergh and Ambassador Alanson B. Houghton walked to the tomb of the Unknown Soldier, where Lindbergh placed a wreath of flowers with the inscription—"In memory of England's unknown warrior—from the American people."

In the evening there was a private dinner at the Savoy Hotel by the Association of American Correspondents in the Abraham Lincoln Room. On the speaker's table before the guest of honor were five sandwiches and a half gallon jar of water. The Chairman gravely announced: "Captain Lindbergh will now partake of his customary meal." After a round of laughing applause, the real dinner was served. [10]

Sometime during the day the Air Ministry had guaranteed to make arrangements for the dismantling and packing of the NYP and shipment back to the United States. As a result of that order and later that evening, Air Chief Marshal, Sir Arthur Murray Longmore, Director of Equipment for the Air Ministry, who was completing some work at his office, was contacted by phone and instructed to go over to the American Embassy at once. He was to meet Lindbergh in person to arrange for the NYP to be loaded on board the United States Line's liner, George Washington, which was to stop at Southampton on the morning of June 2 enroute to New York.

Another shot in the same hangar ***(Mitchell Museum)***

Longmore was not pleased to go. He was shown to Lindbergh's suite and found him changing into formal attire for the Savoy Hotel dinner. Lindbergh immediately apologized for any trouble he might be causing and volunteered to fly the airplane the following morning to wherever Longmore suggested and at whatever hour was necessary.

Longmore set the time at 5 a.m. for them to meet at Croydon Aerodrome, to which Lindbergh readily agreed, as he had to be back in time to go to Buckingham Palace later that morning. According to Longmore, the two of them were to fly south-west to Grange Field (RAF) at Gosport, Hampshire, on the south coast of England.

NYP TO GOSPORT

Tuesday, May 31

Lindbergh was up and out of bed before dawn and was at Croydon Aerodrome at 5:15 a.m. He was immediately met by Longmore together with other Royal Air Force officers.

The plane was wheeled out of the big hangar and after a brief pre-flight took off before the few other people present realized what was happening.

He was accompanied by a Bristol two seat fighter, and a Hawker Woodcock II, s/n J-8295 with Longmore in the Bristol and an RAF officer flying the Woodcock. These two aircraft escorted Lindbergh on the sixty-five mile trip to Gosport.

As Longmore's Bristol was considerably slower, Lindbergh kept contact with Longmore by occasionally doing aerobatics in his vicinity.

Lindbergh landed at Grange Field, Gosport, after a fifty minute flight. [11]

The stop was kept a secret so the press and public could not learn of it and swarm all over Gosport's Grange Field causing heavy damage to the NYP.

Let us imagine the scene at Grange Airfield in the early hours of this thirty-first of May. There was a buzz of expectancy in the air by many who suspected something was up, due to the secrecy of the impending arrival.

When the NYP landed and came to a stop the secret was out. If seeing the tall blond figure climb out of this airplane were not enough, the words "Spirit of St. Louis" painted on the nose confirmed the suspicions that this famous flyer had just arrived in Gosport.

Most of the base officers and military guards turned out to greet him. Apparently, as he was talking to them, giving detailed and explicit instructions on how to remove that one piece forty-six foot wing and other components and how it should be packed and/or crated for its long over-ground and sea journey, a photographer snapped a picture.

MISPLACED PHOTOS

Sometime later after the NYP had been rolled into a hangar and the start of the disassembly had begun by the removal of the outer strut fairings at the wing juncture, another picture was taken. To date these are the only photographs known to exist. Who was the photographer? Were others taken, and if so, where are they and their negatives?

Here may be the answer to that question. Jock Egan was a part of the staff at that time at Grange and said that it was a fascinating place to be and a very busy place. In addition to the permanent resident aeroplanes there were invariably interesting visiting planes to look at either on the field or overhead. Some planes were there just for a day or two for some proposed modification. One keen photographer recalls he took pictures of fourteen different aircraft types on the ground in the course of one day.

There was an ongoing series of VIP visitors to Grange, one of whom was Sir Richard Fairey, a very dynamic person and the founder of Fairey Aviation.

A couple of months after Egan's arrival at Grange, he found himself not tasked for any particular duties. To fill in time he was one day sorting papers in a cabinet.

When he had completed his self-appointed task, he had a great deal of unrelated paperwork left over. In addition to some old looking documents, there was a file folder , the contents of which were held together by rusty paper clips. Then he found a

The Air Ministry Administrative building on Croydon Aerodrome. Photographer: Mr. Satchell. ***(The R. J. Mitchell Memorial Museum, Southampton, England)***

couple of photo negatives which he retrieved from the back corner of one of the drawers where they had been trapped, apparently for some time.

These papers appeared to be assessment reports or test evaluations on four different aircraft during the autumn of 1929. Some of the airplanes covered were the Blackburn Nautilus, The Short Gunard and the Fairey Fleetwing.

The photograph negatives were of an aircraft on the ground, but it looked nothing like any other air machine he had seen previously. Someone provided a magnifying glass to read the logo which was just behind the uncowled bank of radial cylinders. This was deciphered as "Spirit of St. Louis."

This was all taken to the office of Flt. Lt. Jones, BEM (British Empire Medal,) the engineering officer in charge of Air Servicing Flight, who arranged for the negatives to be printed. Some days later he stated that the file apparently had been forwarded from the Aeroplane and Armament Experimental Establishment at Martlesham Heath when the aircraft, with the exception of the Short, were transferred to Gosport.

How the file came to be in the cabinet remained a mystery, although the civilian cleaners recalled that some of the furnishings had been moved from an unused office in the Fort several years previously. All of the relevant papers were returned to Martlesham which was still a going concern at the time.

It was determined that the negatives of the NYP were of course taken at the time of Lindbergh's May 31st visit to Grange. One of the officers in a picture with Lindbergh was Air Commodore Masterman, who was in command of the Naval Airship section.

Finally Flt. Lt. Jones stated that as part of the then current Operation Goodwood (the planned rundown of the airfield towards ultimate closure) one of the educators had been tasked with compiling a history of everything. The photographs would, therefore, be sent along to the education section. As it was nearing lunch time Egan elected to deliver them on his way. Neither of the two education officers was available when Egan called, but when he told the typist about the photos she put them in a large file box marked in bold lettering—History of Gosport Airfield. The lid snapped shut and that was that.

At that point Egan would normally have asked to see the other material in the box, but pangs of hunger were urging him elsewhere. More time for the box later.

It is also reported that an "unknown" photographer accompanied the NYP from Gosport to Southampton . However, his name or any resulting photographs have never been found. [12]

In the meantime the NYP was safely stored in the hangar and under guard all night. One of those guards, Arthur Freeman, (now deceased) was the only surviving guard from that exciting event when interviewed in 1992. As an Air Craftsman 2nd class in the RAF at that time he remembered well being in the hangar all night at Gosport and spending a good two hours just sitting in the cockpit admiring all the "gadgets", and he stated that a photographer, name unknown, did accompany the crates from Portsmouth to Southampton.

Tuesday, May 31, 1927

For Lindbergh's return flight to the London area the RAF had provided him with a Hawker Woodcock II, s/n J-8295, powered with a Bristol Jupiter IV nine-cylinder, direct drive, not supercharged (400 hp @ 1575 RPM) radial engine. This one was from the No. 17 Squadron, based at Upavon, Wiltshire. The Woodcocks were the only RAF fighters specifically tasked for night fighting from 1925 to 1928 and the first to enter squadron service in such a role. The Woodcock was the first new British fighter to go into production after WW I, and the second design by the new H.G. Hawker Engineering Co. Ltd., formed in 1920 to succeed the celebrated Sopwith Company. It broadly resembled the Sopwith Snipe, which it followed into RAF service and was evolved as a night fighter.

Interestingly enough, as prearranged by Longmore, the Hawker Woodcock was issued to Lindbergh after he had signed a simple but official Royal Air Force "receipt for equipment on temporary loan." It was dated June 2, 1927 at RAF Station Kenley. So it is not known if he signed if after he was back at Kenley three days later or not. It appears as though he did not sign this release until after he had already flown the aircraft. [13]

Lindbergh took off in the Woodcock, accompanied by Longmore in the Bristol fighter and a Fleet Air Arm officer in an Avro Bison. Before this day Lindbergh had never seen a Woodcock, so due to its single cockpit, it was naturally a "self" checkout. Once they were on course and Lindbergh realized again that he was much faster than the Bristol or the Avro, he proceeded to become a bit more acquainted with the machine by looping and rolling it and running circles around the two all the way to Kenley, south of Croydon. Today the Kenley Aerodrome still exists as a glider training facility where the Surrey Hills Gliding Club is based, along with an RAF gliding detachment. [14]

When Lindbergh arrived over Kenley, he proceeded to entertain the few spectators on the ground with what was described as a perfect exhibition of every kind of aerobatics imaginable. The people on the ground did not realize at the time who was flying the airplane and probably thought it was one of their own Royal Air Force officers, thoroughly familiar with the fighter.

Lindbergh's next engagement was at 10:00 a.m., when he met with Mr. & Mrs. Stanley Baldwin, the Prime Minister and his wife, at Number 10 Downing Street in London. For part of the time all three watched from the garden wall the rehearsal of the ceremony of Trooping the Color taking place on the Horse Guards Parade Grounds.

Then Lindbergh met with General Porter and the group travelled to Buckingham Palace to meet King George V and Queen Mary. The audience lasted about twenty minutes and during that time the King bestowed the Air Force Cross upon Lindbergh, who carried it in a case as he left the Palace. This decoration was instituted in 1918 to be awarded to officers of the Royal Air Force for acts of courage or devotion to duty when flying other than against an enemy. It is also awarded to non-members of the RAF who render important services to aviation. The only other Americans who ever received this cross were the crew of the NC-4, which crossed the Atlantic via the Azores, and Commander Zachary Lansdowne, who was killed on the Shenandoah dirigible in a crash in Ohio in 1925.

From Buckingham Palace, Lindbergh was driven to York House to be received by the Prince of Wales, where he spent ten minutes in private. The Prince wanted to know what he was going to do in the future and Lindbergh replied, "I'm going to keep on flying." [15]

At a luncheon given by the Air Council at Claridge's Lindbergh was presented with the London Daily Mail's gold aviation cup, which had been instituted many years previously by the late Lord Northcliffe. [16] Secretary of State for Air, Sir Samuel Hoare, presided and welcomed Lindbergh on behalf of the British government and the Air Council. [17]

In the afternoon Lindbergh managed to work in a visit to the Houses of Parliament as a guest of Lord and Lady Astor. He was received by the Speaker at the House of Commons and also spent a short time visiting in the Distinguished Strangers Gallery. He had tea on the terrace and met many members of Parliament. At the House of Lords he carried on a brief conversation with Lord Balfour. [18]

Aerodrome Hotel at Croydon. It is still there and looks the same as it did in 1927. Photographer was Mr. Satchell. ***(The R. J. Mitchell Memorial Museum, Southampton, England)***

Excellent photo of Lindbergh in the cockpit of the Hawker Woodcock II s/n 8295. ***(Peter Little, England)***

In the evening Lindbergh was invited to the Royal Aero Club for dinner as a guest of that club and the Royal Aeronautical Society, the Air League of the British Empire, and the Society of British Aircraft Constructors. The dinner was held at the Savoy Hotel in London. [19]

There were nearly five hundred guests at this event, including not only many distinguished persons but prominent aviators such as Sir Alan Cobham and Sir Arthur Whitten Brown, navigator for the late Sir John Alcock on the first direct flight across the Atlantic in 1919.

Still later in the evening Lindbergh was invited to a reception with the Anglo-Swedish Society at the Mayfair Hotel. It would bear witness that the people there regarded him as another bond, strengthening the friendship between the Swedish and English-speaking worlds.

The Swedish Minister for London, Baron Palmstierna, in a humorous opening to his speech remarked that his friend, the American Ambassador, presented him with a question as to whom Lindbergh belonged. America had claims on Lindbergh, but by the laws of nature he was more of a Swede.

At midnight Lindbergh attended yet another function, this after being out of bed since 4 a.m. and continuing his "endurance" record, proceeded to the Derby Eve Ball being held at Royal Albert Hall, accompanied by Lord Lonsdale and the Prince of Wales. While there he was able to mingle amongst the dancers unmolested until—again—at 4 a.m. he finally went to bed. [20]

(Still Tuesday, May 31)

While all this intense, hectic schedule of Lindbergh's was taking place, another intense and hectic schedule was underway at Grange Field at Gosport.

Things were humming as the NYP was being dismantled. Secrecy was still being exercised to the fullest. Guards were on hand to make sure that souvenir hunters could not steal any parts from the airplane. Their efforts were quite effective and successful, as the press, always on the alert for stories, never did learn of this "secret mission."

On the one hand they saved the NYP from being damaged or mutilated, which was their main intent. However, historical documentation of this operation has suffered greatly over the years and much mystery has surrounded research efforts to complete this documentation.

No official military orders have been found in existing archival sources from the Public Records Office at Kew, Air Ministry, the RAF, the Royal Navy, Port Authority of Southampton, or local railway archives or marine museums or archives. No photos, other than the two previously mentioned, have been found which show any part of the operation such as the removal of the one piece wing, the construction of the crates and the movements of the crates via rail car to Southampton.

It is not presently known which hangar this took place in or if that hangar still exists at Grange Field, now known as H.M.S. Sultan of the Royal Naval School of Marine Engineering in the United Kingdom.

From existing photographs taken at San Diego, showing the assembly procedure of the mating of the wing to the fuselage, one can see that it took fully eight or ten rather tall and strong men to lift the wing either on or off the fuselage, usually by "walking" it off and to the rear of the fuselage and over the tail assembly. This was after removing the landing gear-to-wing struts and disconnecting the aileron control cables, the wing tanks fuel lines, and the main wing to fuselage mounting bolts.

This photo was taken on May 30th, just after Lindbergh landed the NYP at Gosport. He is probably giving these gentlemen instructions on how to dismantle the airplane for crating it up for shipment back to America. ***(Keith Howard, England)***

Only one photograph has turned up showing the NYP in a hangar with only the right wing strut fairings having been removed. However, they are not shown on the ground or anywhere in sight in the photo. But this does indicate the dis-assembly was apparently begun in the hangar.

With regard to the two crates, and their shipment to Southampton, some mysteries prevail. With such short notice, and without official papers or military orders, was the base so equipped with enough wood and hardware to tackle such a project or did they have to go into town, so to speak, to obtain the necessary supplies? Perhaps it was a matter of calling a supply depot in the Southampton area, a center of shipping and packaging expertise for sea and/or salt water shipments of goods. Were there personnel with this kind of experience stationed on Grange Field at the time or did they have to call in outside help?

When one examines the existing crate today there is no doubt as to its 'professional' type of construction and the quality of the materials. The design was well thought out and clever; the strapping supports, lifting eyes (so important considering the weights involved.) How cumbersome it must have been for riggers to consider when attaching shackles and cable to the crates. It appears that the size of the wing crate was 2 ft. thick x 10 ft. wide x 48 ft. long. The crate for the fuselage on the gear, including the engine, was 9 ft. 6 in. tall x 11 ft. 4 in. wide x 26 ft. 5 in. long; the tail surfaces were mounted separately on the inside wall.

How did the crates get from Grange the eighteen to twenty miles to Southampton? Sixty foot long Queen Mary lorries large enough to carry such cargo were not in existence until 1938. What about bridge clearances at the time if by either rail or road?

Wednesday, June 1

After sleeping for part of the morning, Lindbergh had been invited by Lord Lonsdale to go to the Epsom Downs Horse Derby.

In the evening there was yet another banquet, again at the Savoy Hotel in London given by the American Society in London, the American Chamber of Commerce and the American Club. [21]

All during this day the NYP was being packed and crated at Grange Field in Gosport. It is not known if the crates were

shipped up to Southampton toward the end of that day, or the next morning.

Thursday, June 2

In the early evening of May 31st, a coded telegram was sent to Lord Crewe at the Foreign Office in Paris with the following message—Important: Captain Lindbergh desires to fly from London to Paris most probably on June 2nd in British service aircraft. Please seek permission of French government for this flight and for machine to be flown back to England by Royal Air Force pilot. [22]

This was the day that Lindbergh was scheduled to depart for another visit to Paris where Parisians had insisted he return for more honors. He had earlier made a promise that having landed in France from America, he would leave from France to return home. Imagine the logistics alone to work out his itinerary and arrange for his transportation both by the British as well as the French.

However, the weather had deteriorated. There was a low pressure system moving through the area at the time, causing widespread fog and rain over the English Channel. So the trip was postponed one more day. [23]

In the meantime he was invited to a luncheon party by Mrs. Houghton at the American Embassy which included many high ranking guests.

After this affair Lindbergh was invited back to Croydon Aerodrome where the pilots of Imperial Airways were anxious to present him with a memento of his visit to England. It was a rather quiet meeting, including only a dozen pilots who were off duty and was held in a room in one of the larger hangars.

Later that day he was taken by motorcar to Kenley Aerodrome, where he spent the night in the Officer's Mess as a guest of the Royal Air Force. The Hawker Woodcock II, which he had flown up from Gosport, was kept there in a hangar ready for him to fly to Paris. [24]

The weather forecast for London, SE, E., SW, Midlands etc. for the next day was calling for wind between W. and NW, light or moderate; fair apart from a few scattered showers, visibility moderate to good, moderate temperatures.

Friday, June 3

This day turned out to be a very active one. The command was given by the President of the United States, Calvin Coolidge, to dispatch a naval light cruiser instead of utilizing the liner, George Washington, as previously suggested, to Southampton, England to pick up the NYP.

The U.S.S. Memphis, under the command of Vice Admiral Guy H. Burrage and Capt. Henry Ellis Lackey, was at that time tied up at the dock in Rotterdam, Holland. Interestingly enough the Memphis had just arrived in Cadiz, Spain on May 20th, the day Lindbergh took off from New York headed for Paris. On the 25th she departed Cadiz and arrived in Rotterdam on the 28th where she stayed until June 2nd.

On June 2nd it left Rotterdam and steamed down the English Channel, arriving at Ocean Dock (White Star Line Dock) harbor of Southampton on June 3rd at 11:21 a.m. [25]

When the ship initially arrived several officials were waiting on the quayside, including Mr. J.M. Savage, the American Consul, and Mrs. Savage and the mayor of Southampton, (Ald. P. V. Boryer who attended in his capacity as Admiral of the Port.) Also in the group was Capt. E.W. Harvey, M.B.E., Dock-Master and outdoor assistant, who represented the Southern Railway Company. Capt. Harvey's presence suggested the crates went by road to a rail siding to be loaded aboard a rail flat car for shipment to Southampton where rail lines fed all the main piers? [26]

This is the Hawker Woodcock II, s/n 8295, flown by Lindbergh back to the RAF Station Kenley, south of Croydon. This picture was taken at Le Bourget, near Paris, France, after he had flown it from Kenley by way of Lympne, near the town of Ashford. ***(Leo B. Kimball collection)***

KENLEY TO LE BOURGET (June 3)

At 3:30 in the morning Lindbergh was awakened with the announcement that the weather was clearing over the channel. So with little sleep he dressed and had breakfast with the officers at Kenley.

He was to fly the Woodcock but due to the small and limited accommodations of the small aircraft the wireless apparatus had to be removed to make room for his suit case and hat box.

By 6:50 a.m. he took off from Kenley in the Woodcock (s/n J-8295) escorted by two Gloster Gamecock biplanes, piloted by Flight Lieutenant J.A. Boret and Flying Officer R. H. Horniman, both from the No. 23 Fighter Squadron.

The three aircraft took off in formation, Lindbergh in the middle. They climbed rather steeply and headed south eastward toward the coast at an altitude of about 1000 feet. [27]

However, eight minutes later they ran into heavy fog over the channel and had to land at a little town called Lympne near the town of Ashford, now known as Ashford Airport. They touched down at 6:58 a.m.

The three of them remained there for an hour and fifteen minutes until conditions improved. They took off again at 8:13 a.m. They headed for Paris, flying over the narrow neck of the English Channel.

F/O (Flight Officer) S.A. Thorn was dispatched to Paris via Imperial Airways on June 2nd to ferry the Woodcock back to Gosport, England. Thorn was known among his fellow flyers as "Bill," and during World War II became the Chief Test Pilot for A..V. Roe, builders of the Lancasters, Manchesters, Ansons, Tudors, etc. [28]

FOOTNOTES

1. *The Story of Croydon, An Introductory History*, W.C. Bersick Sayers, Chief Librarian, Croyden Public Libraries, 1925. Courtesy of Raymond Billings, England.

2. Careful study of photographs in the author's collection, revealing aircraft types, models and registration letters.

3. *The First Croydon Airport, 1915-1928*, Bob Learmouth, Joanna Nash, Douglas Cluette (Editor,) Sutton Libraries and Arts Services, Sutton, Surrey, England, 1977, page 70

4. *Aeroplane Monthly* magazine, IPC Magazines, Ltd., London, England, June 1, 1927, page 644.

5. Ibid, page 644.

6. *First Croydon Airport*, Ibid, page 72.

7. *Aeroplane Monthly*, Ibid, page 648.

8. *Flight* magazine, June 2, 1927, Iliffe & Sons, Ltd., Dorset House, London. "London's Welcome to Lindbergh," page 347.

9. Letter to the author from Sir Peter G. Masefield, Surrey, England, October 8, 1992, whose wife was at Croydon at the time of Lindbergh's arrival on May 29, 1927.

10. *The Aeroplane* magazine, IPC magazines, Ltd., London, England, June 8, 1927, "Captain Lindbergh's Busy Visit."

11. Charles A Lindbergh's personal pilot log. Copy at Yale University, Sterling Memorial Library, Manuscripts and Archives Department, New Haven, CT. Log dated from November 11, 1926 to July 7, 1928.

12. *The Journal of the Gosport Aviation Society*, Issue 4, The Museum, Priddy's Hard, Gosport, Hampshire, England, dated 1991, published quarterly by the Gosport Aviation Society and written by Jock Egan "Bits from the Past," pages 4-6.

13. Royal Air Force, Form 108, Receipt for Equipment on Temporary Loan. Received of - O.O. RAF Station Kenley, June 2, 1927. RAF Museum, Hendon, Longdon, England, 1991.

14. *The Times* newspaper, London, England, June 1, 1927, "A.F.C. For Captian Lindbergh, Reception by the King, Departure Tomorrow."

15. *The Times*. Ibid, page 1.

16. *Aeroplane Magazine*, Ibid, page 678.

17. *The Spirit of St. Louis*, Charles A. Lindbergh, Charles Scribner's Sons, New York, NY, 1953, page 518.

18. *Aeroplane* magazine, Ibid, page 678.

19. Ibid. page 678.

20. *We*, Charles A Lindbergh, G.P. Putnam's Sons, New York, NY and London, England, The Knickerbocker Press, 1928, with a forewaord by Myron T. Herrick, American Ambassador to France, page 260.

21. *The Aeroplane* magazine, Ibid, page 684.

22. Code telegram to Lord Crewe, (Paris), Foreign Office, May 31, 1927, 6:00 pm. No. 146 (R) Ref: No A 3215/3097/45. Also noted "NO DISTRIBUTION." Photocopy in author's collection.

23. *The Times* newspaper, London, England, "The Weather," "Forecasts for Friday, June 3, 1927."

24. Operations Record Book, RAF, Form 540, of (Unit or Formation,) RAF Station Kenley, dated June 2 and 3, 1927. (June 2 "Col. Lindbergh arrived at Kenley to fly from there to Paris in a Woodcock aeroplane. His departure was delayed owing to bad weather conditions & Col. Lindbergh remained overnight in the Officer's Mess") (June 3 "Col. Lindbergh left Kenley for Paris at 06.50 hrs escorted as far as Lympene by two Gamecocks from 32 Squadron pilots Fl/Lt A.J. Boret, M.C. AFC & F/O R.H. Horniman.")

25. *Southern Railway Magazine*, Docks & Marine column, Vol. V. No. 55, July, 1927. This publication is incorporated with the South Western Railway Magazine, page 197 and 198, and was found at the National Railway Museum, York, Yorkshire, England.

26. *Southern Daily Echo*, Southampton, Hampshire, England, Friday, June 3, 1927, "Lindbergh's Plane Homeward Bound, Spirit of St. Louis Shipped at Southampton," "Flight to Paris," "Suitcase Displaces Wireless in RAF Machine."

27. *Southern Daily Echo*, Ibid.

28. Operations Record Book, RAF Form 540, of (Unitor Formation) No. 17 (Fighter Squadron, UPHAVON, (June 2, 1927,) page 11, May 26 through July 25, 1927. Letter from F/Lt. Donald K. Healy, No. 17 Fighter Squadron, Parkstone, Poole, Dorset, England, dated February 21, 1993, to Phil Munson, South Coulsdon, Surrey, England, on behalf of this author.

ENDNOTES

National Geographic maps of Ireland, England, France, in addition to appropriate road maps by Rand-McNally, the American Automobile Association, and maps as published by Dressee par la Manufacture Francaise des Pnaumatiques Michelin, France, were checked by the author for correct general compass headings over specific towns, cities and bodies of water in addition to correct distances between specific points.

Careful study of photographs in the author's collection revealed details of the NYP structure, etc. while in England from May 29, 1927 to May 31, 1927.

Letter dated 31 May, 1927 from Wing Commander, Air Staff, Headquarters, Fighting Area, Royal Air Force (his signature unreadable) to Station Commander O.O. No. 17 (F) Squadron, The Officer Commanding, Royal Air Force Station, Uphavon, Wiltshire, England. Subject: Visit of Captain C. Lindbergh. Letterhead shows—Headquarters, Fighting Area, Royal Air Force, Hillingdon House, Uxbridge, "URGENT."

Personnal research visits to the National Newspaper Library, Hendon Way, North London, England and the Public Records Office, Kew Gardens, London, England.

De Havilland Aircraft Since 1915, A. J. Jackson, Putnam & Company Limited, London, England, 1962.

The Daily Telegraph newspaper, London, England, Monday, May 30, 1927. "London's Welcome to Captain Lindbergh."

The New York Times newspaper, New York & London, Tuesday, May 31, 1927, "Lindbergh Starts For Home This Week; Has day of Comparative Ease in London, But Rivals Derby in Public Interest." by J.S. MacCormac.

Personal inspection of the *Spirit of St. Louis* by author at Smithsonian National Air & Space Museum, Washington, DC.

Southern Daily Echo, Southampton, Hampshire, England, Monday May 30, 1927, Wednesday, June 1, 1927, Thursday June 2, 1927, page 4 "Round the Port, Lindbergh's Plane," Friday, June 3, 1927, and Saturday, June 4, 1927.

From Sea to Sea, 1910-1945, Sir Arthur Longmore, Air Chief Marshal, Goeffrey Bles, London, printed by Butler and Tanner, Ltd., Frome and London, England, Chapter X, "Andover, Air Ministry and Inland Area," 1925-29.

Royal Air Force, Form 108. Receipt for Equipment on Temporary Loan, received of O.O. RAF Station Kenley, June 2, 1927. RAF Museum, Hendon, London, England. 1991.

Aerosphere 1939, edited by Glenn D. Angle, Aircraft Publications, New York, NY & Detroit, MI.

Aeroplane Monthly magazine, IPC Magazines, Ltd. London, England, May, 1991, "On Silver Wings."

Log Book of the U.S.S. Memphis light cruiser, first rate, Commanded by Captain Henry E. Lackey, U.S. Navy, U.S. Naval Forces, Europe, Squadron, Commencing June 1,1927 at Rotterdam, Holland and ending June 30, 1927 at New York, NY.

The Times newspaper, London, England, Saturday, June 4, 1927, "Lindbergh's Paris Flight, R.A.F. Escort to the Coast. Delay by Fog."

Profile Publications, The Gloster Gamecock, No. 33, Francis K. Mason, Profile Publications, Ltd. London, England.

CHAPTER 12

Second Trip to Paris

Friday, June 3 through Saturday, June 4

TO PARIS, LESSAY, CHERBOURG, U.S.S. MEMPHIS

Initially Lindbergh was scheduled to come to Paris the previous day, Thursday, June 2nd, which generated a very large crowd at Le Bourget. They waited all day in the rain. Due to their obvious disappointment when Lindbergh did not show, except for a few hardy souls, they did not return the next day.

When he arrived on Friday, the third, the crowd consisted mainly of police, soldiers, cinema people, press photographers, and journalists.

A squadron of French military aircraft took off from Le Bourget a short time before his arrival and flew over Paris as a sign of welcome.

After circling the Aerodrome, Lindbergh landed close to the assembled crowd at 10:01 a.m., but he was invited to move his airplane to a location nearer to the hangars across the field. Without more ado he took off and "flew" just ten feet above the ground to the other side of the airport where officials, men with cameras, and the rest of the crowd ran helter skelter across the ground to catch up. Lindbergh preferred to pay the Woodcock the compliment of flying it rather than running it along the ground for such a distance.

He was welcomed by officers of the 34th Aviation Regiment, representatives of the American Embassy and Mr. B. Franklin Mahoney, president of Ryan Airlines, Inc., who had been there since the previous week. Mahoney had come to Paris aboard the steamship Mauretania especially to discuss future plans with Lindbergh, and he was among the first to shake hands with the aviator.

After a brief reception by the Franco-American authorities, Lindbergh motored off to the American Embassy to fulfill another heavy social schedule.

He had lunch with the French League des Aviateurs at the Bois do Boulogne, which included the Lafayette Escadrille, the famous American volunteer squadron that fought for the French Army. Later he attended a reception given by the Swedish Minister and members of the Swedish Colony at the Swedish Church in Paris.

In the evening he was given a last farewell dinner at the American Embassy, where he stayed that night.

After a tremendous two weeks of being feted and honored, Lindbergh was out of bed by 6 a.m. on Saturday, June 4, 1927 and by 8 o'clock had breakfast and bid farewell to the Embassy staff. At 8:30, accompanied by Ambassador Herrick and the Ambassador's son, Parmely Herrick, Lindbergh was driven to Le Bourget to prepare for his return to America.

Meanwhile the operation at dock-side in Southampton, England, was progressing. Swinging the two heavy crates on board the Memphis occupied considerable time, and it was with much difficulty that they were finally mounted and secured on the after deck, starboard side, which was covered with guns, two small biplanes and other naval equipment. It appears that the two crates were actually set on one of the seaplane catapult structures. [1]

During the operation the ship's kangaroo mascot (yes, a real live kangaroo) danced merrily about as if quite pleased at the chance of seeing the NYP.

Lindbergh said in his book Autobiography of Values, page 315, "I feel there was something improper about putting my *Spirit of St. Louis* on board a boat. It seemed like imprisoning the future within the past to bind my silver wings into a box that would be rocked and tossed, back to America by the very ocean they had conquered in their flight. I suggested that, instead, I fly back by way of Ireland, but Ambassador Houghton was not at all impressed. A destroyer would be sent to get me, he continued. The time spent on the voyage back by ship would be needed in Washington and New York to arrange for my reception." [2]

This is the little aerodrome observation building with Lindbergh's name still there. ***(M. Michel Pinel, France)***

Lindbergh memorial plaque which is still on the little grass field at Lessay. ***(M. Michel Pinel, France)***

Local people running to greet the two French Brequet XIX airplanes as they landed at Lessay. ***(M. Michel Pinel, France)***

About 12:30 p.m., June 3rd, the cruiser set sail at 1:01 p.m. for Cherbourg, France. The ship steamed across the English Channel and came into Cherbourg Harbor at 6:21 and fired a twenty-one gun salute with the French National Ensign "at the main truck" (a small, circular piece of wood placed on the top of a mast to protect it and give a more finished appearance.) A few minutes later Fort du Hornet returned the twenty-one gun salute.

At 8:35 the Memphis moored to Buoy #1 in the Inner Harbor for the night. Soon the U.S.S. Breck came alongside to port and commenced fueling the Memphis. The operation was completed the next morning at 6:37. [3]

The plan was for Lindbergh to leave Paris by air and fly to Cherbourg to meet the Memphis and land at the Aerodrome at Querqueville, 5 km northwest of Cherbourg. However, the authorities conferred for a long time and finally decided that the airfield was not very safe, though the reason for this is unknown. So Lessay, the nearest town with a suitable Aerodrome, was selected for the destination.

Lindbergh walking from his airplane with local officials at Lessay Airfield. ***(M. Michel Pinel, France)***

On the fourth, Lindbergh was loaned a brand new Breguet XIX by the French for the flight to the Naval field at Lessay, a grassy field, as it is today. Lindbergh carried one passenger, the French Sargent Charpentier. They were to be accompanied by a second Brequet XIX piloted by Sargent Brillant, with Commandant Tom Weiss, 34th Aviation Regiment Le Bourget Commandant as his passenger. It was Weiss's job to ferry the Lindbergh Breguet back to Paris.

The Breguet XIX (19) is of particular interest due to the numerous long distance flights accomplished in this model. The 19 was a two place, open cockpit biplane, used both as a fighter or bomber and sometimes as a reconnaissance / observation aircraft. It was fitted with either the Hispano-Suiza, Farman, Salmson, Renault, Lorraine-Dietrich or Gnome-Rhone "Jupiter" engines. With an upper wing span of forty-eight feet eight inches of mostly metal construction and fabric covered, it was a very large, solid and stable flying machine. [4] This particular Breguet was powered by the Hispano-Suiza engine of 450—600 hp. The serial number of the one flown by Lindbergh has never been determined. [5]

After a pre-flight inspection and explanation of the Breguet's controls, Lindbergh and the other Breguet took off from Le Bourget at 9:23 a.m. They were accompanied by escort, a fleet of

no less than twenty-two French military aircraft for the first thirty miles of the 180 statute (290 km) miles from Le Bourget to Lessay. The flight was rendered rather difficult by strong winds, rain and mist, but Lindbergh made a perfect landing on the grass strip at Lessay at 11:36 a.m., followed by Weiss in the second Breguet XIX.

A guard of 125 French sailors and 50 gendarmes awaited him on the landing field, where about 1500 people from Lessay and neighboring villages had assembled to see and welcome him.

He was received by Monsieur Admiral Renault and Monsieur Paul Jeanson, mayor of Lessay, accompanied by his town council, and many other officials and dignitaries. Music was provided by the municipal band of La Haye-du-Puits, that immediately struck up the American national anthem. School children of Lessay were there as well as war veterans carrying flags, and many of the local societies. Also in the reception group were American dignitaries who were at Le Bourget when he landed there after his ocean flight.

Three young girls of Lessay, the misses Henriette Yvetot, Denise Auger, Edith Clisson, all of the Ecole Pratique, presented three bouquets of flowers: one from the schools of Lessay, one from the town council, and one from the Prefect of La Manche.

At the Hotel de Ville (town hall), which was decorated in American and French colors, Lindbergh signed the guest register and some autographs and waved to the crowd from the balcony, to the sounds of an endless ovation. [6]

After being entertained at a luncheon given by the mayor of Lessay, at the Lessay chateau, Admiral Renault welcomed the flyer. The Mayor said that the commune (town) was grateful for the honor of his presence. [7]

This whole event was a tremendous boost to the town. City fathers had been attempting to improve the Aerodrome facility for some time, and any progress made had been slow. Aviation was still in its infancy over there and politicians were reluctant to approve funds for further development.

The Lessay airfield had only been in existence officially since December 2, 1923, when the Navy was authorized to take possession of the land. [8]

The event of having Lindbergh come there in 1927 would establish permanently the importance of the Lessay Aerodrome. It is today named the Aerodrome Charles Lindbergh, inaugurated August 24, 1980.

At 1:10 pm. Lindbergh, in a motorcade of thirty cars, departed Lessay for the thirty-three and a half miles (54 km) to Cherbourg. They drove via today's routes D.900, D.2 and N.13, taking them through La Haye du Puits, St. Sauveur le Vicomte, Valognes, and on to Cherbourg. During the journey they passed gaily decorated villages whose inhabitants lined either side of the road and filled his car with bouquets as he passed by. Another great reception awaited him as thousands had assembled in the streets and dock area of the ancient port of Cherbourg to see him off. [9]

In Cherbourg he was received at the City Hall and presented to the crowd. He was officially received by Monsieur Quoniam, President of the Chamber of Commerce, who welcomed him with a most eloquent speech describing him as the messenger of the New World. He showed him the plaque that would commemorate forever his magnificent feat. That plaque was mounted at the Gare Maritime (Marine Railroad Station) in Cherbourg, commemorating the spot where Lindbergh had approached the French coastline on his way to Paris after leaving New York. He was also greeted by the mayor, M. Jules le Brettevillois. The stations was later destroyed by the Germans when they bombed the port in July 1944, sending the plaque to the bottom of the sea. [10]

Lindbergh is shown at Lessay with local greeters. The second man from the left with mustache is Octave Lucas, an attorney, who was the Mayor of Lessay. ***(Brooklyn Public Library—New York)***

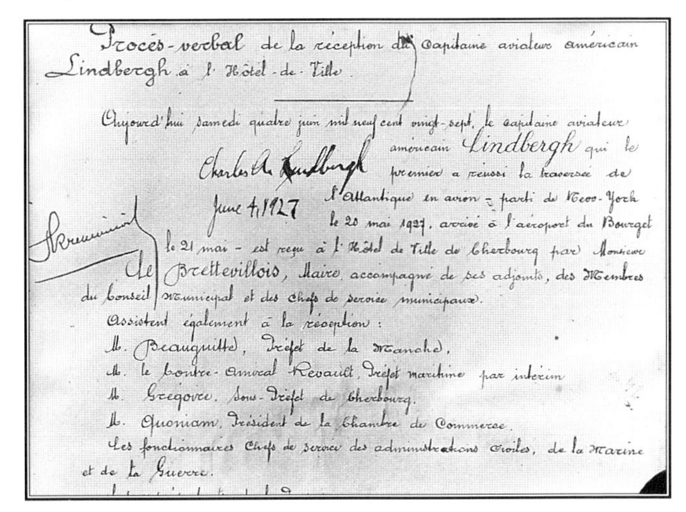

Procès-verbal de la réception du Capitaine aviateur américain Lindbergh à l'Hôtel-de-Ville.

Aujourd'hui samedi quatre juin mil neuf cent vingt-sept, le capitaine aviateur américain Lindbergh qui le premier a réussi la traversée de l'Atlantique en avion - parti de New-York le 20 mai 1927, arrivé à l'aéroport du Bourget le 21 mai - est reçu à l'Hôtel de Ville de Cherbourg par Monsieur Le Brettevillois, Maire, accompagné de ses adjoints, des Membres du Conseil Municipal et des Chefs de Service municipaux.

Charles A. Lindbergh
June 4, 1927

Assistent également à la réception :
M. Beauguitte, Préfet de la Manche.
M. le Contre-Amiral Renault, Préfet maritime par intérim
M. Gregoire, Sous-Préfet de Cherbourg.
M. Quoniam, Président de la Chambre de Commerce.
Les fonctionnaires Chefs de service des administrations civiles, de la Marine et de la Guerre.

This is the guest book at the city hall of Lessay, where Lindbergh signed-in on June 4, 1927. ***(M. Michel Pinel, France)***

Lindbergh is seen here in the front cockpit of the French Brequet XIX with French Sargent Charpentier in the rear cockpit. ***(John Underwood)***

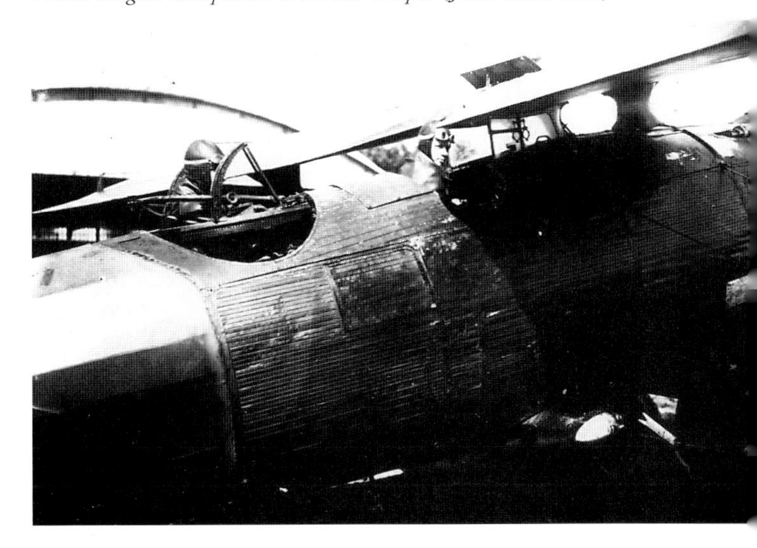

"Come back soon," someone shouted from the dock as he climbed aboard the motor launch that was provided to take him from the dock area to the U.S.S. Memphis, which had arrived the night before. As the launch pulled away someone rushed through the crowd and tossed a disreputable looking package wrapped in brown paper. It was Lindbergh's baggage sent by train from Paris.

Earlier that morning Franklin Mahoney of Ryan Airlines reported on board for passage to the United States, as did William Hellman of International and Universal News Service, Mr. Benner of International News Reel, Raymond Rosseau of Pacific and Atlantic Photos, Mr. J. Glenn of Pathe News, Albert Sozio of Paramount News Reel, and Carlyle MacDonald.

At 3:43 p.m. Lindbergh accompanied by Dick Blythe of the Wright Aeronautical Corporation, came aboard the ship. They were greeted by Admiral Burrage and Captain Lackey, while the ship's band played the American and French national anthems. Lindbergh was immediately given the Admiral's cabin, where they had already hung a portrait of his mother on the wall. He was quite touched by this. [11]

At 4:35 the Memphis unmoored from Buoy #1 and, escorted by a squadron of French sea planes, steamed out of the harbor and on course at about twenty-three knots. [12]

Lindbergh's last sight of France was just a few miles from where he had first sighted the country two weeks previous. His only regret was that he had to return on the sea rather than by air.

FOOTNOTES

1. Log Book of the U.S.S. Memphis light cruiser, first rate, Commanded by Captain Henry E. Lackey, US Navy. US Naval Forces, Europe, Squadron, Commencing June 1, 1927 at Rotterdam, Holland and ending June 30, 1927 at New York, NY, page 419.

2. Ibid.

3. Ibid.

4. *Janes All the World's Aircraft,* Vol.1, 1980, pages 348 & 349.

5. Charles A. Lindbergh's personal pilot log. Copy at Manuscripts & Archives Department, Sterling Memorial Library, Yale University. Log dated from November 11, 1926 to July 7, 1928.

6. Excerpt from the "Journal ed de l'arrondissment." (Newspaper of Coutances and surrounding district,) Saturday, June 11, 1927. Lindbergh's departure and reception at the Lessay Flying Club. Translation from French by French instructor, Laura Longacre of the Cheshire Academy, Cheshire, CT, October 1994, pages 1-14.

7. Ibid.

8. Ibid.

9. Ibid.

10. Letter to the author from Ronald M.A. Hirst, Wiesbaden, germany, August 13, 1997.

11. Log Book

12. Ibid.

CHAPTER 13

Aboard the U.S.S. Memphis

Cherbourg to America

The U.S.S. Memphis, CL-13, was the fourth Navy ship with the name Memphis, named after the city in Tennessee. The first one was built in Philadelphia in 1853 and was a five gun screw steamer. The second was a seven gun screw steamer built in Scotland in 1861. The third was originally named the Tennessee, an armored cruiser, commissioned July 16, 1906 and renamed May 25, 1916. [1]

This fourth one was built by William Cramp & Sons Shipyards, Philadelphia, and launched on April 17, 1924; sponsored by Miss Elizabeth R. Paine, daughter of Mayor Rowlett Paine of Memphis, Tennessee, and commissioned at Philadelphia Navy Yard on February 4, 1925 (Lindbergh's birthday) with Capt. Henry E. Lackey in command. [2]

Few ships, if any, in the United States Navy up to World War II have had a more colorful career. It is almost as though she had been singled out to represent our country overseas.

She received Kings and Presidents aboard, explored the Alaskan coasts, put landing parties ashore in far off China and attended important conferences at which the strategy of World War II was planned.

Until 1945 the Memphis sailed on missions of good will to every corner of the globe, including the dedication of Naval bases and the receptions of Kings and Presidents. Such duty took the

June 3rd, at the dock (quay) side at Southampton showing the main crate being hoisted aboard the U.S. Navy light cruiser U.S.S. Memphis before sailing over to Cherbourg to pick up Lindbergh for the return trip home. ***(U. S. Navel Historical Center photo)***

A good aerial view of the U.S.S. Memphis, photo of which was actually taken on May 31, 1934. ***(National Archives)***

Lindbergh having conversation with the skipper of the Memphis and two of its aviators. Note the NYP crates in the background. ***(Robert W. Arehart)***

Lindbergh getting the feel of a Vought 02U-1 "Corsair" powered with a Pratt & Whitney "Wasp" engine, floatplane on the Memphis. ***(Robert W. Arehart)***

Memphis on voyages totaling approximately eight hundred thousand miles, a distance roughly equivalent to thirty-three trips around the world at the equator.

Even though Lindbergh was quite disappointed at the thought of returning to the United States on a ship rather than by air in his NYP, the idea still held some fascination. Since his boyhood he had seen Navy vessels in the Washington Navy Yard and always had a desire to ride aboard one.There would be suitable and convenient space on the cruiser for the bulky and rather cumbersome crates. During this trip he did get to know the inside workings and operations of a Navy ship, as well as learn much about the surface of a large ocean.

Lindbergh was quite impressed with the ship and did not waste any time during the nine day voyage. He was shown every corner and learned in detail its operation and how one navigates on the high seas. He could easily compare his methods of aerial navigation with that of the US Navy.

The Memphis was always in radio communication with land facilities and its navigators could pinpoint their position at any

Here the Memphis is shown as it pulled up to the dock at the Washington Navy Yard in Washington, D.C. with Lindbergh and the NYP on board, June 11, 1927. ***(Edward E. Barr via U.S. Naval Historical Center)***

given time within a ten mile radius. Lindbergh felt that future development of aviation technology would bring aviation to the point of being able to communicate and navigate as well, if not better. His thoughts drifted back to when his cousin, Emory S. Land, a United States Navy Commander, had made an Atlantic crossing as an Annapolis cadet. He had done this aboard a "square rigger" only thirty years before. The ship and crew had been becalmed in the Sargasso Sea, without food or any method of communicating their plight or seek help. How far technology had come, he thought.

But other more pressing and important thoughts were on Lindbergh's mind during the trip too—money matters. He was concerned about his financial situation. Of the $15,000. he had raised when the flight was planned, he had $1500. in his pocket.

Before leaving New York he had signed a contract with The *New York Times* newspaper to write his version of the historic flight. That would produce several thousand dollars. However, he could not live on that money and whatever else he had in his bank account. He needed a survival plan in which he could earn a steady income. At the same time he needed as much free time as possible to pursue his deep interest in the future development of aviation and air travel.

An agreement to write a book had also been drawn up with publishers G. P. Putnam's Sons of New York before he left for Paris. Because it would be written in the third person, via interviews, with Lindbergh doing the Preface, an experienced New York Times correspondent was hired to do the actual writing aboard the Memphis. Much of Lindbergh's time was spent working with this correspondent on the book, We, eventually one of his most well known books.

One man who was part of the crew on that voyage was Chief Harvey L. "Deacon" Wynn, who was the only man still living in 1997 from that original crew. He lied about his age when he joined the Navy. He was actually only sixteen years old, quite below the recruitment required age of eighteen.

Wynn had reported for duty aboard the Memphis on January 9, 1926, as a seaman second class. He spent a total of twenty years without interruption aboard the Memphis, a record that few Navy men can equal.

Wynn remembered that the cruiser's radio officers handled more than 75,000 words of congratulatory messages for Lindbergh. The whole crew became intimately acquainted with the flyer. [3]

Wynn worked in the engine room so he missed many of the up-on-deck activities, such as loading the two crates at Southampton.

Admiral Guy Burrage, who was aboard the Memphis, was from Hopkinton, New Hampshire. He owned a small piece of property in Contoocook, NH, where he thought he might retire some day. During the trip Burrage asked Lindbergh if he had any special plans for the crates when they reached America. Lindbergh had not really given it a thought, and when Burrage asked if he could have them to make into a vacation cabin on his retirement property, Lindbergh gave the O.K. Originally Burrage thought of putting the crate on his daughter's property known as "Ingleside", near Norfolk, Virginia, but finally decided upon New Hampshire.

As the ship neared the coast of the United States on Friday, June 10th, they met the U.S.S. Humphreys which came alongside. Both slowed to appropriate speeds in order to transfer movie film from the Memphis to the Humphreys. This film was probably of Lindbergh aboard the ship or other activities of his European visit. [4]

That same day another ship came alongside, the U.S.S. Goff, to transfer aboard a custom official named Mr. Haywood.

The Memphis left the high seas of the Atlantic Ocean and at 4:00 p.m., June 10, 1927 entered the Chesapeake Bay just north of Virginia Beach, Norfolk, Virginia, and Cape Henry. It sailed northward toward Point Lookout, Maryland, where the ship entered the Potomac River.

At 8:33 p.m. the Memphis anchored for the night in eight fathoms (48 feet) of water off Piney Point Light. Sometime that evening Pilot Luckett came aboard to plan for the arrival in Washington the next day. Lindbergh and the crew rested well before the official arrival in Washington.

The ship had made a record trip from France to the United States in six days, five hours, thirty minutes. [5]

FOOTNOTES

1. *Dictionary of American Naval Fighting Ships,* Volume IV, 1969, Navy Department, Office of the Chief of Naval Operations, Naval History Division, Washington. Superintendent of Documents, US Government Printing Office, Washington, DC, pages 317-320.

2. Ibid.

3. U.S.S. Memphis, CL 13, 1925-1945. A history of the ship and its crew given to the author by retired Chief Harvey L. "Deacon" Wynn, US Navy. Date of printing and publiusher unknown.

4. Log Book of the U.S.S. Memphis light cruiser, first rate, Commanded by Captain Henry E. Lackey, US Navy. US Naval Forces, Europe, Squadron, Commencing June 1, 1927 at Rotterdam, Holland and ending June 30, 1927 at New York, NY, pages 437-439.

5. Ibid.

The welcoming crowd at the dock before Lindbergh walked down the gangplank. Note the steam powered crane #11 in position for off-loading the crates. ***(U.S. Naval Historical Center)***

CHAPTER 14

Washington, DC: Anacostia-Bolling Field

June 11, 1927

At 4:26 a.m. the Memphis, weighed anchor and proceeded up the Potomac River toward Washington, D. C.

At 9:30 a.m. the U.S.S. Los Angeles dirigible appeared overhead to join the escort. In addition there were eight Coast Guard cutters; #233, 193, 187, 228, 144, 138, 200, and 196.

Then at 11:09 a.m. the Washington Navy Yard fired a salute of fifteen guns, which was returned with a salute of thirteen guns from the Memphis.

After a triumphant journey up the Potomac River and into the Anacostia River, the Memphis docked port side at 11:34 a.m. at the Mayflower dock at the Washington Navy Yard (largest naval ordinance plant in the world and home of the US Naval Gun factory) on the north side of the Anacostia River. After securing the ship and the gangplank, Secretary of the Navy Curtis D. Wilber came aboard.

Shortly thereafter Admiral Burrage came down to the dock to escort Mrs. Evangeline Lindbergh aboard the ship to spend some quiet moments in private with her son in his quarters.

After a brief and somewhat informal greeting by dignitaries, Lindbergh was surrounded for protection and escorted down the gangplank to a waiting car and whisked away to attend function after function in his honor in the city.

Now for the off-loading of the two crates, the re-assembly of the NYP, including any necessary repairs and other adjustments, had to be worked out. Just as in England, security to avoid any possible physical damage to the planewas of top priority. Just imagine the coordination and responsibility of those in charge. Without a doubt, this would be a major undertaking.

In preparation and for mechanical convenience, the Memphis was moved aft at the dock by the tugs Choptank and Tecumseh.

The main crate carrying the fuselage with the engine attached together with the tail assembly and wing supporting struts weighed in at 5600 pounds. It was twenty-six feet five inches long, eleven feet four inches wide, nine feet six inches in height and reinforced with steel straps. The other crate carrying the wing was forty feet long, ten feet wide and about two feet thick. It weighed 1600 pounds.

The main crate being maneuvered on or off the Yard Explosive at the Washington Navy Yard. ***(Donald Albert Hall family)***

When the Memphis was docked at "Ocean Dock" in Southampton, England its hook (derrick) had experienced some injury during the loading of the crates. Although it was basically in good condition, the crew did not wish to take the risk of trusting this valued cargo to this uncertain machinery. A hurried conference was called and someone related the point that nothing but the biggest and mightiest crane in the Navy Yard should be given the task of getting the airplane ashore. [1]

Word was sent to the Naval Yard for the best crane on the premises and Unit No. 11, commanded by John K. Daniel, 760 9th St. SE, was given orders to get up steam on that warm afternoon. Finally, after the patience of the waiting mechanics at the Naval Air Station at Anacostia, where the NYP was to be re-assembled, had become almost exhausted and waiting throngs began to leave, No.11 chugged around the corner on its combination locomotive and arrived alongside the ship. [2]

It was not a question of just hauling it off. The hook was put in place and the fastenings were gathered up and placed in it. The crane moved up and down, back and forth, to make sure it was in proper balance. More time was lost getting miscellaneous adjustments secure.

Finally Daniel put all his steam to work and the big package rose off the deck. Swinging in mid-air as it was turned toward the land, Navy officers directly concerned with its safe delivery registered concern and openly expressed the hope that the cable would not part, despite the fact that No. 11 could lift forty tons (80,000 pounds). [3]

Gracefully it was heaved around and slowly lowered. It came to rest on the ground without so much as a jolt. Then the hook went back for the wing crate.

It is possible this picture was taken just after the NYP was removed from the crate at Anacostia Naval Air Station. ***(Donald Albert Hall family)***

A Navy mechanic/artist touching up the lettering on the nose of the NYP. He looks quite happy, too. Wonder what his name is. This is in the double hangars. ***(U.S. Navy photo)***

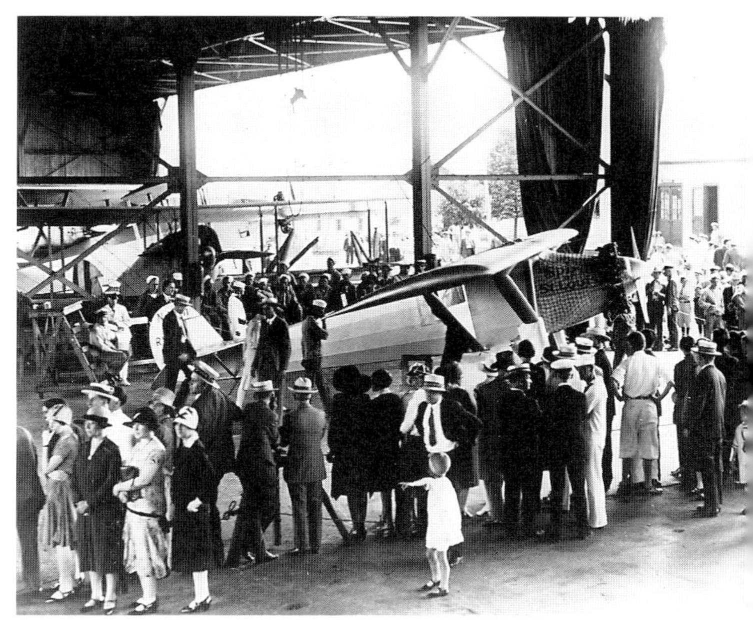
About June 15th or 16th, showing the NYP in the double hangars at Anacostia Notice only 2 fuel caps are visible on the top of the wing. ***(Leo B. Kimball collection)***

There were only a few spectators at the yard, but immediately some of them dug into their pockets for pocket knives and began peeling off splinters from the case. They ripped into the sides and on the corners and attacked the box with vengeance. Finally one or two blue jackets put a stop to the souvenir hunters.

A Navy vessel supposedly named the "Yard Explosive" but not found in official Navy archives was supposed to have had a crane with a hook. It is only speculation that such a vessel existed. No photos of such a boat have surfaced after exhaustive research on the part of this writer and U.S. Navy historians. The name has only appeared in newspaper reports. Therefore, It appears that the term "yard explosive" was derived as a slang expression by Navy personnel when referring to the barge later used to carry the boxes and later yet the assembled NYP. The Navy Yard at the time was an ordinance depot, and this barge more than likely was used to transport explosive types of equipment; thus the term "yard explosive."

Altogether it was a little more than an hour from the time the crane began transporting the first box until it had swung the wing box through the air a few feet and placed it aboard the "yard explosive" barge. Then it went back after the bigger box and lifted it from the ground and it towed it to the barge.

Among the interested spectators aboard the Memphis was Capt. Lackey, skipper of the ship. He felt responsible for delivering the airplane to Lindbergh in good order. When the single box sailed over the side he sent up a cheer and shouted his congratulations to Chief Boatswain W. C. Fitzpatrick of the Naval Air Station and those assisting him. The Memphis had done her duty and all aboard turned to other things.

On January 1, 1926 a flight section had been established as a separate department at the station with a Lt. Henderson in

This is the happy looking Navy crew that worked on the assembly of the NYP at Anacostia, prior to the U.S. Tour. ***(Library of Congress)***

Soon after the NYP was assembled and checked, this photo was taken of Lindbergh being admired by Navy personnel. ***(Leo B. Kimball collection)***

charge. Henderson's credentials included setting a world altitude record for Class C seaplanes in April, 1927.

The two cases aboard the vessel with such an un-romantic name floated slowly over to the Naval Air Station sea wall. This operation was supervised by Boatswain Fitzpatrick and Lieut. Comdr. A. C. Miles and Lieut. George R. Henderson.

Impatient to get at their task, mechanics on board the barge, while floating down the river, had opened the wing box and were ready to put the wing ashore. The task of getting the wing ashore involved the employment of nearly thirty blue jackets, who were hustled to the sea wall from all parts of the station. Groaning and puffing under their load, one group lifted one end of the wing down or over to the grassy area, while another crewman pushed up on the opposite end. The wing was placed on the shoulders of the sailors and, resembling a centipede, was conveyed around to a hanger (Seaplane Hangar No. 2) which had been roped off to permit work without interference.

A blast of hot air rushed out as the end was removed, despite the fact that the British packers had placed a large ventilator on the case.

It is assumed that the large box with the fuselage was off loaded at the sea wall as well, and somehow put on rollers to be moved across the grass area to one of the hangars (Seaplane Hangar No. 2).

The other possibility is perhaps they opened the large crate, rolled out the airplane on its gear, over to the hangar.

Rare view of the NYP on the barge, giving an indication of how the airplane was loaded and off-loaded on the barge for display off Haines Point. Appears the "Yard Explosive" is in the background, which probably had something to do with moving the barge around. ***(Else Hale, Portland, CT)***

No photographs or other type of documentation have been found to confirm any of this. Photographs of the air station taken at that time, aerial and otherwise, only show a ramp into the water for seaplanes and a small dock suitable only for small craft. The small dock is still there.

Once the large box was in place at the hangar, six bolts at one end were removed. The end was moved aside and a blast of hot air rushed out despite the fact that the British packers had placed a large ventilator on the case.

This much of the airplane was intact; propeller, engine, fuselage, landing gear and wheels and vertical fin. Wrapped in burlap and strapped to the sides of the roomy case were four wing support struts, the stabilizers, elevators, rudder and various pieces of strip metal cowling which were removed when the wing was taken off.

Blocks nailed around the wheels and tail skid held the fuselage in place. These were knocked away and the ship was rolled out in ten minutes after the end was opened and through a lane of about one hundred spectators who had remained for the sight. As far as could be determined, no souvenir hunters attempted to get a slice of fabric or other item from the airplane. Lt. Commander D.C. Watson, Commandant of Anacostia, took no chances after what had happened in Paris and assigned a detail of sailors with fixed bayonets to guard the airplane.

Donald Hall, chief engineer of the Ryan company, Kenneth Lane and Kenneth Boedecker, both of the Wright Aeronautical Corporation were present most of the evening while the airplane was being assembled.

Officially it was 7:00 p.m. on Saturday night, June 11, when the NYP was accepted and/or received at the station and the crew of Navy personnel began the task of re-assembly of this prized airplane. [4]

The erection or re-assembly commenced immediately by the Navy Flight Test Rigging crew, supplemented by a portion of the Assembly and Repair Crew.

The crew assigned to this work, under the direction of Aviation Chief Machinist Mate William J. Morris were mechanics Erickson, Sommons, Bowersooka, Criptenden, Cook, Christensen, and Salva. [5]

Again without official documentation and very few photographs it appears the NYP was assembled in seaplane hangar no. 2. The crew first began the re-assembly with the tail surfaces, hooking up the control cables and checking the trim mechanism for the stabilizer.

The job was progressing well until the discovery of a cracked wing attach fitting. Information has not come forth as to exactly which fitting it was.

Rare view of the NYP on display near Haines Point for public viewing as it sat on the barge. ***(Cradle of Aviation Museum)***

A considerable amount of time was spent in deciding how to either remove the fitting to replace it or having it repaired. No photos or drawings, if in fact a drawing was made, have been found.

It appears the fitting was firmly built into the wing proper (main spar most likely) and had to be removed with much difficulty.

Eventually a new fitting was made and installed in the wing. The repair required about two hours of labor.

All this work went on through the night until about 6:00 a.m. Sunday morning when the Wright engine was given a ground run-up test.

After the airplane was completely assembled, it was rolled through the grass area to the sea wall. At that point seamen bridged over to the barge with large wooden planks. The NYP was rolled along the planks to the barge and secured solidly to the vessel. The barge was decorated with much bunting, and in photographs can be seen that it was equipped with a railroad track. It must have been used to transport railroad cars from one place to another in the course of its Navy service.

The barge was then towed or propelled by a small boat visible in some photographs to be anchored off Hains Point for exhibition purposes. The reason for this arrangement was so the public could view and photograph the airplane and not get their hands on it. None of those public photos have turned up at this writing. The barge spent all of Sunday anchored off Haines Point.

At 8:00 p.m. that same day, June 12th, the airplane was returned to Anacostia and placed in the hangar under guard.

On June 13th the NYP was made ready for the proposed arrival of Lindbergh. It was fueled and the oil tank filled under the direction and supervision of Kenneth Lane of the Wright Company.

The engine was started. It seemed to function properly up to 1100 rpm. Then the warming up process was turned over to Lindbergh. When he opened the throttle to full power No. 8 cylinder began to cut out. The trouble was traced to a cam follower on the intake side of No. 8 cylinder frozen in the guide at the full up position, thereby holding open the intake valve, almost cutting out this cylinder. The cam follower was actually cracked. At this time the engine had about 66:40 hours total time. [6]

The defective cam follower was removed from the engine and replaced by a spare cam follower of an older type which they found at the Naval Air Station. Repairs were completed by 1:30 p.m. that same day, and the airplane was then transferred to the landplane hangar and placed under guard. That landplane hangar was a smaller one north-east of the seaplane hangars and no longer in existence. [7]

Aftermath of the incredible ticker-tape parade in New York City on June 13, 1927 ***(Air and Space Collections, Nassau County Museum)***

Lt. George R. Henderson, standing on the center float of a Vought 02U-1 "Corsair", at Anacostia Naval Air Station, about April 1927. ***(Library of Congress)***

Washington, D.C. Celebration and Honors

Saturday, June 11

All official business at the Nation's capitol was suspended as Lindbergh was greeted by statesmen, jurists, cabinet members, foreign ambassadors and other distinguished people.

He and his mother were driven in a White House car in a parade, through a sea of humanity along the streets of Washington, directly to the Washington Monument.

250,000 people were there to greet the flyer. With the President and Mrs. Coolidge, ambassadors, diplomats of many nations and other U.S. Government officials, with their wives.

It was at this time that Lindbergh received the very first Distinguished Flying Cross (D. F. C.) USA. It was the first one struck and approved by The Fine Arts Commission on May 28, 1927, produced at the Quartermaster's Depot at Philadelphia. [9]

Lindbergh gave his first speech in his home country, where he said, in part—"I bring a message home to you, the affection of the people of France and of Europe for the people of America," a

This photo was taken from the Brooklyn Bridge on June 13th, and shows the reviewing stand at City Hall in New York City. ***(Air and Space Collections, Nassau County Museum)***

(Above) *This is an aerial view of the reception for Lindbergh at Roosevelt Field on Long Island on June 16th. One of the only such photos in existence. One would think that scores of photographs would have been taken of this historic event. Notice the dirt runway that stretches from the left, through the circles of cars, diagonally up and to the right. This is the runway Lindbergh took off from on the morning of May 19, headed for Paris.* **(Smithsonian Institution)**

(Below) *June 16, 1927, at Bolling Field, adjacent to Anacostia Naval Air Station, just before he took off for the reception at Roosevelt Field on Long Island. Notice Army personnel near the airplane, and Navy people in white uniform beyond the NYP.* **(Charles Augustus Lindbergh Papers, Manuscripts and Archives, Yale University Library)**

simple but diplomatic message, that was broadcast over radio throughout the country.

From here they went to the temporary White House at Dupont Circle where he dined with the President and other officials, and later attended a National Press Club dinner at the Washington Auditorium.

Sunday, June 12

On Sunday morning, Lindbergh and his mother attended church with the President and his wife and later they all went to Arlington Cemetery where Lindbergh placed a wreath on the tomb of the unknown soldier.

Lindbergh visited soldiers of WW I at the Walter Reid Hospital, and attended a ceremony on the national capitol steps to honor the 150th anniversary of the American flag. Here he was presented with the Cross of Honor by the former secretary of state, Charles Evans Hughes.

Later in the day he attended a function at the National Press Club, and in the evening a Fellow Minnesotans banquet at the Willard Hotel.

New York and the Ticker Tape Parade

Monday, June 13

In the early morning, Lindbergh borrowed a military Curtiss Hawk and flew from Bolling Field to Mitchel Field on Long Island, to be in position for an incredible celebration in New York City.

From Mitchel Field, he piloted a Loening amphibian to a landing in New York Harbor, where hundreds of boats were waiting to be part of a celebration near the Statue of Liberty (given to America by the people of France,) a most appropriate tribute to both countries.

Soon he boarded the mayor's yacht, the Macon, where he rode on the top of the pilot house, and was taken to the Battery, where began a parade into the city.

During the parade up Fifth Avenue on that hot June day, he was inundated with millions of paper shreds, or 'snow' known for years as the "ticker tape parade." It was like no other fete in the history of New York City.

Mayor James J. Walker, son of an Irish immigrant, welcomed the flyer, the son of another immigrant, and presented Lindbergh with the keys to the city. The parade had all the color of New Orlean's Mardi Gras.

The presentation was made at the City Hall. After those ceremonies, with Lindbergh riding in the mayor's car, they drove to Madison Square where Lindbergh placed a wreath at the Eternal Light. From there they cruised to Central Park, where over 300,000 people awaited the flyer's visit and a speech.

Lindbergh was presented to the throng by New York Governor, Alfred E. Smith, who decorated him with another medal of honor from the State of New York. Lindbergh was accompanied during all of this by his mother.

From Central Park, Lindbergh and his mother were taken out to the Mackay Estate on Long Island to attend a dinner.

Lindbergh attended other functions during the afternoon as well. One occurred at the Hotel Commodore, another at the Merchant's Association and later attended a banquet of the Aeronautical Chamber of Commerce at the Waldorf. Lindbergh and his mother stayed overnight at the Mackay estate.

While on Long Island, Lindbergh was given a chance to fly a Curtiss Oriole belonging to Casey Jones for ten minutes. Jones and Lindbergh had briefly met at Curtiss Field before the Paris flight. It is possible that the Oriole was the same one that took the last pictures of the NYP heading out over the north shore of Long Island on the record flight.

Charles Lindbergh accepts the congratulations for his accomplishment from France's Raymond Orteig at the Hotel Brevoort on June 16, 1927. ***(Raymond Orteig III)***

Wednesday, June 15

Apparently this was a day of rest, as there were no official functions to attend for the tired aviator.

Receives the Orteig Prize

Thursday, June 16

Sometime after midnight, in the early hours of the day, Lindbergh took off in the Curtiss Hawk and headed for Anacostia Field in Washington. He was accompanied by Captain Street of the Army Air Corps. At Anacostia the NYP had been rolled out and the engine warmed.

When the NYP was ready, and after a thorough pre-flight, Lindbergh climbed in and took off at 4:05 am. by the light of the moon for Roosevelt Field on Long Island. On this flight, he was accompanied by Lt. Commander H.C. Wick, USN, Lt. Commander A.C. Miles (cc) USN, and Captain Street, in other aircraft. The flight was completed at 7:00 am. EST.

This was the first time Lindbergh had been back at Roosevelt Field since his May 20th takeoff for France. Thousands of people and vehicles formed a large circle on the field, in the center of which had been prepared a grandstand. After many ceremonial messages there, Lindbergh flew the NYP to Mitchel Field where it was temporarily housed in one of the hangars. He was then taken back to New York City.

Originally the big meeting with Raymond Orteig was to be a breakfast, but Mr. Orteig and the trustees of the $25,000 prize fund agreed to change the occasion of the presentation to a "Tea at six o'clock." This was because Lindbergh needed time to return to Mitchel Field to prepare the NYP for a flight to St. Louis the next day. The tea was held at the Hotel Brevoort at Fifth Avenue and Eighth Street in New York City.

According to Vice-Chairman Colonel George W. Burleigh, spokesman for the trustees, Lindbergh was the only aviator whose

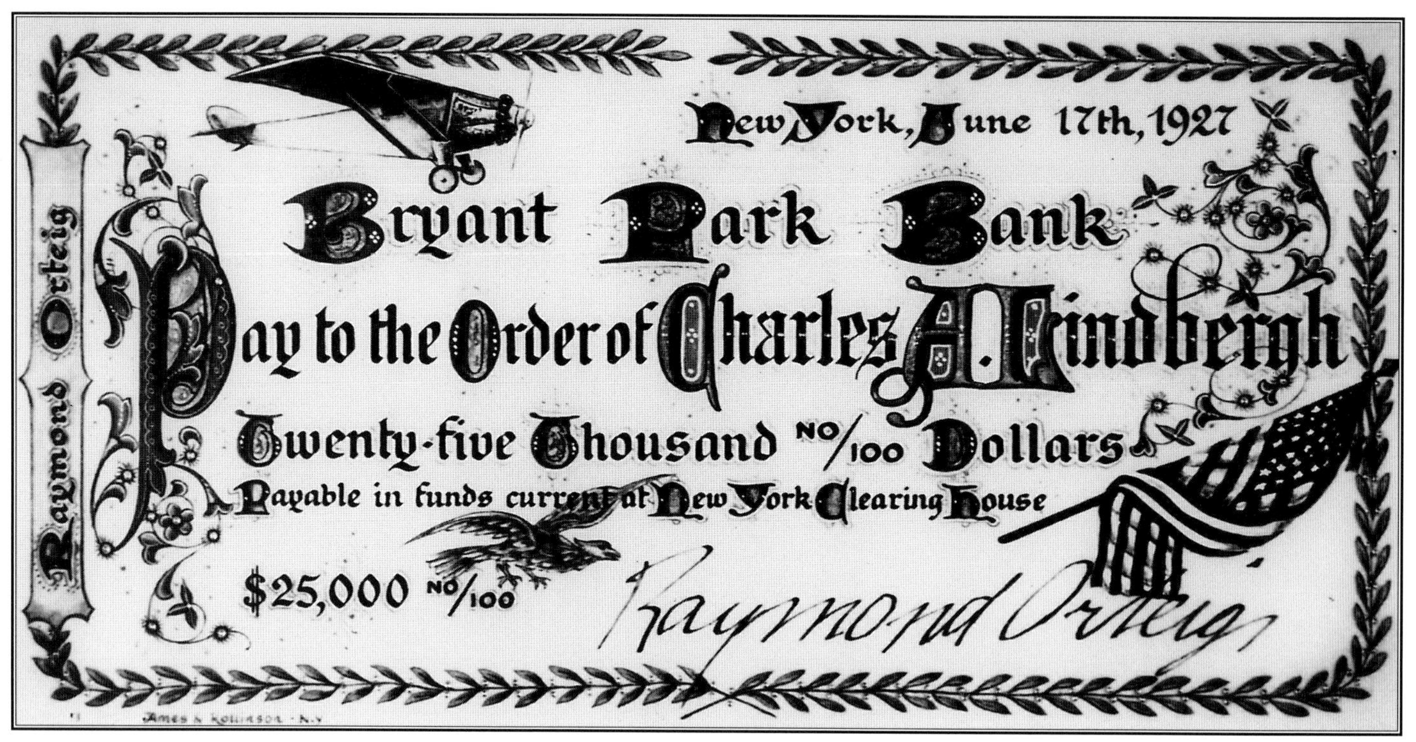

The $25,000 Orteig Prize check given to Charles Lindbergh for accomplishing the goal of becoming the first person to cross the Atlantic from New York to Paris nonstop ***(Cassagneres collection)***

entry complied with every detail of the requirements of the NAA, and the rules and regulations of the flight. He also felt that "the high character and earnest purpose of Colonel Lindbergh will have the greatest influence upon the youth of all the world, and we shall see its results in the coming generations of boys who will be influenced to mold their character and life after the wonderful modesty and firmness of this man and his marvelous achievement."

Burleigh went on to read—"Whereas, Captain Charles A. Lindbergh of Little Falls, Minnesota, an officer of the Missouri National Guard and a United States Air Mail pilot, alone, in a single engine Ryan monoplane, *The Spirit of St. Louis,* successfully made the first non-stop flight from New York City, United States of America, to the City of Paris, Republic of France, leaving Roosevelt Field, New York at six fifty-two o'clock am., New York time, on Friday the twentieth day of May, nineteen hundred and twenty seven and landing at Le Bourget Field at ten twenty one o'clock pm., Paris time, on the twenty-first day of May, nineteen hundred and twenty-seven after a flight of thirty six hundred miles, in an elapsed time of thirty three hours and thirty-three minutes, at an average speed of one hundred and seven miles an hour and

"Whereas, the National Aeronautical Association of Washington, D.C., has certified that Captain Lindbergh and his plane conformed to all the regulations of entry and the rules of the flight competition, as well as those of the National Aeronautic Association of the Federation Aeronautique Internationale of Paris, France, Now Therefore Be It

"Resolved, that the $25,000 Prize, offered by Raymond Orteig of New York City, May 22, 1919, for five years, and given to the undersigned Trustees by Deed of Trust dated June first, nineteen hundred and twenty five, and pursuant to said agreement, be awarded to captain Charles A., Lindbergh, for his wonderful personal achievement in flying alone from New York to Paris, as the first aviator to achieve a non-stop flight between the United States and France; and said amount be paid to him.

"It gives me great pleasure to present to you this engrosses copy of the Resolution, signed by all the Trustees."

Sometime later he was Awarded another $25,000 from the Woodrow Wilson Foundation for the contribution his flight had made to international friendship.

After the day's festivities, Lindbergh flew the NYP over to Mitchel Field, taking all of five minutes, to have the airplane in position for the start of his pre-planned flight to St. Louis, Selfridge Field in Michigan, and Ottawa, Canada, on the next day, June 17th.

Thus ended the journey that took Lindbergh to prominence, began the ground swell of aviation-mindedness around the world, planted the seeds of interest in long-distance air travel, and set the stage for the next big adventure in Lindbergh's life, the famous Guggenheim-sponsored air tours.

FOOTNOTES

1. *The Sunday Star*, newspaper, Washington, DC, June 12, 1927, "Cracked fitting discovered as noted plane is unpacked." Sunday morning edition.
2. Ibid.
3. Ibid.
4. Flight Test Department, Bureau of Aeronautics News Letter, Navy Department, Washington, DC, No. 160, June 29, 1927, pages 5 & 6.
5. Ibid.
6. Ibid.
7. Ibid
8. *The New York Times,* newspaper, Friday, June 3, 1927.
9. Flight Test Dept. News Letter, No. 160, pages 5 & 6
10. Ibid.

ENDNOTES

Careful study was made of photographs in the author's collection revealed details of the NYP structure, etc., its various locations while being worked on in hangars at Anacostia, and personnel of the US Navy involved with the assembly of the NYP. Additional photos taken in that era of the station itself, both on the ground as well as from the air also provided information.

Personal inspection of the Anacostia and Bolling sites near Washington, DC, at various times from 1989 to 1997 was made. Photographs were taken of hangars, both outside as well as inside, showing details of construction and their site location and orientation. Construction drawings of the hangars were obtained from the archives of the US Navy Yard for study of details of construction to compare with original photos taken in 1927. Similar visits to the Washington Navy Yard studying and photographing the docks, yards, and historical buildings.

Several visits were made to the Naval Historical Center, Building 27, Washington Navy Yard, Washington, DC and consultations were made with Historian Roy A. Grossnick.

Further help was received from E.C. Finney, Jr., Curator, Photographic Section, Naval Historical Center (CUP,) Washington Navy Yard, Washington, DC, Comptroller, Naval Imaging Command, Naval Station, Washington, DC.

Log Book of the U.S.S. Memphis, light cruiser, first rate, Commanded by Captain Henry E. Lackey, US Navy. US Naval Forces, Europe, Squadron, Commencing June 1, 1927 at Rotterdam, Holland and ending June 30, 1927 at New York, NY.

Round Shot to Rockets, A History of the Washington Navy Yard and US Naval Gun Factory, by Taylor Peck, United States Naval Institute, Annapolis, Maryland, 1949.

United States Naval Aviation 1910-1970, prepared at the direction of the Deputy Chief of Naval Operations (Air) and the Commander, Naval Air Systems Command 1970. United States Government Printing Office, Washington, DC.

Lindbergh, His Story In Pictures, G. P. Putnam's Sons, New York and London, 1929, by Francis Trevelyan Miller, pages 171-210.

Program - Testimonial Dinner, given to, Mr. Raymond Orteig, by his Friends, Wednesday, November 2, 1927, Waldorf-Astoria Hotel, New York, N.Y., pages 3-66.

Personal interview with Raymond E. Orteig, III, New York City, October 7, 1933.

CHAPTER 15

NYP at Smithsonian

The Smithsonian Institution is a non-profit organization of scientific, educational, and cultural interests. Partially federally funded, it is located between the National Capitol and the Washington Monument on the Mall in Washington, DC. The Institution is dedicated to saving, preserving, and displaying the country's heritage.

The Institution was founded by a British scientist, Sir James Smithson, who willed his fortune to the United States for the establishment of a scientific institution. The gift was accepted by Congress in 1846 to establish an institution "for the increase and diffusion of knowledge among men."

It has since carried out the will of its founder by increasing knowledge through explorations, research, the collecting of significant objects, and by diffusing knowledge through publications, lectures, and exhibitions, embracing every form of life, science, and human accomplishment.

This world famous campus of art, history, and science museums preserves and displays items representing the arts, American history, aeronautics and space exploration, science and technology, and natural history, and engages in many educational programs centered around those subjects.

Paul Edward Garber at age 85, at the National Air and Space Museum in Washington, DC, about February 1985. Notice the Wright flyer in the background. ***(Ev Cassagneres collection)***

Astronomer Samuel Pierpont Langley built up the great tradition in aeronautics at the Smithsonian. When he became third Secretary of the Institution in 1887, he continued his researches in aerodynamics and the construction and testing of his now famous aircraft, ranging from very small models to the large "Aerodrome". Not only do examples of Langley's work reside at the museum, but the examples of many of his contemporaries do as well; men such as Lilienthal, Hargrave, Nerring, Huffaker, the Wright Brothers, and Chanute. Langley's interests also resulted in the acquisition of a valuable aeronautical library which he assembled to form the basis for the Museum's extensive reference files and archives.

Over the years many historically significant aircraft were acquired and put on display at the red brick Arts and Industries building on the Mall. Since 1917 there had been a World War I surplus airplane hangar on the west side of the building. It was provided to house part of the aircraft collection. Several military airplanes of the time were the first to be housed in that building. It is no longer there.

I can vividly remember, as a boy, going there and being allowed to walk around, under the wings, and actually touching the airplanes, feeling the fabric covering if I wished. The general public respected those airplanes then. Most people would not dare do any physical damage to them. There was a certain awe in that setting. The hanger and airplanes were a bit dusty, but seemed as though they had just come in from a flight.

As one entered the front entrance of the Arts and Industries Building into the North Hall, the first airplane seen was *The Spirit of St. Louis* suspended by cables. Off to the left wing was a Curtiss "Jenny" suspended on cables and in the right wing Wiley Post's Lockheed Vega "Winnie Mae", hanging in all its glory.

As the aircraft collection grew, Congress created Public Law 722, resulting in the world famous National Air Museum in 1946 as a bureau of the Smithsonian Institution. The museum was renamed the National Air and Space Museum in 1976, supported jointly by the government as well as private funds. On July 1, 1976 the spectacular and new Air and Space Museum building officially opened on the Mall. It began to be filled with some of the most prized airplanes in existence in the United States.

Every spring school children and their teachers come from all over the country and overseas to view this spectacular display of airplanes. Consider a Douglas DC-3 and Boeing 247D, sizable airliners of the 30's, suspended on cables from the ceiling, along with many other aircraft. It has been the most visited museum in the world.

Drawing as many as 30,000 people in an average day, the National Air and Space Museum is the most popular exhibit building in Washington, DC. It has often been called the most attended museum in the world. To keep up with the times, space exploration vehicles are a big draw, where one can view numerous historical rockets, space craft, and related equipment.

PAUL E. GARBER, HISTORIAN EMERITUS AND RAMSEY FELLOW

When one speaks of the National Air and Space Museum, the name Paul Garber nearly always becomes part of the conversation. He is probably the one man most responsible for the air museum as we know it today, including many of its aircraft and other memorabilia. This includes the new air museum on the Mall, which he fought for, starting before World War II.

Garber was hired by the Smithsonian in June 1920. His love for aviation was evident, but his other deep interest centered on the kite. He spent hours teaching children how to build and fly kites, showing by his example that anyone can make something that flies.

Garber early on envisioned the airplane's eventual historic importance and sought out flying machines for the national collection with unique wisdom and foresight. These historic aircraft might otherwise have been lost to time and the human tendency to scrap yesterday's history.

He was the first curator of the National Air Museum. He developed a personal relationship with such outstanding aviation personalities as Jimmy Doolittle, Orville Wright, Charles Lindbergh, Billy Mitchell, Glenn Curtiss, Amelia Earhart, and many others.

Sixty-seven years after beginning his work at the Institution, he was named Honorary Director of the National air and Space Museum for one day, August 14, 1987. He had never before been the director of his own creation. The day was marked by a Presidential proclamation, deservedly making the day unique in the annals of the museum.

Many years ago, as I was getting involved with research into aviation history, I can recall meeting Mr. Garber in his office. As were the archives of that time, it was located high in an attic in the Arts and Industries building, without air conditioning. I would first stop by for a brief visit and chat with Mr. Garber, and do some hangar flying. Then he would say, "Well, Ev, you know where the files are, go have fun." After checking with archivist Robert Wood, I would open file drawers on Ryan and other aircraft that I was familiar with, then check for misfiled items and straighten it all out as well as I could. Sometimes Mr. Garber and I would do some trading, so that the collection had a new item. There was a high trust in those days among many of us. It was an accepted procedure, without stress. We all accomplished much, and could usually find what we were looking for, and by contrast help them with questions they had. We helped each other.

SILVER HILL, SUITLAND, MARYLAND

The behind-the-scenes workshop of the National Air and Space Museum is known today as the Paul E. Garber Restoration, Preservation and Storage Facility of the National Air and Space Museum. It is located across the Potomac River at Silver Hill in Suitland, Maryland. The place houses the most interesting and unusual aircraft of our time in the collection, including space vehicles and equipment.

The facility has been used as an artifact storage and restoration center since the mid-1950's. It was not until 1977, however, that some of the buildings were opened to the public as a "no frills" museum.

On display one can find about 160 aircraft as well as numerous spacecraft, engines, propellers and other aviation related memorabilia. Artifacts consisting of very delicate material are stored in an environmentally controlled building.

Free tours are available via special arrangements, to individuals or groups. The Garber facility was named in honor of Paul

A rare photo of the NYP as preparations were being made for the NYP's final resting place at the Smithsonian Institutions Arts and Industries Building on the Mall in Washington, DC. Taken May 13, 1928 ***(Leo B. Kimball collection)***

The NYP fuselage as it was being rolled into the Arts and Industries Building at Smithsonian Institution. ***(Library of Congress)***

Photo shows the process of hoisting the NYP into position in the Arts and Industries Building main hall, where it was to hang for many years. May 14th. Three cables, each of which could sustain 3800 pounds. ***(Leo B. Kimball collection)***

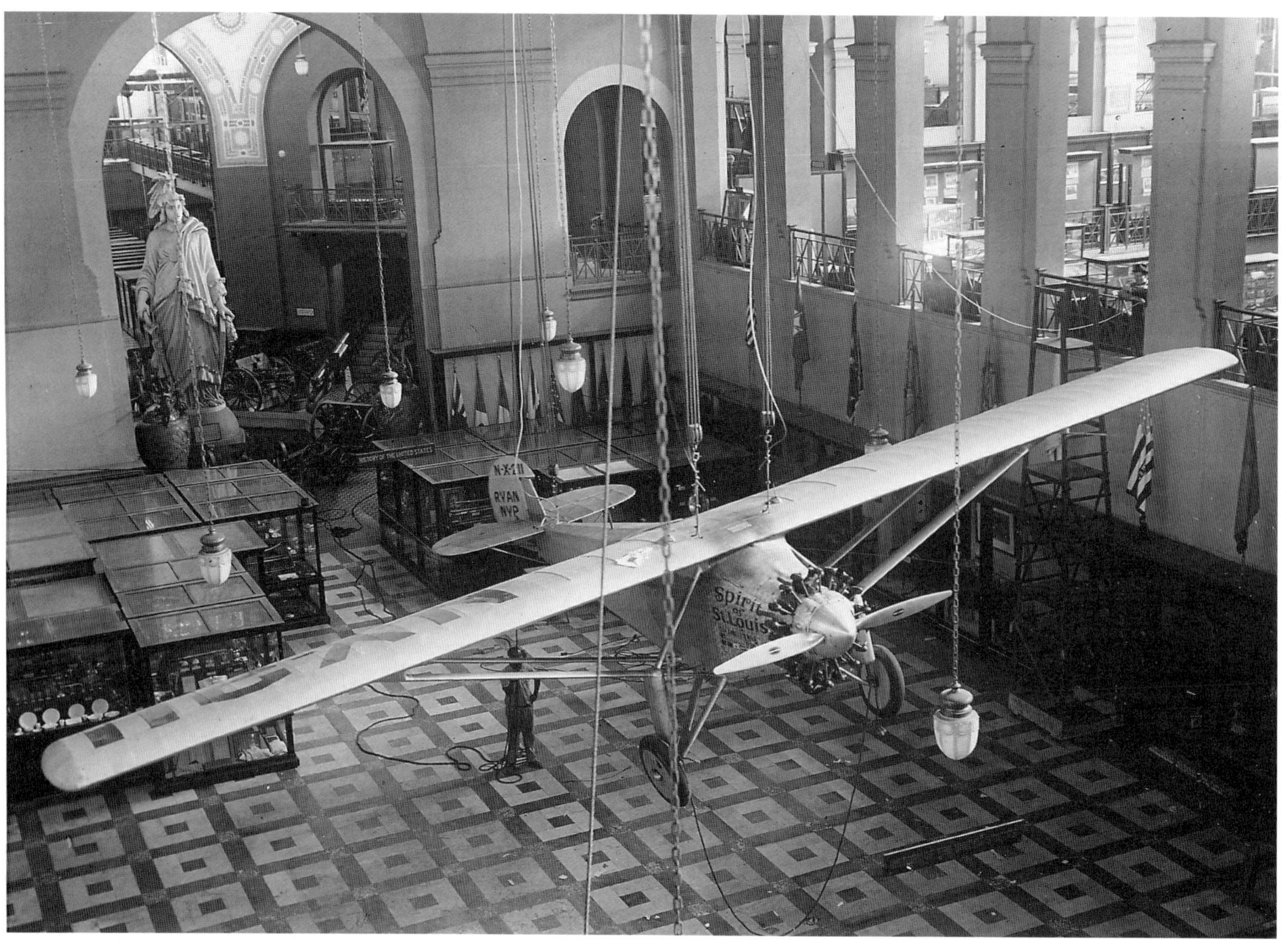

(Above) **The Spirit of St. Louis being hoisted to the ceiling of the hall of the old Smithsonian Arts & Industries Building. (Smithsonian Instituition)**

(Below) **Finally suspended, with Lindbergh's photograph just below and a space display to the right. Date of photo unknown. (Smithsonian Institution)**

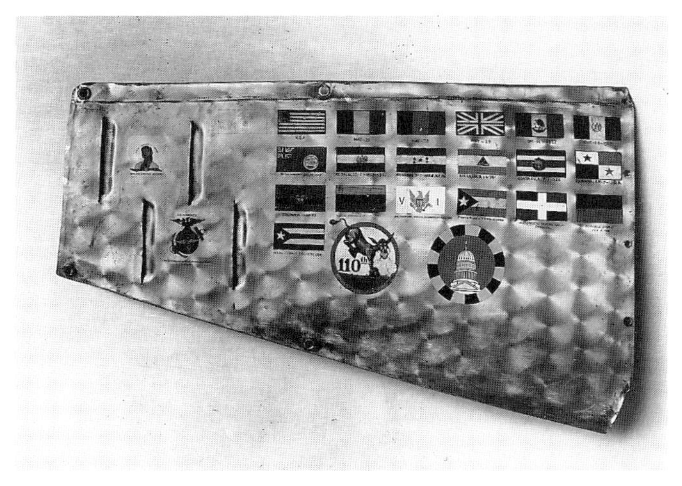

Close up view of the left engine cowling, taken shortly after the airplane was put into the museum. ***(Leo B. Kimball collection)***

Garber in 1980.

Paul Garber was married to Irene "Buttons" Tusch. Irene was the daughter of "Mother Tusch", owner of the famous Mother Tusch 'hang-out' for flyers located in Berkeley, California.

Paul Garber passed away at the age of 93 on the morning of September 23, 1992. He had spent more than seventy years at the museum!

NYP ACQUISITION

When the news of Lindbergh's successful take-off from Roosevelt Field, New York on that wet May 20, 1927 morning reached a small, soft-spoken, but greatly determined young Paul Edward Garber, he immediately had the foresight to approach his boss about obtaining the airplane for the museum.

Garber suggested to the non-aviation-minded Dr. Charles Greely Abbot that they wire ahead to Paris and request that the NYP be donated to the Smithsonian. The latter almost threw Garber out of his office as he, like many people, did not expect Lindbergh to make the flight in the first place.

With the success of the flight, and his acceptance of the request, the picture changed, and Dr. Abbot was most cooperative.

TELEGRAM

Washington, D.C. May 27, 1927
Captain Charles A. Lindbergh,
American Embassy, Paris,

SMITHSONIAN INSTITUTION CONGRATULATES YOU ON GLORIOUS ACHIEVEMENT STOP HOPE Spirit of St. Louis WILL EVENTUALLY JOIN LANGLEY'S MACHINES THE ARMY WRIGHT FIRST PLANE EVER OWNED BY ANY GOVERNMENT THE NC4 CHICAGO AND OTHER HISTORIC AMERICAN PLANES IN OUR UNITED STATES NATIONAL MUSEUM.

C. G. Abbot, Acting Secretary.
Smithsonian Institution.

PREPAY—Charge Smithsonian—Govt. rate. NAM 106 [1]

This photo was taken at the Silver Hill restoration facility in Suitland, Maryland, in 1975. ***(National Air and Space Museum)***

Good view of the underside of the NYP showing clearly the flair tubes and other details. ***(Smithsonian Institution)***

On April 30, 1928 Lindbergh took off from Lambert Field at St. Louis, Missouri and flew non-stop to Bolling Field, Washington, DC. This trip of 725 miles took 4 hours 58 minutes, with an average speed of about 145 mph due to a strong tail wind.

Soon after landing the airplane was rolled into one of the large Army hangars. It must have been a sad occasion for Lindbergh, after such a profound relationship in the air with his trusty machine, and to know it would never fly again. [2]

Lindbergh sat quietly in the cockpit as the engine came to a stop, contemplating this last flight in his famous airplane. He picked up his blue sweater and some baggage before climbing out of the cockpit. He had kept his promise of donating the NYP to his country, and now he must get on with his life.

Total flying time was 489 hours 28 minutes, with 174 individual flights to its credit. [3]

Soon the workers, some Army personnel and Smithsonian people, including Paul Garber, began the task of removing the

The NYP dismantled at the Arts and Industries building about September 9, 1975, to be shipped to Silver Hill for some restoration work. ***(Smithsonian Institution)***

A close up view of the wing removal before going over to Silver Hill. September 9, 1975. ***(National Air and Space Museum)***

large wing. The wing was placed on mattresses on the floor. Then they removed the full six piece engine cowling and propeller, as well as the horizontal stabilizer and elevators and wing struts. The vertical fin and rudder remained on the airplane.

A large canvas tarpaulin was secured over the forward half of the fuselage, covering the cockpit forward to the engine.

Photographs show that the wing was placed on a long four wheel flat bed pulled by a tractor. The horizontal tail surfaces were placed in an Army truck with a canvas top.

Sometime during the early morning or nighttime, the somber procession got underway, through the city streets toward the Smithsonian Institution.

MAJOR GENERAL HOWARD C. DAVIDSON

In the early part of 1928 Major General Howard C. Davidson became the Commanding Officer of Bolling Field. In 1928 he was a Major.

Partly his responsibility, Davidson recalled many years later details of moving the NYP to the Smithsonian..

"We had to disassemble it. We made all arrangements with the police. They had put up 'No Parking' signs all along the route. We tied the tail to a truck and moved the plane after 1:00 a.m. He remembered that the wheels of the airplane were an unexpected problem. "We never thought how defective they were. As the plane was being towed through the streets of Washington, the wheels caught fire once or twice."

Taken sometime in January 1992 at the new National Air and Space Museum building's Milestones of Flight Gallery, supported on the floor on Walkswagon type wheels. ***(National Air and Space Museum)***

"Oh, I thought if I burned up the *Spirit of St. Louis* I might as well take off from the United States." He recalled also that the police would go on ahead along the route to pick up illegally parked cars and move them. [4]

It appears that after leaving Bolling Field, the movers went over the 11th Street bridge, proceeded to Independence Avenue westward by the Capitol, and directly to the Arts and Industries Building just past 7th Street.

The NYP was put on display in the North Hall of the Arts and Industries Building on May 13, 1928.

On May 23, 1928, Secretary Abbot reported to Colonel Lindbergh that the *Spirit of St. Louis* was in the North Hall of the Arts and Industries Building. The deed of gift was signed by the ten St. Louis benefactors who financially supported Charles Lindbergh's New York to Paris flight. The deed of gift stipulates that the *Spirit of St. Louis* be placed on permanent exhibit and that the cabin area (cockpit) would be visible. During his lifetime, Lindbergh was the sole judge to decide whether these conditions were satisfied. Upon his death, the deed transferred this prerogative to the Washington, DC Commission of Fine Arts.

When the airplane was hung, it was supported by three steel wire cables from the roof members of the building. Two 5/8" cables were attached to diagonal struts and transverse cross members of the fuselage and up both sides of the wing spar passing through holes made in the wing to the roof of the building.

The third steel cable of 5/16" diameter supported the tail of the airplane. The lower end of this cable is fastened to the upper longerons just forward of the leading edge of the vertical fin.

It was at this time that the Smithsonian awarded Charles Lindbergh the Langley gold medal for aerodromics in recognition of the importance of his flight. [5]

The NYP hung in the Arts and Industries Building for 47 years before plans were made to move it to the new air museum building on the Mall.

In a letter dated March 31, 1933 from Lindbergh to Dr. C. G. Abbot he wrote, "I have replied to all inquiries in regard to moving the plane for temporary exhibition, that I am unalterably opposed to ever moving it from its present location in Washington. I feel it is a great mistake to subject museum articles to the wear, risk, and damage of transportation." [6]

In another letter from Lindbergh to Dr. C. G. Abbot of the Smithsonian Institution, dated May 31, 1933, he wrote, "It is my request and understanding that neither the *Spirit of St. Louis*, nor any part of its equipment, will ever be removed from the Museum for temporary exhibition elsewhere."

MISSING SERIAL NUMBER

In the meantime, while the airplane was still in its original location, the question arose as to the correct airframe serial number. Through extensive research, checking photographs and other documentation, such a number was not visible.

On November 28, 1969 arrangements were made through my friend, Paul Garber, for me to physically check a lead I had found in a conversation in 1968 with former Ryan employee O. R. McNeel in Twenty Nine Palms, California. He said that with the blunt end of a file he had scratched the number on the inside of the top cowl, toward the trailing edge in the center.

National Air Museum staff erected a special scaffolding so I could climb up to the airplane and remove the cowling pieces. After extensive checking and photographing of the details of the six pieces, no number was found. Many initials and names were inscribed in these pieces, however.

Here the airplane is seen suspended in the Milestones of Flight Gallery at the National Air and Space Museum, where it has been for many years. ***(National Air and Space Museum)***

After exhaustive research over the years, the following story has been pieced together.

It does not appear that Ryan Airlines, Inc. ever assigned a serial number to the airplane. It was just referred to as the "NYP". In the list of Ryan airplanes built around that period, serial number 29 was assigned to a Hispano-Suiza powered Ryan, a B-1 or B-2 with registration C-3007. There is also a possibility that serial 30 or 31 was assigned to 3009, but that can't be confirmed.

Aviation writer and historian Richard Sanders Allen has done considerable research in FAA files on many aircraft, including the NYP. He did not find any mention of a serial number for the airplane in the original NYP FAA (CAA) files.

The only other Ryan airplane vying for inclusion in this serial number question would be the Robinson ordered "Gold Bug", which was sold to Frank Hawks and renamed "Miss Maxwell House". This Mahoney Ryan was also known as the "Pride of San Diego". During its life it carried 3009 and 1105, which was a temporary license number.

As a side note it is interesting to see what became of the original "NX211" registration number over the years.

In 1926 or 1927 the number 211 was assigned to an airplane known as the Irwin M. T., built in the fall of 1924 by the Irwin Aircraft Company, location unknown.

After the NYP was officially taken out of service, the "211" was next assigned to Lindbergh's Lockheed "Sirius" serial number 140 as NR211. Then it was later assigned to his Lambert Monocoupe s/n D-125 as NR211.

In 1947 N-211 was assigned to a North American AT-6 (SNJ-4) serial 9845.

In 1958 the N211 was assigned to a Beechcraft s/n 6009 and in 1964 N211 was assigned to a Cessna (195 series) s/n 7294.

On September 9th, 1975 the NYP was lowered to the floor of the Arts and Industries building and shipped to Silver Hill for some restoration work before being put on display in the new Air and Space Museum on the Mall.

While at Silver Hill the NYP underwent minor cleaning and repairs. A restoration report prepared by Patricia Williams and John Cusack and approved by Donald K. Merchat was made.

The airplane was re-hung in the Milestones of Flight Gallery at the new National Air and Space Museum in time for the July 2, 1976 grand opening.

Eventually, the museum staff decided that the NYP needed a proper and thorough inspection and decided to lower it to the floor in the Milestones of Flight Gallery. This was completed on January 23, 1992.

The task was accomplished with the use of an oversize "mite lift" that possessed an extended capability at least equaling the height of the main landing gear wheels on the airplane. The original wheels were removed and Volkswagon "travel" wheels installed on the axles. The crew consisted of Bill Reese, George Vencelov, Will Lee, and Matt Nezzaro.

A Conservation Condition and Treatment Report for the NYP was prepared and printed in April 1992. It indicates the following items were attended to:

A Plexiglas sheet was installed in the door opening to prevent dust and dirt from entering the airplane and still allow viewing access to the public.

A portion of fuselage fabric just ahead of the vertical fin on top of the fuselage was replaced. It was Grade A cotton, which was doped with multiple coats of clear nitrate and finished with butyrate silver dope.

The right and left wheel axle fairings were replaced after repairing the wooden inserts which are installed inside the hollow axle shaft.

The left wheel access point for the tire valve stem required new fabric edging, finished in Grade A linen fabric, with the usual butyrate dope.

The center wing fuel tank vent on top of the wing (a facsimile made prior to this conservation work) was attached with epoxy to a metal stiffener (plate), which is not part of the airplane.

A stress analysis was made by Dr. Marion Mecklenburg, C.A.L. using modern technological equipment. It was centered on the structural airframe, engine mount and the tubular airframe.

In the final report it was stated that the *Spirit of St. Louis,* although basically in good condition, has deteriorated more than expected.

Conservators contributing to the report were from the Conservation Analytical Laboratory of the Smithsonian, specifically the Paul E. Garber Facility in Suitland, Maryland, under the direction of Edward McManus, Chief Conservator—A.I.C. Fellow.

The NYP was re-suspended on March 25, 1992 in the Milestones of Flight Gallery in the new building on the Mall.

NOVEMBER 2000 TEMPORARY MOVE

On October 31, 2000, the NYP was lowered to the floor of the Milestones of Flight Gallery and moved to the West Wing, where it was re-suspended in a temporary location.

The Air & Space Museum building had been undergoing a major restoration in phases, gallery by gallery. This move was part of a major restoration of the building. The NYP was suspended in its original location in the Milestones of Flight gallery sometime during the last week of June, 2001, in preparation for an anniversary celebration that took place on July 1st.

INTERESTING FACTS

The original 32" x 4" wheels that made the flight to Paris are not on the NYP and have not been since they were removed about August 23 or 24 at Minneapolis, Minnesota during the tour. The replacement wheels have been on the airplane ever since, including all of the time during display in Washington.

The original wheels have been in a humidity controlled environment at Silver Hill all these years. This writer had the pleasure of examining them; taking photographs, measuring the wheels and tires, etc. a few years ago.

The wheels on the airplane presently are the ones that were installed during the U.S. tour at Wold-Chamberlain Field in Minneapolis. They are 30" x 5" in size.

When the six piece cowling panels were removed several years ago by this author, the following names were found scratched on the inside.

They are the names of people who worked on the NYP over the years during its flying years. They scratched their names on the inside of the sheet metal as listed below.

This is one of the original two 32" x 4" wheels that were on the NYP during the New York to Paris flight. They were removed at Wold-Chamberlain Field, St. Paul, MN during the U.S. Tour on August 23-25, 1927. and are now in storage at the National Air and Space Museum in Washington, DC. ***(Ev Cassagneres)***

TOP COWLING (Obviously done at Bolling Field)
December 13, 1927

To C. A. Lindbergh
With sincerest hopes that you may
Be successful we thank you for en-
Trusting to us the work of prepairing
Your plane for the flight.
Very truly yours,
R. H. Hooe, S. Borecki, J. E. McQuade
C. C. Rockenbaugh, I. L . Kallmyer, D. H. Stewart
(written across above),

TOP COWLING
John Daley, Frank E. Field, Canal Zone, Jan 19, 1928
Lela Williams, St. Louis, Mo.
Miss F. Rohr, 3722 Art Zona, San Diego, Cal.
F. C. Mitchell, 4453—39th St., San Diego, Cal.
Pop Daly—Canal Zone

RIGHT HAND SIDE COWL
W. G. E., W. G. Edwards,Portland
JNO R. Lester, San Diego, Fred Maguda
Fred Rohr, San Diego, Calif.
Original builders of this cowling.

ON ENGINE COWLING AROUND CYLINDERS
P. R., L. B., L M, J.B Bobin, A. H. L., P C. Nations
W. D., Haiti, W. B. 28, Sgt. Psierra, Feb. 11, 1928

ON PROP SPINNER
Prest Rose, 1946, May. 28, West Indies Express

WOMAN'S COMPACT MIRROR

It is known that a woman in the crowd gave Lindbergh a small circular compact mirror just before he left Roosevelt Field for his historic flight. It was installed on the upper center portion of the instrument panel.

On July 1, 1998 this writer made a special trip to the museum to do further inspection of details of the NYP.

Concentrating on the cockpit and instrument panel area, I removed the famous mirror from the top center of the panel. To my surprise, when the mirror was turned over it was painted all red, with gold letters—"STARRETT TOOLS"—inscribed on the surface. Analyzing the situation I determined that this could not be the original mirror given to Lindbergh by Mrs. Loma Oliver, Jr. More than likely she would have had one in her compact that had been made by a major cosmetic company.

Contact was made with the L.S. Starrett Company, in which I described the mirror with an accompanying photo of the Starrett one.

Mr. D. R. Starrett, Chairman and CEO, replied, "The mirror was made for us as an advertising giveaway in the very early days of our company. I do not have the actual dates, but it had to be in the late teens or early twenties. This was kind of a handy tool for a workman to have if he wanted to use it to read a dial indicator that was being rotated, or a guy could take it out of his toolbox to see if he had a small cut on his face, or something like that.

At any rate, these mirrors with our name and logo on them were made by Bastian Brothers in Brooklyn, New York. They were made in the small size that you photographed, up to something like 8" diameter. These were discontinued about the time of World War II.

Since this was a giveaway, we don't have any reference to it in our catalogs, but I am sure there are a lot of mirrors out in the country. In fact, I still have one that I picked up from my father, who also had it in his toolbox." [7]

In conclusion, it appears that the original mirror was perhaps removed by a mechanic for his own souvenir and then replaced by the Starrett mirror, which is still in the NYP. Where that original mirror is today is anyone's guess. My own opinion is that it was removed sometime during the NYP's stay for maintenance at Teterboro, New Jersey.

Today, as it hangs in the National Air and Space Museum building, it is still the most popular single exhibit.

LINDBERGH VISITS THE NYP IN 1940

On Thursday, February 29, 1940, while on business in Washington, Lindbergh spent about an hour at the Smithsonian and had the following to say about his visit to view the NYP for the first time in several years.

"Had the afternoon free, so took a taxi from the Army & Navy Club to the Smithsonian Institution. I have not seen the *Spirit of St. Louis* for several years, and I wanted to know how it is being cared for. It is nearly twelve years now since I last flew in it.

"I was anxious to get in the building without being recognized so after leaving the taxi I walked around the building in the hope of finding a side door open, but there was none. A dozen or so people were sitting on the benches on each side of the front entrance, watching all passers-by. Another dozen, including guards, were inside the door where the plane is hanging. However, by blowing my nose at the right moment, I got by them all. I did not want to have to talk to the guards, be taken to call on the museum officials, and look at my plane with a crowd of people gathered around.

"Immediately after entering, I turned right, into the room of Presidents' wives and dresses. I never thought I should have such a close personal debt of gratitude to Martha Washington, but her dress and figure, and the glass case which contained them, were in exactly the right position for me to stand behind and look through into the adjoining room at the *Spirit of St. Louis*. No one took notice of me there, for if they looked at all it was at Martha Washington's dress, and not at me. I felt she and I had something in common as we watched the *Spirit of St. Louis* together. I rather envied her the constant intimacy with the plane that I once had.

"How strange it seemed, standing there looking at the plane, and what a chasm of time and circumstances separated us. Yet in another sense how close we still were! I could feel myself in the cockpit again, taking off from the rain-softened runway at Roosevelt Field, skimming low over the waves of mid-Atlantic, or brushing past a high peak of the Rockies. Such a little plane, it seemed to me today; I felt about it as I once felt about the old Wright biplanes. Still, there was a trimness about the *Spirit of St. Louis* that even now gives me a feeling of pride. I felt I could take it down from its cables, carry it to some flying field, and feel perfectly at home in that cockpit again. (I have in my dreams, flown the old ship several times since that last landing on Bolling Field in 1928, and I have always felt worried, and sorry I had taken it from the museum lest it crash in that post last flight. I was always relieved when I woke and found I had not really violated my decision that the plane should never be flown again.)

"People stopped beneath it as I watched, and looked up at the plane and at the articles of equipment in the showcase. The plane is in excellent condition—perfectly cared for. I stood looking at it for nearly an hour, I think, losing all count of time. Finally, I noticed two girls looking at me—they were not certain—in a moment they would ask. It had been the most pleasant visit I had ever made to the museum—the first one on which I could really think about and appreciate my old plane. I did not want to talk to people. I left." [8]

Clear view of the instrument panel as it looks now at the museum. Notice the compass correction sheet (blue print) on the right side. The mirror at top dead center is not the original (see text) . The cover plate below the clock is missing. ***(National Air and Space Museum)***

FOOTNOTES

1. Original telegram found in the Archives of the national Air & Space Museum, washington, DC NAM 106.
2. *The Spirit of St. Louis*, Charles A. Lindbergh, Charles Scribner's Sons, New York, 1953, page 513.
3. Ibid.
4. Comments by Major Howard C. Davidson, USAF, (Ret.) in a conversation with Lt. Col. Raymond H. Fredette, USAF (Ret.) in Washington, DC on December 14, 1974.
5. *Webster's Third International Dictionary of the English Language,* unabridged, A Merriam-Webster, G & C. Merriam Company, Publishers, Springfield, MA, USA, 1966, page 33.
6. Copies of both of the original letters are in the author'collection.
7. Letter to the author, dated September 1, 1998, from D.R. Starrett, Chairman and CEO of The L.S. Starrett Company, Athol, MA.
8. *The Wartime Journals of Charles A. Lindbergh,* Harcourt, Brace, Jovanovich, Inc., New York, 1970, pages 319-320.

ENDNOTES

Other Reference Material Used for this Chapter

Conservation Condition and Treatment Report, *Spirit of St. Louis* airplane, Washington, DC, April 1992. This document was assembled by the National Air & Space Museum staff and individually written by: Frank Florentine, Lighting Designer; Lin Ezell; Robert van der Linden; Edward McManus; Patricia Williams; John Cusack; Donald K. Merchat; Natt Nazzaro; Bill Reese; Dr. Marion Mecklenburg (stress analysis); Dr. Mary Baker; Robert Mikesh; Donald S. Lopez.

The National Aeronautical Collections, Exhibited by the National Air Museum, under the Administration of the Smithsonian Institution, by Paul E. Garber, Head Curator, National Museum, 1956, Publication 4255, published by the Smithsonian Institution, Washington, DC.

The Smithsonian Book of Flight, Walter J. Boyne, 1987, Smithsonian Books, Washington, DC and Orion Books, New York

The Aircraft Treasures of Silver Hill, Walter J. Boyne, 1982, Rawson Associates, New York, NY.

Letters of correspondence between Paul Edward Garber and the author over a period of 20 years.

The Wright Brothers, Fred C. Kelly, 1943 & 1950, Ballantine Books, Inc., New York, NY

F. Robert van der Linden, Ph.D, NYP curator, National Air & Space Museum, Washington, DC.

Dan Hagedorn, Research Team Leader, National Air & Space Museum, Washington, DC.

CHAPTER 16

The Crate Story

Who would ever believe that one of the two packing crates, built in England by the Royal Air Force, would end up in a little town in Maine as an historic artifact? It is a true "Americana" experience to visit that site today and see first hand a "final " resting place of a wooden crate and what it means to our American aviation heritage.

The story started aboard the U.S.S. Memphis on the high seas of the Atlantic Ocean during the voyage from Cherbourg, France to Washington, D.C.

Vice Admiral Guy H. Burrage, Lindbergh's official escort, happened to have a summer place in Contoocook, just west of Concord, New Hampshire, that he felt needed a cabin on it. He asked Lindbergh what he might be planning to do with the larger of the two crates. He had no plans and said the Admiral was most welcome to have it.

At first it looked as though the crate might be shipped to the property of Barton Myers, Jr. in Ingleside, Virginia, home of Adm. Burrage's daughter, Mrs. Myers. Certainly the logistics of moving the crate from the Washington Navy Yard to Ingleside, near Norfolk, would be somewhat simpler than sending it to New Hampshire. [1]

After the NYP was off-loaded at the U.S. Navy Yard in Washington, D.C., the crate was possibly taken by U. S. Navy ship to Boston, then by rail to Contoocook, New Hampshire. [2] There it was set up on a corner of the Burrage family property. The family referred to the crate as "The Shack". The crate was so well built by the RAF that the Burrage family had the outside walls turned inside out to make best use of the pine finish. Inside one could see the outside latches, which are still on it. [3]

Local carpenters at the time sheathed the outside—"England's pine covered by New England's pine," said Larry Ross, the present owner on whose property it rests today. This work provided a double siding. Added to that were doors, windows and a back porch. For many years the Burrage family used the shack as a guest house for family and friends. A grandson remembers that when he was small he and his sister slept there when they visited. In 1954 Admiral Burrage passed away and from that time on the shack began to deteriorate. [4]

Here "the shack" (crate) is shown on the bank of the Blackwater River in Contoocook, New Hampshire. ***(Larry Ross)***

In the early 1960's a grandson had the shack moved across the property to be put on the bank of the Blackwater River. It became a "stopping place" (a Hippie retreat) for anyone who would like to stay there. A pregnant woman stayed there a few days and gave birth to her child, a girl, and named her Amelia for Amelia Earhart. [5]

In 1990 thirty-eight year old Larry Ross, the director of Sebasticook Farms, a social service agency for the disabled, learned that the shack was up for sale. Being an avid historian, he just could not resist. Ross was not a Lindbergh buff and is not a pilot, but has a weakness for unusual memorabilia. Ross just had to have this crate. [6]

The deal was made, and Ross had planned to get the crate to his home on Easy Street in Canaan, Maine, to restore it to the condition that it had in 1927. A volunteer donated his truck and loaded the crate aboard a flatbed for the journey. Ross was able to accomplish the restoration with volunteer assistance from a group he affectionately referred to as the "schemers and dreamers."

The crate made it to its present resting place on top of a hill in Maine as a lasting tribute to the NYP flight of 1927. Larry Ross once said that it was his hope that the crate serve to promote the idea that people with vision, with well planned and articulated goals, working in cooperation with each other, can accomplish things that otherwise may appear impossible. He went on to say, "That to me seems to be one of the lessons we can still learn from Lindbergh's flight." [7]

In a local effort under the direction of Larry Ross, the crate was mounted on the hill facing east toward Paris, France. Scores of people donated granite, gravel, wood and many hours of their own labor to the project. The area around the crate was landscaped. New wood sheathing, a new roof and "wrap-around" porch were added. Outside the crate looks like any other small

Mrs. Burrage (wife of Vice Admiral Guy H. Burrage) with the contractor who did the initial work on the crate at Canaan, Maine. ***(Larry Ross)***

The crate being moved along the road to Canaan, Maine to its final resting place and glory. ***(Larry Ross)***

The crate as it looks today, on a hill overlooking a valley in Canaan, Maine. ***(Larry Ross)***

gray-blue bungalow. On the grounds are a small monument and flag pole.

Inside one can find all sorts of historical memorabilia; photographs, letters, artifacts, buttons, flags and banners and technical data on the Lindbergh story. All of this is available for children and adults to study and learn.

Ross's intention is to make the crate available on a non-commercial basis to schools groups and people interested in its odd but nevertheless significant role in history.

Opening dedication ceremonies took place on May 22, 1992. It has become an annual event, known as "Lindbergh Crate Day", to focus on the importance of having a vision of what you would like to achieve with your life.

Mr. Ross provides children an educational experience filled, with not only excitement, but also examples of values and role models for them to aspire to. Using Lindbergh's flight as a backdrop, the children participate in a variety of educational activities. A cross-section of people are invited to the event, people who have achieved some aspect of their own visions. It makes for a powerful learning experience and has been a successful and well-received event.

Now known as the Lindbergh Crate Museum, it is open to the public free of charge and is especially geared to school children with a message coined by Ross.

"BE SOMEONE"

"Lindy flew his ocean blue.
If he can do it, so can you."
Lindy made his dream come true.
With some planning, so can you.
Pick your target, keep on track.
Keep on moving; don't look back.
Find some friends to lend a hand,
Think it through, work your plan.
Choose a place you want to fly.
Always, always, always try.
Lindy flew his ocean blue,
If he did it, so can you.

Larry Ross

ENDNOTES

1. *Virginian Pilot,* June 11, 1927. Magazine article, "Historic Packing Cases Housing Lindbergh Plane May Be Brought to Norfolk," author unknown, unpaged.

2. *Yankee Magazine,* Yankee, Inc., Dublin, New Hampshire, November, 1974. "Where's the Crate That Carried 'Lucky Lindy's' Plane Home," Robert Ganley, pages 254-255.

3. *Smithsonian Magazine,* Washington, DC, Sptember, 1993, "Around the Mall and Beyond," Ewards Prk, pages 16-20.

4. Ibid.

5. *Yankee Magazine,* Yankee, Inc., Dublin, New Hampshire, August ,991, Quips, Quotes and Queries "Living in Lindbergh's Crate," Larry Ross, pages 16-17.

6. *Down East, The Magazine of Maine,* Camden, ME, June, 1990, "Lindbergh's Legacy," page 43.

7. *Sport Aviation,* experimental Aircraft Association, Oshkosh, WI, February, 1991, "The Lindbergh Crate," Larry Ross (Letter from Ross to Mr. Paul Poberezny, President of EAA.)

CHAPTER 17

Survival Equipment

As with any research study of this magnitude, the researcher needs to reach people "who were there". As the years go by, it becomes more difficult to find such people and such was the case when I began to look for Kenneth Lane. Lane worked for Wright Aeronautical Corporation in Patterson, New Jersey in 1927 as their Chief Engineer in charge of aircraft structural design. It was in May of that year that the firm assigned him as a technical representative to Curtiss Field to assist wherever necessary any of the flyers using their products who were planning and/or attempting to make the New York to Paris flight.

After a five year search, I located Mr. Lane then living in Florida in the winter and Madison, New Hampshire during the summer.

Arrangements were made for me to visit Madison on July 25, 1973 to interview Mr. Lane. I flew a Piper Apache twin engine aircraft to Conway, New Hampshire, where Mr. Lane picked me up and we drove to their home in the little town of Madison.

After a pleasant lunch prepared by Mrs. Lane and time getting acquainted, I got into the appropriate questions on his career in general, eventually concentrating on his Curtiss Field duties.

We had covered considerable ground with about two questions to go when he casually remarked to his wife Elizabeth, "Didn't we have Lindbergh's kit bag (the survival equipment carried from New York to Paris, which I did not realize existed at this time) out in the barn?" She replied that she thought they did, and he suggested that shortly he would go out to look for it. He came back with two small cardboard boxes, and we proceeded to lay the contents out on the living room floor. It included three cans of Army emergency rations, four red flares each of which was sealed in a rubber bicycle tube, one ball of cord, one coil of heavy string, two fishing hooks, one large needle, one match container with matches manufactured by Marbles Company, one hack saw, one seat air cushion, and the cloth bag which held these items during the flight to Paris. That was all in one box.

Items that were in the survival equipment kit bag, as described in the text. ***(Ev Cassagneres photo)***

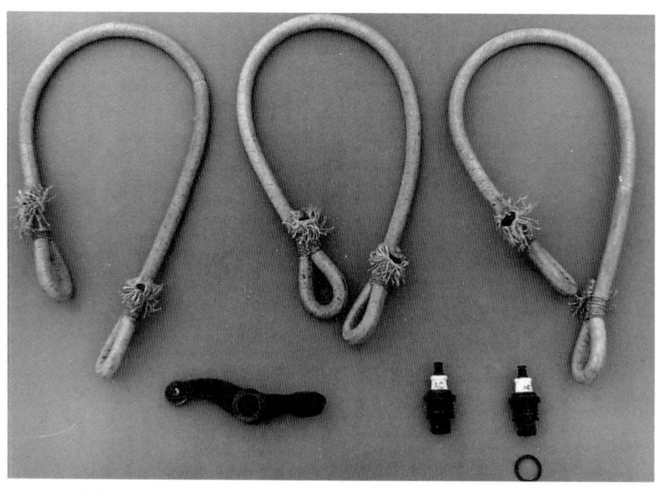

Three of the individual landing gear shock chords, one rocker, two AC type N spark plugs, and one of the spark plug washers. ***(Ev Cassagneres photo)***

The other box contained two AC Type N spark plugs, two rocker arms from the Wright J-5, nine individual landing gear shock cords, three pieces of damaged fairing strips (right aileron possibly), fuel or oil tank cap, one half of a two piece seat belt. The seat belt was apparently used to support a passenger next to Lindbergh when a flight was made in the NYP. Other items included an unidentified can with curved end tubes, three unidentified miscellaneous pieces, including a piece of metal fairing.

Upon inspection of these historically significant artifacts, I felt that when the Lanes passed away these items could fall into the

One of the two rocker arms from the Wright J-5 "Whirlwind" engine. ***(Ev Cassagneres photo)***

hands of some collector who would put an exorbitant price tag on them and put the items on the market for sale. Another possibility was that someone would find it in the barn, think it was junk, and throw it away. As it turned out, the Madison residence was broken into in 1978 and ransacked. [1] I felt very strongly that some of these items really belonged with the original airplane at the National Air and Space Museum, where they could be put on permanent display. So I suggested that I take it all, identify, photograph, document each and every item, and notify Lindbergh and the Smithsonian. I would, after this documentation, hand carry it to Washington, rather than trust it to the mail system.

The Lanes agreed to this arrangement and several weeks later I drove to Madison, picked up the two boxes, brought them home, and photographed all of the contents. I sent the pictures to Lindbergh then living part time on Maui in the Hawaiian Islands. He seemed quite pleased at the discovery and promptly replied in two letters authenticating the collection. [2]

On June 9, 1978 I delivered the survival equipment to the Smithsonian National Air and Space Museum in Washington where they were put on display on the Mezzanine, not far from the original NYP.

Some other items went to the Lindbergh Interpretation Center in Little Falls, Minnesota on September 14, 1978 and are still on display there. The rest of it was given to the San Diego Aerospace Museum in San Diego, California. On September 27, 1978 unfortunately all of the material in San Diego was either stolen or disappeared sometime after the delivery and have yet to be found.

Getting back to the Lanes at Madison, my immediate question was how did they acquire the material in the first place.

Mr. Lane explained that when Lindbergh returned from Europe and before starting on the US Tour, he flew the NYP on July 4, 1927 into Teterboro Airport, New Jersey, from Ottawa, Canada. Lindbergh asked the Wright Aeronautical Company to make Mr. Lane available to undertake some alterations in the plane. Lindbergh and Lane discussed the matter and agreed upon the changes to be made. In the matter of the kit, which was stored in the fuselage behind the seat, Lindbergh felt that it obviously would not be needed on the upcoming US tour, and that Lane should take it to his home in Ridgefield, New Jersey to keep it

The author (seated) the day he donated Lindbergh's survival equipment to the National Air and Space Museum. Left to right: Kirsten and Bryan Cassagneres: Don Lopez: Melvin B. Zisfein, Deputy Director of NASM; Eline Cassagneres; and Dr. Paul Garber, curator. ***(National Air and Space Museum)***

safe from souvenir hunters until such time as he needed it. Mr. Lane agreed, and Lindbergh never did return for the kit.

Lindbergh apparently developed both a friendship and a trust for Lane while they worked together at Curtiss Field, which made Lindbergh feel that the items were safe with him. Lane kept them all those years, taking it with them as he and his wife moved from place to place and he changed jobs and locations.

When Mr. and Mrs. Lane retired in 1961 they moved to the property in Madison, taking the boxes with them and storing them in the barn where they had been until the time I met Mr. Lane for the interview in 1973.

ENDNOTES

1. Letter to the author from Elizabeth lane, May 3, 1978 from Miami, FL.

2. Letters to the author from Charles A. Lindbergh, January 29, 1974 and January 30, 1974. His residence at this time was Hana, Maui, HI.

CHAPTER 18

Other Spirits

We all know that the original NYP, the Spirit of St. Louis, was built for one purpose, not a prototype for production and not to prove a design concept. The airplane would only serve one purpose, to fly a long distance, non-stop, successful flight to win a prize. Lindbergh made no specific plans for future use of this airplane other than perhaps personal travel around Europe.

Therefore the NYP, as far as the Ryan company was concerned, was completed and sold to one customer. They did not plan on reproducing this model in quantity to be sold to the public.

However, the success of Lindbergh's flight to Paris so stirred up aviation all over the world, aviation minded people figured that if any more records were to be broken or long distances were to be conquered, this must be the type airplane to use. So now a "market" had developed.

William Randolph Hearst suggested to his son, then living on the West Coast, to contact the Ryan Company and have them build a duplicate of the Lindbergh NYP, to fly to Hawaii in the August 1927 Dole race. But the Ryan Company declined, as they were just too busy at the time. [1]

After Lindbergh's success in 1927 two NYP types were built; one in San Diego for the Japanese, and the other one built in France for an east to west Atlantic crossing. It's a toss up which one was built first, but the Japanese version was built by Ryan and was officially designated the NYP-2.

NYP-2 FOR THE JAPANESE

Even before Lindbergh's much-heralded flight across the Atlantic Ocean, it was accepted that the vast Pacific Ocean was another challenge to be met, another immense stretch of ocean to be conquered by the airplane. When at times it looked as if one of his competitors would beat him to Orteig's prize, Lindbergh himself contemplated "Plan B"—a transpacific flight with the NYP to be modified for the longer, more arduous assignment.

The only photo ever taken of the Japanese NYP-2 in the United States. The scene is Dutch Flats near San Diego, where the airplane was temporarily assembled for the picture by Ryan employees, before being shipped to Japan. ***(Ryan Aeronautical Company via William Wagner)***

The Japanese, experiencing a surge of nationalism following victories over China and Russia and annexation of Korea, became obsessed with the idea of a transpacific flight. Success in the venture would be worth any risk involved, as worldwide acclaim would accompany their successful effort. A prize of $25,000. was offered by two of the leading Japanese newspaper chains and pioneers in promoting aviation, Asahi Shimbun *(Rising Sun News)* and Mainichi Shimbun *(Every Day News)* Announced in 1927, the reward would go for the first nonstop flight from Japan to the United States.

Sponsors of the contest also joined in the competition. Because of Lindbergh's success with the custom-designed NYP, they asked the Ryan Company to duplicate the NYP for a Pacific flight.

This airplane, which is really the very first replica, was officially designated the NYP-2 and carried the Ryan Company airframe serial number 36. It carried Japanese registration number J-BACC and Japanese Certificate of Airworthiness No. 1616 issued in December 1927. The airplane was powered by a Wright J-5 "Whirlwind" of 220 hp and was painted silver overall with black lettering. Like its "brother/sister" it had the large 46 foot wing with ailerons inboard of the wing tips. It was licensed under the name of Osaka Mainichi Simbunsha (Osaka Office of the Mainichi Press).

On the rudder was inscribed Tonichi Daimai No. 11, these two words being abbreviations for the newspapers in Tokyo and Osaka. The designation signified that this was the eleventh airplane to be purchased jointly by these newspapers.

Ryan test pilot Red Harrigan test flew the NYP-2 and did not like its handling characteristics. The Japanese spent some time in San Diego to oversee its construction, while the project was shrouded in secrecy lest some other world famous flyers might decide to beat the Japanese to such a flight across the Pacific Ocean. [2]

The NYP-2 was ordered in the summer of 1927 at a cost of $10,000 or $15,000 and after testing it was dismantled, packed into wooden crates and loaded aboard a freighter bound for Yokohama, along with a B-1 Brougham (s/n unknown) which the Japanese had ordered from Ryan at the same time. [3] The crates arrived at Yokohama on October 30, 1927. The two airplanes were shipped by rail from the port city to Tokorozawa Army Airfield for assembly with a Ryan mechanic, whose name is unknown, accompanying them to supervise setting up. [4]

The Japanese pilot chosen to fly NYP-2 was Fumio Habuto, who had become chief pilot for the Mainichi newspaper organization in 1923. Following graduation from the Tokorozawa Aviation School, he had been a test pilot for the Japanese Army. By the end of World War II Habuto had logged 6400 hours in American aircraft (Lockheed "Altair", Douglas DC-3) and numerous Japanese variants.

From the beginning Habuto had problems with NYP-2 because of its lack of forward visibility. As training to overcome this difficulty he rode local trains on curving routes. "I tried to keep in mind the entire outside scene as I viewed it in fragments, laterally, through the windows," he explained. Because of the visibility problem, chase planes accompanied Habuto on these first test flights. The first test flight was on December 4, 1927.

Still another unexpected hindrance developed. When owners of the plane applied to the Japanese Aviation Bureau for Airworthiness Certification, the Bureau imposed the restriction that NYP-2 could carry only enough fuel for twenty hours of flight. No explanation has ever been found. [5]

However, NYP-2 was never to attempt the transpacific crossing. With the lack of accurate weather forecasting over that vast ocean and with navigational problems resulting from the absence of land masses in the Pacific to use as reference points, this flight was infinitely more perilous than anyone had anticipated. In fact, the 2400 mile Dole Race from San Francisco to Honolulu in 1927 stands out as the most disastrous air race in history. Ten pilots lost their lives before Arthur Goebel captured the $25,000 prize.

Meanwhile, NYP-2 did achieve a measure of fame during her relatively brief time in use.

With hopes for a transpacific flight grounded by the Aviation Bureau's restriction, Mainichi Shimbun proposed a record endurance flight between sunrise and sunset as a worthy assignment for their highly-prized NYP-2.

In the pre-dawn hours of April 26, 1928, NYP-2 was prepared for flight on a large flat grassy area known as Kagamigahara, Gifu Prefecture, Central Japan, about twenty-eight miles northwest of Nagoya.

The pilot's seat had been decorated with floral bouquets presented by a group of hotel waitresses. Other well-wishers arranged for a pre-takeoff ceremony featuring tiny rice cakes, green tea, and chocolate. International as aviation was becoming, cultural differences added variety and spice to the undertaking.

On the morning of the flight the weather was clear and calm. Clouds over southern Kyushu, however, indicated there might be some rain by the end of the flight.

Just before the sun rose the Wright J-5C engine was started, and Habuto taxied to the end of the runway. Mechanics stood back and Habuto started his take-off at precisely 5:02 a.m. NYP-2 lifted gracefully off the ground after a run of only 300 meters (1000 ft.). It is not known how much fuel Habuto had on board.

The silvery aircraft glinted in the sun's first rays as the pilot circled over the field and headed southeast to Mamamatsu, northeast past beautiful Mt. Fuji with its shining snow cap to Odawara on the coast of Sagami Nada, north-north-east to Tokorozawa Airfield northwest of Tokyo, where Habuto received some sort of ground signal that indicated fine weather over Sendai. He then flew northeast to Mito north-north-east to Onahama on the coast line near Iwake and north to Sendai, where he made a 180 degree turn over that large city to head south past the Tsukuba Mountain to Tokyo. There Mainichi Shimbun employees waved Habuto from the roof of the newspaper building. He then headed west to fly over Tokorozawa again, south-south-west to Odawara, southwest over Suruga Wan (Bay) to Shizuoka, southwest to Hamamatsu, over Ise Wan west to Tsu, west to Osaka, west over Osaka Wan and Harima Nadato Okayama, southwest to Onomichi. He then took a sharp left turn to head east over Hiuchi Nada to Takamatsu, then east-north-east over Harima Nada and Osaka Wan again to land at the Osaka Military drill field at 6:25 p.m. sundown.

French-built Avimeta 92, built for an east-west trans-Atlantic crossing, piloted by Michel Detroyat. ***(John Underwood)***

This is the scaled-up version of the NYP-2 built by the Japanese, designated as the K-12 Sakura, and carrying the first NYP-2 registration J-BACC. Notice they had a windscreen and side cockpit windows installed for better visibility. ***(Mainichi Shimbun)***

During the thirteen hours and twenty-three minutes in the air Habuto had covered a distance of approximately 1300 miles (2091.7 km) for an average speed of 97 mph.

More than 2000 cheering spectators greeted Habuto upon his landing and hailed him as the "Japanese Lindbergh". He was awarded the Transportation Minister's Prize and the Japanese Aviation Association Prize for setting a new non-stop flight record in Japan.

Soon after Habuto's big flight the NYP-2 was modified to eliminate the poor visibility which caused him landing difficulties. Perhaps his shorter stature was a factor in this situation; Lindbergh, at six feet, three inches tall, adapted well to the airplane's interior design.

The Japanese removed the front fuel tank, replacing it with a pilot's seat. However, the modifications proved unsatisfactory. After a number of test flights in which the airplane developed serious stability problems, plans for further modifying NYP-2 were abandoned. After damage occurred on one landing, the airplane was repaired and demoted to the lowly role of "crew training."

Years later it was learned that the plane had been restored to its original configuration and not used after the outbreak of the Manchurian Incident, the first phase of the Japanese-Chinese war, 1931 to 1939. With the outbreak of World War II NYP-2 was put into "mothballs,." according to Habuto.

Post World War II terms imposed on the defeated Japan led to the total demolition of NYP-2. Since Japan was not permitted to have "any" airworthy aircraft, U.S. occupation forces in 1945 took the silver monoplane from the Mainichi Shimbun hangar at Tokyo airport and destroyed it with a bulldozer!

Habuto sadly recalled in 1968, "The glorious Ryan, imported from America as Japan was about to enter a new age of international affairs, regretfully could not accomplish more for civil aviation here." Records of the NYP-2, which Habuto had kept at home, were burned during American air raids in World War II. Total flying time logged for the plane up to that time was a mere 120 hours. [6]

When NYP-2 proved unsuitable for a transpacific flight, the Teikoku Aviation Association raised funds for construction of a "scaled up" version of the same plane, to be approximately twice the original size. Designated the K-12 Sakura, (Cherry Blossom) the airplane went into construction in the fall of 1927 at Kawanishi Aircraft Works of Osaka. The designer was Eiji Sekiguchi. Officials had proposed a transpacific flight in August of that year. The K-12 had a wingspan of sixty-two feet six inches and was powered by a Kawasaki-licensed and produced BMW (Bavarian Motor Works) Type IV V12 water-cooled, 12 cylinder engine of 500 hp. [7]

Supposedly the construction of the K-12 was begun in October 1927 and completed in June 1928. It was the largest aircraft produced by Kawanishi up to that time and optimistically christened the Kawanishi K-12 "Nichi-Bei-Go" (The Japan-U.S. Model.) So closely did the Japanese follow details of the smaller plane that they even duplicated a dent in the cowling that had occurred during shipping of the NYP-2 from San Diego.

Intended for a crew of two and constructed mainly of wood, the K-12 grossed out at a full 5500 kgs (12,125 lbs), which made it the largest single-engine landplane of domestic design yet produced in Japan.

In preparation for the great transpacific flight, sponsors of the project carefully plotted a North Pacific course which provided some assurance to the crew that they would not be lost at sea in the event of a ditch. To aid in identification at sea, they had three bold red stripes painted on the wingtips.

The bold stripes were never necessary because the vaunted K-12 never left its home airport. Test flights were abandoned when the Japanese government agency for aviation grounded the airplane for "insufficient power and flying range". The sheer bulk of the K-12 proved too much for the engine. The fuel range would have been much too short for the more than 5000 mile transpacific flight. Even that serious deficiency never became a practical problem, as the airplane failed to reach a height of 500 feet after a take-off run of 853 meters (2800 ft.)

When Ryan employees learned of the K-12's fate, they nicknamed it the "Rucky Rindy."

Thus the Japanese dream of winning worldwide acclaim by flying the Pacific " a la Lindbergh" was never realized.

Finally in 1931, Clyde E. "Upside Down" Pangborn and Hugh Herndon won the $25,000 prize when they flew their Bellanca monoplane from Japan to Wenatchee, Washington, Pangborn's hometown. Years later, in August 1939, a partial crossing was made in a modified Mitsubishi twin-engine transport known as the "Nipon".

What happened to the K-12? A 1930 report said it was suspended from the rafters over the assembly shop of Kawanishi Kokuki K.K. as a reminder to workers of how not to build a special-purpose airplane. [8]

FRENCH AVIMETA 92

There existed in 1926 an aircraft manufacturing firm by the name of Avimeta (Societe Avimeta.) They were in business only until 1928. [9]

After Lindbergh's successful 1927 flight Avimeta produced their model 92, a modified copy of the NYP with similar configuration, but of all-metal construction. Rumor says that the French were planning an Atlantic crossing with this airplane, east to west, to be piloted by Michel Detroyat, the highly skilled test pilot.

The Avimeta 92 was powered with the very same engine as the NYP, the Wright J-5 "Whirlwind" of 220 hp, but was also designed to accommodate the 230 hp air-cooled Salmson 9 A.B.

It had a one-piece strut-supported high wing. It was covered with aluminum, known in France as Alferium, similar to duralumin. The tail surfaces and wing were covered with corrugated Alferium.

Hollywood actor Ray Milland and Miss Lillian Fette, an American Airlines stewardess. Miss Fette was a technical advisor for certain scenes in the film "Men With Wings," by Paramount Pictures, 1938. ***(American Airlines, Inc. via John Underwood)***

The landing gear was of the exact same configuration as the NYP. The fuselage was provided with a windshield and windows all around and both sides of the passenger cabin. The windows could be opened and were constructed of non-splinterable glass. Seats were provided for four passengers, plus the pilot up front, a similar set-up as the Ryan B-1 Brougham. The fuselage was covered with Alferium, with stiffening ribs running for and aft along the fuselage sides.

Wing span was 41 ft 4 in. Length 31 ft 3 in. Height 9 ft. Wing area was 313 sq. ft. Maximum speed for the airplane was 124 mph (200 kph) with a landing speed of 44 mph (70 kph) and the ceiling was 19,400 ft (6000 m). It was intended as a commercial monoplane. Final disposition is unknown.

HOLLYWOOD MOVIE NYP COPY

In 1938 Paramount Pictures made a film titled *Men With Wings,* staring Ray Milland, in which they used a "Spirit of St. Louis" copy, that appears to have been one of the Ryan B-1 "Broughams" reworked to look like the NYP. No further information has been found as to its serial or registration numbers or final disposition.

One photo exists that shows Milland standing in front of the airplane, accompanied by an American Airlines stewardess by the name of Miss Lillian Fette, who was a technical advisor for certain scenes in the film. The photo clearly shows the curved cockpit side windows so prevalent on the B-1 series. Aluminum panels were fastened on the inside and painted over in black lettering "Spirit of St. Louis" with the curved structure still plainly visible.

THREE RYAN B-1 JIMMY STEWART MOVIE REPLICAS

After a lapse of nineteen years another NYP duplicate was required. What perpetuated this series was the Warner Brothers film "The Spirit of St. Louis" in 1957 starring Jimmy Stewart.

A Star of the Warner Brothers movie, Jimmy Stewart stands proudly by one of the NYP replicas, and looks pretty determined to portray Lindbergh, his idol. ***(Cassagneres collection)***

This film, of proportions almost as heroic and adventuresome as the events it depicted, was produced in Cinema-Scope and was based on Lindbergh's Pulitzer Prize-winning autobiography by the same name.

Via personal association with Lindbergh, co-producers Leland Hayward and Billy Wilder arranged to adapt the widely-read book to the screen. At the time Stewart was the nation's number one box-office attraction. An actor singularly destined and completely qualified for the leading role, he did a fine job of portraying Lindbergh at age twenty-five when he himself was forty-eight. He gave a flawless performance in a part that involved both depth and range. The filming of that great flight had been considered inevitable by all of Hollywood's film makers ever since the original landing in Paris.

No expense was spared to give the film scope and authenticity. At Lindbergh's suggestion, his old friend, Harlan A. "Bud" Gurney, was hired by the film company as a technical advisor. Gurney was flying DC-6s, as a Senior Captain, for United Airlines at the time and had to take a leave of absence for what he considered a fun job. During production, Lindbergh himself was a pleased and interested visitor on the set, both in Hollywood and New York. One day the crew and staff were deeply moved to silent and respectful nostalgia when Lindbergh climbed into the cockpit of one of the copy Spirits. Then they watched him tenderly reach out to make a small adjustment to one of the instruments.

Ryan B-1 Brougham s/n 153, NC7206, used in the movie Spirit of St. Louis starring Jimmy Stewart. This was taken before the modification. ***(Bob Baker)***

Here is s/n 153 made up as the NYP replica for Jimmy Stewart movie. ***(John C. Barberry)***

Stewart, ever since his early days in Indiana, Pennsylvania, had nourished a great respect for the flier. He cherished the hope that he might someday be called upon to play Lindbergh. A skilled pilot as well as actor, in World War II he had distinguished himself by winning the DFC and Air Medal with three Oak Leaf Clusters. He even bore a certain physical resemblance to Lindbergh. It was only necessary for the makeup artists to lighten his hair and switch the part from "starboard" to "port" to recreate young Lindbergh.

Playing the part of the "mirror girl" was twenty-three year old Patricia Smith, a green-eyed blond from New York. Smith attended Neighborhood Playhouse in New York and later Skidmore College. She gained some Broadway experience and was chosen for this part by Leland Hayward himself who said, "I've been waiting for a chance to use that wonderful face on the screen, and this role as the 'girl with the mirror' was exactly it." He went on with, "Although it isn't a very big role in the picture, it's a long way from a bit role. The incident and the girl's face will haunt the

Another shot of s/n 153, showing the filming crew from Tallmantz Aviation, Inc. Paul Mantz, himself, can be seen by the nose, with his right hand up and wearing a flashy sport shirt. ***(Cassagneres collection)***

1928 Ryan B-1 Brougham s/n 156, NC7209 before the movie makeover, at McBoyles Dells Airport, Lake Delton, Wisconsin. ***(Cassagneres collection)***

audience throughout the rest of the film just as it did Lindbergh during his flight." [10]

Patricia Smith remarked at one time that "If they want a soulful look in my eyes when I stare up at him (Stewart) as I hand him the mirror, they've got it. What girl can help but look soulful when she looks at Jimmy Stewart..." Smith was smitten with Stewart. Smith later married actor John Lasell and went on to a career in motion pictures and television.

When it came to doing the airborne scenes, no expense was too much. With the original NYP hanging impressively and forever in the Smithsonian, it was necessary to build one for the movie. In fact, it was decided to build three so that two of them could be photographed simultaneously at different locations with the third on hand as a spare in case of the frightening possibility of a crash. A sound-stage mockup was also built.

Paul Mantz, pioneer film pilot and at the time president of Tallmantz Aviation, Inc. based at Santa Ana, California, was consulted for the job. He had been supplying aviation props for movies for many years and was well qualified for this phase of the endeavor.

Immediately Tallmantz began to search for a Ryan B-1 "Brougham", which they felt could be reworked into an NYP copy. After several months of following up on many leads, they found one Ryan C-1, s/n 402, NC-558N, and three B-1s.

Ryan B-1 s/n 156 made into the NYP replica for the Warner Brothers Spirit of St. Louis movie. ***(Thomas E. Peter via Cassagneres collection)***

Here is s/n 156 as it can be seen today at the Henry Ford Museum, Dearborn, Michigan. ***(Ev Cassagneres)***

Imagine, after all those years, finding the last remaining B-ls so close to each other in production serial numbers. They were 153, NC-7206; 156, NC-7209; and 159, NC-7212. The C-1 was cut up for parts with not enough left to rebuild, which is unfortunate, as not a single C-1 exists today.

B-1 number 153, after passing through a series of owners (mostly in Pennsylvania, Indiana and Michigan) found itself in Ceresco, Michigan, owned by Benjamin J. Carnes. Paul Mantz purchased 153, and had it ferried across the country to his facility in Santa Ana, to be made into a replica for the movie.

After the movie, the airplane was purchased in 1962 by a group of investors from St. Louis, Missouri and given to the Missouri Historical Society of that city. After some commemorative travels it was displayed in the International Wing of the main airline terminal at Lambert Field. Over the years it was decided to restore the Ryan due to deterioration. So in 1998, it was given to Langa Air, Inc. of East Alton, Illinois (St. Louis Regional Airport) to do the work. The work was completed in 1999 and the plane

Ryan B-1 Brougham s/n 159, NC 7212 in an early photo. ***(Doug Anderson - Canada)***

was installed in the Grand Hall of the Emerson Electric Center of the Missouri History Museum in Forest Park in downtown St. Louis.

B-1 number 156 spent most of its early life in Indiana and Colorado. Actor Stewart and his friend Joe De Bona bought it in Greeley, Colorado for $1,000, where it had been tied down in derelict condition for a long time after being used to carry fishermen into the high meadow country of the Rockies. After the picture was produced and in circulation across the country, the plane was donated to the Henry Ford Museum in Dearborn, Michigan next to Greenfield Village, where it can be seen today. [11]

B-1 number 159 spent most of its early life in the northwest, flying vacationers into remote areas of Idaho. It did a stint in Montana on timber inspection flights and ferrying hunters for Flathead Air Transport out of Kalispell, Montana. Mantz purchased the plane from Peter Fountain in Moscow, Idaho, in August 1956. After the movie was completed, old 159 was auctioned off by Rosen-Novak Auto Company of Omaha, Nebraska. David Jameson of Oshkosh, Wisconsin was high bidder and exhibited it in air shows around the country. It is now owned by the Long Island Early Flyers Association and is on permanent display at the Cradle of Aviation Museum in Garden City, Long Island, New York. It was flown in May 1977 to commemorate the 50th anniversary of Lindbergh's 1927 take-off from Roosevelt Field, not far from the museum

Over the years and since the movie's release, there has been much talk among the aviation history community suggesting that Lindbergh himself may have flown one of the movie replicas. Through research by aviation history writer John Underwood, and Stan Raiehle, of the Cradle of Aviation Museum, it appears he may have flown s/n 159, registration NC—7212 (or N 7212). However, it has only been speculation and to date no actual documentation in the form of aircraft logs (s/n 159) or pilot log (Lindbergh) or photograph has appeared to substantiate such a claim.

S/n 159, NC 7212 after the modification into a Spirit of St. Louis replica for the Warner Brothers movie. ***(Dick Stouffer via George Gentsch)***

S/n 159 as the Spirit of St. Louis for the movie. October 30, 1955. ***(Cradle of Aviation Museum)***

To the layman, they all appeared exactly the same. To the critical aviation historian and buff however, some very noticeable differences appeared. For instance, the style and size of lettering in black paint on the nose ("Spirit of St. Louis") was quite different on all three. Even the cut of the cowling was not the same. The pitot tubes were not identical, nor were the tail skids or tail wheels. The hinges in the cockpit door differed as well as the design of the tires and the fabric wheel covers. One major modification not seen by the film viewers was the design of the windshields and cockpits. While they were filming the ship on the right side and so the pilot had better visibility, especially forward, they would leave the left side open behind Plexiglas as the pilot was actually sitting up front in the normal B-1 pilot seat. The pilot who flew most of these scenes was Stan Reaver.

The copies actually logged more flying time than the original NYP. The movie planes flew something close to seven hundred hours compared to the NYP's total time of four hundred eighty-nine hours. Most of the flying scenes were shot at such places as Zahn's Airport, Amityville, Long Island, NY, which is no longer in existence, and Edwards Air Force Base in California.

The film's premier

PROJECT "WE"

The scene: *The Eiffel Tower, Paris, France.*

The action: *a small single-engine silver monoplane with the wording "Spirit of St. Louis" painted on her nose has circled the tower and gone on to land at Le Bourget Airport just northeast of Paris.*

Only this was not at night in 1927. It was on a sunny Sunday afternoon on May 21, 1967. They say history repeats itself and, in this case, it did just that. Only the pilot this time was Frank G. Tallman, not Charles A. Lindbergh.

April 20, 1977. This is the Tallmantz-built replica, shown with a blunt spinner cap similar to the one on the original NYP. ***(Cassagneres collection)***

Hollywood movie pilot, Frank Tallman, shown in his flight suit, similar to Lindbergh's original suit worn on the New York to Paris flight. ***(Frank Tallman)***

*Ed Morrow, former Ryan employee, standing by the Spirit II which was lost in the San Diego Aerospace Museum fire in 1978.(****A. Roselle****)*

The airplane was a copy of the original, not one of the reproduction B1s used in the movie. This was a brand new airplane built from scratch and appropriately named the Spirit of St. Louis II. Pilot Tallman, popular stunt flier, corporation president, and owner of Tallmantz Aviation of Santa Ana, California was a tall, lanky man looking very much like Lindbergh except for graying black hair and a mustache.

How did this all come about? A program aimed at building an NYP for static display on the 40th anniversary of the flight of 1927 was initiated by the San Diego Aerospace Museum, in part headed up by two of the men who built the original at the Ryan factory and since deceased. They were "Dapper" Dan Burnett, who died June 13, 1976, and Ed Morrow, who died on December 7, 1994. They received able assistance from such others as Jon van der Linde, Fred Rohr, Hawley Bowlus and William Wagner.

To set the stage for United States participation in the 1967 Paris Air Show, it was planned to land the Spirit II on Le Bourget Airport.

The original plan was for the retired former employees and friends of Ryan Airlines to construct this airplane in spare time. By being in San Diego where the original company still had files on the early ships, they were able to work from original data. In addition, 1927 photos which showed the NYP in different phases of construction were located and studied. Other forty year old documents gave additional specifications. A set of original shop drawings was found and painstakingly reproduced by Ed Morrow, an expert draftsman with the memory of a computer.

Work began at the Aerospace Museum in Balboa Park, San Diego. Little by little, fittings and other small parts started to take shape, but progress was slow. With time running out and finances rather slim, they decided to have Tallman take over and complete the project. On April 25, 1967 the plane was rolled out of his shop, glistening in the southern California sun. After assembly, Tallman took the plane up for its first test flight. Upon his return, he said he was satisfied that it not only looked like the original but flew like it as well. "It is as close to a perfect reproduction as anyone could hope for." The only visible difference from the original was the addition of a radio, (due to air traffic regulations), needed when they were requested to fly it into a controlled airport for display. Inside the plane had only one fuel tank instead of the five of the original NYP.

It is interesting to note that the take-off weight of the Spirit II was 2,177 pounds compared with the original's 5250 pounds, the difference being fuel load.

The Spirit II was flown to Paris in a U.S. Air Force C-141 jet transport. There it was assembled and stored at a field just forty miles from Paris on a former Air Force base in the town of Evreux. It was again test flown by Tallman. On May 21st, at exactly 3 p.m. Paris time, he took off and flew down the Seine River, circled the Eiffel Tower, and landed at Le Bourget about 4 p.m.

A scale model of the 630 foot "Gateway to the West" arch in St. Louis, Missouri, which was erected on Le Bourget, honored the city where Charles Lindbergh lived at the time of the flight in 1927. The Spirit II was mounted on a pylon beneath the arch. It turned out to be a crowd-stopper throughout the Paris Air Show, a world-wide aircraft trade show.

The Spirit II was returned to the U.S., where it was sold to the city of San Diego and placed on permanent display in the San Diego Aerospace Museum in Balboa Park. Unfortunately, it was lost in a fire at the museum in February 1978.

NYP III

After the loss of NYP II a group of dedicated people at the San Diego Aerospace Museum began construction of a replacement NYP to be put on display in a new museum in Balboa Park in San Diego. This latest copy was completed in December of that same year and was registered as N-211SD and flown by Ryan company pilot Ray Cote. He logged a total time of two hours and forty-two minutes in NYP-III before it was put on permanent display in the museum in 1979.

CANNAVO NYP

This writer had the pleasure of visiting the shop of young David Cannavo in Philadelphia, Pennsylvania in 1978, where he was building from scratch another NYP copy. He began construction in 1976 and completed it in 1980. He even duplicated the original 450 gallon fuel tank and the 25 gallon oil tank. Of all the duplicate NYP's up to this time, it is the most accurate with the exception of the use of a Lycoming R680-11 225 hp radial engine instead of the Wright J-5.

Cannavo flew it to the 1980 Sun-n-Fun fly-in in Florida and later in the summer flew it to Oshkosh, Wisconsin to the annual EAA convention.

Mr. Cannavo had originally planned to fly his airplane from New York to Paris, France to make what would be the first re-creation of the 1927 Lindbergh flight. Cannavo never did make the flight. He did, however, bring it to many air shows around the eastern United States. For a few years it was hangared at Philadelphia International Airport, and later Wilmington, Delaware. The airplane was sold in the fall of 1994 to Kermit Weeks of Florida, where it was put on display in his museum at Polk City, Florida. [12]

EAA NYP

To celebrate the fiftieth anniversary of the 1927 U.S. Goodwill Tour, the Experimental Aircraft Association of Oshkosh, Wisconsin built the next NYP copy, which they flew on a duplicate tour around the United States in 1977. They covered forty-eight states and made eighty-two stops. In 1978 they flew it throughout Canada on two goodwill tours.

When the idea of building another NYP copy arose, the EAA searched for a Ryan B-1 Brougham to modify, as was done for the movie copies. They located and purchased an original B-1, s/n 104, NC-5216, in Alabama. But when it was brought to the EAA shops at Oshkosh and closer examination was made, they found the fuselage too far deteriorated to rebuild and other parts were in poor condition. Very few of the original airplane components were usable. However, a copy was built up from useable remains into a full flying NYP copy, powered with a Continental W-670 220 hp engine. They also equipped it with modern, up-to-date radio and navigation equipment. They made provision for a windshield up front in the normal position, where the pilot, sitting up front also, could look straight ahead.

The airplane was flown by several EAA pilots on various stages of the U.S. tour. Among them were Paul Poberezny, Vern Jobst, Gene Chase and Bob Heuer. Today this NYP copy can be seen in the EAA Air Adventure Museum in Oshkosh, Wisconsin.

This is the Cannavo NYP replica, built in Philadelphia, PA in 1976-1980. ***(Ev Cassagneres)***

This is a cockpit shot of one of the Spirit IIs, not the original. ***(Terry and Penny Bieritz)***

ANOTHER EAA NYP

The newest of the copy NYPs, built by the Experimental Aircraft Association's "Aviation Foundation" staff and volunteers, was completed in 1991. Part of the project was financed by the David Claude Ryan Foundation. On the outside and from a distance this one appears similar to the original and all the other copies, but in fact it has many modifications built in, mainly for safety and convenience. It is registered as N-211 rather than NX-211 as on the original. It has a fuel capacity of 100 gallons and a wing span of 44 feet.

This example was built to be flown around the country to tell the story of who Lindbergh was and what he did for aviation, and to interest youth in aviation as well. It also advertised the Experimental Aircraft Association and their other educational programs.

The replica was built to accommodate a "working" cockpit in the original location, aft of the wing, with the pilot in command up front with a windshield. With this unique arrangement a

This is the Experimental Aircraft Association's NYP #1 in flight. ***(Experimental Aircraft Association)***

Experimental Aircraft Association, Oshkosh, WI, NYP #2. ***(Experimental Aircraft Association)***

One of the German NYP replicas in Frankfort, Germany. ***(Ronald M.A. Hirst)***

"guest" could sit in Lindbergh's seat and fly the airplane. This second pilot has a set of rudder pedals, a stick, and throttle and trim control, plus working instruments from the 1927 era. This has been a pilot's fantasy for many years, and scores of people have had the chance to live Lindbergh all over again. As of 2001 it was still in airworthy condition and based at Pioneer Airport at Oshkosh, Wisconsin, home base of the Experimental Aircraft Association.

TWO NYP'S IN GERMANY

Through the efforts of Herrn Manfred Pflumm and his wife Margot, there exists, as of 1997, two reproductions of the NYP in Germany.

The Pflumm's own and operate the totally private International Aerospace Museum at the airport outside the city of Schwenningen, which opened on May 28, 1988. Due to their interest in preserving aviation history, and especially world famous aircraft, they have constructed a collection of reproductions that made world aviation history. Two NYP reproductions were built at Schwenningen.

One is hanging in the Departure Hall of the Frankfurt International Airport, outside the city of Frankfurt, Germany.

The other one is hanging in a private museum collection in the city of Hanover, Germany. The Luftfahrtmuseum Laatzen there is owned and operated by businessman Herr Gunther Leionhardt, and opened on November 15, 1992. Most of the aircraft in this museum are also reproductions, with a handful of originals salvaged from around Europe.

Both of the NYP reproductions are fabric covered, but it is not known what type of construction materials was used for the main structures.

The accuracy of both aircraft is fair, and gives a general representation of what the original NYP looks like. It is not known if the dimensions are the same as the original.

SWEDISH NYP

A brand new NYP copy is now flying in Sweden, and appropriately so, considering Lindbergh's heritage. Now the Swedish people and other Scandinavians will be able to view and observe a full size copy of their countryman's famous airplane.

Through the efforts of Pierre Hollander of Balsta, near Stockholm, Sweden, this long time dream has come to fruition. Pierre is the owner of the renown Scandinavian Air Show AB, based in Vasteras, some 100 km west of Stockholm. Pierre is also the chief pilot.

Unlike most NYP copies, Pierre intended to build up the airplane as close to the original as safely and physically possible, to be used on a regular basis during their air show season throughout Scandinavia.

It was built at Nurmsi, outside Paide, 100 km south of Tallin, in Estonia, on a former Soviet Air Force grass airfield that was used for bombers and transport aircraft. Two parallel grass runways are five hundred feet wide by twelve thousand feet long.

The only remaining building, after the Soviets left Tallin in 1989-90 was a barracks, which was used as a shop/hangar for the NYP construction.

The reproduction was built by Konstantin Knoll, Paul Juurma, Rauno Raak, Valeri Kuznetsov and Illar Link, who together with his son Limar also was Pierre Hollander's contact and organizer in Estonia. The plane was built in about five years. Roll-out and first test flight was on August 20, 1997 (Ev check). It was registered in Estonia as ES-XCL (CL for Charles Lindbergh). The airplane is powered by a 220 hp. Continental W670-6A, which was obtained in the United States.

This NYP is configured to represent the Lindbergh NYP when it made the flight from New York to Paris, so it does not have Central and South American flags or the cowling louvers. The airplane is flown with a tail skid, but does have expander type brakes on the main wheels. The pilot seat is in the same place as Lindbergh's, and the plane is flown from that position. Therefore there is no windshield with a forward pilot position, as in the EAA NYPs. The instrument panel is original in equipment and configuration, as Pierre has either had made or found original working instruments and they are used in flight. No radio is installed.

During the initial test flight with Pierre at the controls, the airplane flew quite well, to the joy of all the workers and friends.

Pierre remarked that it flew like it looked, very heavy and slow on ailerons, unstable like a Tiger Moth and floated like an old glider without brakes on landing. It was flown with no more than one hundred gallons of fuel in the main fuselage tank.

After several test flights, the plane was ferried to Sweden for final fitting out and preparation for the 1988 air show season.

The first cross-country flight was from Paide via Tallin, over the Gulf of Finland, the Sea of the Archipelago, the Aland Sea and on to the grassy pasture next to Hasslo Airfield at Arlanda, Sweden.

COLE PALEN / RHINEBECK NYP

The most recent NYP copy is under construction at the Old Rhinebeck Aerodrome, Rhinebeck, New York.

It was started by Cole Palen, creator of the world famous World War I Aerodrome, back in the early sixties. Cole and his staff held popular weekend air shows until his death in 1993. The full operation continues today.

This latest copy will be the most accurate of all thus far. It is being built at Rhinebeck, by aircraft and engine mechanic and air show pilot, Ken Cassens. The workmanship is superb, with not one detail left to the imagination.

The airplane will fly without brakes of any kind, and with a tail skid fashioned just like the original, and the pilot will fly it from the same position as Lindbergh.

Configuration will be the same as the Swedish copy, to represent the New York to Paris flight. It will be powered by a Wright J-5E "Whirlwind." It will carry FAA (showplane) registration No. N211XC.

Instruments and all controls are as close to original as is possible. Mounted on the nose is an original ground adjustable Hamilton Propeller.

At this writing, (2001,) the fuselage is welded up, the tail surfaces are complete, and it is on the landing gear. The wing is complete. Attention to detail has not been spared. It will be flown in their regular weekend air shows as well as on special occasions elsewhere.

SAN DIEGO AIRLINE TERMINAL—NYP

Another full scale reproduction of the NYP was under construction to be a center piece in the new airline terminal at Lindbergh Field in San Diego, CA.

The desire to re-live Lindbergh and fantasize what it must have been like to fly the Atlantic Ocean in the original Spirit of St. Louis continues in the minds of not only the aviation community but also the general public. Through these replicas and copies, the fantasies have remained to be lived; in person, in the air, on the ground, and in museums.

A non-flying replica NYP built by Warner Brothers and Tallmantz in 1955 as a sound-stage background mockup for the movie Spirit of St. Louis. Now hanging in the Minneapolis-St. Paul International Airport's Lindbergh Terminal in Minneapolis, Minnesota. Recently refurbished by a crew of Minnesota Aviation Hall of Fame and Minnesota Air Guard Museum volunteers. ***(Noel Allard)***

The Swedish NYP replica built up by Pierre Hollander for his airshow work. Shown at Mora, Sweden. ***(Carrie Högland)***

The only unfortunate thing that has happened as a result of these copies being built is that slowly and subtly the original NYP has been lost in the minds of the general public to some degree. They bring their children to a museum and take their pictures of it with their children or themselves in front of the copy and make such remarks to the offspring as "That's the Spirit of St. Louis that Lindbergh flew to Paris in 1927." They say this because the little plaque in front of the airplane only has it written in small lettering that this is a copy or reproduction or replica, which the public sometimes misses altogether because of the initial excitement of seeing this particular "Spirit".

Meanwhile the original NYP proudly hangs in our National Air and Space Museum in Washington, having had some of its due glory stolen by these many copies.

A wonderful photo of Anne Morrow Lindbergh standing by the Experimental Aircraft Association NYP replica #1. The occasion was the 1977 replica tour by EAA. This was at the first stop, Brainard Field, Hartford, CT, on June 15, 1977. ***(Virginia Welch)***

Interestingly, the original NYP has been duplicated/replicated more than any other historically significant airplane of the twentieth century.

As of late 2001, another replica NYP is being considered, but no actual construction was yet underway.

Builders are Randy Smith and Joe Hunt of Durham, North Carolina. They had begun collecting actual original instruments and other necessary hardware.

Their NYP would represent the configuration of the airplane at the time of the New York to Paris flight in 1927.

It would be full scale and as close to the original as physically possible, and would be flown regularly, powered by a Lycoming nine cylinder engine.

REPLICA, REPRODUCTION, COPY ORIGINAL OR FACSIMILE

The first NYP was the original and the Japanese version (NYP-2) was the second original or duplicate, having been built by the original manufacturer, Ryan Airlines, Inc. The same people who built the original also built the NYP-2

Three original Ryan B-1 Broughams were modified to an NYP configuration for a Hollywood film, depicting the New York to Paris flight. Clearly, as described in the text, there followed a series of these airplanes for various reasons. Now the question becomes, "What are they?"

Standard language used in the museum world:

Replica: *An object constructed to represent to a greater or lesser degree of accuracy an object which existed at some previous time.*

Reproduction: *A copy of an existing object. Copy, likeness, reconstruction. duplicate, facsimile or replica mean: A thing made closely resembling another. Reproduction implies an exact or very close imitation of an existing thing. Duplicate, a double or counterpart of a thing, exactly corresponding to it. Copy, a more general term, anything reproduced by printing or striking off at the same time or by making separately. Facsimile, a close reproduction in identical materials, but often differing Iin scale. Replica, an exact reproduction of a statue, a painting or an airplane made by the same artist and not clearly distinguishable from the original.*

In other words, there was an original, a duplicate, and the rest were replicas or reproductions.

FOOTNOTES

1. *One Pilot's Log,* the Career of E.L. "Slonnie" Sloninger, Jerrold E. Sloniger, Howell Press, Inc.;, Charlottesville, VA, 1997, page 72.
2. *Ryan Broughams and Their Builders,* William Wagner, Historical Aviation Album, Temple City, CA, 1974, page 35.
3. Letter to the author from James E. Marquis, United Aircraft International, East Hartford, CT, November 28, 1968, Item 10.
4. Ibid.
5. Letter to the author, November, 1968 from Fumio Habuto, Tokyo, Japan.
6. Ibid.
7. *Aeroplane Monthly,* August, 1966, pages 20-21.
8. Ibid.
9. *Janes, All the World's Aircraft,* 1928, pages 84c and 85c.
10. Warner Brothers Studios, Burbank, CA, HO 9-1251, "Biography of Patricia Smith," August, 1956, found in the Library of Motion Picture Arts & Sciences, Hollywood, CA
11. Telegram from James Stewart, Beverly Hills, CA to William Clay Ford, President, Board of Trustees, Henry Ford Museum and Greenfield Vilage, Dearborn, MI, October 20, 1959.
12. Interview with David Cannavo, Aero Taxi, at the Greater Wilmington International Airport, Wilmington, DE, december, 1994.

ENDNOTES

Historical data on the three Ryan "Broughams" made into NYP copies for the movie *Spirit of St. Louis* starring James Stewart, were gleaned from the author's files. The individual files for each airplane contain numerous letters from former owners and operators of these airplanes, the FAA, and other sources, and are a result of over 35 years of correspondence and research.

Miscellaneous letters and notes to the author from retired Ryan employees Ed Morrow, "Dapper" Dan Burnett, O.R. McNeal, Jon harm van der Linde, Walter Locke, and others, was invaluable in piecing together the story of the NYP II and NYP III. These fine gentlemen, in their retirement, helped build these airplanes.

Other people and organizations who have contributed extensive information are John Underwood, Noel Allard, San Diego Aerospace Museum, Experimental Aircraft Association (Dennis Parks, Susan A. Lurvey, Tom Poberezny,) Pierre Hollander, and Ken Cassens.

Japan Air Lines, Washington, DC office, April 19, 1968 via George H. Kronmiller, United Aircraft International, Washington, DC office.

Germany Bibliographia:

Aeronautics, November, 1929, "Japan's Hampered," E. Percy Noel.

Letter from A.M.E. Pflumm to Ronald M.A. Hirst, June 6, 1997

Aeroplane Monthly, March 1993, "Laatzen," by Bob Ogden.

CHAPTER 19

Ryan B-1X Story

At one time there existed two Ryan airplanes that to the average person on the street looked for all the world like the *Spirit of St. Louis,* and was often mistaken as such, even up to the present time. This writer has been shown or given countless photographs from people all over the country who claimed they saw and photographed Lindbergh's airplane. Well, the second one was Lindbergh's airplane, but not the NYP.

Let us digress a bit as we get into the story of the first Ryan, to the winter of 1928. Lindbergh was loaned a Ryan B-1 Brougham to use for his travels in and around the eastern United States. Three photographs exist that show Lindbergh both in the cockpit as well as outside, pre-flighting the Ryan. It was manufacturer's serial number 63, and carried registration number 4034 (no C or NC). He had a forced landing with it while carrying Henry Breckenridge, an attorney who was Lindbergh's legal advisor at the time. The incident was due to bad weather, and he landed on the farm of Ammor R. Way, near Coatesville, Pennsylvania. The two flyers stayed overnight in the farmhouse of Charles Elkington, who lived nearby. Lindbergh and Breckenridge were on their way to Washington, DC.

It is not known at this writing who the owner was of this Ryan, or where it was based, or what the arrangement was between the owner and Lindbergh. The date of the forced landing was March 13, 1928. Final disposition of the airplane is not known either.

Regarding the second Ryan, let us digress again.

While Lindbergh was on his goodwill tour of Central America, at Tegucigalpa, Honduras, he sent on January 4, 1928, a telegram to Franklin Mahoney in San Diego.

TELEGRAM; LINDBERGH TO MAHONEY:
TEGUCIGALPA, HONDURAS

DEAR FRANKLIN, JANUARY 4, 1928

I AM DELIGHTED TO HEAR THAT YOU ARE MOVING TO ST. LOUIS, AND THAT YOU WILL BE THERE WHEN I RETURN FROM CUBA. I BELIEVE THAT ST. LOUIS IS UNUSUALLY WELL LOCATED GEOGRAPHICALLY FOR A PLANE FACTORY AND THAT YOU HAVE MADE AN EXCELLENT DECISION.

THE SPIRIT OF ST. LOUIS IS IN PERFECT CONDITION AND PERFORMING AS WELL AS EVER ON THIS FLIGHT.

I HAVE BEEN CONSIDERING PLACING THIS PLANE IN THE SMITHSONIAN SOON AFTER RETURNING TO THE STATES, ALTHOUGH I DO NOT WANT ANY PUBLICITY GIVEN UNTIL I AM SURE. IF SO, I WILL NEED A PLANE TO FLY AROUND IN AND AM WONDERING IF YOU HAVE DONE ANYTHING ALONG THE LINES WE TALKED ABOUT IN SAN DIEGO.

IF HALL HAS NOTHING IN VIEW AT PRESENT IT MIGHT BE BEST FOR ME TO TAKE ONE OF THE REGULAR MODELS TEMPORARILY AT LEAST. WILL TALK TO YOU ABOUT THIS IN ST. LOUIS.

WITH BEST WISHES TO ALL,

CHARLES A. LINDBERGH [1]

Apparently when Lindbergh was in Dan Diego in September during the US tour following the Paris flight, he discussed the above subject with Franklin Mahoney. It is assumed that Mahoney had offered Lindbergh a plane for his personal transportation needs, a new Mahoney Brougham. It was to be a gift from the manufacturers and suppliers whose equipment was used on the NYP for the Paris flight.

It was variously known as the custom built Lindbergh Special. It turned out to be a near duplicate of the NYP with the same 46 foot wing span rather than the standard 42 foot wing. In order to avoid any instability which was characteristic of the NYP the factory increased the size of the tail surfaces to some degree, and the ailerons were set into the trailing edge some distance from the wing tip for lateral stability. As in Frank Hawks "Gold Bug", a set of landing lights were installed in the leading edge of the wing,

This is the Ryan B-2 or B-1X, s/n 69, NX4215, just after assembly at the Mahoney/Ryan facility on Dutch Flats. Note the control wires not yet connected to ailerons and that the cockpit fairing is off. ***(Erickson photo via Ev Cassagneres collection)***

One of the early photographs taken after it was test flown and ready for Lindbergh to accept. ***(Erickson photo via Ev Cassagneres collection)***

Rare photo of Lindbergh with the B-1X. Location is unknown. Note that the spinner assembly is missing. ***(Charles A. Lindbergh)***

just inboard of the tip. It proved to be undesirable because of their disturbing the airflow over the wing and especially to the aileron area.

The construction of the plane was begun about February of 1928, as a "factory special" with engine, instruments and accessories etc. given by the various companies who expected to receive some credit and a bit of publicity for their generosity.

The plan was to present the Brougham to Lindbergh when he made a trip to San Diego in the coming spring. The engine, a Wright J-5C "Whirlwind" was donated by the Wright Aeronautical Company and had a hand cranked starter, as can be seen in most photos on the right side, between the engine and the forward part of the cockpit.

This was the only Brougham in which the engine had the chromed rocker-box covers and polished case, a "special" from the Wright company.

According to Ryan company publicity man Tom Mathews, "There were many other special features in the luxuriously appointed B-1X. Items such as night parachute flares which Lindbergh suggested be added as we went along. One thing he did not want was any publicity whatever about the new ship, although he was agreeable that pictures be taken of the actual delivery."

"Most of the suppliers were donating the original and extra equipment just for the publicity so I was in a real bind. Mahoney told me to go along with Lindbergh's request, but that it was OK

Here the B-1X is shown at the Mahoney/ Ryan facility at Dutch Flats shortly after it was assembled. ***(William Wagner)***

to take pictures of the various equipment items 'for the files.'"[2]

The airplane was delivered to Lindbergh on April 5, 1928 at San Diego. It was a basic B-2, although the ATC number had not yet been assigned to the company for production. So it was given the model designation B-1X. It carried registration number NX-4215, and mfg. serial number 69. The Wright "Whirlwind" was serial number 7771. The airplane was officially built by B. F. Mahoney Aircraft Corporation, owners of Ryan Airlines, Inc.[3]

It was test flown initially by Red Harrigan, Ryan test pilot. Harrigan did some fancy flying with the ship to demonstrate its characteristics and safety, according to Mathews. One interesting maneuver was a nose-high power slip, with directional changes by opening and closing the doors (in case rudder control was ever lost) and rudder turns with dead ailerons. According to Mathews, who was a passenger in the plane with Art Mankey when Harrigan was doing one of his demonstrations, "We were with Red when he tried that nose-high power slip over the electric pole wires at the end of the field. It had to be the shortest brake-less landing on record!"[4]

Donald Hall, not actually involved with the building of this airplane, did have a ride in it one day but showed no interest, and in fact felt its performance unsatisfactory.

Lindbergh test flew the B-1X on April 5, 1928 and the next day took off for a week at a ranch near Santa Barbara, California. His passengers were Harry F. Guggenheim and three of his St. Louis backers—Knight, Bixby and William B. Robertson.

On April 13th he left with Knight and Bixby for St. Louis and made an overnight stop at the Grand Canyon. In a letter to the author in 1968 Lindbergh explained,

"On the flight over the Grand Canyon, which ended (for the day) with a night landing at Williams, I had Harry Knight and Harold Bixby on board. (possibly Bill Robertson too-I am not sure.) I had planned on landing on a field that had been described to me as lying not many miles from the hotel on the south brim of the canyon. We arrived over the area in early evening, and I could not find the field. I decided to continue south to Williams, where I knew a satisfactory landing area existed. Since I had planned on landing well before nightfall, I had not checked to see

The B-1X at Grand Canyon Airport with St. Louis backers Harold M. Bixby on left, Lindbergh in the center, and Harry H. Knight on right. ***(William Wagner)***

A nice view of the instrument panel and cockpit flight controls of the B-1X. ***(Aero Digest, New York)***

Shortly after it was first assembled, at Dutch Flats. ***(Carl Shory)***

that the parachute flares were releasable. (It was the practice to safety the bottom of the flares with cotter-pins for daylight flights.) These cotter-pins were reachable by a man lying on the bottom of the cabin. [5]

"I told Bixby and Knight that somebody would have to check on the cotter-pins and pull them out if they were in place. Actually, it wasn't either difficult or dangerous; but a good deal of humorous discussion resulted. Finally, Bixby held on to Knight's legs while he pushed through the cracked-open door, bent under the fuselage, and pulled out the cotter-pins with a pair of pliers."

"When we circled over Williams, a number of cars drove out and threw their head-lights over the grass-field area. I landed without using either of the flares"

"To make the flight from New York to California in two days (against the west winds that usually prevailed) meant cutting down on sleep during the intervening night. I remember once getting only two hours at Wichita. The cruising speed of the Brougham (as I throttled the engine) was about 85 mph." His letter was dated April 7, 1968, Darien, CT.

Lindbergh flew the B-1X all over the United States, crossing the country often. He never landed in Canada or Mexico although he did overfly Ontario on a flight from Ford Airport in Dearborn, Michigan to Curtiss Field in New York on August 5, 1928.

The only other person to fly the airplane, solo, during the time Lindbergh owned it, was the Mexican pilot Capt. Emilio Carranza, who took it on June 30, 1928 from Curtiss Field to the south shore of Lake Erie (airport or location of the field not known) and then out to Ford Airport. [6]

Lindbergh never flew it into New England but did come close on August 12th when he flew from Curtiss Field—Barrett Air Port to Armonk, New York in the White Plains area, and on back to Curtiss the next day. [7]

According to Ryan factory worker during the NYP construction, O. R. McNeel, he saw the airplane on display at an automobile show in Los Angeles one time, about a year after it was built. This story might not be plausible as Lindbergh only had the airplane for about six months.

So final disposition of the B-1X is still not clear. There is speculation that it was turned over to Mahoney in October of 1928. According to Art Mankey, who was working as chief engineer for Mahoney-Ryan, a letter existed that was written to Henry Breckenridge, Lindbergh's attorney, stating, "This ship can now be licensed permanently under the B-2 type class." If so, this would have allowed issuance of an unrestricted license and permitted its resale as a commercial airplane.

According to Lindbergh's log, his last flight in the B-1X was on October 18, 1928. He flew from Curtiss Field on Long Island to Teterboro, New Jersey, and from there to Lakehurst, New Jersey, with a return to some Long Island "training field" and from there back to Teterboro for his final landing. He had as his passengers on that last flight Anne Morrow and a Mrs. Graham, although the flight from Teterboro to Curtiss (:25) was solo. He had flown the airplane for a little over six months. [8]

Lindbergh logged a total time of 310:55, with 176 flights, carrying 311 passengers in the B-1X.

It appears that the plane was relicensed and resold to someone on the West Coast, possibly via some connection at the Teterboro Airport in New Jersey. No records have turned up to confirm any of this, except that according to the FAA, the registration was canceled at the owner's request, no date given.

FOOTNOTES

1. *Ryan Broughams and Their Builders,* William Wagner, Historical Aviation Album, Temple City, CA, 1974, pages 47-49.

2. Ibid.

3. *Log from Ryan Brougham-Experimental B-2-NX 4215,* dated from April 5, 1928 through October 18, 1928, a copy of which was found at the Manuscripts and Archives, Sterling Memorial Library, Lindbergh Collection, Yale University, New haven, CT.

4. Wagner. Ibid.

5. Letter to the author from Charles A. Lindbergh, April 7, 1968, Scotts Cove, Darien, CT, pages 2 -3.

6. Ibid.

7. Ibid.

8. Ibid.

CHAPTER 20

Last Flights of Charles A. Lindbergh

Over the years I have been asked about Lindbergh's last flight. Actually there were two "last flights." One has to do with his being Pilot In Command and the other as a passenger in an airplane.

It is appropriate to consider what the circumstances were leading up to his last Pilot In Command flight. The youngest Lindbergh daughter, Reeve, then married to photographer Richard Brown, lived in the Northeast Kingdom area of the state of Vermont. They planned to write a book which was eventually published in 1992 and titled View From the Air. It consisted of many outstanding photographs taken from the air by Brown, accompanied by text written by Reeve.

Charles Lindbergh was always concerned with the condition of our planet, which he loved, and what man's impact had on the future of Mother Earth. In the text, Reeve movingly writes for her father, while sharing his perspective on his life as an aviator and his concern with preserving the earth he loved.

Richard Brown was not a pilot but needed some aerial photos of the countryside. Who better to fly him around on such a mission than his father-in-law?

At the Edward Knapp Airport in Barre, Vermont they rented airplanes owned and operated by Mr. & Mrs. Emando Roberti of the Vermont Flying Service based on the field.

Lindbergh was eventually checked out in Cessna 172, N4211F in January, 1968. Check pilot was Emando Roberti. Over the next four years, Lindbergh flew Cessna 150s N5443Q, N8526J, N21966, and Cessna 172s N4211F and N2831L.

The last flight Lindbergh made as Pilot In Command took place on Tuesday, October 12, 1972. It appears that his passenger was Richard Brown. The flight was in Cessna 172H, N2831L. (1)

LAST FLIGHT AS A PASSENGER

When it was discovered that he had lymph node cancer in 1972, arrangements were made to fly Lindbergh from New York to Hawaii. The flight was made on August 8, 1974 on United Airlines Flight Number 987. The airplane was a DC-8 flown by Captain William Arnott.

He was flown in a twin-engined Beechcraft from the island of Hawaii to the island of Maui.

Lindbergh died on the morning of Monday, August 26, 1974.

As Lindbergh was in his final hours of life, his attending physician, Dr. Milton M Howell had the following to say about the experience:

"He (Lindbergh) stated that he wished his death to be a constructive act in itself. His example of simplicity, his careful planning, his unfailing politeness and consideration for those around him, his public refusal of medical heroics, and his humble funeral are evidence of that wish. Death was another event in his life, as natural as his birth had been in Minnesota (author: actually Detroit, Michigan) more than 72 years before." (2)

This is how Cessna 172H N2831L looked when last flown by Lindbergh. ***(Dick Mansfield)***

Charles A. Lindbergh standing with Roger Roux by Cessna 172 N2831L at the Vermont Air Service facility at Barre, Vermont. ***(Mrs. Mary Roberti—original photo property of George V. Landry, Jr.)***

This is Cessna 172H, N2831L as it looks today. Photo taken near Syracuse, New York, and is flown on a regular basis, ***(Ev Cassagneres photo)***

Cessna 150L N5443Q as it still looks today, with the same paint scheme as when Lindbergh flew it. It is still active and flown regularly in Massachusetts. ***(Ev Cassagneres photo)***

FOOTNOTES

1. Note from Charles A. Lindbergh to Emando Roberti dated October 13, 1972. Letter related to charges, etc. regarding the flight in the 172, N2831L on Thursday, October 12, 1972.

2. Milton M. Howell, MD, Editorial Board of JAMA, "The Journal of the American Medical Association," May 19, 1975, Vol. 232, No.7, page 715.

Mr. & Mrs. Emando Roberti at the Vermont Flying Service in Barre, Vermont. ***(Ev Cassagneres photo)***

Another view of the Vermont Flying Service facility at the Edward Knapp Airport, Barre, Vermont. ***(Ev Cassagneres photo)***

CHAPTER 21

Epilogue

In ancient Greece, the architect and inventor Daedalus strove to acquire a oneness with the birds by creating wings of feathers and wax for himself and his son, Icarus. While both soared successfully into the air with their wings, Icarus carelessly flew too close to the sun, the wax melted and he plunged to his death in the sea.

As an airmail pilot, Charles A. Lindbergh also flew toward the sun every day when flight was still considered a risky adventure—but he made his way safely back to earth each time, showing earthbound humans that flying was no longer just a dream, but had become a living reality. He accurately predicted that aviation would not only be commonplace in the future, but would actually become our primary means of long-distance transportation.

In the early 1960s, Lindbergh was asked by Pan American Airlines to be their representative at a worldwide meeting of airline executives in Paris, France. As he entered the lobby of his Paris hotel, an attractive young woman welcomed him with the greeting, "Welcome, Mr. Lindbergh. is this your first trip to Paris?"

It is sad to realize, that as time passes, Lindbergh's name will fade from the consciousness of our younger generations, and his phenomenal accomplishments in the field of aviation may be reduced to a short passing reference in school text books.

The human spirit fuels the pursuit of progress. Without a doubt, both the dreams and the reality of aviation have always stimulated human creativity. The idea of human flight in any form addresses and inspires the human needs for conquest, creation, and recognition, and provides an environment in which these dreams and aspirations can be realized in continually astonishing ways.

Since an airplane's performance, speed, height, range and endurance can be measured specifically at any moment, the sense of human accomplishment with every new development is both immediate and verifiable. Early aviators recognized the airplane's ability to provide instant gratification as they set and broke aviation records during the 1920s and 30s. The results opened the eyes of not only our nation, but the entire world to the capabilities and potential benefits of flight.

With out the ingenuity of the early engineers and designers and the courage of those first daring pilots, who undaunted by foul weather, lack of decent navigational tools, and threatening terrain, regularly risked their lives to carry the U.S. mail to areas relatively inaccessible by more conventional means, our society would not know the advantages of air (and even space) trans-

Charles and Anne, possibly over California, in their Lockheed "Sirius", named the "Tingmissartoq". ***(United Technologies Archive)***

Charles and Anne Lindbergh standing by their Lockheed "Sirius" when it was in the landplane configuration. ***(United Technologies Archives)***

portation we take for granted throughout the world today.

Lindbergh's amazing accomplishment of flying non-stop from New York to Paris in May of 1927 really opened the doors to the possibilities of a viable commercial aviation industry. Starting in July, 1927, Lindbergh proceeded to make a series of "good will tours"—first through the United States and later in Canada, Mexico, Central and South America, the Caribbean and Cuba. At every stop, he brought with him the message of rapidly developing aviation in the United States, providing a living example of its possibilities. In his talks, he brought to life an imaginative picture of regularly scheduled airlines crossing and recrossing the United States. A true "Ambassador of Air Travel," Lindbergh went so far as to visualize that someday there would be regular air traffic between the United States and Europe as well.

By his New York to Paris flight, Lindbergh had accomplished his initial goal of linking together continents of our western hemisphere by air, hugely increasing the political significance of the future growth of both national and international air travel.

In the summer of 1928, having met Juan Trippe of Pan American Airways, Lindbergh joined the airline as a consultant. In this capacity, he flew Pan Am's Sikorsky S-38 flying boats throughout Central and South America and the Caribbean. Lindbergh believed that these flights were a step toward flying regular passenger routes over the Atlantic and Pacific oceans as well.

The Arctic was also ideal for air routes and terribly tantalizing to Lindbergh. One could avoid the oceans if one was willing to fly far enough north; only 50 miles separated America from Asia across the Bering Strait, and it was less than 700 miles from Labrador to Greenland, which was the biggest water gap that would separate America from Europe on a northern land-hopping route.

The trade-off, of course, was the fierce weather conditions such flights would encounter. Lindbergh faced a real challenge trying to get the executives and planners sitting in the New York offices of Pan American to understand the dangerous realities of both options by stretching a piece of string across the surface of a globe to find the shortest (and therefore, in their minds, the most efficient routes.)

In the winter of 1930-31, Lindbergh planned his flight over the great circle route between New York and Tokyo, including his wife Anne as co-pilot and radio operator. They purchased a Lockheed Sirius and named it the "Tingmissartoq," an Eskimo word meaning "the one who flies like a bird." Leaving from New York, their route took them over Canada, Alaska—down the Kamchatka Penninsula and over the Kirile Islands to Tokyo (Kasimiquara) Japan, eventually reaching Hankow, China.

Encouraged by their initial success, Charles and Anne made a 1933 survey flight around the North Atlantic Ocean in the same Lockheed Sirius. The purpose of this flight was to study the possible air routes between America and Europe. Their flight included crossing from South America to Africa in the south, and Scandinavia to Iceland, Greenland, and Canada in the north, covering over 30,000 miles.

At that time, the commercial air routes of the world were entering their final stages of development. Countries had already been crossed and the continents connected. It remained only for the oceans to be spanned, which was the last major barrier to the business of air travel over the North Atlantic Ocean. The routes developed by Charles and Anne Lindbergh offered some viable solutions to the problem. As a result of his flights with Anne, Lindbergh had no further doubts about the wisdom of establishing the first air routes to Europe and to the Orient.

Other faces of Charles A. Lindbergh

Not everyone realizes that Lindbergh's accomplishments were not confined solely to aviation. From 1930 to 1934, he collaborated with Dr. Robert Goddard to help develop the basics of rocket power, the same power that would eventually send our spacecraft to the moon and beyond.

Lindbergh also devoted years of his life to the protection of threatened animals and primitive people, and helped save many

Here the flying couple are shown again by the Lockheed "Sirius" when it was equipped with the floats. ***(The Hartford Times)***

species from extinction. His work in later years with Dr. Alexis Carrel on the perfusion pump were determining factors in the state of heart transplant surgery being done today.

The Spirit of St. Louis

The *Spirit of St. Louis* referred to by Ryan Airlines as the model NYP is one of the most important artifacts of the national aeronautical collection at the Smithsonian Institution in Washington, DC. Over the years, it has been referred to as a "tiny' or "dinky" little airplane; frail, put together with sticks, some cloth, bailing wire and glue, as though it were the mere whim of some crazy aviator and a bunch of simple mechanics who threw it together without much thought.

But as this book has tried to clarify, it was in fact one of the most carefully planned and built aircraft of its time, and was built to last for a long time, under the worst conceivable conditions—wind, rain, sleet and fog. This airplane, difficult to fly, was landed on all kinds of unimproved surfaces, with no brakes, no steerable tailwheel, blind to forward visibility and without a radio. No, the NYP was not by any stretch of the imagination a "tiny" or "dinky" little airplane.

Lindbergh, the pilot and master of the NYP, never lost control. Having been involved in the most minute details of the *Spirit's* design, he knew the aircraft intimately, and accordingly, the plane responded to his slightest touch. Man and machine were truly one.

I would venture to say that if the NYP were allowed to be put on an airfield today, checked out thoroughly, with fuel and oil and necessary repairs made, would fly just as well now as it did in 1927 and 1928.

What has become of Ryan Aircraft?

What about the old Ryan Airlines, Inc. of San Diego, California, and the part it played in history?

Ryan is still very much in business. Ownership of the company has changed several times over the years: Mahoney/Ryan, Ryan Aeronautical Company, Teledyne-Ryan, Allegheny-Ludlum, and now Northrup-Grumman.

Lindbergh on the right, with Harry Guggenheim on the left and his other friend, Dr. Robert Goddard, the famous rocket scientist. ***(United Technologies Archive)***

Many years after Lindbergh's 1927 flight, one of the people who worked on the NYP for Ryan said that if Ryan Airlines, Inc. had been more firmly established as a company in 1927 with full-time engineers, Lindbergh's request would have been denied as impractical, and the NYP would never have been built (at least not by Ryan.)

Had the NYP been of poor design and the aviator much less skillful, Lindbergh would have become either another statistic in the cross-Atlantic race, or simply lost among the many other pioneer aviators and adventurers of the time who quietly faded from view.

The fact remains, however, that the highly intelligent aviator and the extremely well-designed and carefully built NYP made incredible history together. Their union gave the aviation industry, and air travel in particular, the boost it needed to move ahead with further development and trusted acceptance throughout the United States and the western world.

One of Pan American Airways Sikorsky S-38 flying boats. ***(Leo B. Kimball collection)***

A young 25-year-old Charles A. Lindbergh as he looked when first appearing at the Ryan Airlines facility. ***(Donald Albert Hall family)***

Lindbergh as a United States Air Force Brigadier General. ***(Ev Cassagneres collection)***

Flying boat and helicopter pioneer Igor I. Sikorsky, and close friend Charles A. Lindbergh, seated in one of the Sikorsky flying boats ***(United Technologies Archive)***

Charles A. Lindbergh in his later years. ***(The Hartford Times)***

Igor I. Sikorsky and Charles A. Lindbergh standing by the first successful Sikorsky helicopter, the VS-300. in Stratford, Connecticut, now preserved in the Henry Ford Museum, in Dearborn, Michigan. ***(United Technologies Archive)***

(Ryan Aeronautical Company)

The Wright J-5 Engine

The success of the Lindbergh flight 75 years ago is due in no small part to one man and one component that never received the recognition they deserved. Donald Hall, the engineer and the Wright J-5 "Whirlwind" engine.

One may contemplate as to what person or component played the most important part in the success of that flight. Fully and clearly, it was a combination of high intelligence in more than one person, together with a perfectly designed and built airplane, powered with the best engine available at the time.

There were any number of aviators with skills that perhaps equalled Lindbergh's and airplane builders with resources and experience enough to build the best airplane to do the job.

But let us look into the engine situation. At the time there were only four significant airplane engine companies worthy of consideration. The Wright Aeronautical Corporation, Pratt & Whitney Aircraft, the Curtiss Company and Packard.

In 1924, Wright had emerged as the most outstanding aircraft engine manufacturer in the country. Curtiss had their 400 hp. D-12, and Packard was just about ready to announce their high-powered liquid-cooled aircraft engine.

However, a young fellow by the name of Frederick B. Rentschler had resigned as president of the Wright Aeronautical Corporation in September, 1924. Rentschler was deeply engrossed in aircraft engine development, and eventually started his own firm to do just that. That company became the world renowned Pratt & Whitney (named after Francis A. Pratt and Amos Whitney) Aircraft.

By early 1926 the newly formed company in Hartford, Connecticut had designed and successfully run an air-cooled radial aircraft engine, named the "Wasp," that could produce 410 to 420 hp. The very first Wasp s/n 1, still exists and is on display at the Franklin Institute in Philadelphia, PA.

Soon the Wasp revolutionized American aviation. Within a year an experimental version shattered its first world record and went on to eclipse existing standards for both landplanes and seaplanes for the next seven years, carrying airframes and pilots higher, faster and farther than they had ever gone before. It was reported that the Wasp incorporated some of the finest workmanship and engineering yet seen in aircraft engines, for which Pratt & Whitney was and still is known.

But one of the reasons for Lindbergh not using the Pratt & Whitney Wasp was that it was really not a proven design or in regular production in time for his planned flight. The third experimental Wasp was completed in October, 1926, while the J-4 and J-5 Wright Whirlwinds had become proven equipment.

Had the Wasp been a proven engine and available at the time Lindbergh needed it, there is no doubt in this writer's mind that his flight could have been just as successful. One could not have made such a statement in 1927, however.

Timing is everything in life, as they say, and Wright won out due to good timing.

Pratt & Whitney is still in existance, but the Wright Aeronautical Company, after being absorbed more than once, is only a few cartons of papers stored in a museum in New Jersey.

The Wright engine was ahead of its time, and it was the choice of other aviators who were planning the flight to win the Orteig prize. Any one of them could have made it with the Whirlwind, if it were not for the extremely well planned and executed flight of Charles Lindbergh.

Passengers carried in the NYP

Donald A. Hall, May 3, 1927, San Diego, CA
Major James Erickson, May 3, 1927, San Diego, CA
A.J. Edwards, May 8, 1927, San Diego, CA
O.R. McNeal (or McNeel), May 10, 1927, North Island, CA
Brice Goldsborough, May 13, 1927, Curtiss Field, NY
Kenneth Boedecker, May 14, 1927, Curtiss Field, NY
Edward Mulligan, May 14, 1927, Curtiss Field, NY

On U.S. Tour

Henry Ford,August 11, 1927, Detroit, MI
Edsel Ford, August 11, 1927, Detroit, MI
Evangeline Lindbergh (Mother), August 12, 1927, Grand Rapids, MI
B. Franklin Mahoney, September 23, 1927, San Diego, CA
Donald E. Keyhoe, September 30, 1927, Oklahoma City, OK
Earl C. Thompson, October 4, 1927, Memphis, TN
Governor Harry F. Byrd, October 16, 1927, Richmond, VA
Harry F. Guggenheim, October 16, 1927, Richmond, VA
C.C. Maidment, October 16, 1927, Richmond, VA

No passengers were carried during the south of the border tours.

Two other pilots flew the NYP

Major Thomas Lanphier, July 1 or 19, 1927, Selfridge Field, MI
Philip Rockford Love, August 8, 1927, Louisville, KY

A final thought

Think of this—man has actually traveled to the moon. Neil Armstrong and Buzz Aldrin's heroic and pioneering act of traversing the far reaches of space to set foot on an alien world would surely rank with Lindbergh's pioneering flight. What amazing hero, cut from the same cloth as these men, will step forward to handle the controls of some exotic machine in the future, the first ship to land on Mars!

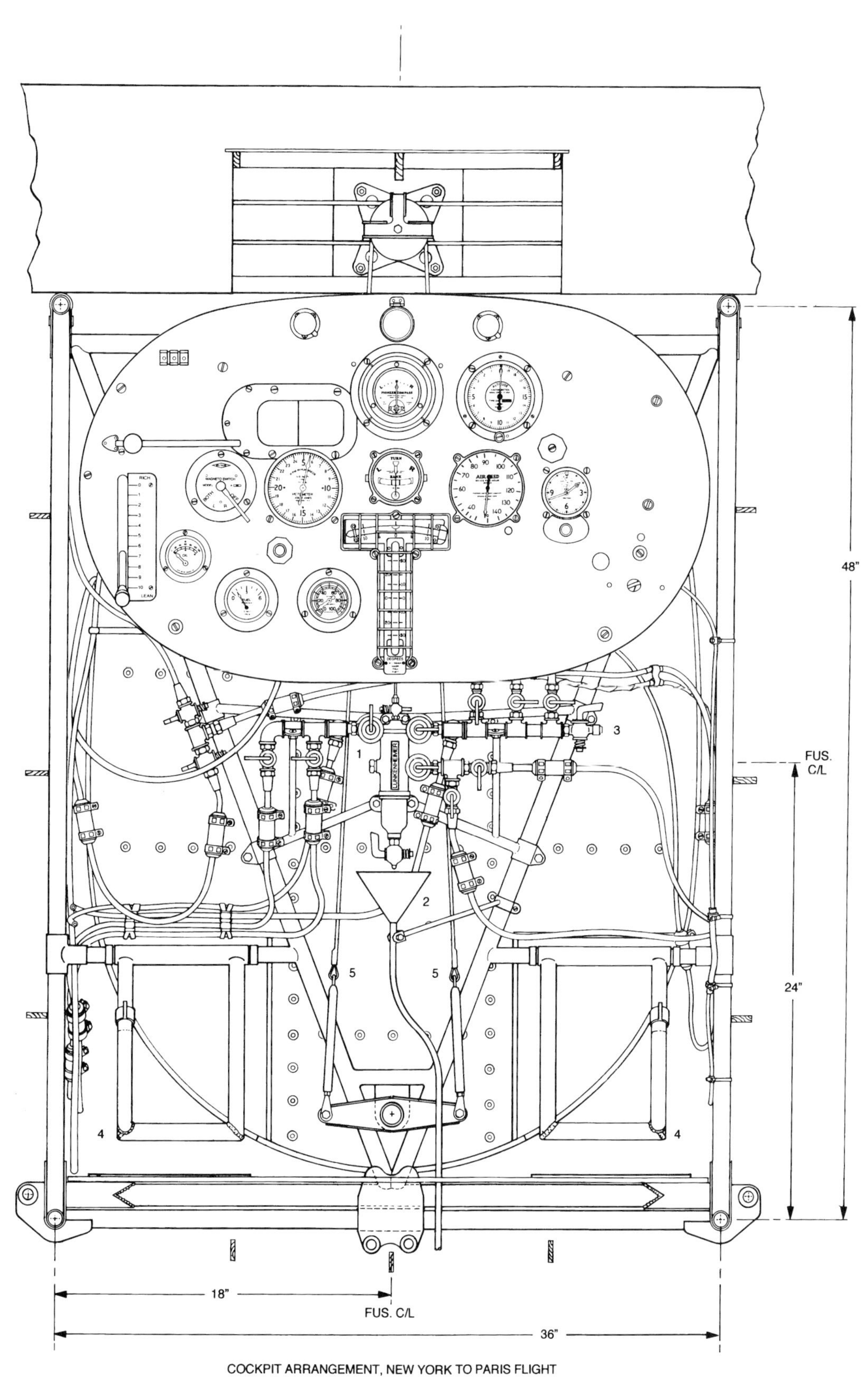

COCKPIT ARRANGEMENT, NEW YORK TO PARIS FLIGHT

1. LUNKENHEIMER FUEL LINE DIRT SCREEN AND WATER TRAP
2. DRAIN LINE
3. FUEL LINE CONTROL VALVES
4. RUDDER PEDALS
5. AILERON CONTROL CABLES

RYAN NY-P "SPIRIT OF ST. LOUIS"

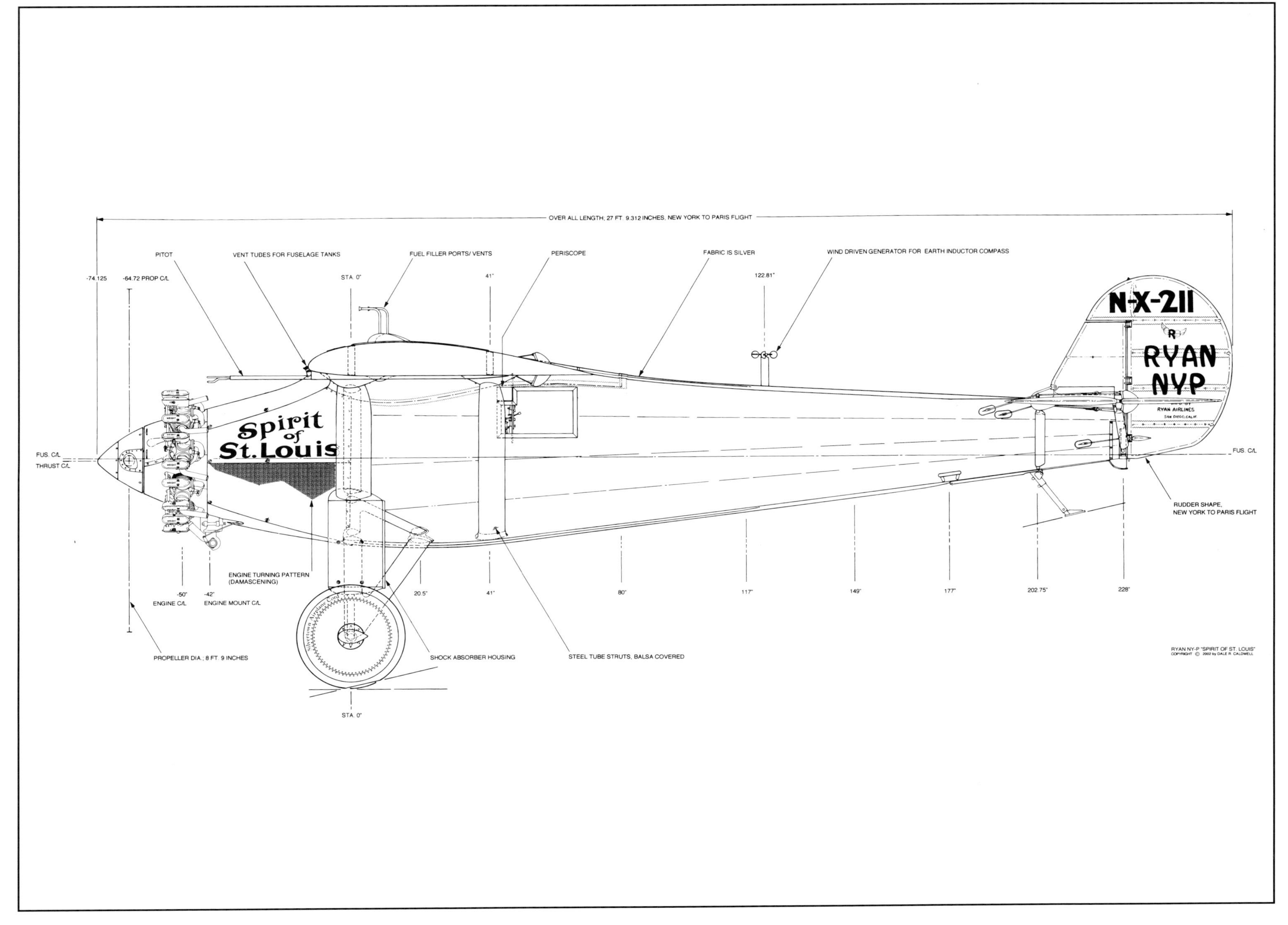

OVER ALL LENGTH; 27 FT. 9.312 INCHES, NEW YORK TO PARIS FLIGHT
PITOT
VENT TUBES FOR FUSELAGE TANKS
FUEL FILLER PORTS/ VENTS
PERISCOPE
FABRIC IS SILVER
WIND DRIVEN GENERATOR FOR EARTH INDUCTOR COMPASS
-74.125
-64.72 PROP C/L
STA. 0"
41"
122.81"
N-X-211
R
RYAN
NYP
RYAN AIRLINES
SAN DIEGO, CALIF.
Spirit of St. Louis
FUS. C/L
THRUST C/L
FUS. C/L
RUDDER SHAPE,
NEW YORK TO PARIS FLIGHT
ENGINE TURNING PATTERN
(DAMASCENING)
-50"
ENGINE C/L
-42"
ENGINE MOUNT C/L
20.5"
41"
80"
117"
149"
177"
202.75"
228"
PROPELLER DIA.; 8 FT. 9 INCHES
Silvertown Airplane Cord
SHOCK ABSORBER HOUSING
STEEL TUBE STRUTS, BALSA COVERED
STA. 0"
RYAN NY-P "SPIRIT OF ST. LOUIS"
COPYRIGHT © 2002 by DALE R. CALDWELL

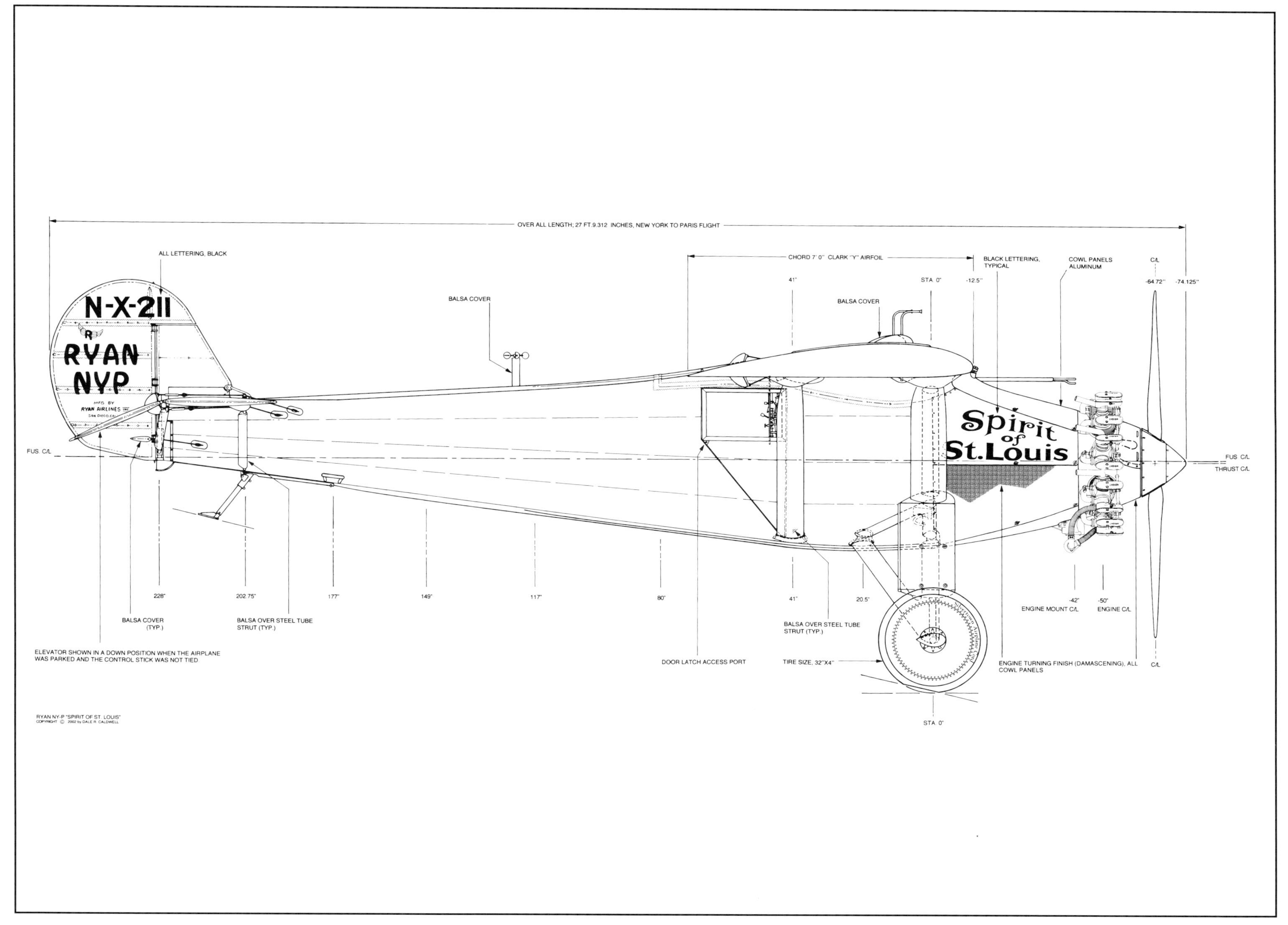
OVER ALL LENGTH; 27 FT.9.312 INCHES, NEW YORK TO PARIS FLIGHT
ALL LETTERING, BLACK
N-X-211
RYAN
NYP
MFG. BY
RYAN AIRLINES INC
SAN DIEGO, CAL
BALSA COVER
CHORD 7' 0" CLARK "Y" AIRFOIL
41"
STA. 0"
-12.5"
BALSA COVER
BLACK LETTERING, TYPICAL
COWL PANELS ALUMINUM
C/L
-64.72"
-74.125"
Spirit of St. Louis
FUS. C/L
FUS. C/L
THRUST C/L
228"
202.75"
177"
149"
117"
80"
41"
20.5"
-42"
ENGINE MOUNT C/L
-50"
ENGINE C/L
BALSA COVER (TYP.)
BALSA OVER STEEL TUBE STRUT (TYP.)
BALSA OVER STEEL TUBE STRUT (TYP.)
ELEVATOR SHOWN IN A DOWN POSITION WHEN THE AIRPLANE WAS PARKED AND THE CONTROL STICK WAS NOT TIED
DOOR LATCH ACCESS PORT
TIRE SIZE, 32"X4"
ENGINE TURNING FINISH (DAMASCENING), ALL COWL PANELS
C/L
STA. 0"
RYAN NY-P "SPIRIT OF ST. LOUIS"
COPYRIGHT © 2002 by DALE R. CALDWELL

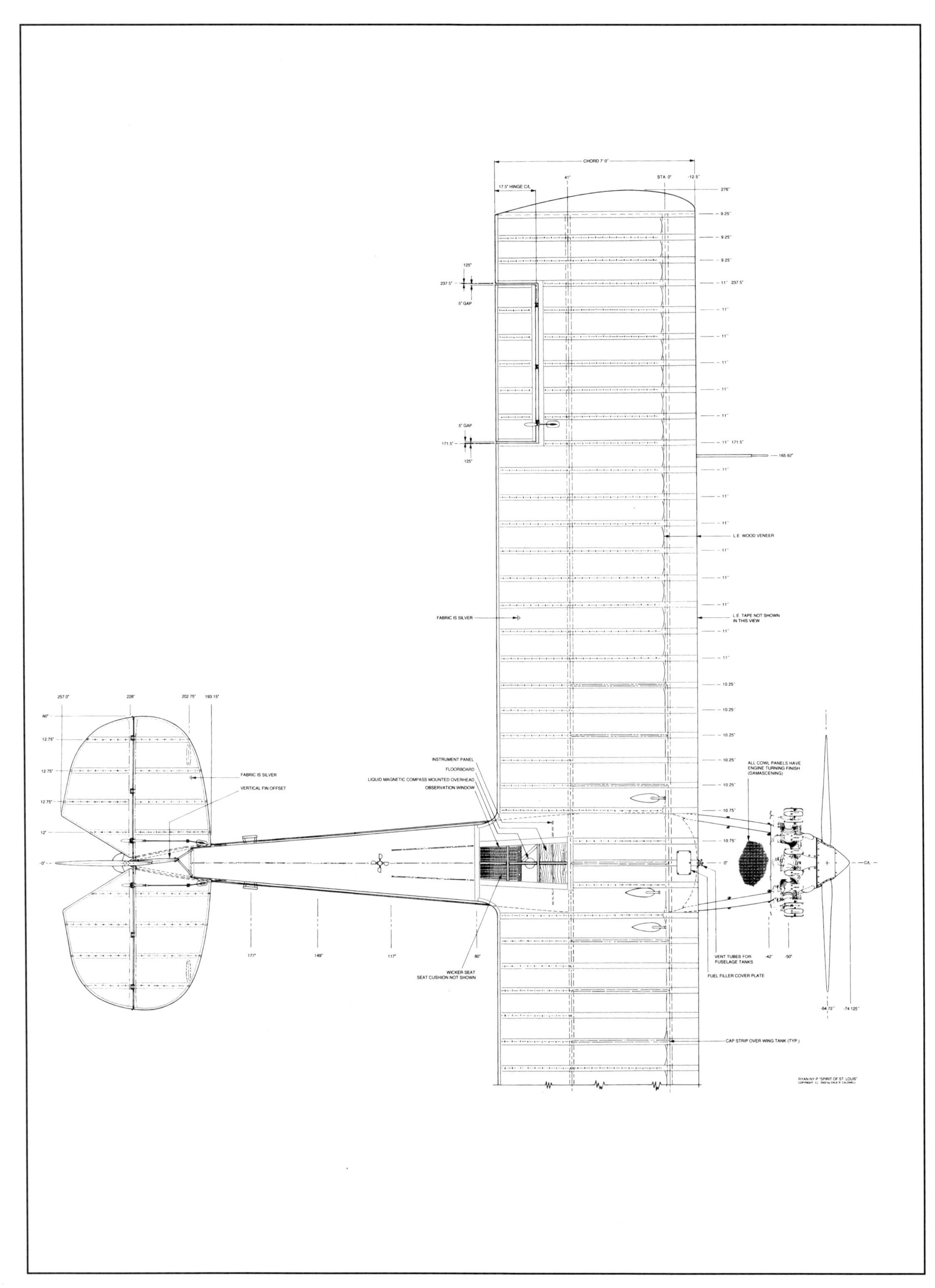

CHORD 7' 0"
17.5" HINGE C/L
41"
STA. 0"
-12.5"
276"
9.25"
9.25"
9.25"
11" 237.5"
125"
237.5"
5" GAP
11"
11"
11"
11"
11"
5" GAP
171.5"
125"
11" 171.5"
165.92"
11"
11"
11"
L.E. WOOD VENEER
11"
11"
11"
FABRIC IS SILVER
L.E. TAPE NOT SHOWN IN THIS VIEW
11"
11"
10.25"
10.25"
10.25"
10.25"
10.25"
10.75"
10.75"
0"
C/L
257.0"
228"
202.75"
193.15"
60"
12.75"
12.75"
12.75"
12"
0"
FABRIC IS SILVER
VERTICAL FIN OFFSET
INSTRUMENT PANEL
FLOORBOARD
LIQUID MAGNETIC COMPASS MOUNTED OVERHEAD
OBSERVATION WINDOW
ALL COWL PANELS HAVE ENGINE TURNING FINISH (DAMASCENING)
177"
149"
117"
80"
WICKER SEAT
SEAT CUSHION NOT SHOWN
VENT TUBES FOR FUSELAGE TANKS
FUEL FILLER COVER PLATE
-42"
-50"
-64.72"
-74.125"
CAP STRIP OVER WING TANK (TYP.)
RYAN NY-P "SPIRIT OF ST. LOUIS"
COPYRIGHT (C) 2002 by DALE R. CALDWELL

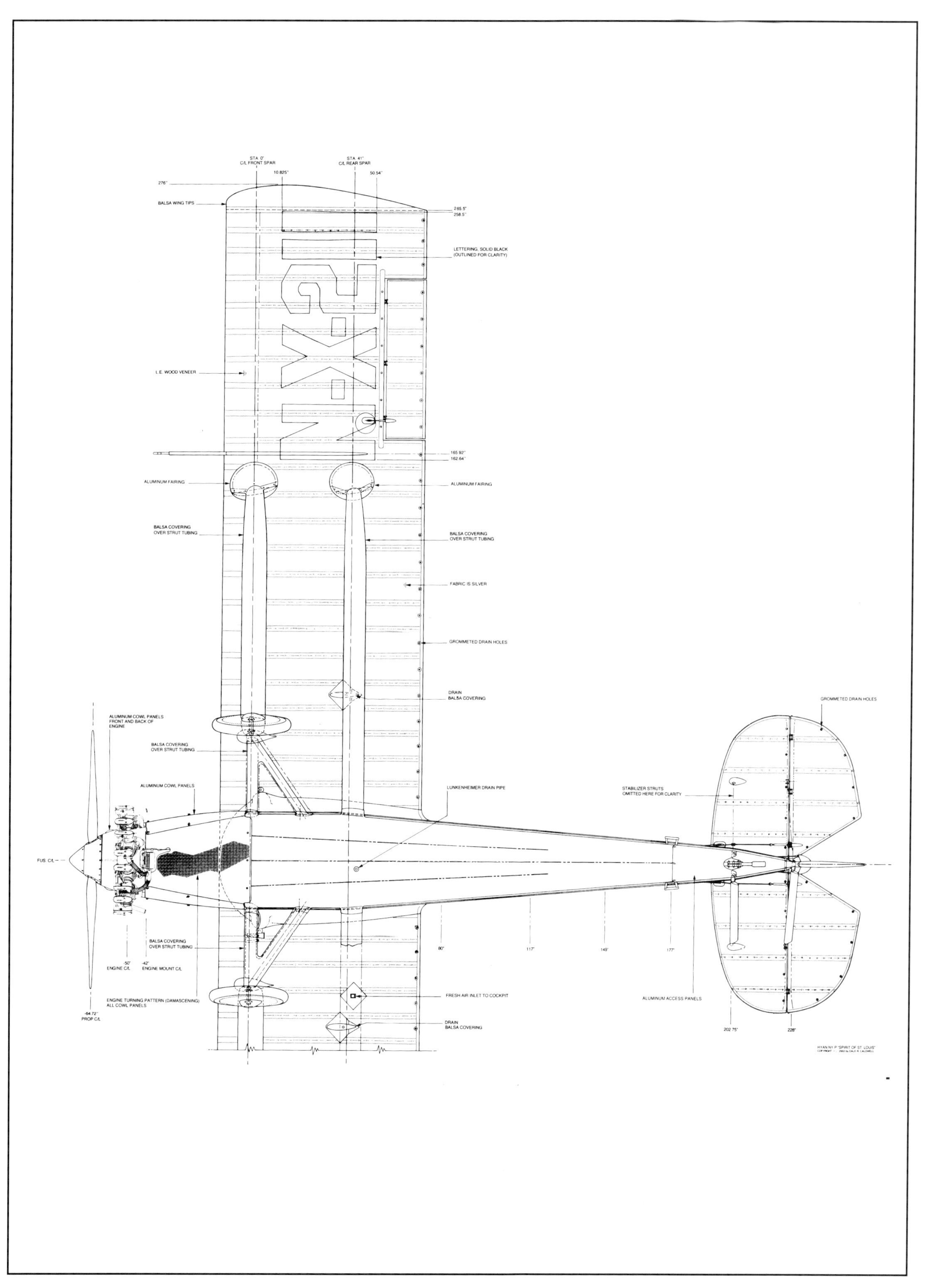
STA 0"
C/L FRONT SPAR
STA 41"
C/L REAR SPAR
10.825"
50.54"
276"
BALSA WING TIPS
265.5"
258.5"
LETTERING, SOLID BLACK
(OUTLINED FOR CLARITY)
N-X-211
L.E. WOOD VENEER
165.92"
162.64"
ALUMINUM FAIRING
ALUMINUM FAIRING
BALSA COVERING
OVER STRUT TUBING
BALSA COVERING
OVER STRUT TUBING
FABRIC IS SILVER
GROMMETED DRAIN HOLES
DRAIN
BALSA COVERING
ALUMINUM COWL PANELS
FRONT AND BACK OF
ENGINE
BALSA COVERING
OVER STRUT TUBING
ALUMINUM COWL PANELS
LUNKENHEIMER DRAIN PIPE
STABILIZER STRUTS
OMITTED HERE FOR CLARITY
GROMMETED DRAIN HOLES
FUS. C/L
BALSA COVERING
OVER STRUT TUBING
-50"
ENGINE C/L
-42"
ENGINE MOUNT C/L
80"
117"
149"
177"
ENGINE TURNING PATTERN (DAMASCENING)
ALL COWL PANELS
-64.72"
PROP C/L
FRESH AIR INLET TO COCKPIT
ALUMINUM ACCESS PANELS
DRAIN
BALSA COVERING
202.75"
228"
RYAN NY P "SPIRIT OF ST. LOUIS"
COPYRIGHT 2002 by DALE R. CALDWELL

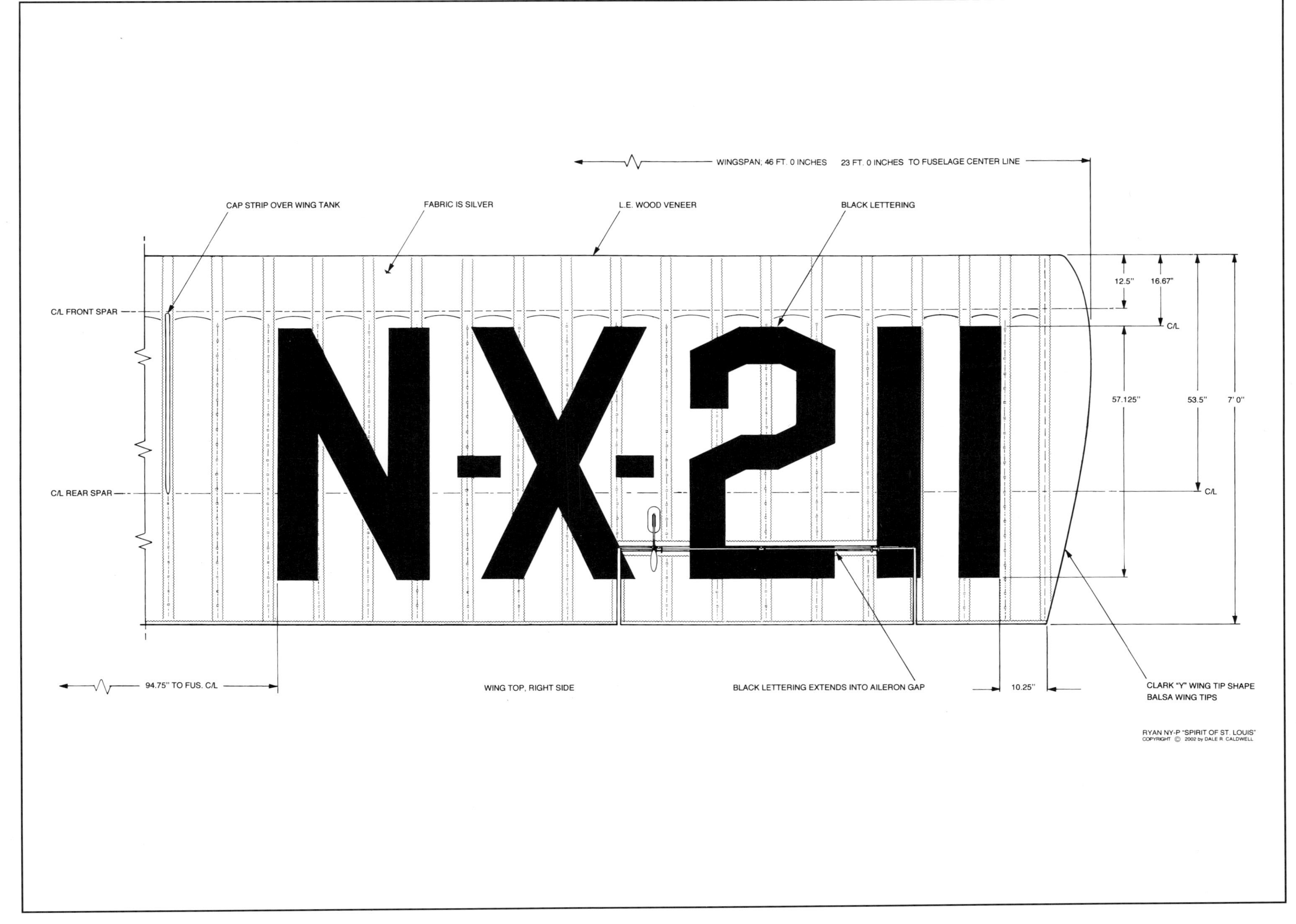
WINGSPAN: 46 FT. 0 INCHES 23 FT. 0 INCHES TO FUSELAGE CENTER LINE
CAP STRIP OVER WING TANK
FABRIC IS SILVER
L.E. WOOD VENEER
BLACK LETTERING
C/L FRONT SPAR
C/L REAR SPAR
N-X-211
12.5"
16.67"
C/L
57.125"
53.5"
7' 0"
C/L
94.75" TO FUS. C/L
WING TOP, RIGHT SIDE
BLACK LETTERING EXTENDS INTO AILERON GAP
10.25"
CLARK "Y" WING TIP SHAPE
BALSA WING TIPS
RYAN NY-P "SPIRIT OF ST. LOUIS"
COPYRIGHT © 2002 by DALE R. CALDWELL

The author checking the original NYP at the National Air and Space Museum, November 28, 1969, looking for the original mfg serial number. ***(Cassagneres Collection)***

About the author

Ev Cassagneres is an internationally recognized historian of Ryan aircraft. He is the pre-eminent specialist on the NYP, having devoted 35 years to its study. His personal archives are considered to be the largest collection of Ryan memorabilia in the world, and include over 3000 photos of Ryan aircraft.

He is one of the 13 founding members of the Connecticut Aeronautical Historical Association which operates the New England Air Museum. He is author of countless magazine articles on Ryan aircraft, and three books, The Spirit of Ryan and The New Ryan, histories of the Ryan Aeronautical Corporation, and the development and history of the Ryan ST and SC respectively, and Supplement A, the individual histories of all Ryan ST series airplanes. Born in 1928, Cassagneres' interest in aviation dates to childhood. He is a licensed professional pilot with SMELS-I and over 56 years has flown more than 50 types of aircraft. He currently owns and flies a Classic 1953 Cessna 170B.

He served in the U.S. Army and took part in the Korean Conflict, winning two purple hearts for his bravery under fire. He is also a bicycle racer and seven-time Connecticut Senior Champion, having retired undefeated. His records include an unbroken 200 mile national endurance/speed record.

Cassagneres is also interested in everything outdoors. He owns a 1945 Old Town HW wood and canvas canoe which he uses on Connecticut lakes and rivers, has partaken in swimming, downhill and cross-country skiing events, camping and travel, contra-dancing, photography, ethnic and classical music and model ship building. He is president of his own company, Aero-Draft, doing engineering and drafting consulting, and Bluebird Aerial Photography Division of Aero-Draft.

He also worked in his adult flying career as a clown pilot for Cole Palen's Old Rhinebeck Aerodrome in New York, where he performed in a Piper Cub comedy act as "Solo" the flying clown. Cassagneres spent a lifetime researching Ryan aircraft and became well acquainted with T. Claude Ryan and Charles A. Lindbergh and his family during the course of his study. He currently lives in Connecticut.